CONTEMPORARY
SUPERVISION

Advisory Editor
W. JACK DUNCAN
The University of Alabama in Birmingham

CONTEMPORARY SUPERVISION

Norbert F. Elbert
Bellarmine College

Richard Discenza
University of Colorado at Colorado Springs

Random House Business Division New York

First Edition
9876543
Copyright © 1985 by Random House, Inc.

Library of Congress Cataloging in Publication Data

Elbert, Norbert.
    Contemporary supervision.

    Includes index.
    1. Supervision of employees.   I. Discenza,
Richard.   II. Title.
HF5549.E485   1985   658.3'02   84–24942
ISBN 0–394–32585–0

Manufactured in the United States of America
Cover design: Levavi & Levavi
Text design: Rueith Ottiger/Levavi & Levavi

ADVISOR'S FOREWORD

A special report in *Business Week,* April 25, 1983, entitled "A New Era for Management" projected a number of important changes for management at all levels. For first-line supervisors, the management job is expected to change radically over the next few years. According to most experts, the supervisor's job will be more of an enabling function, requiring a new type of first-line supervisor. As the report in *Business Week* noted, "the old foreman is on the way out, and the new one will be more important."

Contemporary Supervision by Elbert and Discenza captures the trend of the new era of management as it relates specifically to first-line supervisors. The book provides a balanced mix of theory, practice, and skill building for prospective supervisors.

There was a time when first-level supervisors could perform satisfactorily with a minimum of management knowledge and skill if they were strong enough to "knock heads." A few, no doubt, will retire with little more than this aggressive style. Certainly disciplinary actions will always be required, and high levels of productivity and satisfactory quality control will not take place without the exercise of authority. Yet the next generation of supervisors will not be able to be successful using the same approach.

The new first-line supervisor will experience many challenges and opportunities rarely dreamed of twenty years ago. These supervisors will have to lead rather than command, efficiently use resources—including their own time—to accomplish work group goals, and always keep their minds on training and developing valuable human potential. They will even have to learn new forms of manufacturing as robots begin to do more of the work on typical assembly lines and computers become integral parts of production processes.

Contemporary Supervision begins by developing an appreciation for the supervisor's role and the organizational environment in which the first-line manager works. Understanding and dealing with "people problems," with particular emphasis on leadership and motivation, are discussed in Part Two.

The next major part emphasizes the role of the supervisor as communicator and evaluator. The need for effective performance appraisal and dealing with problem employees is treated thoroughly. Finally, special challenges for supervisors are discussed in Part Four.

The book includes several extremely useful and unusual chapters. Of particular significance are the chapters on personal computers for supervisors and tactics for survival. The final chapter includes a "Supervisor's Action Guide," which provides a very practical approach to the "typical" supervisory problems and deals with individual, interpersonal, and organizational skills.

Contemporary Supervision is a book for the "new era" of first-level management. We are happy to add this exciting title to our increasingly comprehensive management list.

W. Jack Duncan

PREFACE

This text is designed to familiarize students with the activities and skills of the contemporary supervisor. The challenges that supervisors face today are more complex and demanding than ever before; fair employment regulations, foreign competition, declining productivity of the American worker, the increasing number of women entering organizations, and the never ending stream of technological improvements are just some of the pressures thrust on the supervisors' shoulders by middle-level managers, government, special interest groups, and supervisors themselves. To succeed, supervisors need competent training in a wide range of specialized areas, but perhaps none more important than in understanding human behavior and how to work effectively with people.

This book is different from other supervision texts in at least two significant ways. First, we believe that feedback and control skills are of primary importance to effective supervision. Supervisors depend heavily on communication, motivation, leadership, and performance appraisal skills. Our approach is designed to blend the theories behind each of these areas with a liberal dose of "how to's." For example, we offer practical advice on how to make subordinates more productive, how to clarify your expectations, how to give constructive feedback, and how to link performance to rewards, to name just a few. We present a carefully chosen variety of information on how supervision is typically described and prescribed, the research of key behavioral science and management studies, the personal experiences of supervisors, and realistic incidents and illustrations of how some organizations actually perform specific activities. This approach, we believe, will enable you to handle a wide range of first-level management situations.

A second difference is the inclusion of new and non-traditional topics such as values and organizational survival tactics. Values, for example, are known to influence work outcomes such as job satisfaction, productivity, and work attendance. Furthermore, work force composition is becoming more and more varied with the additions of women, senior citizens, minorities, and part-time employees. Most of the members of these groups tend to have shared values. The more the supervisor understands these shared values, the better are his or her chances of learning to effectively cope with these subgroups. Personal survival is also a topic not usually found in supervision texts. We will show you how to build your own network of contacts, how to leave a favorable impression with important people, and how to read the climate of your organization.

This text offers other innovative and practical features, such as reference guides for the supervisor. For example, if you want to know how to conduct a one-on-one meeting with a subordinate, chances are the Job Performance Discussion Guide in Chapter 9 will be of assistance. In addition, the Supervisor's Action Guide is a capstone section that appears at the back of the book and encapsulates most of the material presented throughout it. This section is designed as a quick reference tool for the reader who requires immediate insight into a pressing management problem. Current and concise explanations, along with a list of simple guidelines, are presented in a "do's and don'ts" format with references.

While we use a conversational writing style and a liberal dose of marginal comments, we have not sacrificed rigor or content. Complex material, such as Title VII of the Civil Rights Act, is presented in a clear manner that is appropriate for practicing and aspiring supervisors and managers. In making the text understandable, however, we have been careful not to omit or oversimplify any of the basic principles.

As with any text, this book is a result of the efforts of a great number of people. Their collective wisdom helped us to improve earlier drafts of this book.

Among our colleagues we would especially like to acknowledge Neil Jacobs of the University of Denver and Jason Schweizer of Arizona Public Service Company. Their ideas, suggestions, and especially their criticisms made a significant difference in helping to produce a better product.

There were also a number of helpful suggestions provided by reviewers throughout the book's lengthy process. Specifically, we would like to thank Charles Beavin, Miami-Dade Community College; John W. Boyer, Jr., Labor-Management Relations & Arbitration Services, Ltd.; James Boyle, Glendale Community College; Don R. Brown, Antelope Valley College; Leo Chiantelli, Shasta College; Marie Dalton, San Jacinto College; Norman Ellis, Tarrant County Junior College; Alexander Farkash, Canisius College; Charles R. Flint, San Jacinto College; Newton Godnick, Fashion Institute of Technology; Lawrence Hoover, University of California at Davis; John Minch, Cabrillo College; Edward C. Mirch, West Valley College; Robert A. Myers, St. Petersburg Jr. College; Lee H. Neumann, Bucks County Community College; Richard Sabo, California State Polytechnic University; and Charles Watson, Miami University.

Many of the ideas contained in this text were stimulated by conversations with several of our colleagues and associates throughout the past four years. We would specifically like to extend appreciation to Chris Bavasi, Jim Belohlav, Jack Dittrick, Gene Grape, Carroll Halterman, William Kehoe, Sue LeTerneau, Robert Myers, Mark Ortman, Jon Ozmun, Jackie Priser, Allan Service, Richard Scudder, and Robert Zawacki.

The people at Random House, Inc. also deserve a special thanks. Paul Donnelly somehow managed to hold the project together during the darkest of days. Valerie Raymond, Senior Developmental Editor, was a constant source of encouragement and made significant contributions to the style of the book. We were also impressed with the professional expertise and cheerful cooperation of many employees we never met, but whose skill and contribution were effectively tapped and expertly managed by Steve Young, Manuscript Editor.

We are indebted to Dianne Minner and Sally Calton for the many grueling hours they devoted to editing the initial drafts and to Cathy Abeyta and Sue Svanoe for typing. A special thanks goes to Cathy Howard, who spent many hours typing preliminary drafts, getting source material, and suggesting current thoughts on various topics. Together, these people helped us to meet our deadlines.

Finally, the personal support each of us received from our families and their willingness to make sacrifices while we were writing this text cannot go ignored. Barb Elbert not only typed and edited a major portion of this text, she was an inspiration when the authors needed it the most.

N. F. E.
R. D.

CONTENTS

CONTEMPORARY SUPERVISION

PART 1

MEETING
THE SUPERVISORY
CHALLENGE

CHAPTER 1

SUPERVISION: FOLKLORE AND FACT

I'm not allowed to run the train
Or see how far it will go.
I'm not allowed to let off steam
Or make the whistle blow.
I'm not allowed to pull a switch
Or even ring the bell.
But let it jump the track
And see who catches —!

—ADAPTED FROM STANLEY J. SEIMER

Chapter Outline

Where the Supervisor Fits in the Organization
What Supervisors Do and Don't Do
The Operating Roles of a Supervisor
   The Decision-Making Role
   The Interpersonal Role
   The Informational Role

Objectives

Organizations are social devices that enable the accomplishment of objectives that are too large and too complex to be executed by individuals. The management of these organizations is a subject of increasing importance in society. The supervisor or first-level manager has an important role in the management of these organizations. This chapter provides the basis for understanding this role and how it is carried out at the supervisory level. Specifically, in this chapter you will become familiar with:

1. The level of a supervisor in the management structure
2. The role of the supervisor in the organization
3. The individuals the supervisor works with
4. What a job in supervision involves
5. The decision-making role of a supervisor
6. The interpersonal role of a supervisor
7. The informational role of a supervisor

Major Concepts

Supervisor	Delegating
Subordinate	Brainstorming
Responsibility	The interpersonal role
The traditional approach	The informational role
The behavioral approach	Transmission patterns
The decision-making role	

CHICAGO—The way Peter Schmidt tells it, his first 18 months as a boss have been pretty traumatic. "Sometimes I feel like I'm being drawn and quartered" on the job, he says.

As chief accountant at a medium-sized gear company here, Mr. Schmidt supervises a handful of bookkeepers who previously worked without supervision. One underling has frequently chastised him "for not picking up the in-house system quickly enough," he says. Another tries to boss him around. "She's old enough to be my mother—and she acts like it," he maintains.

So, like many a troubled manager these days, Mr. Schmidt has turned to consultants for help. . . . He and 170 other new supervisors are jammed into a ballroom at the O'Hare Motor Inn, waiting for . . . enlightenment.

Promptly at 9 A.M., seminar leader Jay Terry strides to the podium. He's a fast-talking former teacher and corporate personnel man who promises six hours of practical advice.

"You probably know all the technical information you need to do your job," he begins. On the other hand, most new supervisors need to learn a lot about dealing with people on the job.

One of the best ways to motivate employees, Mr. Terry says, is to tell them exactly what you are trying to accomplish as boss. But few supervisors communicate this "big picture" effectively, he adds. To prove it, he gives a quick test. "How many of you know the five most important things that measure the success of your immediate boss?" Mr. Terry asks. Only a few hands go up. "That's the first thing you should ask your boss when you go back to work tomorrow."

But it probably isn't a good idea for a new boss to ask employees about *their* individual goals right away. Probing too early, he says, can make a subordinate suspicious. Until boss and subordinate have begun to trust each other, the employee is apt to wonder, "Are we setting goals to catch me or to help me grow and develop?"

One way to help a subordinate grow is to learn the proper way to praise him, Mr. Terry says. The wrong way is to give the employee a quick slap on the back and say, "Good job" or "Attaboy." Better to say, "I'm happy about the way you processed those invoices so quickly. You really saved us a lot of bucks. Thanks." Taking the latter approach, the boss has told the subordinate how he feels ("I'm happy") and told him exactly what he's happy about, so the employee knows how to repeat the praiseworthy behavior.

Mr. Terry also suggests that there's a right way and a wrong way to interrupt a subordinate while he's working. The wrong way is to stroll over to his desk and say, "Are you busy right now?" "That's a hard question to field," Mr. Terry says. If the employee says, "No, I'm not busy," he sounds like he's goofing off. If he says, "Yes, I'm busy," he sounds a little rude. Better to ask, "Is this a good time to interrupt?"

Mr. Terry isn't just a corporate Amy Vanderbilt, however. He's all for being the tough guy on certain occasions. Consider how he recommends dealing with chronically tardy subordinates:

Tell the employee, "We have a problem and it has to be resolved. I'm upset that you keep coming in late because it really screws up the invoice processing," or the telephone load, or whatever. The key thing is to let the employee know how you feel and to let him know that his tardiness messes up the office and makes life difficult for the people around him.

The latecomer is likely to offer some kind of excuse. The boss, Mr. Terry says, should brush aside all excuses until the employee admits he's creating a problem. Only then is the employee likely to vow to get better. About 5% of the time, however, the latecomer simply won't admit he's causing a problem. In that case, the boss should say that the latecomer is passing up any chance of being promoted and might be fired.

What's more, the boss must be willing to back up his threat, or he loses credibility and authority. That's a particular problem for new supervisors, who frequently find their authority put to the test right away.

Al Sporny, manager of a tire store in downtown Chicago, is one seminar participant who remembers facing such a test his first day as a manager. On the same day that Mr. Sporny was promoted from mechanic to service manager, the tire store decided to extend hours until 9 P.M. on certain evenings. But despite Mr. Sporny's orders, none of the mechanics would agree to take a night shift.

"So I fired the ringleader," the 33-year-old Mr. Sporny recalls, and he told the other mechanics, "if I have to fire all of you, I will." Mr. Sporny said the blowup prevented him from sleeping for two nights. The ringleader "had a family; he had a girl six months old," Mr. Sporny recalls. "But it was his career or my career." Fortunately, he adds, the

*I*n this century, American society has become increasingly organizational. Many tasks that a century ago were carried out on the farm and in the home by various family members are now performed by organizations. These organizations, whether nonprofit institutions (hospitals, schools, or universities) or profit-making business enterprises, are run by professional managers and supervisors. The job of these individuals is to make the organization perform in a way that will produce results consistent with the organization's objectives.

Where the Supervisor Fits in the Organization

Before beginning a discussion of what a supervisory job involves, the reader should understand where the supervisor fits into the administrative structure of an organization. Every organization functions on at least three distinct but overlapping administrative levels. These levels—technical/operations, managerial/administrative, and strategic—are shown in Figure 1.1.

The strategic level controls the managerial level and mediates between the organization and the environment served by the organization. In a nonprofit organization, the strategic level can consist of boards of trustees,

FIGURE 1.1
Levels of Management

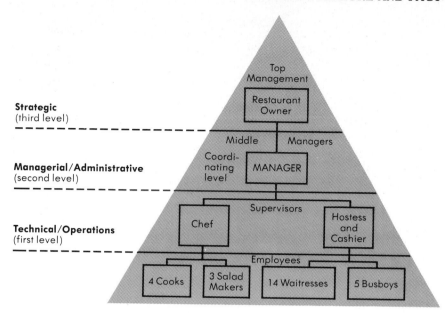

Strategic
(third level)

Managerial/Administrative
(second level)

Technical/Operations
(first level)

such as the board that runs Goodwill Industries, or it can be made up of school boards that represent the community and guide the district superintendent. In profit-oriented organizations, the board of directors, along with a president and a group of vice presidents or similar executives reporting to the president, make up the strategic level of management. This level is concerned with how the organization can most successfully operate within the social system and determines the goals of the organization.

The managerial/administrative level performs two functions in the organization. First, it administers and provides support services for the technical/operational level of the organization. Second, it mediates between the technical level and those who use the products of the organization. This may include customers, taxpayers, or homeowners. For example, the parent who is unhappy with his child's teacher goes to the school principal to work out a solution. Decisions at the managerial level determine how the operations level functions. Managerial/administrative personnel also procure resource input for the lower levels and ensure that the organization's output is sold.

Since every organization performs certain functions or operations in the actual production of goods and services, one part of the organization has the responsibility to make sure this function is carried out effectively. This is the technical or operations level. In the case of manufacturing, for example, there are two coexisting areas of responsibility: the processing of material and the supervision of those operations. Thus the operations

A supervisor defined

level of the organization's management has the primary responsibility for the development, use, and interaction of resources (money, people, facilities, information) to provide the goods and services for which the organization was established. A supervisor is anyone at the operations level who has the responsibility for getting the hands-on-the-work employees to carry out the plans, goals, and objectives of the organization.

This book deals with the supervisor. Organizations may have different titles for this individual. A supervisor may be called a foreman, a floor chief, a section head, or a department head, or be referred to as a first-level or first-line administrator. Regardless of the title, we are concerned with the individual who supervises subordinates who have little or no administrative duties. Supervisors are individuals who are on the first step of the administrative ladder. They are typically people who have had little or no administrative experience prior to accepting the supervisory position.

The relationship between the supervisor and the individuals that he or she deals with are shown in Figure 1.2. The following discussion will provide some additional insight into these relationships.

FIGURE 1.2
The Relationship
Between the
Supervisor and
Individuals Within and
Outside the
Organization

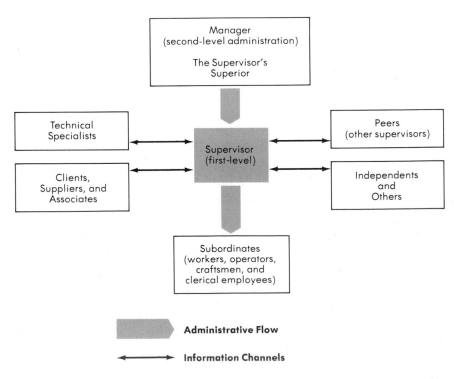

What Supervisors Do and Don't Do

Having established where the supervisor fits into the administrative hierarchy, the next part of the discussion centers around the actual duties of a supervisor. In spite of the importance of the supervisor to the organization, relatively few studies have examined what supervisors do. The total number of managers and supervisors actually studied is small, and many studies have included top executives and middle- and lower-level managers as well as supervisors.[1]

The traditional approach to the study of management is a functional one. This means, for the purposes of analyzing the components of a manager's job, the functions of planning, organizing, controlling, and directing have been identified. Scholars frequently have concerned themselves with the order in which these managerial functions should be undertaken. Theoretically, planning comes first; organizing, staffing, leading, and controlling follow. This logic assumes that the organization carries out a simple sequential master plan, each part of which, once completed, is never revised or modified. This conception is unrealistic, however, since practicing managers oversee many plans and operations at various stages of execution. They are more likely to move from one function to another, devoting their attention to the most pressing issues. What do supervisors actually do?

The traditional approach

The works of Guest, Ponder, Mintzberg, and LaForge and Bittel show that the duties of supervisors include a considerable amount of variety. Guest conducted a study that observed in detail the activities of fifty-six production supervisors in an automobile assembly plant.[2] The study showed that supervisors handled an average of 583 incidents over a full eight-hour shift. The high incident rate was usually due to operational circumstances beyond the control of the supervisor. The supervisor experienced little idle time during the shift, since he had to handle many pressing problems, with constant interruption, in rapid-fire order. He had to retain many problems in his mind simultaneously while juggling priorities for action. It became obvious that the supervisor's job involved interruption, variety, and discontinuity.

More recently, a nationwide survey of production management supervi-

---

[1] Some representative studies include: Robert Guest, "Of Time and the Foreman," *Personnel,* 32 (May 1956), pp. 478–486; Quinton Ponder, "The Effective Manufacturing Foreman," in Edward Young, ed., *Industrial Relations Research Association, Proceedings of the Tenth Annual Meeting,* Madison, Wis., December 1957, pp. 41–54; Henry Mintzberg, *The Nature of Managerial Work* (New York: Harper & Row, 1973); and R. Lawrence LaForge and Lester R. Bittel, "A Survey of Production Management Supervisors," *Production and Inventory Management,* vol. 24, no. 4 (1983), pp. 99–110.

[2] Guest, "Of Time and the Foreman."

sors was carried out by LaForge and Bittel. Overall 2,098 participants responded to 149 questions relating to the nature of a technical operations supervisor's job in a wide variety of organizations. A number of questions dealt with the general conditions under which these supervisors work. Under the category of time utilization, the supervisors were asked to indicate which production-related activities took an "above average" amount of time. Table 1.1 summarizes these results.

TABLE 1.1 Supervisors' Rating of Production-Related Activities Requiring an "Above Average" Amount of Time

ACTIVITY	LINE SUPER- VISORS		STAFF SUPER- VISORS		BEHAVIOR SKILLS
Planning production schedules for the department	24.3	(1)	23.1	(6)	
Solving production-schedule problems	23.1	(2)	23.6	(4)	
Dealing with supervisors and staff people from other departments	22.7	(3)	35.1	(1)	*
Devising improved methods and procedures for the department	21.2	(4)	26.5	(3)	
Preparing routine paperwork, production records, time cards, etc.	19.7	(5)	23.6	(4)	
Solving quality control problems	19.0	(6)	16.2	(11)	
Making daily job assignments	19.0	(7)	9.1	(15)	
Discussing personal problems and/or job performance with individual employees	18.5	(8)	22.6	(7)	*
Training employees for improved performance	17.9	(9)	17.0	(10)	*
Meeting with the boss on work-related problems	17.5	(10)	19.5	(8)	*
Solving cost- or expense-related problems	15.9	(11)	27.4	(2)	
Being involved in safety-related matters	14.0	(12)	7.4	(16)	
Attending departmental or company meetings	13.2	(13)	14.3	(12)	*

TABLE 1.1   (*Continued*)

Being involved in employee grievance and/or disciplinary matters	9.7	(14)	9.2	(14)	*
Solving customer-related problems	8.1	(15)	18.8	(9)	*
Interviewing and/or placing new employees	7.6	(16)	9.6	(13)	*

Rank of each activity is recorded in parentheses.

Adapted from R. Lawrence LaForge and Lester R. Bittel, "A Survey of Production Management Supervisors," *Production and Inventory Management,* vol. 24, no. 4 (1983), p. 103.

Besides showing the importance and the number of production activities that supervisors perform, the table shows a large number of activities that require behavioral skills. The supervisor deals with a variety of people in the operating and service departments, and with individuals on different levels of management. In many cases a supervisor's job involves getting things done with a diverse set of people, over many of whom he or she has little control. Nonetheless, the supervisor probably has more contact with people during a workday than anyone else in the managerial structure.

While most textbooks stress the functions and duties that a supervisor should perform, they fail to offer realistic help in areas where the supervisor spends a majority of his or her time and energy. There is a considerable difference between what a supervisor should do and what he or she can do. With the supervisor jumping from one incident to another, there is simply not the time or inclination to follow the traditional managerial approach. Out of this need to provide the supervisor with tools that actually improve his or her on-the-job effectiveness came the behavioral approach.

The behavioral approach emphasizes the interpersonal aspects of organizational effectiveness. Figure 1.3 presents a model of the behavioral approach to supervision. Given a specific organizational environment, the approach involves plans, implementation, behavioral elements, and results. Plans center around organizational objectives, groups, and individuals. Implementation consists of establishing standards, correcting deviations from established policies, and measuring the performance of the organization or work group.

The behavioral elements depicted in Figure 1.3 point out the critical variables that are present to some degree in job performance. Specifically, individual characteristics, work effort, and organizational support are the

The behavioral approach

FIGURE 1.3
The Behavioral
Approach to
Supervision

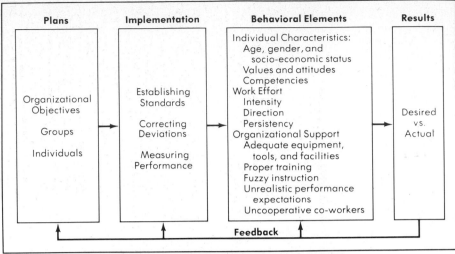

Plans	Implementation	Behavioral Elements	Results

Organizational Objectives
 	
Groups
 	
Individuals
	Establishing Standards
	
	Correcting Deviations
	
	Measuring Performance
		Individual Characteristics:
		  Age, gender, and
		    socio-economic status
		  Values and attitudes
		  Competencies
		Work Effort
		  Intensity
		  Direction
		  Persistency
		Organizational Support
		  Adequate equipment,
		    tools, and facilities
		  Proper training
		  Fuzzy instruction
		  Unrealistic performance
		    expectations
		  Uncooperative co-workers
			Desired
			vs.
			Actual

Feedback

THE ORGANIZATIONAL ENVIRONMENT

Individual characteristics cannot be ignored

elements that essentially produce the intended or unintended results that come from supervising employees on the job. Alone and in combination, these elements influence performance. Consequently, this book is devoted largely to treating the more important variables that comprise each of the behavioral elements beginning with individual differences.

As everyone knows, people are different. Because no two employees are exactly the same, there is no guarantee that what motivates one person will have the same effect on another. Nevertheless, in spite of individual differences, there is much that can be gained from an understanding of values, competencies, and the demographic characteristics (i.e., background variables such as age, sex, and socioeconomic status) that have helped shape what a person has become. The more knowledgeable supervisors are of "work ethic" values, for example, the better the likelihood of staffing their work units with people of appropriate characteristics such that, given adequate support and a motivation to work, they will be quite productive.

Develop maximum work effort

Perhaps the most significant element within a behavioral perspective is motivation because it is the one that determines work effort. "Motivation" is a term that describes the intensity, direction, and persistence of effort. Motivation is obviously an internal process. Although we often talk about the supervisor's need to motivate subordinates, in actuality the degree of effort a subordinate makes on the job is totally within his or her control. This, then, is the supervisor's challenge—to figure out the secret formula for getting maximum work effort from his or her people. However, a word of caution is needed. Motivation alone is not enough—competence is an equally important ingredient of superior job performance.

The third behavioral element is support from the organization. When there are inadequate resources; lack of proper training; fuzzy or misleading instructions; uncooperative co-workers; and faulty equipment, facilities, and tools, even the most motivated employees will likely be doomed in terms of meeting performance expectations. Thus, a major part in supervising a work group is ensuring that the opportunity to succeed is real—not fabricated or hypothetical.

A supervisor is in a position to work with each of the three behavioral elements. Although work effort is an internal process, the supervisor can influence employee motivation through such management techniques as goal setting, positive reinforcement, and incentives. However, for performance to be high, all three behavioral elements must be present to some degree. If one or more is ignored, the likelihood of unintended results is increased. This may include subordinate resistance, performance cover-ups, work avoidance, and distructive conflicts. While some negative results are always going to occur, it is important that they fall within acceptable, or manageable, limits—a parameter that is determined as much by the organization as it is by the supervisor's competence.

> **Provide real success opportunities**

The Operating Roles of a Supervisor

The need for effective managers and supervisors has long been recognized. As a result, an enormous amount of study and research has been carried out to try and understand the managerial process. One theme that continually recurs in these studies is that many of the key supervisory processes are enormously complex and mysterious—both to researchers and to those who implement the managerial process, supervisors. What has emerged from this effort is a general body of knowledge describing the characteristics of supervisory work. These characteristics can be classified into three behavioral roles: decision-making, interpersonal, and informational. They are shown in Figure 1.4.

THE DECISION-MAKING ROLE

Many new supervisors do the wrong things first: They try to manage their time or develop their employees' potential before they have learned how to do properly one of the most important parts of their job—making decisions. There is nothing in the world so common and yet so difficult to make as a tough decision. Every day supervisors are confronted with choices.

FIGURE 1.4
The Behavioral Roles
of a Supervisor

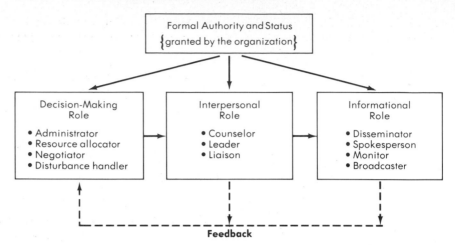

Susy Bankers, a data entry supervisor in a large bank, knows all about tough decisions. A typical day for Susy involves making one decision after another. For example, by 10:30 A.M. on a Monday, she is faced with three out-of-the-ordinary requests.

1. Theresa, one of her clerks, wants to know if she can take off next Friday in order to attend a cousin's wedding in Louisville. Part of her reasoning: "My cousin means more to me than my job."
2. Beth, another data entry clerk in the department, wants to know if she should stop entering data into her computer until it is repaired or replaced. She contends, "My keyboard smells funny; like something is burning or smoking, but I can't find anything wrong in particular."
3. Then there is the phone call from Cheryl, her boss, who has perhaps the most unusual request: "Susy, could you help me out on a delicate problem? A mentally retarded young man has applied for a job with the bank. Actually, we were told he has just a minor learning disability. Do you think you could create a job for him? The bank wants to hire some handicapped people, but we don't know where to put people like him."

Susy's performance at the end of the year will be judged by her track record in making enough "right decisions." Although most of the decisions supervisors are expected to make will not involve the difficulty of Susy's third dilemma, still they will be difficult. Moreover, such decisions don't seem to get any easier with experience.

Most of the decisions a supervisor makes affect, in one way or another, the lives of other people—usually subordinates. Yet no two people are the same in terms of attitudes, background, and needs. Moreover, a decision taken at one moment—such as who works overtime—may not

at all resemble the same decision three months later. Employees may
fight over additional income opportunities in December to help pay
for gifts and other holiday expenses, but when spring fever arrives, working late may be the last thing they want to do.

Although there are no simple procedures for decision making, the
following are some guidelines that can make the task less burdensome
and also improve the quality of the decision:

Determining if a decision is even necessary
Identifying a desired outcome before making a decision
Knowing how to search for alternatives
Using your time efficiently
Learning to glean the best from each alternative, as opposed to adopt-
  ing an "all-or-none" philosophy
Taking action that will get results
Knowing when to delegate

Is a Decision Needed? Not all decisions are unique. In the example
cited above, Susy was faced with two decisions that are probably routine
in her line of work. Theresa's request and Beth's equipment problem
are the kinds of situations that are common and predictable. A typical
office will have a policy statement that tends to cover problems of the
kind presented by Theresa. Policy statements are broad guidelines that
set limits on the types of decisions that are to be made. For example,
Susy might review office policies and remind Theresa that "It is the
policy of this bank to offer every employee one day off (with pay) during
the year for personal reasons when the time off doesn't interfere with
the normal operation of the department. Since you have not exercised
this option this year and the office is running smoothly this week, I
will O.K. your request. But, I do expect to see you back in the office
on Monday morning." Policies are purposely broad, however, and do
require supervisors to exercise judgment and discretion.

> Review company
> policies

In contrast to policies, procedures prescribe what actions are to be
taken in a specific situation. They leave little room for supervisor discretion. Beth's problem, for example, might not involve a decision by Susy
at all. Susy, as the supervisor, might be expected to follow a specific
set of actions, such as immediately reassigning Beth to another computer
or (if none were available) sending her to the control clerk for a nonma-
chine assignment. Procedures are intended to provide a degree of assur-
ance that all similar situations will be handled routinely and consistently.
This frees supervisors to concentrate their efforts on solving problems
that are unique and unpredictable.

> Develop sound
> procedures

Sound policies and procedures are valuable time savers for the supervisor because they guide decision making. They are also valued by employees. Questions regarding what is (or is not) acceptable employee behavior may be answered when policies and procedures are advertised and consistently followed.

Deciding whether to decide

Yet another element to decision making is deciding whether or not to decide. Supervisors should constantly be on the alert for occasions to delegate decisions or at least to consult with others who are in a better position to make a particular decision. Sometimes the complexities involved in a particular matter are not controlled or understood by the supervisor. Thus knowing when and how to involve appropriate others becomes extremely important. Supervisors known to be good decision makers have usually built a network of contacts to call on for advice when faced with a unique problem situation.

Spreading responsibility

Spreading responsibility for a decision, especially a risky decision, is a tactic that may protect the decision maker when a decision turns out badly. Obviously, it is harder to point a finger of blame when several persons were known to be involved in the process than when only one person made the decision. Bringing other people into the process, especially people who are critical to the implementation of the decision, is also a sound strategy for improving decision quality. Moreover, it helps to build commitment, because people are more likely to "buy into" a decision in which they have personal involvement.

To understand these concepts better, consider Cheryl's request for Susy to create a job for a mentally handicapped applicant. Susy recognizes that the problem she faces is one of placing an employee of limited ability. After analyzing the problem and examining the implications, she is faced with these unanswered questions:

> How much supervision will this individual need?
> What should the level of productivity be?
> Do I, or anyone else in the department, have the necessary skills for this type of problem?

Susy is quick to recognize that if the new employee is going to have any reasonable chance of success, other departmental members will need to be brought into the picture. Their cooperation and support—in the form of patience, understanding, and assistance—will be critical to the success of this decision.

Susy begins to meet and discuss her boss's request with key members of her office staff. In effect, she is spending time gathering the information necessary for generating and analyzing alternatives. Since this is perceived by Susy as a decision of great magnitude (hiring decisions usually are), and one that would be difficult to reverse or expensive to change, she is thorough and patient in proceeding. Some of the areas she explores are attitudes toward the handicapped and the willingness on the part of the staff to work with the new employee. In her search, Susy learns that one member of her staff has worked with the mentally handicapped and would be quite willing to work with the new employee when Susy was not available.

Searching for Alternatives.

It is important to recognize that often the quality of a decision is a function of how much effort and skill went into the search for feasible alternatives. Sometimes a poor decision simply reflects a lack of options from which to choose. Thus a wise supervisor spends time, and keeps an open mind, when searching out alternatives. Fresh perspectives are often found in the most unlikely places or people.

When supervisors reach the point of evaluating alternatives, they have two options available: They can make the decision themselves, or they can choose to use the group. Using the group is time consuming; but it is important if the group's acceptance of the decision is critical to its implementation. Susy decides to go with a group decision-making technique called brainstorming. Instead of analyzing each alternative as it is developed, brainstorming requires that a specific amount of time be allocated simply to listing alternatives. Only after every alternative has been identified is each examined. Advantages and disadvantages are listed, with special emphasis on identifying the worst thing that could possibly happen if a proposal were implemented. Brainstorming tends to ensure that every option is considered.

Brainstorming

Once a decision has been made, action plans should be designed that put the plan into operation. For some decisions, such as new accounting policies and procedures, employee commitment is not critical to successful implementation. For other decisions, such as the one Susy is faced with, commitment is vital. Getting key personnel involved in defining the problem and in deciding how to go about implementing the decision was a smart move on Susy's part.

Delegating—Getting More Done in Less Time.

Susy is smart in other ways as well. She knows her limitations and is not afraid to share them with her staff. She asks for their help and she depends on them for useful suggestions. Moreover, she is not afraid to push down to her staff some of the responsibility and challenge that she faces. She knows when and what to delegate, such as letting go of projects for which she has no unique competence. One good rule to effective

TABLE 1.2   What Is Needed to Delegate?

1. Know the difference between "mine" and "thine."
2. Bring judgment to the task.
3. Ensure good controls.
4. Establish limits of authority.
5. Tell the employee how much follow-up he or she can expect.
6. Make delegating an opportunity for two-way communication.

delegation is, if others can get the job done, let them. Table 1.2 summarizes what is needed to delegate.

Delegating work to subordinates is an important way to get more done in less time, but it is risky. If work is delegated to the wrong people, the supervisor is the one who must pay the price. Choosing the right person involves assessing the subordinate's skills, special knowledge, relevant experience, and motivation to do the job. If the subordinate qualifies on one or more of these dimensions then he or she is probably a good candidate for delegation. People who need a great deal of direction are poor choices for delegation. Yet don't wait for the perfect candidate to appear. Expect mistakes, but catch the mistakes before too much damage is done.

THE INTERPERSONAL ROLE

The interpersonal role is the second of the three operating roles for a supervisor. Until recently, the work of management was believed to be best described in terms of such abstract concepts as strategic planning, organizing, and controlling. However, a recent series of studies concentrated on identifying the actual behaviors of supervisors and managers, and their conclusions are dramatic.[3] Supervisors spend their time in a never-ending series of contacts with other people. They must meet, talk, listen, attend endless meetings, plead, argue, and negotiate. For supervisors, these activities may occur in a rapid-fire sequence, perhaps as many as a hundred contacts per day, with many lasting less than a minute.

Be fast on your feet

Being a supervisor means engaging in work that is hectic and crisis-oriented. It demands strong interpersonal skills. The supervisor is a leader and a motivator. When supervisors encourage or cajole a subordinate, they are exercising this role. When supervisors communicate with peers

[3] The best summaries of such studies are John Kotter, "What Effective General Managers Really Do," *Harvard Business Review*, November–December 1982, pp. 156–167; and Henry Mintzberg, *The Nature of Managerial Work* (New York: Harper & Row, 1973), chap. 3. Other important research studies in this field are Rosemary Stewart, *Contrasts in Management* (London: McGraw-Hill, 1976); and Ross Webber, *Time and Management* (New York: Van Nostrand, 1972).

(i.e., other supervisors), or people in other parts of the organization, they are developing a network of contacts to call on when needed. The multitude of personalities the supervisor must work with is incredible. It requires the ability to read people, to understand their needs and motives. It requires the ability to shift from one style and set of movements to another in a matter of seconds—for example, to be articulately coaching an employee at one moment and intently listening to the personal problems of another supervisor at the next moment.

The interpersonal role is always going to take a large part of the supervisor's time. As we will see later in the book, supervisors are in a strategic position when it comes to fulfilling the individual needs of their subordinates. Employees thrive on face-to-face communication. It is the basis for motivating people in organizations.

THE INFORMATIONAL ROLE

The third operating role of the supervisor is the information-processing one. Supervisors are typically the focal point of their departments for the movement of information. Because they are more quickly informed of the latest developments within the company, and because they interact with other supervisors and this interaction often provides suggestions and techniques for information transmission, supervisors are in the best position to pass on decisions that have been reached by higher-ups. In carrying out the information-processing function, the following transmission patterns have emerged: grapevines, verbal, and written.

Transmission patterns

Grapevines are the informal and unofficial communication networks that exist within any organization. Everyone knows that employees often depend on the grapevine to provide them with information inaccessible through official channels that they need or want. What is not so obvious is that supervisors may develop and use their own grapevine.

The grapevine

Subordinates, of course, play a major role in the supervisor's grapevine. A boss may choose to disseminate selective information unofficially through a subordinate that, for various reasons, cannot be divulged officially to the whole group. Although supervisors tend to be more comfortable passing along information that is grounded in "hard facts" as opposed to rumors and hearsay, the grapevine is often utilized when the information the supervisor has is speculative, or "soft" in nature, yet has some potential value to the work group. Because grapevines are usually a fast transmission pattern, they are popular with supervisors who want the information dispersed quickly and with a minimum of personal effort.

Written messages and instructions are the most orderly and systematic method for transmitting information, but they take time, concentration,

Verbal is the preferred medium	planning, and organization. Supervisors do not work in an environment that is orderly and systematic. Crises occur frequently. Therefore, supervisors generally favor the verbal medium of communication. Verbal messages not only save time, they provide the supervisor with immediate feedback in the form of nonverbal cues (e.g., tone of voice, gestures, and facial expressions) from the subordinate.

As with the interpersonal role, the effectiveness of the informational role depends largely on good communication skills. That is why we chose to develop and emphasize one-on-one feedback skills in Part III. Whether the supervisor is operating in a crisis mode or working in a more leisurely environment, the ability to transmit information depends on communicating effectively.

SUMMARY

First-level supervisors are strategically located in every organization. They can always be found where the action is heaviest, which is usually at the operations level. And while they may be called by a wide variety of names (e.g., foreman, section or department head), the one thing all of them have in common is their responsibility for getting the product out the door or for providing the organization's most essential services.

Historically, the study of supervision has been functionally presented. Concepts such as planning, organizing, directing, and controlling have traditionally been the framework for understanding the supervisor's job. Certainly there is justification for such an approach. However, there is some evidence that these functions are not of equal importance to the first-level supervisor. Planning, for example, assumes that the supervisor's work environment is stable and predictable. More often than not, the work environment is just the opposite. It tends to be crisis-oriented, more informal, less organized, and more spontaneous. The nature of supervisory work does not breed reflective planners or systematic deci-

sion makers; instead it produces supervisors who depend largely on their interpersonal, communication, and intuitive decision-making skills.

The approach emphasized throughout this book is a behavioral approach. Woven into the fabric of the behavioral approach are the critical elements of individual differences, work effort, and organizational support. For high performance to occur there must be a good fit between the employee and the job. For this to happen, each of the above mentioned elements must be addressed by the supervisor if he or she is to design a compatible match between person and job.

The behavioral approach also emphasizes three types of roles. The decision-making role, the interpersonal role, and the informational role, as described by Mintzberg, offer a more relevant framework for understanding what supervisors actually do than the traditional approach. Furthermore, it is an approach that highlights the effective use of one's personal time—a critical issue to a supervisor who is always on the go.

TO BE OR NOT TO BE

Mike LaVera was a full-time employee of Standard's Department Store in downtown Louisville. As a salesperson in the garden department, his primary responsibility was selling hardware, outdoor furnishings, and garden utensils and supplies. There were times, however, when he was assigned to the stockroom to unload incoming inventory and supplies (a task that he performed with less than full enthusiasm). In total, the garden department employed four full-time salespeople and six part-time salespeople.

LaVera was a recent graduate of Bellarmine College and he had majored in management. The job market was tight, so he took the first serious income-producing job he could find. However, he had not been hired as a management trainee. The few management trainee slots that existed were filled before LaVera applied at the store. He decided to take a chance and accept a position in sales because he sensed he had strong interpersonal skills and because it offered more money than the only other job offer he received—assistant store manager for a fast-food franchise. He also liked the people who interviewed him at Standard.

After a year of selling at the store, Standard's personnel manager, Greg Hammond, called LaVera into his office. LaVera was noticeably nervous as he walked into Hammond's office.

After a warm and friendly greeting that helped put LaVera at ease, Hammond began praising LaVera for the quality of his work and his patience in working with disgruntled customers. Hammond said he had been hearing good things about Mike for some time. La-Vera's nervousness turned to excitement as Hammond told him that his work over the past year had most definitely been noticed. In fact, Hammond was so pleased that he offered La-Vera the position of departmental supervisor. LaVera's current supervisor was resigning in three weeks.

Despite LaVera's quick acceptance, Hammond said that he didn't want a decision immediately and gave LaVera two weeks to think about the offer. He suggested that during the two weeks LaVera find out as much as possible about supervision before making a final decision.

LaVera left the office elated and certain he would accept the job of supervisor of the garden department. He was also determined to learn as much about being a supervisor as he could. Without thinking, LaVera quickly told a co-worker about the offer, and before the end of the day everyone in the department knew that he had been offered the job as their boss.

The more LaVera thought about it, the more he appreciated Hammond's suggestion to reflect on the offer. Because over the next few days, some strange and trying experiences were in store for LaVera. One co-worker, Bob Burnette, simply made it known to everyone that under no circumstances did he feel that LaVera deserved the promotion. Burnette felt he had more seniority and was actually the more qualified person. LaVera, in the past, had always got along with Burnette, so he was at a loss as to what to do about Burnette's comments. Another co-worker, Rich Hounchens, was becoming noticeably more acquainted with LaVera, offering to do favors and even being

TO BE OR NOT TO BE (Con't.)

willing to pick up the lunch check on more than one occasion. Other co-workers, on the other hand, were becoming more distant with LaVera both on and off the job.

LaVera realized that he didn't actually know what supervision was all about. Although he knew he liked selling, he needed some time to decide if he really wanted to be a supervisor.

1. If you were Mike LaVera, how would you go about gathering information about the job of supervisor?

2. What are the kinds of problems that an employee must expect when promoted to supervise the group he or she has always worked in?

3. Describe the most common types of activities a supervisor must perform.

4. If you were Mike LaVera, what would you do now? Assuming that LaVera accepts the new position, what should he do about Burnette and Hounchens?

DISCUSSION QUESTIONS

1. Explain what a supervisor does.
2. What are the major differences between a supervisor's job and a technician's job?
3. To be a good supervisor, what managerial skills are needed?
4. How is the job of supervisor similar to that of higher-level managers? How is the supervisor's job different?
5. What types of people must the supervisor interact with?
6. Discuss the behavioral approach to supervision. How does this approach differ from the traditional textbook approach to supervision?
7. Identify and discuss the behavioral roles of supervisory work.
8. Discuss the nature of delegating as it applies to a supervisor.

REFERENCES

Bittel, Lester. *What Every Supervisor Should Know.* 4th ed. New York: McGraw-Hill, 1980.

Guest, Robert H. "Of Time and the Foreman." *Personnel* 32 (May 1956): 478–485.

Huse, Edgar F. *The Modern Manager.* St. Paul: West Publishing Company, 1979.

Koontz, Harold; O'Donnell, Cyril; and Weihrich, Heinz. *Management.* 7th ed. New York: McGraw-Hill, 1980.

Kotter, John P. "What Effective General Managers Really Do." *Harvard Business Review* (November–December 1982): 156–167.

LaForge, R. Lawrence, and Bittel Lester R. "A Survey of Production Management Supervisors." *Production and Inventory Management* 24, no. 4 (Fourth Quarter, 1983): 99–112.

Mintzberg, Henry. "The Manager's Job: Folklore and Fact." *Harvard Business Review* (July–August 1975): 73–84.

Mintzberg, Henry. *The Nature of Managerial Work.* New York: Harper & Row, 1973.

Pearce, John A. II. "Problems Facing First-Time Managers." *Human Resource Management* (Spring 1982): 35–38.

CHAPTER 2

SUPERVISORY PLANNING IN ACTION

Ask me for anything but time.

—Napoleon

Chapter Outline

Time: The Critical Resource
Myths About Time and Managerial Effectiveness
Aspects of Time Management
    Avoiding Procrastination
    Planning Effectively
    Setting Priorities
    Developing and Using a Time Plan
Ways to Gain Control of Your Time
    Attacking the Problem of Desk Clutter
    Managing Visitors
    Managing the Telephone
    Managing Meetings
Ways to Improve Your Reading Skills

Objectives

This chapter is designed to aid the supervisor who is confronted with more work to do than there is time available to do it. The material presented here should help the supervisor work smarter, not harder. Initially, several myths of time management are discussed.

Time management begins by learning to manage oneself. This can be facilitated by the use of a time plan. Several additional suggestions are presented to improve the supervisor's effectiveness. Specifically, in this chapter you will become familiar with:

1. Myths about time and managerial effectiveness
2. Ways to reduce procrastination
3. The use and development of a time plan
4. The role of planning in time management
5. Ways to keep your desk clear
6. Ways to manage visitors, the telephone, and meetings
7. Ways to read more effectively

Major Concepts

The workaholic
Time management
Procrastination
Murphy's Law
Nonscheduled time

Standing plan
Time plan
Time wasters
Supervisory planning
Reading improvement

THE ART OF DELEGATING

"You must really be working Robert hard," Della said to Chris Masing. "It seems like the kids and I don't see much of him any more. Ever since he became department manager he leaves the house at 7:30 A.M. and doesn't get home before 6:00 P.M. Then he's usually got an attaché case full of papers, and he works from after supper to around 10:00. Why, he's even been working on weekends lately!"

Chris listened to Della with great interest. Obviously, the company picnic was no time to go into the matter in detail. However, Della's husband had been promoted to department head six weeks earlier, and as Chris's newest manager he might be having some problems. Chris decided to talk to Robert first thing the next week.

The two men met for coffee at 10:30 Monday morning. Robert admitted, quite frankly, that there was a lot to do. "I've got so much work on my desk that I end up taking some of it home every night. I'm so snowed under, I'm even working on weekends."

Chris explained to Robert that he was working too hard. "You've got to delegate some of that stuff, or you'll be snowed under indefinitely. Look, I want you to meet me again this afternoon at 2:30 with all the work that you still have to do."

Later that day, the two men sat down and put Robert's work into three categories: (1) should be delegated to others, (2) could be delegated to others, and (3) must be done personally. Fifty percent of the material went into the first category, 30 percent into the second, and 20 percent into the third. Chris then reviewed with Robert the various people in his department who could be assigned the work in the first two categories. The men agreed to meet again on Friday.

Robert related on Friday that he had delegated three-quarters of the work he had been doing. Furthermore, he reported, the people in his department expressed a willingness to help. One of them told him, "I'm really glad you asked me to do this. When you started taking all the work home with you, I thought maybe you didn't trust us. Now I feel important and involved."

The next week, Della called Chris to thank him. "You really saved the day," she said. "Robert is excited about his job, and we're seeing as much of him as we did before! Thanks for helping out."

Adapted from Richard M. Hodgetts, *Modern Human Relations* (Hinsdale, Ill.: Dryden Press, 1980), p. 280.

*F*or supervisors, planning is the process of systematically organizing what they and their work group will do in the future. Plans are typically classified according to their duration and purpose.

Long-range strategic plans are ones that look forward five or more years; typically they are set by higher management and provide a broad course of action selected from alternatives as the best way to obtain major organizational objectives. Keeping in mind the organization's capabilities, resources, and major functions, these plans outline a strategy that maintains a position of advantage in relation to the organization's competitors.

Long-range plans

Coordinative or tactical plans are directed toward implementing long-range plans by coordinating the work of different organizational units. These plans are a primary tool of middle management, which has the responsibility of deciding specifically how the resources of the organization will be used to help the organization achieve its strategic goals.[1] These plans typically range in duration from one year to five years, depending on the organization and the nature of its activities.

Tactical plans

At the lowest (or operations) level of management, supervisors have the responsibility of following the tactical plans established by middle-level management to achieve the long-range plans formulated by top management. These plans are normally for a period of one year. They

[1] James Stoner, *Management* (Englewood Cliffs, N.J.: Prentice-Hall, 1978), p. 97.

are specific and consist primarily of implementing budgets, procedures, and rules. Often, the activities associated with these plans are routine, and the results of their implementation can be measured quantitatively. Examples include adhering to projected costs and budgeted items or creating a production schedule.

While both long-range and coordinative planning techniques are helpful to supervisors in an overall sense, the day-to-day operational methods of managing one's work are more directly useful for supervisors. Because routine, day-to-day activities are the main domain of supervisors, they usually find the simple operational techniques of time management covered in this chapter the most valuable.

Time: The Critical Resource ▬▬▬▬▬▬▬▬▬▬

As a supervisor, do you find yourself wishing that there were more than twenty-four hours in a day? A great many people in managerial positions regularly complain that they don't have enough time to do everything that they want to do. We all have the same amount of time; the point is, how do we use that time? Surveys have been conducted on managerial personnel, and the results generally indicate that as a person moves higher in administrative ranks, his or her workday and work week become **More responsibility, longer hours** longer. The typical explanation is that the more important a job is, the heavier the responsibility one has and the more people one is held accountable for. All of this requires more time. Another explanation is that as people move up in management, they try to do the whole job themselves rather than delegating it to others. This is done out of fear. That is, people feel they must do the job themselves in order to ensure that it is done properly.

Many managers work a sixty-hour week. Often, over fifty hours are spent in the office and about ten hours are spent working at home. **The workaholic** The term "workaholic" is used in defining these people. A workaholic is a compulsive overworker. Some traits of workaholics are: (1) a hasty sandwich at the desk, (2) a bulging briefcase carried home from the office, (3) boasting that they haven't had a vacation in years, (4) the inability to meet deadlines (they seem to be constantly behind in getting things done), (5) the messy desk (they are too busy to straighten things out, so papers are in disarray throughout the office, (6) the typically late arrival home.

The thing workaholics don't realize is that people who constantly spend so many hours a week on the job tend to become inefficient.

People's productivity tends to decline after eight hours of work. Moreover, when people work long hours, they often adopt the attitude that there is no great rush to get something done because there is always tonight or tomorrow to complete the project. A job that could be done in eight hours often stretches out to twelve or fourteen hours. On the personal side, one characteristic of workaholic administrators is their readiness to sacrifice their family lives for their work. But instead of becoming more effective with longer hours of work, they spend more hours completing a job that could be done in fewer hours. In a word, the workaholic supervisor is an *inefficient* supervisor.

> Long hours lead to low productivity

Are you a workaholic? Take a few minutes to answer the workaholic test in Table 2.1. If you answer correctly to more than six questions, your work habits need to be evaluated and streamlined. The suggestions presented in this chapter, if applied correctly, could greatly improve your effectiveness on the job.

TABLE 2.1   The Workaholic Test

1. Do you frequently telephone friends in the evening just to chat?

2. Do you generally keep your office door closed?

3. If you had to choose, would you rather be admired than liked by friends and co-workers?

4. Do you usually let people finish what they're saying to you?

5. Does your spouse (or closest friend) think of you as relaxed and easygoing?

6. (a) Do you get upset when the car ahead is driving too slowly and you can't pass? (b) If so, do you keep your annoyance to yourself rather than expressing it to others in your car?

7. Do you like to help with household chores such as dishwashing?

8. Do you often bring work into the bathroom?

9. Are you punctual for appointments?

10. Are you usually much annoyed when your spouse (or a friend) keeps you waiting?

11. While you're in a meeting or busy with someone in your office, do you usually refuse to take phone calls?

12. When someone is talking to you, do you often let your mind stray to other lines of thought?

ANSWERS:
1. No. 2. No. 3. Yes. 4. No. 5. No. 6. (a) Yes, (b) No. 7. No. 8. Yes. 9. Yes. 10. Yes. 11. No. 12. Yes.

Warren Boroson, "The Workaholic in You," *Money,* June 1976.

Myths About Time and ━━━━━━━━━━━━
Managerial Effectiveness

Work smarter

Plan before acting

Decisions should be made at lowest level

Delegating improves efficiency

There are several myths about managerial effectiveness, the first being that the harder one works, the more one accomplishes. This is not necessarily true. The better adage is work smarter, not harder. It is often the ineffective supervisor who looks busy but is not really accomplishing very much. A second myth is that managers who are the most active get the best results. In reality, an emphasis on activity for its own sake can lead to disastrous results. Being active does not ensure that one is effective. Planning ensures effectiveness more than anything else. For every hour spent in planning, three hours may be saved in execution. Many activity-oriented managers avoid planning because it takes time initially. But this initial investment typically results in improved execution.

A third myth relates to the level of decisions. Some people believe that the higher the level at which a decision is made, the better the decision. This goes along with the notion that because higher-level people are paid more money, they are able to make smarter decisions. Hence the more decisions that are made at the top, the better off the whole organization will be. However, an understanding of basic management principles indicates that decisions should be made at the lowest level in the organization that has access to relevant facts, as well as good judgment. Lower-level decisions typically cost less because the decision maker has greater familiarity with the circumstances involved. One of the most common failings of supervisors is the tendency to continue making the same kind of decisions that they made at a lower level of responsibility.

A fourth myth concerns delegating. Many supervisors avoid delegating work because they are convinced that they can get things done faster and better themselves. They want to save the time it would take to tell others how they want the job done, plus the time it would take to determine whether or not the job was done right. The primary fallacy of this approach is that by refusing to delegate work and to take the time to see that it has been done right, supervisors are ensuring that they will be forced to do the job next time—since no one else will have learned how. Inability to delegate is a common trait of entrepreneurs who enjoy success initially. They feel that their success is a result of their own activity. They conclude that no one else can do the job as well as they can and insist on doing many things that should be delegated to subordinates. In short, they don't have time to manage. However, growth in an organization or unit demands that the supervisor delegate.

Aspects of Time Management

Management has been defined by a number of people as consisting of seven basic functions:

1. Planning: The systematic examination of future events to meet company or organizational objectives; a process by which a supervisor looks to the future and examines certain alternative courses of action open to him or her

Seven functions of management

2. Organizing: The structuring of one's activities and those of subordinates
3. Decision making: The process by which a course of action is chosen from the available alternatives for the purpose of achieving a desired result or goal
4. Controlling: Maintaining direction by means of feedback; the process by which ideas are transmitted to others for the purpose of obtaining a desired result
5. Directing: Influencing others to work; the process by which actual performance of subordinates is guided toward a common goal or goals
6. Communicating: The process by which ideas are transmitted to others for the purpose of affecting a desired result
7. Staffing: The process by which supervisors select, promote, develop, train, and terminate subordinates

Time management may be thought of in terms of these same activities but applied at the individual level. In short, time management involves managing oneself. Remember, it's your time, and you're spending it; therefore, you should be its master and not vice versa. The key factor in time management is that supervisors must be willing to master themselves so that they can begin to master their time.

AVOIDING PROCRASTINATION

All of us are at times guilty of procrastination when confronted by some unpleasant task that we wish to avoid. But procrastination is a major

Procrastination is normal

time waster, and when it becomes an excuse for incompetence and inefficiency, the manager or supervisor should become concerned. Habitual procrastinators become interruption prone; they invite interruptions. Countering an inclination to procrastinate requires self-discipline and perseverance.

Procrastination puts off a sometimes painful confrontation between one's actual abilities and one's imagined talents. Individuals who fall below what they feel are their subjective standards perform extraneous functions and then offer the handy excuse, "If I only had had more time, I could have done it better." This pattern reflects the individual's need for self-esteem. One is afraid of finding out that one's abilities are limited. To overcome procrastination, one must learn to feel good about oneself; accept what one can and can't do. The following are some techniques for countering procrastination.

Set realistic goals

First of all, set realistic goals. For example, don't try to write a report at one sitting. This only reinforces the feeling that report writing is drudgery. Instead, break the report down into segments, and then alternate periods of writing with some other kind of work.

Murphy's Law

Second, adjust your concept of time. If you think it will take two hours to write a report, allow yourself four days to accomplish it. Remember Murphy's Law of Time—it advises that you multiply by two the amount of time you think a task will take, and then use the next highest time unit.

Set aside nonscheduled time

Third, develop nonscheduled time. This seems at first to be contrary to learning not to procrastinate. However, it is important to have time available for things not scheduled. Set aside time for doing things that make you feel good and stay healthy—such things as taking a coffee break, watching your favorite TV program, visiting with friends, or jogging. By scheduling time for leisure, you'll be less troubled by guilt. And when you allow time for recreation, you will be less tempted to stray from work to be done while at the office.

Take a break if you've earned it

Reward yourself. Immediately after doing an unpleasant task, no matter how small, plan to take a break, read a magazine, call a friend, or take a walk. (However, keep in mind that these types of rewards should be approved by the boss.) The most mundane rewards can make boring jobs more tolerable. One should learn to be firm, yet kind, to oneself. This is important. In fact, it is like learning to be one's own parent.

Don't demand perfection

Don't let perfectionism limit you. As a supervisor, you should learn to realize that your work will never be perfect. Settle for your best effort. This may sound obvious, but for a lot of bright people it takes a long struggle to recognize.

PLANNING EFFECTIVELY

Planning is the rational predetermination of where you want to go and how you intend to get there. When good results occur without good planning, it is the result of good luck and not good management. Planning saves time and can be an effective tool for managing one's time.

One of the measures of an effective planner is the ability to distinguish between the important and the urgent. One of the reasons managers often give for failure to plan is that they have to "put out today's fire" because it has a much higher priority than planning for tomorrow. Typically, however, managers concentrate on attending to urgent matters to feed their own sense of gratification in overcoming a crisis.

Avoid firefighting

Planning prevails in good management. When planning for a cooperative group of people, decisions should contain elements provided by all members of the group. Planning may begin with a vague hunch or an element of intuition onto which the individual or group stumbles. However, good managers will quickly visualize a clear pattern for handling current thought about future actions.

A plan is a predetermined course of action. It may be tailored to a specific project or established as a standing plan for future actions. A standing plan can be used when the action required is rather routine. At the operational level, standing plans are sometimes called standard operating procedures. Standard operating procedures have the advantages of economizing on thought processes and making control more uniform. Check lists are often developed after detailed study of a routine set of actions, and these lists can serve as a predetermined path of action.

Use a standing plan for routine tasks

Planning involves more than the selection of a predetermined course of action, however. It also includes mentally searching for possible future problems. Sometimes the alternatives are limited by the economic considerations of a manager's time. Plans, in effect, become premises for future decisions.

The planning process involves the following steps:

1. Analysis of the situation.
2. Relevant assumptions. Alone or with the group, the supervisor must develop relevant assumptions concerning a given situation.
3. Establishment of objectives. A plan should be directed toward well-defined objectives that have been prioritized.
4. Alternative strategies. When faced with a need for alternative courses of action, a supervisor has two sources from which to draw. The

The planning process

first and most commonly used is his or her own experience; the second is the experience and practices of other people.

5. Implementation in the form of action plans. Generally, two steps are involved in the implementation phase: (1) the development of necessary procedures; and (2) an action plan that is communicated to those involved and affected by it.

6. Feedback and control procedures. Feedback is the process of adjusting future actions on the basis of information about past performance. Any alternative that has been implemented must be responsive to changing conditions. This is generally termed the control function and, if effectively carried out, it will provide the supervisor with continual feedback on exactly where the alternative stands at a given point in time with respect to achieving the desired objective. Ideally, feedback pertains not only to the overall picture, it also pinpoints some specifics. When objectives are not being achieved, or their accomplishment is behind schedule, the supervisor will use available information to identify areas that are causing problems and will develop other alternatives to overcome these problems.

The control function

SETTING PRIORITIES

Every plan is based upon an identified objective. Developing meaningful objectives, however, is not always easy. A good objective is one that motivates you to take action and provides direction for that action. The following criteria may help you improve your efforts and enable you to develop objectives that really work for you. Objectives should:

Ingredients of an objective

be your own
be written
be realistic and attainable
be specific and measurable
have time schedules
be compatible

Once objectives are clarified, some time management concerns are almost automatically solved. Those people who have only one objective can rest easy; for them, most of the hard work is over. Most people, however, have more than one important objective or goal in their work. For them, the next step is setting priorities.

Most of us have a fuzzy definition of "priority." We usually use the word to mean "an important project or responsibility connected with one's work." Under this definition, we would say that a small portion of our time is devoted to priorities.

It is impossible to work always on the basis of priorities; if you don't make an attempt, however, you allow any urgent activity to control your time while items of greater importance go unattended.

Set priorities to accomplish difficult and unpleasant items first. Determine what you really want to accomplish. Develop a "to do" list. Your "to do" list may be as simple or complex as you desire. Prioritize the list each day and allocate time for planning and meeting established goals and objectives. Proceed from complex to simple or low-value tasks. Do not schedule every minute of the day; save time for distractions. However, do not allow the distractions to take you away from the main goal.

Construct a "to do" list

Investing time to save time is not the easiest concept to get across. Managers who resist planning because they "don't have time" are failing to look ahead to the significant, long-range time savings and to the improved performance that usually result.

Use your evaluation criteria and review often. Include a look at the various alternatives under consideration. Assess the degree to which outputs meet established objectives or standards. Consider effectiveness as well as efficiency. This allows for management changes and the resulting impacts.

The dictionary defines "priority" as something given precedence; in other words, something done before something else. This definition gets right to the heart of spending time. Everything people do during the day involves a priority decision. Unfortunately, many priority decisions are not made consciously and do not reflect stated objectives or goals.

Managers use a wide variety of criteria in deciding how to use their time. The six listed here are just examples.

1. Demands of others
2. Closeness of deadlines
3. Amount of time available
4. Degree of enjoyment
5. Order of arrival
6. Degree of familiarity

Take control with priorities

Establishing priorities is difficult for many people. Setting priorities is a difficult but necessary task. The alternative to consciously setting priorities is unconsciously reacting to demands as they occur. Reacting seldom brings the best results. Initiating action requires control coupled with decision-making abilities. Actions initiated on the basis of carefully thought-out decisions are almost always better than actions initiated haphazardly. The priorities you establish may not always be the best, but your odds are greater with careful thought.

DEVELOPING AND USING A TIME PLAN

One of the key ingredients of time management is development of a time plan. This is necessary to help change one's time-wasting habits. To make the effort requires conviction of its worth. Supervisors can build on the development of a time plan by learning from the experience of others.

Common Time Wasters. People often think of time as being wasted by external factors such as the telephone. But the development and evaluation of a time plan may give a different picture. Time wasters can be classified into two categories. The first are internal time wasters—a result of the failure to set objectives, priorities, and deadlines. They generally come about from crisis management, a lack of delegation, the open-door policy, and just plain procrastination. Related to an individual's mode of operation, the internal time wasters are the cluttered desk and personal disorganization. They also involve being unnecessarily caught up in routine matters, trying to do too much at once, unrealistic time estimates, and indecision.

Internal time wasters can become bad habits. One way to develop new habits is with self-management. To break old time-wasting habits and adopt new, time-saving ones, the supervisor must develop a new approach with as much determination as possible, since this will help to avoid the tendency or temptation to backslide. No variance from the new regimen should be allowed until it is firmly rooted. And the time to implement that new approach is—as soon as possible.

External time wasters are, by definition, created by others. Typically they are people who have more authority than you, who are outside your sphere of influence, or who have unlimited access to you at work or at home. For example, common external time wasters are the unavailability of key people and delays that are created by outside personnel. Interruptions, too, play a major role in wasting time.

There is a subtle deceptiveness about interruptions. They are seldom recognized as symptoms of inefficiency because they are described by the offending person as legitimate. The supervisor's in-basket is frequently

Internal time wasters

In-basket abuse

FIGURE 2.1
Weekly Time Plan

Week ____

Time	**Monday**		**Tuesday**		**Wednesday**		**Thursday**		**Friday**	
	Planned Activity	Actual Activity	Planned Activity	Actual Activity	Planned Activity	Actual Activity	Planned Activity	Actual Activity	Planned Activity	Actual Activity
8–9										
9–10										
10–11										
11–12										
1–2										
2–3										
3–4										
4–5										

a case in point. It is assumed by most supervisors that anything in their in-basket is there by right. Don't you believe it. This assumption may be the greatest single factor preventing supervisors from routing back to the sender items that should never have been sent in the first place.

How to Set Up a Time Plan. The time plan not only lists planned activities, it provides space for you to record what actually happened. It is a planned allocation of your time as a supervisor—a daily listing of the anticipated tasks for the coming week and a record of how the time was actually spent as compared to the initial plan. A sample form for a time plan is shown in Figure 2.1.

Some experienced observers suggest that a time log, which is simply a record of the supervisor's actions as they happen, should be kept and evaluated for the purpose of analyzing time use. The analysis usually points to the need for remedial action, and it can be used to check the tendency to neglect establishing priorities. The time log can be an effective tool for evaluating your use of time as a supervisor. However, it does have a number of drawbacks. First, it is rarely an accurate record of the supervisor's actions. The log is usually completed at a convenient time or at the end of the day and involves trusting to one's memory— risky at best. Moreover, time logs lack detail. When entries are made in general terms, the effectiveness of the time log is weakened.

The following are specific instructions for use of the time plan:

1. *Plan your time:* You need to decide on priorities and the percentage of time to be allocated to each. Your priorities, in order of importance, might include "checking inventory," "taking delivery," "training a new employee," "meeting with a vendor," "giving daily work assignments," and so on. Use specific terminology; avoid vague phrases. Place each task in the "planned activity" column, and do this for each day of the week.

2. *Keep track of time:* As the week progresses, record the results frequently. Do not wait until the end of the day to fill in the chart. Memory can be deceiving, and the longer one waits, the more errors will creep in.

3. *Summarize and evaluate:* After the plan has been kept for at least one week (two weeks is recommended), add up the total hours spent on each task. It will then be an easy matter to compute the percentage of the total time spent on each category of activity. With this information, you will be able to analyze the areas of your greatest and least effectiveness. On this basis, you will be able to plan a strategy for improvement.

The use of a time plan often indicates that much of a supervisor's work is repetitive and should be delegated or routinized. Many people continue to live with time wasters. Others realize that they must do something to eliminate them if they are to be effective. The time plan can be a useful tool in achieving this goal.

Ways to Gain Control of Your Time

ATTACKING THE PROBLEM OF DESK CLUTTER

An important place to begin organization is at one's desk. A cluttered desk affects the performance of supervisors and other office workers. Why does that occur? People stack things on their desks because they don't want to forget where they are. They often put an item on the top of a stack so that they can actually see that item. The unfortunate result of this habit is that attention is frequently drawn to the item and away from the task at hand. The disadvantages of this habit increase as the stacks grow higher and one becomes unable to remember what is where. One begins to look for something in the stacks and additional time is wasted.

When your desk resembles a paper snowdrift, and its surface hasn't been seen in months, the problem has reached the crisis stage. At this point, you should attack the snowdrift. You should take one stack of papers at a time and begin the operation of working through the pile.

One method for working through the snowdrift is to discard those no longer having any importance, mark others either for routing to the appropriate persons or offices or, if they require your personal attention, file them in order of their priority. Say, for example, that at the top of this pile of papers is an invitation for you to give a talk at the local Rotary Club. You must decide whether you intend to accept the invitation or not. If you do, then the invitation should be placed in a folder marked for your secretary so that the event can be noted on both your calendar and the secretary's. If you decide not to give the talk, you will ask your secretary to send, immediately, a letter of regret. Professional publications—magazines, newspapers, and so on—can be kept in a separate stack so that, as time permits, you can scan them for items pertinent to your business affairs.

As a supervisor, you must learn to develop criteria for the flow of paper as it comes in. You must learn to decide how to act on it, how to put conditions on that decision, and how to arrange things so that you will not have to handle that paper again. As a supervisor you should not, generally, keep your own letters, do the filing, keep your own calendar, or even answer the phone any more than is absolutely necessary.

Since organization is difficult for a lot of people to attain, one suggestion is to spend the first half-hour of the day planning and doing paperwork. If this is inconvenient, spend at least one half-hour at the end of the day planning for the next workday. You must decide what your priorities are before you can attack the snowdrift. Once priorities are set, you can start attacking the pile from the top down. If you find you are having difficulty disposing of an item, for any of a number of reasons (for example, just being in the wrong frame of mind or being unable to decide how to handle a matter), you should go on to the next thing. It is important to continue until the paperwork is finished.

Once the stacks of paper have been cleared from your desk, there are a number of things you can do to make sure that the desk remains in an uncluttered state. A key to maintaining an uncluttered desk is to clear it of everything except items that have top priority at the moment. Another important key is to resist the temptation to set aside a current project for a more appealing task. You should work on the current project until as much work is done as can be done and then go on to another task. Once a project is completed, recheck the priorities of remaining tasks and start on the next most important one. When you arrive at

Work through the piles of paper

Know what to do with each piece of paper that crosses your desk

Keep only top priority items in sight

your desk in the morning, the only thing that should be on it is the job with top priority for the day. The secretary can play an important part in maintaining the uncluttered desk. Have him or her inspect your desk and continue to keep it clear except for the number one priority project.

Use the wastebasket

Learning to use the wastebasket may be one of the most important ways of managing one's work. There is often a tendency to overfile and to retain papers that are never referred to again. Some filing systems become so complex that their value is negated. A good rule of thumb is to discard correspondence that is over a year old. Alec Mackenzie, one noted expert, estimates that over 95 percent of the papers in files are never referred to again.

MANAGING VISITORS

The key to managing visitors is to authorize one's secretary to handle appointments. Appointments should be made in such a way that you can devote a certain part of your day to taking care of tasks without being interrupted by visitors. It is important to protect the most creative and productive time of the day. This time varies with each individual. You should determine your most productive time and use it to maximum benefit.

Protect the most productive time of day

Unscheduled visitors are key time wasters. That is why executive managers have visitors screened. As a supervisor, you should make yourself available only to people who have a legitimate reason to visit. One way to avoid interruptions in your work is to go to the office of a possible visitor before he or she can come to yours. This allows you to finish the matter at hand without unnecessary delay. Moreover, by going to another person's office you control the situation. You can leave when you want to. Also, you are paying that person a compliment by going to see him or her. Another strategy is, after a visitor has been announced, to step outside your office to meet that person. In this way, you are able to limit the duration of the call; the visitor is thus prevented from sitting down and gaining psychological control. Your secretary can also be an important aid in managing visits. Have your secretary monitor the visit. That is, have him or her come in and remind you of another obligation. A typical response to such a reminder would be, "I'll be through in five minutes."

Use your secretary as a screen

Another way to manage visits is by advising visitors at the beginning of a visit how much time you have available. Avoid small talk and try to get right to the point. When time must be conserved, discussion of nonbusiness items should be kept to a minimum. But it is also important to give visitors the courtesy of uninterrupted time—that is, to block interruptions except for an emergency. In summary, visitors should be seen under controlled conditions. It is a myth that the open-door policy improves managerial effectiveness. It can, in fact, encourage dependency on the supervisor as well as being very disruptive.

Avoid an open-door policy

MANAGING THE TELEPHONE

The telephone can be of help in avoiding time-wasting meetings. And it can be used in lieu of making trips and writing letters. However, for a person who desires to be involved in everything and who is unable to terminate conversations, the telephone can also be one of the biggest time wasters. Some people fear that terminating a conversation too quickly will offend the caller. And they are reluctant to have calls screened by a secretary for the same reason. But managing one's telephone calls is yet another important aspect of time management.

Incoming calls should be screened for urgency, purpose, and to clarify who is the most appropriate party to handle the call. Use a call-back system when feasible—that is, save a certain part of the day to return calls that have come in during the day. With regard to outgoing calls, let your secretary save you the time of dialing and getting your party on the line. And keep the conversation to a minimum. Never open the conversation with, "Hi, Jim. How are you?" This may be an invitation to a long conversation. Instead, start out with, "Hi, Jim. If you have the time, I need a couple of quick answers."

Use a call-back system

MANAGING MEETINGS

Time management also involves the effective use of meeting time. Supervisors and other types of management personnel necessarily spend a large proportion of their time in meetings. But much of this time is wasted. Many meetings are called simply because a supervisor is unable or unwilling to make a decision. Or a supervisor may have a compulsion to overcommunicate and may call meetings for the sake of meetings. Poorly planned meetings are time wasters. Avoid meetings whose purpose has not been specifically defined or where critical information is lacking. It is the supervisor's job, when setting up a meeting, to prepare a clear-cut agenda and to consider who needs to be there, rather than involving people for whom the meeting would serve no purpose. Since every meeting represents a high cost in terms of wages and time, supervisors should ensure that the benefits derived from a meeting will outweigh the costs.

Meetings can be time wasters

When setting up meetings, one should discourage time overruns. Try

Discourage time overruns

to schedule meetings before lunch or near quitting time to keep them from running on too long. Those who attend meetings may find comfortable chairs and not wish to move. One hour is sufficient time for most meetings. The supervisor controlling the meeting should get it started on time, follow the agenda closely, get to the point, and stick to it.

Ways to Improve Your Reading Skills

At virtually all supervisory and management levels, the amount of reading required has increased significantly in recent years. Chances are that, as a supervisor, you are stuffing your briefcase with more and more material to read in the evening after work. The fact is that most managers could lessen significantly, or even eliminate, the amount of work that they take home. One way of accomplishing this is to develop more efficient reading habits. Most studies have shown that businessmen typically read below the college level, attaining on the average about 300 words per minute. Furthermore, their comprehension of the material is much less than it could be. Most people find that after taking some sort of reading improvement course, their reading speed has doubled and, more important, their comprehension has increased considerably. To the slow reader, increasing one's reading speed and comprehension seems like an impossibility. Some people even feel that the ability to read fast is a God-given talent possessed by a selected few. But reading rapidly is not a special talent. A person's reading ability is a result of the habits that he or she has developed. With study and determination, a slow reader can usually become a good reader.

One of the methods available to supervisors to improve their reading is a course in speed reading. Most colleges and universities offer courses through which one can double, even triple, reading speed. These courses and programs offer highly scientific techniques for determining one's reading difficulties. For example, there are techniques for recording the actual movements of the eyes. These give a graphic picture of the number of fixations per line and the amount of backtracking that is done.

The first thing to do if one is experiencing reading difficulty is to take a diagnostic test. The test may be one recommended by a university or college connection or by the Better Business Bureau of your city. It is important to examine the instructor's qualifications because there is no certification or other controls in this field. If the test indicates that improvement is needed, you would be wise to invest in a few hours of

Faster reading reduces homework

Get some professional help

instruction. This will enable you to learn specific techniques for improving reading comprehension and speed. And the instructor may be able to provide some material for home use that is suitable to your specific problem. In addition, there are numerous inexpensive reading manuals containing exercises geared to building both speed and comprehension. It's important to be able to obtain 80 percent correct answers to questions in these exercises. Reworking the sections of the manual may be necessary to attain this degree of proficiency. If possible, return to the clinic or class to see how much progress you have made and whether or not you need additional training.

There are several things to keep in mind when engaged in a program of reading improvement. You should not try to read when overtired, and the eyes should be rested frequently. The habit of moving the lips or tongue while reading should be avoided. Nor should you read aloud when trying to increase your speed and comprehension. In addition, your own ideas should not be injected into the material; it is important to follow the author's thoughts whether you are in agreement with them or not.

Do's and don'ts

It is possible to improve reading speed and comprehension without seeking professional help. This approach requires a great deal of individual effort. But, if one is willing to study and practice, reading can be improved significantly. Merely reading a book on how to improve your reading will not increase reading ability—just as reading a driver's manual does not, in itself, enable one to operate an automobile. Concerted practice and discipline are required.

A number of principles may be applied in trying to develop improved reading habits. Many people tend to be perfectionists when reading. That is, they read every word because they are afraid of missing something important. But reading whole thoughts and phrases, rather than single words, increases both speed and comprehension. Start out by picking up some material of average difficulty, such as a popular magazine or a novel. Then time yourself to see how much you have read in, say, a fifteen-minute period. At a later time, preferably the next day, read for the same length of time, but try to read more of the text. While doing this, concentrate on moving forward and avoid looking back to pick up something you feel you may have missed. If you have trouble getting the full meaning, you are reading too fast. The important thing is to continue with concentrated practice in order to achieve improvement. There are a number of books on the market specifically designed to improve reading skills. They frequently contain tests that measure levels of comprehension.

Avoid perfectionism in your reading

Improved concentration is possible

One of the most frequent complaints reading specialists hear is, "I can't seem to concentrate." Thus one of the greatest benefits eventually derived from improved reading performance is an increase in one's powers of concentration. But it is an uphill battle, and students in the early stages of the program often feel that it cannot be won. Obviously, comprehension and concentration are greater if the subject is familiar and interesting. Individual background will determine the degree of complexity that the material holds for the reader. When material is not familiar, there are certain rules one can follow in training and practicing for comprehension. In the case of nonfiction, for example, the first objective should be to find the central thought of each paragraph and each chapter. One can do this by making use of the author's "clues." For example, there are chapter headings, divisions within chapters, and clearly defined subtitles. Another clue is the topic sentence, often the first sentence of the paragraph, which gives the reader a point of focus for what follows in the paragraph. One should keep the author's major and minor themes in mind as one reads and try to determine the essential point of the argument or thought. However, there is a hazard in relying too much on chapter headings and other divisions. For example, a newspaper heading that is an "attention getter" may give an exaggerated or misleading impression. Selective skimming is useful. But sometimes readers skim over great quantities of newspaper and magazine material in a frantic attempt to be "well-informed." All that may be derived from this practice is a useless, sensational version or an erroneous interpretation of what is being said in the article, book, or newspaper.

Retention can be improved by stopping periodically to review what has just been read. Experiments with college students have shown this procedure to be helpful in remembering more material and with greater accuracy. Stopping from time to time strengthens the recollection and the comprehension of what has just been read. When people cram in order to acquire information for an examination or some other short-term need, they soon forget what they have learned. The key to longer retention is repeated review of the material.

To improve retention further, one should clearly determine one's purpose for reading and then select the appropriate method. If you are reading merely to pass the time, you can read rapidly and without concern for details. However, when the material is technical, slow reading is essential to adequate comprehension.

Skilled readers can read short stories, novels, and other light material at around 450 to 500 words per minute. But when attempting to memorize facts or understand mathematical formulas, the material should be read at a rate of 100 to 150 words per minute. If the material is in a textbook of average difficulty, the reading rate should be approximately

Seek the topic sentence

Skim selectively

Review periodically

Be aware of your purpose in reading

Vary your speed

250 to 300 words per minute. An effective method of saving reading time is to skim the material (at a rate as high as several thousand words per minute) to find a few key phrases or thoughts that may determine if the material is relevant to one's need and worth reading at a rate conducive to full comprehension.

The most important habit to develop is that of reading thoughts instead of individual words. This skill requires a great deal of practice—especially for the person who feels that every word must be read. To practice, one should read easy material, such as short, general-interest magazine articles. These should be read rapidly, and one should then try to recall what has been read. The slow reader pauses frequently, sometimes more than once on a single word. On the other hand, a good reader will make as few as two or three fixations on a single line of a book. The goal is to learn to make fewer stops, taking in more words at a time. Speed is gained as one is able to see longer and longer groups of words at a glance. A good reader does this naturally, but a slow reader must be taught. One must learn to select the important words on each line and ignore those that are merely elaborative.

Make fewer stops

SUMMARY

As with all other techniques for effective management, the application of time management principles varies with the individual supervisor. Such things as personality, the make-up of the team, and the circumstances of given situations determine the supervisor's ability to manage details and maintain perspectives on organizational objectives. No two supervisors will use these techniques in exactly the same way. But effective supervisors will employ basic time management principles to one degree or another. Supervisors who manage their time wisely use one or more of the following guidelines. First of all, they organize and delegate. These organizing processes begin with the supervisor's own day. Supervisors who cannot organize themselves, their work, and their subordinates' work schedules are unsuited for supervisory responsibility. Good managers know their own strengths and weaknesses—and those of others. Whenever possible, they assign work to others. And they plan appointments, meetings, telephone calls, and other interruptions at times convenient to them—thereby conserving valuable time. They know the importance of working on one thing at a time. In order to facilitate this, they do not allow the office or the memory to become cluttered. They have a system in which to store information and provide a quick recall when needed. Supervisors can improve their use of time by:

1. Developing and maintaining a more effective secretarial relationship. The secretary should control the three most frequent interruptions—the telephone, drop-in visitors, and mail.
2. Establishing a quiet time during each work day.

3. Protecting the most productive time of the day.
4. Limiting the number of meetings and making optimal use of meeting time.
5. Improving reading habits.
6. Learning to say no.

At the end of each day, the supervisor should take time to review those projects completed and those planned but still unfinished. This gives the supervisor an opportunity to assess progress made or, if necessary, to analyze the reasons for insufficient progress. It also provides a time to plan for the completion of as yet unfinished tasks. Efficient time management demands self-discipline and the avoidance of procrastination. A daily review enables the supervisor to evaluate the degree of success he or she has had in achieving these goals.

HOW TIME GETS AWAY!

Just after the planning conference broke up, George Cox summed up the general feelings of his peers by stating: "Hell, even a 'day-stretcher' wouldn't give us enough time to do our jobs around here!" When several of his colleagues fervently agreed, it made George reflect a little upon what he had said.

Later that evening at home, while talking to a friend from another company, George casually introduced the problem of time management in his job. When his friend, Pete, suggested George run through a typical day in his office, George started by saying that, as a section head, he was responsible for the activities of 25 people. As he described it: "That may be considered a lot of people to supervise but I have an assistant to help me. The lack of help isn't really the problem—it's finding the time to do anything even half-way.

"For example, I am expected in the office about 8:30 A.M., but I'm usually at the desk by 8:00 A.M. This used to be a half-hour's peace and quiet to get things arranged for the day, but not any more. It seems that the minute I walk in these days someone is waiting to hand me the first crisis-of-the-day. And, honestly, we have one 'brush fire' after another all day long! They've been coming so fast lately that I have had to resort to an odd kind of priorities system. First, we decide which ones are more urgent and place those in some order of precedence. Then, within that list, we decide which ones we have to do a thorough job on, those we can just give a reasonable amount of time, and those we can only give a 'lick-and-a-promise.' We know that we are probably going to see this latter bunch again, and at a much increased urgency level, but when we are really pressed for time and people to do the work, as a manager, I have to set priorities on resources like these. It is a shame, though, because many of the things that we suspect we'll be seeing again could be done right the first time around, if we could just give them the attention they deserve."

In answer to a question from Pete, George continued by saying: "No, the job of the section hasn't really changed that much. We're still doing about the same things we were before. It's just the fact that there seems to be a lot more urgent problems coming up now than ever before. We are getting increased demands for more sophisticated planning from up the line and that could create a big problem, if we had time to comply—which we don't! So far, this increased planning demand has taken the form of several conferences, which also used up valuable time we could have spent on solving our problems. Take the conference we had this afternoon. The division manager called a meeting to discuss the long-range planning goals of the division. Heck, we haven't even done any short-range planning in the last two years, let alone sit around dreaming about what our problems are going to be 10 or 20 years from now. Don't misunderstand me. I know the division needs to do some long-range planning, but they shouldn't expect the sections to drop everything and sit around thinking about what we should be doing, or will be doing, in 1990! I said almost exactly that in the meeting this afternoon but got no satisfaction from the division manager. He's one of those guys who thinks everyone should take time to plan whether a person has the time or not."

Pete interrupted the conversation to ask George whether he had some regular plan for operating during the day. George responded by saying that he used to have an informal staff meeting about 9:00 A.M. every morning and a regularly scheduled meeting each Thursday afternoon. The staff meetings were really coordination sessions used to check the progress being made on projects and current problem areas. The formal Thursday meetings were to review ongoing problems. George said he had been forced to discontinue the morning staff meetings "for lack of a quorum," and the Thursday meetings were abandoned after a series of unexpected, but necessary, cancellations. George stated that he, personally, did all of the coordinating now, since some one person needed to know everything that was going on during hectic times, such as the current ones.

George finished the review of his day, stating that: "By lunchtime, I feel like I've already been working 12 hours. The pressure never seems to stop! Lately, I've been eating a sandwich and a glass of milk at my desk. At least it's quiet during the lunch hour. I don't even answer the telephone when it rings. However, it looks like I'm going to have to start locking the door, since some of the boys in the office have started dropping by to ask questions. I can't really blame them for wanting an uninterrupted few minutes with their boss, but it doesn't do much good. Up to now, by the time everybody else got back from lunch, I found I had done quite a few things.

"The division manager saw me eating at my desk last week and told me I ought to get out of the office for a while during the lunch hour. He advised me to take a walk around town. He didn't tell me who would do the work I do between noon and 1:00 P.M. if I left the office to take a walk.

"The afternoons really haven't been as productive as I would like them to be. Of course, most of us are tired after a hard morning's work and then, too, lately we seem to spend a lot of time in the afternoon redoing some of the things we did in the morning. I've wondered if it was my fault that some sloppy staff work kept popping up, but I'm pretty well convinced that it is just the pressure and a lot of problems that we can't seem to solve once and for all that cause our predicament.

"There is one thing that would help us. Neither I nor any of my people go to meetings we can get out of right now. Therefore, we occasionally miss something at a meeting that we should have known that might have saved us a lot of work. But, we just can't afford the time to go to meetings the way things are now in the office!

"There is one other problem that our current pace has caused. I used to have time to talk to the people in the office about new things that were taking place but not any more. Accordingly, when some new program or procedure comes down from higher authority, I just have to distribute it without any amplification of meaning for my people. Ordinarily, that wouldn't be too bad, but lately we have experienced a number of small incidents concerning new regulations where my interpretations and those of some of my people didn't quite coincide. We have learned to live with that situation, but it is not really the way things should be done and it has caused us a few minor problems."

1. What is George's problem?
2. Identify the time wasters that are keeping George from increasing his unit's performance.
3. How would delegation improve George's productivity?
4. What effects might George's work habits have on his own health and career?

Source: William D. Heier, Arizona State University. This case appears in John E. Dittrich and Robert A. Zawacki (eds.), *People and Organizations: Cases in Management and Organizational Behavior* (Plano, Texas: Business Publications, Inc., 1981), pp. 124–126.

DISCUSSION QUESTIONS

1. List and discuss ways that supervisors waste time on the job.
2. What are the habits of a workaholic?
3. What are the advantages of using a time plan?
4. Discuss some ways that a supervisor can manage the telephone better?
5. List and discuss the principles of conducting a successful meeting.
6. Define a standing plan and what a plan of this type is used for.
7. How can a secretary be utilized in order to manage visitors?
8. What does "delegating" mean? Discuss some guidelines that help a supervisor delegate effectively.
9. Supervisor Harry has been burning the midnight oil and can't seem to catch up on the unit's work. His boss, Vera, indicates Harry should use better time management to solve his problems and asks him to write down how he spent the day. The various tasks and corresponding times are listed below. Suggest various ways that Harry could have saved time in performing these tasks.

TIME ANALYSIS OF SUPERVISOR HARRY'S DAY

ACTIVITY	TIME	SUGGESTION	TIME SAVED
Preparing written request to the home office attempting to justify a 20 percent increase in budget next year.	60 min.		
Discussing next month's case load schedule with Mr. G. To be repeated with Mrs. R, Mr. K, and Miss Q later.	15 min.		
Handling thirteen telephone calls only three of which were personal.	50 min.		
Worked on client files alone doing a reorganizing job. Left note to file clerk on work performed.	50 min.		
Interviewing woman sent by Personnel as a possible replacement for Miss Q, who is leaving in two weeks. Decided individual not suitable.	50 min.		
Repairing broken equipment that only I could fix. I asked Mr. K and Mr. G to take an early lunch while I repaired it so they could continue working when they returned.	60 min.		
Typed up an extra five copies of weekly case-load report so that all caseworkers would be informed.	30 min.		

ACTIVITY	*TIME*	*SUGGESTION*	*TIME SAVED*
Struggled again with a new office layout plan that would free about forty square feet for a new piece of equipment on order. Got disgusted and tore up both new and previous plans. Impossible.	50 min.		
Trip downtown to talk to some civic leaders about a controversial program that has been continuing for too long. Meeting took thirty minutes. Transportation time twenty minutes each way.	70 min.		
Meeting with unit employees explaining the vacation policy and schedule for the summer.	45 min.		

REFERENCES

Douglas, Donna N., and Douglas, Merrill E. "Timely Techniques for Paperwork Mania." *The Personal Administrator* (September 1979): 21.

Lakein, Alan. *How to Get Control of Your Time and Your Life.* New York: New American Library, 1973.

MacKenzie, R. Alec. *The Time Trap: How to Get More Done in Less Time.* New York: McGraw-Hill, 1972.

Oncken, William, Jr., and Wass, Donald L. "Management Time: Who's Got the Monkey." *Harvard Business Review* (November–December 1974): 75–80.

Rowan, Robert. "That Filing System Inside Your Head." *Fortune*, August 28, 1978: 82–88.

Schilling, C. W. "Time Planning: How to Divide Up Your Day." *Supervision* 42 (February 1980): 12–15.

PART 2

GETTING
THINGS DONE
THROUGH PEOPLE

CHAPTER 3

NEW VALUES— OLD STYLES

Don't get me wrong. I didn't say it is a *good* job. It's an OK job—about as good a job as a guy like me might expect. The foreman leaves me alone and it pays well. But I would never call it a good job. It doesn't amount to much, but it's not bad.

—BLUE-COLLAR WORKER ON A ROUTINE JOB

Chapter Outline

Objectives

Understanding the differences in values between supervisors and today's subordinates is one of the great challenges in developing the supervisor/subordinate relationship. This chapter provides a basis for understanding these differences, identifies specific values, and presents a practical means of matching the new values with new organizational styles. Specifically, in this chapter you will become familiar with:

1. Job dissatisfaction and its effects on morale and productivity
2. Where values come from
3. Values held by today's workers
4. How to meet new values with new management styles
5. The power of expectations and how to be a positive Pygmalion

Major Concepts ———————————

Work

Job dissatisfaction

Employee stress

Theory X and Theory Y

Values

"New breed" employee

Attitudes

Expectations

The Pygmalion effect

Psychological climate

The supervisor/subordinate process

IS THE WORK ETHIC DEAD?

I am moving at my usual shopping pace: a quick trot, followed by a fast gallop. I dash into a store, zip through my selections, and whirl to the cash register.

The cashier stands behind the counter studying the curve of her fingernails. I place my articles on the counter; she is held entranced by her hands. I stare at her; she ignores me. I clear my throat; slowly the sound waves penetrate her brain. The young woman raises her eyes and regards me as if to say, "Why are you intruding upon my private time with my fingernails?"

"I'd like these, please."

Like molasses in January, she oozes in my direction. With maddening slowness she takes each selection, slowly revolves it to find the price tag, and with what seems great effort, punches the information into the cash register. Her movements remind me of a person struggling through wet cement.

During the entire procedure, her gaze is drifting aimlessly around the store. I wish I could put blinders on her so she would tend to business. Finally, she totals the bill and I hand her my money.

"Oh my," she says thoughtfully as she gazes into the cash drawer, "I'm out of $1 bills."

She stands pondering the cash register as though if she looks at it long enough it might suddenly start producing bills on the spot. "Hmmmmm," she muses and repeats her discovery, "I don't have any $1 bills."

"Why don't you get some?" I inquire, wondering how she can collect a paycheck and not realize the obvious.

"Well-l-l," she sighs. "Hmmmmm." Lazily, she glances around, and seeing another young girl, she visibly brightens.

"Oh, Susie," she calls. "I'm out of $1 bills. Why don't you get some?"

Time passes—no Susie. More time—still no Susie. My schedule now has crumbled.

Perhaps she's gone to pull off a bank robbery, I think, just to get the $1 bills. Maybe she was caught. Maybe we'll wait till they release her from prison.

I hear Susie coming. She is preceded by a wave of giggles as she stands in the aisle telling another clerk-friend all about last night's movie. With every description of the movie's plot she waves the bundle of $1 bills in the air for emphasis while the line of customers behind me lengthens.

Finally, Susie turns off her giggles and slowly plods to the cash register. Now at last, I think, we can get this show on the road.

Miss Molasses starts to gather up my change. "Oh-h-h," she exclaims, in wide-eyed wonder, "I don't have any pennies! Susie, could you get some pennies?"

It has been 25 minutes, and I'm still standing at this slow-motion counter with this turtle-footed child. Mad thoughts rumble through my brain, like: "If you were my daughter, I'd light your fire," or "If I managed this store, I'd fire you—period!"

"Never mind the pennies," I state, "just give me the rest of the change. I have other things to do."

"Well!" Miss Molasses fumes, finally expending some energy by puffing herself up. "If that's the way you want it!"

Change in hand, minus 4 cents, I leave.

Adapted from "Point of View," *Denver Post,* August 9, 1982.

Many of today's managers will recognize "Miss Molasses." She and her male counterpart seem to be everywhere. Why, managers ask, do today's young people not practice the work ethic that built this nation? Why is it they seem to respond so poorly to the supervisor's urgings to "work harder," "do a good job," and "be loyal to the company"?

Consider the effect on the supervisor, who can't understand why employees are not following his or her directives correctly and enthusiastically. Consider also the effect on the new subordinates, who have just joined the organization and find the supervisor's attitude and behaviors to be very much different from what they expected. These people seem, to each other, to be from different worlds. Why do they see things differently, expect different things to happen, and therefore behave differently? It is because *they have different values.*

These differences provide the major focus of this chapter. As discussed in detail later in the chapter, employee values, beliefs, attitudes, and behaviors have changed substantially over the years. If this change in employees had been accompanied by corresponding changes in organizational structure and climate, there would be little problem. However, this is not the case. While there are exceptions, many organizations today continue to use *old styles* in dealing with *new values.* If one views the contemporary employee as "water," and organizational styles as "oil," the old cliché "Oil and water don't mix!" is quite appropriate. Using current terminology, the practitioner and theorist would say there is a lack of "contingency" adaptation. Organizational styles are not being changed to fit different kinds of employees. As a result, many people have dissociated themselves from the workplace—although not from work—leaving literally millions of workers dissatisfied with the job or at least with certain elements that make up the work environment. The effect of job dissatisfaction on the worker is the subject we begin with.

Job Dissatisfaction

Job dissatisfaction is an occupational malady that affects white- and blue-collar workers alike, and it costs employers billions of dollars each year in absenteeism, reduced output, and shoddy workmanship. It occurs whenever there is a "discrepancy between the individual's work values [what is wanted, needed, and/or expected from the job] and what the job delivers. . . . Changes in job satisfaction can therefore result from changes in either or both of those terms" [i.e., values and/or job].[1] How the concept of work itself has changed, the vastness of job dissatisfaction among American workers, and the symptoms of worker dissatisfaction—these are important subjects to the supervisor.

DOES WORK HAVE TO BE "WORK"?

There have been many changes in attitudes toward work over the last few decades. Prior to World War II, work was generally considered to involve physical labor, dirty and sometimes unsafe conditions (as in coal

---

[1] Raymond A. Katzell, "Changing Attitudes Toward Work," in *Work in America: The Decade Ahead,* ed. E. C. Kerr and J. Rosow (Princeton, N.J.: Van Nostrand, 1979), p. 42.

mining), and little opportunity to achieve personal fulfillment. In short, work conveyed a very negative connation to most people. While there are still pockets of people who hold these beliefs, by and large a different orientation toward work has emerged, especially since the early 1960s. Many employees are more concerned about the quality of their work lives—that work should represent a means of satisfying personal needs beyond survival.

What people want from work varies with the individual. Some see work as a way of accomplishing personal goals, others view it as simply a way of passing the time. How a worker views work, whether it is perceived positively or negatively, is influenced not only by the individual's values but by his or her immediate supervisor and by the organization's climate. If the worker belongs to a strong union, the union's influence also affects the perception of work. Government regulations, customers, and co-workers are other variables that influence the attractiveness (or unattractiveness) of the type of work a person does.

Many things can affect worker satisfaction

Does work have to mean drudgery, frustration, and pain? Must it always be an activity that is instinctively despised? Certainly there are risks when it comes to choosing a job or career. A wrong choice can lead to a lifetime of failure and aggravation. But a good choice can open up a lifetime of opportunities for personal growth and fulfillment. When there is a match between person and job, any number of positive outcomes may occur: Wealth, fame, friends, health, happiness, and meaning in life are just a few. People who enjoy their work look forward to each workday—in effect, their work is also their hobby.

Work can be a hobby

THE SCOPE OF JOB DISSATISFACTION

How extensive is the problem of job dissatisfaction? The answer appears to depend on which study one happens to read. For example, the Gallup poll, over the years, has claimed that 80 to 90 percent of workers report positively about their jobs.[2] Does this mean that such high percentages of workers are *really* satisfied with their jobs? Most researchers say no. Longitudinal surveys by the Opinion Research Corporation (ORC) suggest that a substantial proportion of blue-collar workers (a) report being satisfied with their jobs but also indicate they wish to change them and (b) report they would continue working even if they didn't have to but only to fill time.[3] Some of the most recent ORC studies, of

[2] U.S. Department of Labor, "Job Satisfaction: Is There a Trend?" *Research Monograph*, no. 30 (1974), p. 45.
[3] M. R. Cooper, B. S. Morgan, P. M. Foley, and L. B. Kaplan, "Changing Employee Values: Deepening Discontent?" *Harvard Business Review*, January–February 1979, p. 118.

175,000 workers in 159 companies, show that most employees (a) believe their company is not as good a place to work as it once was, (b) regard their pay favorably but are of the opinion that their pay does not offset job dissatisfaction, and (c) increasingly expect their organizations to respond to their complaints.[4] The ORC studies also estimate that 25 percent of all U.S. workers—24 million people—are unhappy in their jobs for one reason or another.[5] If this is true, it represents a significant increase over the 20 percent of workers who were dissatisfied in the Gallup poll mentioned earlier.

Conclusion—a lot of workers are unhappy

Perhaps the most distressing revelation, at least for supervisors, is that made by the noted pollster Daniel Yankelovich. He suggests that an overwhelming 84 percent of all Americans "feel a certain resentment; a belief that those who work hard and live by the rules end up on the short end of the stick." [6] He adds that only 13 percent of all working Americans find their work truly meaningful and more important than their leisure-time pursuits.[7]

On balance, it appears that there are enough studies reporting increasing worker dissatisfaction to believe that the problem is indeed a serious one. While estimates of numbers are imprecise, there does appear to be major discontent that leads to all kinds of morale and productivity problems.

JOB DISSATISFACTION AND THE BOTTOM LINE

Yankelovich estimates that up to $20 billion a year is lost in productivity and in additional labor expenses because of absenteeism.[8] Nearly half of those absences, say experts, are due to poor attitudes and lack of commitment to the job. Furthermore, when times are good and workers perceive themselves as having other options, employees tend to quit jobs in which they are unhappy. This results in both lower productivity and higher labor costs, as new employees have to be trained. Poor workmanship and, in some cases, sabotage also run up business expenses for firms. Dented door panels on cars coming off a Detroit assembly line were traced to an angry worker who had been hitting the passing panels with his fists.[9]

Active resistance

---

[4] Mark Mindell and William Gordon, "Employee Values in a Changing Society," AMA Management Briefing, 1981, p. 8.

[5] Cooper et al., "Changing Employee Values," pp. 117–125.

[6] "Why So Many Workers Lie Down on the Job," *U.S. News & World Report,* April 6, 1981, p. 71.

[7] Ibid.

[8] Ibid., p. 72.

[9] Ibid.

Less dramatic evidence of worker dissatisfaction can be found in the ready admission of employees that they have little energy or enthusiasm for their work. Some perform their tasks adequately, some even exceptionally well, but they reject additional responsibility, even though it would mean a promotion and more pay. An example is the twenty-four-year-old machinist who turns down a promotion to foreman.

Passive resistance

Not even supervisors are immune from worker dissatisfaction. It would appear logical to expect supervisors to be more dedicated about their jobs because they have a greater personal stake in the organization. But this is not necessarily the case. One study reported a significant increase in supervisory and managerial discontent.[10] It might appear in such subtle ways as refusing to cooperate with co-workers who are experiencing particular job-related difficulties, or it might surface in more noticeable ways such as allowing obviously defective units to pass through an assembly station because taking the time to report them would interfere with a scheduled racquetball match.

Supervisory discontent

JOB DISSATISFACTION AND EMPLOYEE STRESS

There are other, less tangible costs of employee dissatisfaction. Research continues to document the association between job-related stress and its undesirable human consequences: mental illness, physical illness (e.g., hypertension, stomach disorders, heart disease), and alcoholism, to name a few.

Needless stress is not good for people or organizations. Supervisors need to be particularly conscious of the type of atmosphere they create for their workers. If the management style encourages an attitude of "every man for himself," for example, needless stress will usually follow.

What can the supervisor do to minimize this problem? Maybe very little when the employee doesn't fit the job or is experiencing personal problems outside of the work environment. On the other hand, the supervisor does have a large influence in the type of psychological climate that exists in the employee's immediate work environment. In that light, the supervisor becomes partially responsible (a responsibility that is shared with management) for providing a humane job climate—one that does not reward employee self-centeredness and insensitivity to co-workers. Instead, employees should be encouraged and rewarded for demonstrating kindness, consideration, and mutual support to their fellow workers. The ideal psychological climate is one that treats each worker with personal respect. Even routine and boring jobs can become palatable to workers when co-workers and management are supportive and considerate.

The supervisor creates the psychological climate

[10] Cooper et al., pp. 117–125.

When Styles and Values
Don't Match ▬▬▬▬▬▬▬▬▬

It's been more than twenty-five years since Douglas McGregor first began telling managers that their styles did not fit employees' values.[11] *Conventional* organization structures, managerial policies, practices, and programs reflect a philosophy of management that McGregor labeled Theory

Theory X

X. In essence, Theory X views workers as lazy, lacking ambition, disliking responsibility, resisting change, not particularly intelligent, inherently self-centered, and indifferent to organizational needs.[12] To meet this perceived challenge, management methods for directing employee behavior include coercion and/or disguised threats, close supervision, and excessive external controls—such as severe penalties for tardiness.

Theory X, of course, is an extreme view of the worker. Most organizations today would never willingly admit to holding such beliefs. Instead, a more popular philosophy is expressed as being "firm but fair" with the worker.

Theory Y

At the other end of the spectrum is a philosophy that McGregor referred to as Theory Y. Basically, this philosophy of management views the worker as self-directed, hard working, committed to the organization's objectives, intelligent, a willing learner, creative, and having unlimited potential.[13] Of course, most organizations fall somewhere in between these two extreme views.

What happens when management holds one set of assumptions about workers (e.g., Theory X) and workers don't fit the mode? One need only witness the rash of lawsuits, confrontations and hostility, and the overall adversarial relationship between management and unions to have an idea of the immensity of the problem. Such noteworthy organizational practices as monetary incentive systems, goal setting, and job enrichment strategies have been rendered ineffective because of management's failure to read what employees really perceive as important.

Value differences, to many managers, represent the core of the problem. Common sense suggests that when a group of people share values, there is greater cohesiveness, friendliness, and cooperation among the group. Even when values within a group differ, there is merit in taking

Some reasons for identifying employees' values

the time to identify and understand them. For one thing, motivational strategies, to be effective, must be based on an understanding of individual values. What turns people on? What is important to them? For another,

[11] Douglas McGregor, Proceedings of the Fifth Anniversary Convocation of the School of Industrial Management, MIT, April 9, 1957.
[12] Douglas McGregor, *The Human Side of Enterprise* (New York: McGraw-Hill, 1960), p. 33.
[13] Ibid., p. 34.

such organizational processes as decision making and communication are affected by the employees' values. How important is employee participation, for example, in such traditional management strongholds as scheduling work? Do employees expect or desire to share in important organizational decisions?

The challenge to management, and hence to the supervisor, is to identify the basic value structures of the work force so that the work experience can be structured in such a way that the employees' needs and the organization's needs can be integrated. Ideally, such integration would allow employees to satisfy their own needs while at the same time serving the needs of the organization. The net result would be that both parties come out winners. Only by first understanding values can the supervisor hope to begin to match the job with the needs of the employee.

Matching employees' needs to the organization's needs

Feeling, Thinking, Doing— Understanding the Individual

A total human being is made up of three separate but interacting parts. Figure 3.1 represents those parts: feelings, thinking, and doing. The three interact to produce the image one presents to others. And they represent one's total set of values, attitudes, needs, and motives. An attitude, for example, results from interaction between what one logically thinks and intuitively feels. How one behaves tells others what one's attitude is.

The set of values that an employee brings to the organization comes from a variety of sources. But basically, people's values tell them how to order their environment. Although often changed by logical thinking processes, values are typically the result of deep personal feelings concern-

The world is seen through one's values

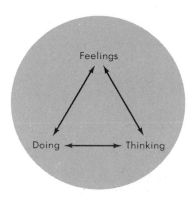

FIGURE 3.1
Elements in the
Individual's Makeup

ing what work, play, or life should be. These values become the basis for needs and motives that develop in all aspects of an individual's life.

Behavior may be in conflict with values

Typically, the individual makes an effort to keep attitudes and values in balance with behavior, but often this is not possible. In other words, people sometimes feel they should behave one way, but for a variety of reasons they do not behave that way at all. Or people may rationally think something is right, proper, or correct, and yet must behave quite differently (e.g., a supervisor may favor pollution control but avoid using pollution control devices because the organization says it's too expensive). As a supervisor it is important to recognize that although individuals usually strive for consistency between values and actions, occasionally they are required to act inconsistently with either their feelings or their logic.

WHY VALUES ARE IMPORTANT

Typically, employees believe that they are capable and responsible. If given no responsibility or autonomy by the supervisor, however, they are forced merely to ask questions, not to make decisions; they have to do only what they are specifically told to do. Their value of what work should be like is not consistent with what work actually is for them. Although the inconsistency is obvious to the subordinates, it is often not so apparent to the supervisor. In the example just given, the subordinates are displeased with the lack of responsibility given them and may react to fit the misperception. In other words, if they are treated as incompetent and incapable, they might as well act like it! This keeps feelings, thinking, and actions in balance. The supervisor, seeing how the subordinates behave, is assured that he or she is treating them the way they should be treated, because otherwise they would "goof off," "screw up," or shirk their responsibilities.

Supervisor cannot see employees' values, only their behavior

The supervisor assumes that the subordinates' actions reflect their internal values and beliefs. Although the subordinates are indeed trying to match attitudes and behaviors, they often cannot when old management styles are in conflict with the subordinates' contemporary values. As a supervisor, you should try to understand and appreciate the contemporary values, needs, and motives of today's subordinates so that both you and they can function effectively.

What, then, *do* subordinates feel and think? How are their individual values determined? What factors influence people so that when they join an organization they have a full set of values and beliefs that guide their actions?

Although an understanding of *how* values are developed may not seem as important to the supervisor as *what* values subordinates hold, both understandings are critical. The next section identifies some of the factors that determine how values are developed.

FACTORS DETERMINING INDIVIDUAL VALUES

Although the influence of specific factors varies among individuals, some factors have a more substantial impact on the development of an individual's values than do others.

Values development begins in early childhood. The family is usually the major source of values. For instance, the idea of working hard to get ahead is typically derived from the things children see and hear at home. If constantly told to work hard, and if they see their mothers and fathers working hard and achieving success, they are likely to carry those values with them through life. On the other hand, the child who sees much hard work but few rewards may develop negative values, that is, that hard work is *not* the way to get ahead. Some families living on assistance have produced a generation of young people who have never learned what it means to be gainfully employed. Supervisors faced with this type of person must realize that in these employees they probably have people whose values do not incorporate the traditional work ethic.

The impact of the family

Many other factors leading to values development are related to family background. Economic conditions, for example, affect each person's family life. Depressions and recessions typically create serious difficulties for families and, in fact, often cause the breadwinner in the family to take a job in another city, state, or country. This has an immediate and substantial impact on family life and specifically on the values development of the children. They may develop the attitude that a job and support of family are more important than being with the family all the time. Thus they may be much more willing to accept a remote assignment or relocate their own families. But the reverse may also occur. Children of persistently absent parents may, when they become parents, turn down promotional opportunities rather than be willing to be absent from or uproot their own families.

Additionally, people's religious affiliation, schooling, neighborhood, social groups, and even their geographic location can influence the development of their values. Figure 3.2 represents the variety of factors that influence an individual's values.

As individuals move through life, their values continue to develop. Early childhood factors are either replaced or modified as individuals grow, relocate, and associate with different people, different educational

FIGURE 3.2
Factors That Shape an
Individual's Values

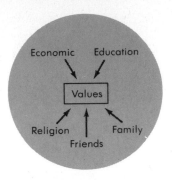

systems, and different cultural backgrounds. Over time, values usually become more stable and less subject to change. By the time people enter the work force, the rate of value change has decreased substantially, such that the eighteen-, nineteen-, or twenty-year-old has a relatively permanent set of values. An individual's values may change because of significant incidents in the adult years; but basic values remain pretty much intact throughout an adult's life. As a supervisor, then, you should be aware of the individual and aggregate values likely to be held by your employees.

> Only significant events will affect established values

Value Comparisons

As a supervisor, you should be aware of the values generally held by today's work force. Additionally, you need to recognize how your own values may differ from those of your subordinates. This section identifies not only the values currently held by the average worker, but also the values held and management styles practiced by the typical supervisor.

SOME MISCONCEPTIONS ABOUT TODAY'S WORKER

Probably the biggest complaint heard in industry and government today is that employees no longer seem to subscribe to the idea that one should work hard and be loyal to the organization. Employers repeatedly comment that employees today do not want to give a "fair day's work for a fair day's pay"; they want to "do a little and get paid a lot"; they're "undermotivated"; they "only care about money"; or "you can't trust them." Many employers feel that employees in the past were better than the employees of today—that they had better *work values.*

> The "demise" of the work ethic

These sentiments might create the belief that today's workers are not producing as much as workers did in the past. We believe, however, that this is false (see accompanying box). The fault seems to lie not with the inappropriate values of the "new breed," [14] but rather in a failure to match those new values with new styles of management.

The Opinion Research Corporation indicates that there has been a major shift in values over the last twenty-five years. Yet it does not depict the American worker as lazy, irresponsible, or dishonest. Instead, it characterizes the shift as one of increasing demand for, as well as tolerance of, self-expression, self-fulfillment, and personal growth. M. R. Cooper and his associates attempt to explain this shift in values:

> There seem to be at least three possible explanations for this trend: (1) that the newer work force values different things; (2) that the older work force has changed what it values; and (3) that the work force is just beginning to overtly articulate what it has always covertly valued. [15]

While traditional values encouraged the individual to sacrifice himself for the sake of family, employer, community, and country, "new breed" values place more emphasis on being true to oneself. This preoccupation with self does not mean that family, community, and country are any less important. It suggests only that the execution of these obligations must take place within the context of self-fulfillment.

Rather than being lazy or expressing a "don't care" attitude, workers in general appear to be disappointed and disillusioned with the atmosphere in which they must often work. Employees in the United States today are better educated, more vocal, and more aware of personal and organizational rights. Employees are no longer content to work hard and hope that appropriate rewards will follow. They want a greater voice in matters that concern the quality of their organizational life. This kind of attitude, and workers' willingness to assert themselves, have created a formidable force—one that needs to be recognized and dealt with by the supervisor in today's organization.

People are more egocentric

Employee expectations are higher

SUPERVISOR VALUES AND MANAGEMENT STYLES

As a supervisor, you are faced with a group of employees whose values are likely to be fairly well established before you even meet them. If your values match those of the group, you will likely have little problem communicating with, motivating, and controlling them. Often, however, this is not the case. Even when supervisors have been promoted from within the group, they often find that their values and beliefs suddenly

---

[14] A term coined by Daniel Yankelovich and one we have chosen to use in this text when comparing contemporary values to more traditional values.

[15] Cooper et al., "Changing Employee Values," p. 125.

THE WORK FORCE: A NEW DIVERSITY

In 1950, the typical American worker was a white male, aged 25 to 44, who worked at a blue-collar job to support a wife and family.

In 1980, there was no typical American worker. Jobholders were almost as likely to be female as male; to be young as to be old. Less than 15% fit the description of the so-called traditional worker: a married male wage earner whose wife does not work.

That radical shift in the composition of the American work force resulted from equally radical changes in social values and economic conditions during the last three decades. It, in turn, has created new social values that affect the workplace—and will continue to do so throughout the 1980s.

The 1950s worker was scarred by the Depression and World War II. He saw self-denial and hard work as the road to the security, stability, and material well-being he longed for. The economy, fueled by the postwar demand for goods and services, rewarded him by doubling his disposable income during the next decade.

Yet the 1960s worker was less certain of the worth of financial rewards. Prosperity had not brought him or the nation the contentment he sought. Another war fueled social unrest and economic uncertainty. His children resisted simple obedience to authority and carried that resistance with them from classrooms into companies. They were better educated than ever before; the average worker now had almost one full year of training after high school. More of them were women, too, as females under 35 moved into the labor force at unprecedented rates.

By the 1970s, the American worker was turning from an ethic of obligation to others—his family, his employer, his country—that he had felt so strongly in the '50s. He stopped believing that self-sacrifice automatically paid off and turned instead to an ethic of duty to oneself first. So did his wife and the wives of his co-workers as they moved into jobs in large numbers: Nearly half of all married women were working by the end of the decade.

differ from those who used to be their peers but are now their subordinates.

A move to supervision can alter one's values

The movement from subordinate, with little authority or responsibility, to supervisor, with considerable authority and responsibility, is an example of one of the "significant events" in life that can alter a person's values. Supervisors are expected to behave in certain ways, and they will typically conform their values to be consistent with the responsibilities of the new position. As a newly promoted supervisor, one emphasizes cost control, higher productivity, less absenteeism, better motivation, and so forth. In short, one now stresses things that one may never have thought about as a subordinate. One's own neck is now on the chopping block, and all of a sudden one finds that things which were once unimportant are now very important. As a new supervisor, one needs to keep in mind that one's beliefs, values, and attitudes probably differ now from those of former co-workers.

The two key changes within the work force that evolved during the '60s and '70s—more women, more educated workers—will make their clearest mark on the workplace of the '80s.

Most female workers will be strongly work-oriented, anxious for job success; at the same time, many will ask for personal satisfaction from work, as well as greater flexibility at work to accommodate their roles as wives and mothers. Their husbands may become less work-oriented since they are no longer the sole support of their families, and may also put a premium on job flexibility and more leisure time.

More and more working people will have training after high school, and will come from middle-class families. They will care less about jobs that simply pay the bills, more about work they feel is self-fulfilling. They are apt to be frustrated by work they feel does not use their skills.

A third change will complicate these two. Because of the low birthrate of the '60s, the number of younger workers will drop. This fact and the aging of the baby boom generation will result in an overabundance of the prime-age work force—people aged 25 to 44 who are usually trying to move up a career ladder. There will be fierce competition for promotions and great frustration for those who fail to attain them. As a result, some of these workers are likely to put more emphasis on traditional rewards—security, earnings, benefits, promotion, and retirement.

Throughout the '80s then, the mark of the work force will be diversity: in the types of workers, in the attitudes and values they bring to work, and in the benefits they seek.

Sharon Frederick, "Why John and Mary Won't Work," *Inc.,* April 1981, p. 74.

THE POWER OF SHARED VALUES

It is one thing to understand how people's values are formed and what effect those values might have on their behavior, but the impact that *shared* values have on organizational norms is also important. Values can positively influence the organizational climate when those values reflect the essence of a company's philosophy for operating a business. For example, Delta Airlines is known around the industry as "the people company." The slogan might sound like a worn-out cliché until one hears some of the comments of Delta employees: "This airline takes care of its people." One pilot we talked with commented, "I don't mind loading or unloading baggage because I know that times are tough and everyone needs to pitch in." Delta's employees feel so strongly about their company that they recently purchased a 767 jetliner and gave it to the company.

Shared values can influence organizational climate

Company slogans
don't have to be
meaningless

Company slogans such as Delta's often indicate the overall philosophy of management. The slogan may even filter down to supervisors and subordinates in the form of specific beliefs and practices. In effect, organizational values define the customs, rites, and rituals that communicate exactly how management want their employees to behave (e.g., attitudes toward customers, personal appearance, willingness to work weekends, and so on).

How do shared values affect organizational performance? Deal and Kennedy suggest that corporate culture (i.e., shared values) represent a powerful force in the work setting in three ways:

(1) Managers and others throughout the organization give extraordinary attention to whatever matters are stressed in the corporate value system—and this in turn tends to produce extraordinary results. An oil company produces crude . . . much more efficiently than others because efficient operation is what it values and what its managers concentrate on. One of this company's principal competitors values trading and financial management most highly. Accordingly, its managers worry less about production operations and concentrate instead on squeezing every cent of potential revenues from their sales.

(2) Down-the-line managers make marginally better decisions on the average because they are guided by their perception of the shared values (e.g., heavy emphasis on people concerns). When a manager at Dana Corporation is confronted by a close question—like making a particular investment in increased productivity versus one in new product development—the manager is likely to opt for productivity (because the slogan at Dana is "productivity through people").

(3) People simply work a little harder because they are dedicated to the cause. "I'm sorry I'm so late getting home, but the customer had a problem and we never leave a customer with a problem." [16]

Shared values can
improve employee
productivity

Deal and Kennedy believe that an organization's culture is an important variable in any strategy for improving productivity. How employees perceive what the organization stands for, and thus what behaviors and attitudes are rewarded, can have an amazing effect on productivity. Deal and Kennedy estimate that strongly shared values can mean an increase in productivity of as much as one or two hours of work per employee per day.[17] When employees are proud of their organization (e.g., "I work with Delta"), they identify with the company. As a result, the next time they have a choice of helping the company or goofing off, they will probably choose the former.

[16] Terrance Deal and Allan Kennedy, *Corporate Cultures* (Reading, Mass.: Addison-Wesley, 1982), p. 33.
[17] Ibid., p. 15.

Expectations—The Pygmalion Effect

Recall that earlier the concept of Theory X and Y was introduced. We suggested that management's assumptions concerning the basic nature of people can, and often do, conflict with the values of the work force. Now we would like to point out how a supervisor's assumptions about people can lead to a self-fulfilling prophecy. Specifically, what happens when supervisors assume that the group is lazy and needs their constant attention? On the other hand, if supervisors' expectations are high, is productivity likely to be high? Is it possible that supervisors' expectations influence subordinate performance?

In numerous research studies, expectations, particularly those of the supervisor, have been consistently shown to influence subordinate performance. Even though values may differ, communicating high expectations of performance to the subordinate appears to result in high performance. The Pygmalion effect, also known as the self-fulfilling prophecy (SFP), is the tendency of people to perform in accordance with what is expected of them, as well as in accordance with their own expectations of success or failure. The existence of these expectations leads to their fulfillment. Expectations can exercise a significant positive or negative influence on job performance.

The self-fulfilling prophecy

Rosenthal's classic study in the classroom examined the influence that expectations have on performance.[18] Rosenthal randomly selected elementary school students, gave all of them IQ tests, and then told their teachers that a random group of students were "intellectual bloomers." Later he retested them and compared their scores to those of a control group of students, children whose teachers had not been given any expectations. The students who were *labeled* as "intellectual bloomers" showed a greater improvement in IQ scores. Even though students were randomly assigned to either the control or the experimental group, the experimental group had higher scores. These results were attributed solely to the "expectations" of teachers who had been told their students were "intellectual bloomers."

The power of expectations

Additional studies on this subject have been conducted in universities, institutions, private industry, and government. Repeatedly, the results support the Pygmalion effect; that is, we get what we expect from people. If we expect subordinates to perform well, they will; if we expect them to do poorly, they will!

[18] Robert Rosenthal, "The Pygmalion Effect Lives," *Psychology Today*, September 1973, pp. 56–63.

How is this possible? If I expect my brother to pay me the $10 he's owed me for five years, will I get the money? It doesn't seem likely that just expecting things to happen will cause people to behave accordingly. But if we want to understand what happens when a supervisor expects a subordinate to perform well or poorly, we need only look at how the supervisor behaves toward the subordinate in each case.

According to reinforcement theory, discussed in detail in a later chapter, people behave according to the way they are treated. Ask a poor worker why she is not a better worker, and she will often say it's because she's not treated fairly, properly, or with respect. The reverse is often true of the good performer. The way the supervisor behaves, then, contributes to that subordinate being a good or a poor performer.

The secret—
expectations +
treatment = SFP

LEARNING TO BE A POSITIVE PYGMALION

What are some strategies that the supervisor can use to bring about desired behaviors from the subordinate? Rosenthal suggested four factors (groups of behaviors) that contribute to better subordinate performance:

1. Climate—The supervisor creates a supportive atmosphere for employees with more "potential."
2. Feedback—The supervisor gives plenty of verbal clues to help improve subordinate performance.
3. Input—The supervisor "stretches" the subordinate by constantly "inputting" more difficult tasks.
4. Output—The supervisor encourages questions and creativity.[19]

What is being suggested here is that the supervisor treats the high-expectation subordinate differently than the low-expectation subordinate. The supervisor actually "creates" high-performance workers by behaving in positive ways toward them. More time is spent with high-expectation workers (listening to their problems, coaching them when they need advice), and the supervisor is constantly on the alert for opportunities that will further these subordinates' personal development. These subordinates are guided to become what the supervisor expects them to become.

Avoid being a
negative Pygmalion

However, there is also the chance that supervisors may be negative Pygmalions—possibly without being aware of the effect of their behaviors. As McGregor noted in his Theory X and Y propositions, we often "create" Theory X people by treating them as Theory X. If you, as the supervisor, expect a person to be a poor performer, you will likely behave in distinctly opposite ways than you do toward the high-performance

[19] Ibid., p. 60.

subordinate. Instead of the feedback and supportive atmosphere provided the good performer, you might have minimal contact, provide little feedback, and generally utilize punishment in dealing with the low-expectation subordinate. Is it any wonder, then, that the subordinate performs as poorly as expected?

THE PROCESS—CREATING THE HIGH-PERFORMANCE SUBORDINATE

The first step in creating a high-performance subordinate is for you, as the supervisor, to convey your expectations clearly. It is not enough simply to tell the subordinate what is expected. You must ensure that the employee understands your directions (i.e., there must be two-way communication), and you must ensure that all your actions support that verbal communication. If your words say "I expect you to do well," but your actions do not reinforce, provide feedback to, or exhibit trust in the subordinate, you will have conveyed an expectation of failure and the subordinate will fail.

Actions speak louder than words

The case of the "hard-core unemployed" type of worker provides a good example of how supervisor expectations can negatively influence the employee. Here is an employee who has never developed good work habits (e.g., going to work five days a week and being on time each of those five days), because he has had few regular jobs. The supervisor expects him to show up on time, and she tells the employee so. However, what happens the first time the employee is late? "I knew it!" says the supervisor. She had just confirmed to the employee her expectation that the employee would fail.

Be aware of negative stereotypes

Perhaps the supervisor has not taken the time to ensure that the employee knows what is expected of him. While the supervisor expects the worker to be there each day, the worker's understanding may be that being a good employee simply means being there three or four days out of the week. It is the supervisor's responsibility to break in the new employee, state her expectations, and then possibly have the subordinate rephrase what he was just told. The rephrasing would confirm that the subordinate knew what was expected of him. In addition, using positive cues (such as "Glad to see you today" or "Good, you've been here on time every day this week") will reinforce the expected behavior.

Clearly identify expectations

Second, the supervisor should regularly measure the subordinate against the standards (expectations) conveyed to him. Regardless of what the particular standards are, they must not change during the measurement process. The supervisor should tell the subordinate how he will be measured, collect the data, and then share that information with him, includ-

Identify measures for the employee

ing positive comments of things well done and suggestions for improvement.

Measurement standards should be understandable to the employee. In dealing with the disadvantaged worker, for example, the supervisor should not only keep track of the number of absences and late arrivals; she should make certain that the employee receives a regular reminder that this information is being recorded. An attendance record issued with the worker's weekly or bimonthly paycheck would be one way to do this.

Provide frequent and constructive feedback

Feedback and reinforcement of expectations complete the process of creating a high-performance subordinate. Following the initial conveying of expectations and identification of measurement standards, the supervisor should feed back to the employee an evaluation of his performance. Reinforcement for having correctly fulfilled the supervisor's expectations would typically be included with this feedback.

Recognize improvements

Reinforcement tells the disadvantaged employee, for example, that the supervisor *expects* him to be at work every day and on time. When the supervisor gives out the paycheck, she should take notice of an employee's attendance and provide reinforcement if attendance has been good. "Good job, Sam, you weren't late or absent at all in the last two weeks. Keep this up, and we'll try to get you onto that fork-lift job you want," is an example of the kind of verbal reinforcement that a supervisor can use.

J. Sterling Livingston has summarized the effect of the self-fulfilling prophecy on employee performance as follows:

> What a manager expects of his subordinates and the way he treats them largely determine their performance and career progress. A unique characteristic of superior managers is their ability to create high performance expectations that subordinates fulfill. Less effective managers fail to develop similar expectations, and as a consequence, the productivity of their subordinates suffers. Subordinates, more often than not, appear to do what they believe they are expected to do.[20]

When the employee uses the supervisor's comments to improve his future performance, the supervisor/subordinate *process* is working. As the process continues, the supervisor must constantly identify new and different expectations that stretch the subordinate's talent.

However, while stretching subordinates is generally recommended because it fills their jobs with challenging assignments, the supervisor must exercise caution. Should the subordinate experience frequent failure and few, if any, successes, be prepared to step in and readjust job expectations,

[20] J. Sterling Livingston, "Pygmalion in Management," *Harvard Business Review*, July–August 1967, p. 82.

as well as your personal expectations of his or her capabilities. It is most important to acknowledge the progress that occurred, thus protecting the subordinate's fragile self-confidence. Unrealistic expectations can lead to intensive frustration. At the worse, subordinates who believe they cannot "make the grade" tend to withdraw from the boss, put in an excessive amount of time on the job (no one can say they didn't try), and then voluntarily exit the organization should an opportunity arise.

> Be on the watch for unrealistic expectations

SUMMARY ▬▬▬▬▬▬▬▬▬▬▬▬▬▬▬▬▬▬▬▬▬

For many of today's employees, the conventional symbols of success are not enough. Contemporary workers are demanding more and giving less, or so say those who hold traditional values. Employees today speak of fulfilling one's potential, the need for psychological growth, and the desire to be true to oneself.

Today's employees are more vocal about jobs that are not sufficiently fulfilling, that lack flexibility and the opportunity for self-expression. Workers feel entitled (not privileged) to enjoy the better things in life. Second, they demand challenging and meaningful work and react negatively when assigned work they consider dehumanizing. Finally, they seek greater participation in the decisions that affect their work environment.

Organizations that are designed with old-fashioned job hierarchies and career paths in mind are finding this structure increasingly inappropriate for the contemporary worker. It is not uncommon, for example, to hear complaints from contemporary employees concerning the excessive time it takes to be promoted.

Knowing the employees' value systems is not simply a luxury, it is a necessity if management is to design an effective motivational system and reduce employee turnover. It makes good dollars and cents to consider an applicant's values profile so that a better and more long-term match can be made between job and worker.

Supervisors whose values more closely coincide with the traditional sector must be willing to accept the views of others with different values. It is important that we continually remind ourselves that values are neither right nor wrong. Values describe what individuals consider to be important. Yet an understanding of values is only a prerequisite to a more complex process that occurs between the supervisor and the subordinate.

The values supervisors hold will influence the kinds of expectations they have about subordinates. Theory X assumptions about employees can result in a self-fulfilling prophecy; subordinates who under different conditions would be categorized as Theory Y find themselves acting much as the Theory X supervisor expected. It is particularly important for supervisors to practice the act of being positive Pygmalions. For the supervisor, the process involves clearly defining expectations for the subordinate, measuring performance against those expectations, giving feedback, reinforcing desired behaviors, and redefining unrealistic expectations. Constant alterations and refinements in expectations and behaviors are important elements of this process.

ARNIE BENTLY—HOUSEHUSBAND

October in southern California can be warm. It was, in fact, about ninety degrees on the Tuesday afternoon that your author first spoke with the familiar bearded face in the supermarket checkout line.

"Hi," I began. "Seems like every time I'm in this place I see you."

"Yeah," he responded, "you retired, too?"

"No, afraid not. I'm a professor over at State. I teach on Mondays and Wednesdays, and the rest of the time I research and write at home. I try to hit the market during the day to avoid the crowds."

The bearded face, who had now introduced himself as Arnie Bently, told your author that he, too, liked to shop when most people were working.

"Are you retired?" I inquired. "Hell, you can't be thirty-five years old!"

"I'm thirty-three to be exact," began Arnie. "I graduated from State in 1971, with a degree in computer science. Worked for San Diego Gas and Electric for six years but hated it. So I retired."

Arnie's story fascinated me. How did he make ends meet? What did he do with himself every day? I really wanted to get to know more about Arnie Bently. I asked him if I could buy him a cold soda, and the two of us spent the next couple of hours sitting in a small restaurant—Arnie doing most of the talking and me listening.

Arnie's "retirement" was, in actuality, a voluntary decision not to have a real job. Married, with two children, Arnie is far from well fixed. His wife is an elementary school teacher and earns $21,000 a year.

"When I left the gas company in 1978, I was making $24,000 a year. If I stayed I'd be probably making $32,000 now. But I'd be a nervous wreck. No, I'm perfectly convinced that making more money is not so all-important.

We're now in a time where society offers new alternatives to working for a living. I'm not into the work ethic thing. So I've chosen to stay home and take care of the house. I guess you could say I'm a househusband. I see the kids off to school, cook, clean, do the laundry, shop and maintain the house. I also do the typical husband chores like taking care of the yard and doing repairs."

When I asked Arnie how his wife felt about his life-style choice, he became quite serious. "At first Maggie was really upset. During the first six or nine months, I thought it was going to break up our marriage. But I held my ground. Maggie is a career woman. She's studying for her master's degree at night and she fully expects to be a school principal within five years. I really respect her ambition but the career thing isn't for me. I think Maggie finally understood where I was coming from when I put it into the framework of the liberation movement. We talk a whole lot about women's lib. Well, I'm into male liberation! Just as women want to be free to choose, so do I! . . . I've opted for a life style that makes me happy and I don't care what others think."

1. Given Arnie's choice of life style, what do you think caused him to leave SDG&E? What could the company have done to retain someone like Arnie?
2. Could Arnie's life style be the beginning of a new trend in North America? Explain.
3. Might Maggie approach her job differently because of Arnie's decision to be a househusband than if Arnie were earning $32,000 a year as a computer specialist?

Source: Stephen R. Robbins, *Organizational Behavior: Concepts, Controversies, and Applications,* 2nd ed. (Englewood Cliffs, N.J.: Prentice-Hall, Inc., 1983), pp. 40–41.

DISCUSSION QUESTIONS

1. Why is job dissatisfaction at such a high level in this society?
2. How does job dissatisfaction relate to performance, absenteeism, turnover, and worker alienation?
3. What are the basic characteristics that reflect a Theory X management style? a Theory Y management style?
4. Why is an understanding of employee values important to the supervisor? Once subordinates' values are known, what can the supervisor do to make the work environment more pleasant, and possibly more motivating, to the subordinate?
5. What role does the family play in the formation of values?
6. What does it take for the organization to change the values of its employees? Give some examples.
7. Is the work ethic dead? Defend your answer.
8. How might a promotion to supervisor affect one's values?
9. Define the "self-fulfilling prophecy." What role might it play for the supervisor who is training a new employee?
10. Describe how a supervisor can learn to be a positive Pygmalion.
11. Explain why old organizational styles might turn off contemporary workers.

REFERENCES

Borbash, Jack. "Humanizing Work—A New Ideology." *AFL-CIO American Federationist* 84, no. 7 (July 1977): 8–15.

Cooper, M. R.; Morgan, B. S.; Foley, P. M.; and Kaplan, L. B. "Changing Employee Values: Deepening Discontent?" *Harvard Business Review* (January–February 1979): 117–125.

Deal, Terrance, and Kennedy, Allan. *Corporate Cultures.* Reading, Mass.: Addison-Wesley, 1982.

Katzell, Raymond A. "Changing Attitudes Toward Work." In *Work in America: The Decade Ahead,* edited by E. C. Kerr and J. Rosow. Princeton, N.J.: Van Nostrand, 1979: 35–57.

Livingston, J. Sterling. "Pygmalion in Management." *Harvard Business Review* (July–August 1967): 70–83.

McGregor, Douglas. *The Human Side of Enterprise.* New York: McGraw-Hill, 1960.

Mindell, Mark, and Gordon, William. "Employee Values in a Changing Society." AMA Management Briefing, 1981.

Rosenthal, Robert. "The Pygmalion Effect Lives." *Psychology Today* (September 1973): 56–63.

Schrank, Robert. *Ten Thousand Working Days.* Cambridge, Mass: MIT Press, 1978.

Turkel, Studs. *Working.* New York: Pantheon, 1974.

"The Unemployed Shun Much Mundane Work, at Least for a While." *Wall Street Journal,* December 5, 1980: 1.

Yankelovich, Daniel. "Work, Values, and the New Breed." In *Work in America: The Decade Ahead.* ed. E. C. Kerr and J. Rosow. Princeton, N.J.: Van Nostrand, 1979: 3–26.

CHAPTER 4

MOTIVATING THE TROOPS

A pat on the back, though but a few vertebrae removed from a kick in the pants, is miles ahead in results.

—ANONYMOUS

Chapter Outline

Objectives

Supervisors are expected to get the most out of their work group. Some use a "get tough" approach. Others depend on the organization's rewards to move their people. Finally, there are supervisors who structure the job in such a way that motivation takes care of itself. The last category is an example of a self-motivated work force and reflects the general direction of this chapter. Specifically, in this chapter, you will become familiar with:

1. Individual needs and motivation
2. Typically used motivators
3. How to link performance to rewards
4. Strategies for designing and implementing reward systems
5. How jobs can be scheduled and restructured so that they capitalize on employee motivation
6. Trust as the key to developing and building a motivating climate

Major Concepts

Needs
Motivation
Maslow's hierarchy of needs
Herzberg's motivator-hygiene factors
Monetary incentives
Rate busters
Status symbols
Praise

Positive and negative reinforcement
Punishment
Valued rewards
Job rotation
Job enrichment
Goal setting
Trust

MOTIVATION FROM FEAR

Many working stiffs can sympathize with the New York Yankees. They, too, know what it is like to have a demanding boss look over their shoulders while they are trying to do a job. It makes them nervous—sort of like the Yankees appeared to be in the 1981 World Series.

But the Yankees' employer not only looks over their shoulders, he makes notes of their sins and blabs to reporters about them. George Steinbrenner seemed to want the nation to know that he knew his players and managers were messing up and that he didn't like it.

Some observers think that his public flogging of his players and his second-guessing of his manager—which is usually the province of sportswriters—cost Steinbrenner's team the championship. For whatever reason, the Yankees certainly were not themselves. They ran the bases like amateurs.

Was Steinbrenner to blame for that ineptness? Did he put too much pressure on his team, which won two games then lost four?

For one thing, people react differently to fear, one of Steinbrenner's tactics. According to Thomas Tutko, sports psychologist, "If you use it, you'd better know the people underneath you and how they respond." Some people produce if they are threatened, but others try so hard they end up too tight to respond, and perform poorly. Others may react with hostility. "The hell with you; you're not going to tell me what to do."

While there are times when a motivation through fear strategy may work, most of the time it puts too much pressure on the employee to produce. Furthermore, he is less willing to put up with a threatening job environment and may look for employment elsewhere, for example, the exodus of superstar Reggie Jackson. When it comes down to performance and the boss is always looking over your shoulder, your behavior *is* going to be different. But different doesn't always mean better.

Adapted from an article by Bill Shirley, *Los Angeles Times,* October 1981.

A fundamental function of supervision is to get things done through people. Few would dispute that motivating workers to excel on their jobs is a primary supervisory responsibility. But how does one motivate? This is a question asked by every conscientious supervisor. There is, of course, no single answer, because there is no universal prescription for motivating everyone. A situation that causes one worker to be marginal and unsatisfactory might be the perfect motivator for another. People are different. And because this is true, the effective supervisor is one who is capable of identifying individual needs, providing a means for satisfying those needs, and at the same time accomplishing the objectives of the organization.

For most of this century, the predominant method for motivating the work force depended on a single incentive. Monetary incentives (including both direct and indirect benefits) were all that was thought needed to maintain motivation. Other motivators were largely ignored. It was almost coincidental when an employee found something about the job task that was personally meaningful or challenging.

Emphasis is on monetary incentives

While it is naive to think that every aspect of any job must be completely satisfying, some of it must be. There are too many alternatives in our society for a worker to be forced into staying indefinitely in the same boring and unsatisfying job.

How does one recognize potential motivators? What is necessary to reward desired behaviors? Why isn't job enrichment for everyone? These are just a few of the questions that will be addressed in this chapter. Practicality will be the theme. In-depth analysis of various motivational theories is not attempted. Instead, the most useful elements of each are presented and integrated into a meaningful strategy that supervisors can immediately implement on the job.

Motivation: From the Inside Looking Out

A widely accepted belief about human behavior, proposed by Abraham Maslow, is that people are motivated and influenced by a more or less predictable set of physical and psychological needs.[1] There are things we must have, such as food, water, and a safe and secure environment. These physical needs are paramount to our survival, and when endangered, they demand and get our full and undivided attention. Other needs, while not a physical necessity, are nevertheless important to our psychological well-being. The desire to be liked and appreciated and the desire to master and control the environment around us are examples of psychological needs.

Unsatisfied needs cause behavior

When a need occurs, motivational tension develops and is directed toward satisfaction of the felt need. The intensity of the effort is a function of how strong the need is.[2] Most behavior is directed toward unsatisfied needs. Satisfied needs do not motivate. A hungry person will seek food, but upon eating will not be hungry (for the next few hours, anyway). There is a reason for every behavior that people engage in, and that reason is almost always related to an unsatisfied need. People work, for example, because it provides a means for satisfying a wide variety of unsatisfied needs—such as security, socialization, and self-esteem. Conversely if people don't perform, it's usually because they see no way in which performing will lead to the satisfaction of their personal needs.

---

[1] Abraham H. Maslow, "A Theory of Human Motivation," *Psychological Review* 50 (1943), 370–396.

[2] Behavior may also occur as a result of instinct (e.g., a bright light causes rapid blinking), or as a result of learned responses (e.g., one develops a routine of getting up and going to work at the same time every morning).

MASLOW'S HIERARCHY OF NEEDS

Perhaps the most intuitively appealing motivation theory for supervisors today is Maslow's hierarchy of needs.[3] In essence, this theory suggests a five-level need hierarchy, ranging from physiological wants to self-actualization needs (see Table 4.1). At any point in time each of us operates at one of these levels, although we are capable of fluctuating in either direction over short periods of time.

Maslow, in his hierarchy, specifies that needs are arranged in order of importance. According to his theory, people move up a need hierarchy, from basic physical needs to self-actualization needs. As their lower-order needs are satisfied, their higher-order needs, such as self-actualiza-

TABLE 4.1   Management Practices That Satisfy Various Levels of Human Needs

PHYSICAL NEEDS	1. Furnish pleasant and comfortable environment.
	2. Provide for ample leisure time.
	3. Provide for "comfortable" salary.
SECURITY NEEDS	1. Adhere to protective rules and regulations.
	2. Minimize risk-taking requirements.
	3. Provide strong directive leadership and follow chain of command policy.
	4. Provide limiting position descriptions.
	5. Minimize negative stroking and threatening behavior.
	6. Provide information about firm's financial status and projections.
	7. Provide "just" compensation and supportive fringe benefits.
SOCIAL NEEDS	1. Encourage the team concept.
	2. Systematically use organization-wide feedback survey.
	3. Use task groups to execute projects.
	4. Provide for firm and/or office business and social meetings.
	5. Provide close personal supervision.
	6. Encourage professional group participation.
	7. Encourage community group participation.
	8. Compensate on basis of total team performance.

[3] Maslow, "A Theory of Human Motivation."

TABLE 4.1   (*Continued*)

ESTEEM NEEDS	1. Include subordinates in goal-setting and decision-making process.
	2. Provide opportunity to display skills and talents.
	3. Provide advancement recognition—e.g., publicize promotions.
	4. Provide recognition symbols—e.g., name on stationery.
	5. Assign associates and support staff for coaching and development.
	6. Provide personal secretary to associates.
	7. Use positive reinforcement program.
	8. Pay attention to office size, location, parking spaces, etc.
	9. Institute mentor system.
	10. Compensate as recognition of growth.
SELF-ACTUALIZATION NEEDS	1. Provide for participation in goal-setting and decision-making processes.
	2. Provide opportunity and support for career development plan.
	3. Provide staff job rotation to broaden experience and exposure.
	4. Offer optimum innovative and risk-taking opportunities.
	5. Encourage direct-access communication to clients, customers, suppliers, vendors, etc.
	6. Provide challenging internal and external professional development opportunities.
	7. Provide supportive supervision that encourages a high degree of self-control.
	8. Adopt specialization strategies.
	9. Compensate as reward for exceptional performance.

One need at a time

tion, become more important. In essence, Maslow suggests that needs are arranged like a ladder that must be climbed one rung at a time. People will be concerned with self-actualization only when their physical needs, their security needs, and so on, are satisfied. Furthermore, if the satisfaction of a lower-order need is threatened, that need immediately becomes predominant, and all higher-order needs are temporarily neglected until the needs beneath are satisfied. This explains why job security becomes a high-priority issue among workers in a recessionary period. Other rewards may actually satisfy more than one need. Compensation tends to satisfy not only physical and security needs of most employees but their self-esteem (see Table 4.1).

WHAT MASLOW'S HIERARCHY MEANS TO THE SUPERVISOR

Once an individual moves above the physical and security levels of the hierarchy, the other needs will vary in importance depending on the individual in question. Esteem needs, for instance, could well be of greater importance to some workers than are social needs. The exact order of the need hierarchy is still a matter of speculation. From a practical viewpoint, however, it makes little difference whether one need (e.g., social) has to be satisfied before another need (e.g., self-esteem). More important is the supervisor's ability to correctly identify which need is operating in the case of a particular worker and whether it is or is not being satisfied by some elements of the job.

Order of needs is not important

While the hierarchy may be of secondary importance to the supervisor, the needs themselves represent a logical starting point in understanding why people behave the way they do. Each level of the hierarchy suggests a number of potentially powerful motivators.

Beginning at the most basic level, what compensation systems are available that conceivably could satisfy an employee's physical needs? In our affluent society, it is rare to find organizations that do not meet the employees' physical needs. Organizations in general provide decent wages, enabling employees to afford, if not a comfortable life style, one that could hardly be called deprived. The supervisor's ability to influence this most basic need is practically nonexistent. And when one recalls that satisfied needs don't motivate, it would seem futile for supervisors to be concerned over this basic need.

Physical needs

The second-level needs of security and safety are also, like physiological needs, found across most organizations. Examples of how these needs are met would include unemployment compensation, safe and clean working conditions, job security, air conditioning, guaranteed annual wage plans, social security, medical and hospitalization plans, life insurance, retirement, fitness centers, and employee assistance programs. Most of these benefits are given to employees regardless of performance. In terms of motivating an employee to be more productive, these benefits probably do not have much of an effect. In terms of high morale, low turnover, and absenteeism, however, these programs are useful; from that perspective, they make the supervisor's job easier.

Security needs

Social needs, the third level of the hierarchy, represent the desire all of us have to be accepted, to belong, and to be loved by people we respect. Whether the people are relatives, friends, or co-workers, this need seems important to most people. Organizations are filled with people who do not particularly like the work but do like the people they work with. An old assumption that many organizations adhered to for years

Social needs

was the belief that women had strong social needs; therefore, boring, repetitive tasks would be acceptable as long as these women could interact among themselves. Perceptive supervisors are able to identify workers with strong social needs and will assign them to tasks that lend themselves to the formation of informal work groups. Unlike in the case of the two prior needs, supervisors are able to exercise some degree of control over the structure and flow of the work setting, thus affecting the satisfaction of employees' social needs.

Wherever we go, whatever we do, we want to feel that we are making a worthwhile contribution to the activities in which we are engaged. One of few universal truths in organizational behavior is that people like to feel that what they are doing is worthwhile and significant. They wish to feel good about themselves and have others recognize their capabilities and accomplishments. In the workplace, ways of meeting the

Esteem needs

esteem needs of employees are many and varied. They include such things as praise for a job well done, additional responsibilities, challenges that allow achievement, advancement opportunities, and symbols that support self-esteem (e.g., titles, privileges, etc.). Many supervisors have experienced the effectiveness of timely words of praise to a subordinate. Other examples of management practices that satisfy the esteem needs of individuals can be found in Table 4.1. In terms of control and distribution, esteem needs are the supervisor's most efficient and effective tools for rewarding desired performance. Consequently, more will be said about this important human need later in this chapter.

Self-actualization needs

Maslow's highest-level need, and one that is the ultimate in human growth, is the need for self-actualization. Becoming everything that one is capable of becoming is self-actualizing. Whereas the satisfaction of esteem and social needs is largely dependent on someone external to oneself, self-actualization, by itself, is determined intrinsically. Of course, reaching this level in the hierarchy depends on the satisfaction of prior needs, which implies at least a minimum of external assistance. A self-actualized employee competes only with himself or herself and is not overly concerned with what others think. For the majority of workers, perhaps the supervisor's best bet for creating a self-actualizing work environment is to help the employee see opportunities for self-actualization in their present jobs. Giving competent subordinates optimum risk-taking opportunities is one way self-actualization may occur. In fact, any time the subordinate is given greater self-management opportunities is a step toward self-actualization—as long as the employee is ready and willing to accept the challenge. Supervisors are often limited in how much they can redesign existing jobs. But when redesign is possible, they should include challenge to the extent that it allows the employee to achieve maximum competence. It is not nearly as simple as it may sound, yet it is not as difficult as many supervisors are led to believe.

LEARNING TO READ PEOPLE AND THEIR BEHAVIORS

The ability to figure out what makes each worker tick is absolutely essential. Some supervisors are able to identify employee needs correctly on the basis of intuition alone. They are the exception, however, rather than the rule. More systematic methods of need identification would include attitude surveys, interviewing, and counseling. The primary problem with these methods is that the skills of a trained psychologist are often required to administer and score the results. Since few organizations offer this luxury, the burden falls on the supervisor.

A skilled psychologist is needed

Unfortunately, simply asking employees what their needs are doesn't always work either. Employees are not always candid about disclosing their needs, either on paper or in person. Furthermore, since it is impossible to observe someone's needs (e.g., one cannot directly observe the need to achieve), supervisors are left with observing behavior and making inferences (e.g., one can infer a person's competitive nature when he or she is continually the top salesperson in the office). While asking employees what their needs are might result in accurate information, it would be risky to rely on the direct approach. There are important needs (e.g., self-worth) that are seldom expressed in words and even more difficult to infer from a behavioral pattern.

Asking and observing

Often the more critical needs are not discussed because (1) employees are not consciously aware of them or (2) employees are not willing to discuss them with supervisors. When one considers that motivation is basically an unconscious process, it is not surprising that employees are not always able to define verbally, even to themselves, precisely what they want from their jobs. Their most important needs may be unconscious ones.

Unconscious needs

A possible solution to this motivational maze is to concentrate on getting to know each worker. One way for anticipating how a worker might react to a motivational strategy is to empathize. For example, the supervisor might put herself, figuratively speaking, into the shoes of the subordinate and visualize how she (the supervisor) might react to the situation. By asking oneself such questions as What would *I* do? What is it *I* want? How would *I* like to be treated? the supervisor might be able to anticipate the reactions of the subordinate. However, because people are different, a motivational strategy that works for the

Empathy

Active listening

Observation

supervisor might not work for the subordinate. A better method is to engage in frequent and open discussions with the subordinate. The key to this approach is *active* listening. Supervisors who monopolize "discussions" are missing opportunities for learning what makes the employee tick. Listening is hard work and demands total concentration. The supervisor who is a good listener will be able to pick up the subtle cues divulged by the subordinate. A truly perceptive supervisor could even pick up on a subordinate's unconscious needs. Skilled observation is another useful technique for identifying employee needs. When a desired behavior is repeated, it is helpful to make a mental note of the circumstances. What led to the desired behavior and what followed it? It might have been praise from the supervisor or simply comments by co-workers.

Empathizing, active listening, and perceptive observation—techniques discussed in later chapters—are useful tools for developing a profile of each subordinate's needs. The choice of the tool (or combination of tools) depend on the individual subordinate, the situation, and the supervisor. It is essential to gear the approach to all three. Attempting to use the same approach in all cases will certainly be ineffective and may create problems.

What Motivates People?

Motivators are present within every job; but it takes a creative supervisor to identify what they are and how they could be implemented. For example, a perceptive supervisor might notice that one of her female employees (let's call her Joan) tends to take on a maternal role with new workers. The supervisor sees an opportunity for gradually increasing Joan's responsibilities by giving Joan responsibility for "employee orientation" and delegating significant authority to her. Over time, the supervisor starts routing periodic reports on employee orientation through Joan, gives her the authority to sign correspondence, and has others report to her for questions in this area of expertise. Will Joan be motivated? Evidence suggests that this type of motivational strategy is quite effective because it increases the employee's sense of contribution while building new challenges into the job instead of asking the employee just to do more of the same.[4] There are all types of motivators. The only limitation is the supervisor's ingenuity in identifying the appropriate ones.

Build challenge into the job

[4] J. R. Hackman and G. Oldham, "Motivation Through the Design of Work: Test of a Theory," *Organizational Behavior and Human Performance* 16 (1976), 250–279.

HERZBERG'S THEORY OF MOTIVATION

Perhaps one of the most useful frameworks for categorizing motivators is Frederick Herzberg's concept of motivator-hygiene factors.[5] Whereas Maslow applied his theory to motivation in general, Herzberg applied his specifically to the workplace. The theory was developed as a result of research that Herzberg conducted with accountants and engineers in an attempt to learn the extent of their satisfaction with their jobs plus the factors that provided the satisfaction. Herzberg reported that satisfaction and dissatisfaction were not simple opposites. Poor working conditions would result in dissatisfaction; yet ideal working conditions did not necessarily lead to satisfaction. He referred to the factors that prevented dissatisfaction as *hygiene factors*. Herzberg reasoned—by way of an analogy—that a town's poor sewage system will lead to greater health problems for its citizenry; however, a good sewage system does not ensure that the users will be free of disease and ill health. The same principle holds for organizations.

Herzberg's approach

Hygiene factors, such as salary and working conditions (see Figure 4.1), reflect the context of the job. They are external to the employee and to the job. For this reason they can be thought of as *extrinsic* incentives. In other words, they are items that are essentially controlled by someone other than the employee. Herzberg contends that hygiene factors are much more difficult to administer effectively, and more important, they don't really provide long-run motivation. They are necessary for preventing dissatisfaction, and their absence prevents the employee from concentrating on higher-level needs. But they are insufficient in themselves to provide motivation. Furthermore, the more resources that are poured down the hygiene drain (for example, by increasing fringe benefits), the more resources will be required in the future, because with hygiene factors it takes ever-increasing amounts to produce the same effect.[6] Indeed, this argument makes sense when one considers how salary issues never appear resolved (e.g., six months after a significant raise, some employees and unions are again clamoring for "more").

Hygiene factors

The second category that Herzberg described consists of motivators. Note that these factors are more *intrinsic* in nature; they reflect the content of the job itself. Instead of the supervisor disbursing them to subordinates, the subordinates administer the rewards to themselves. No one can give a feeling of achievement to another; it must be intrinsic to the individual, and only the individual can assess whether it is present

Motivators

[5] For a more detailed examination of his theory, see Frederick W. Herzberg, *Work and the Nature of Man* (Cleveland, Ohio: World Publishing, 1966).
[6] Ibid., p. 169.

FIGURE 4.1 Herzberg's Theory: Factors Affecting Job Satisfaction

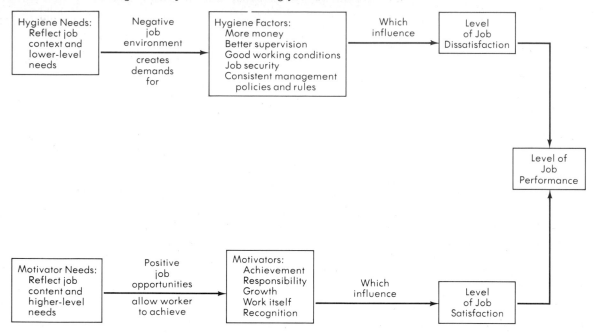

on the job or not. Individuals who find a task intrinsically rewarding tend to satisfy Maslow's higher-order needs. Only motivator factors, according to Herzberg, provide long-term incentives.

Many supervisors (as well as academicians) find Herzberg's theory intuitively appealing. When we think about pay, for example, we generally think of it being an ineffective motivator. Yet it always seems to be an item on everyone's agenda when the fiscal year is coming to an end. Are attempts at using hygiene factors—salary, for example—as motivators a waste of time, effort, and money? Should pay incentive plans be scrapped? Would it be better to give everyone the same extrinsic rewards rather than rewarding only the deserving workers? Can a hygiene factor such as salary become a long-term motivator under certain conditions? These questions and others suggest there might be problems with Herzberg's theory of hygiene factors.

What's wrong with hygiene factors?

CONFUSING GRATITUDE WITH MOTIVATION

The awarding of merit

Ironically, incentive plans, such as bonuses and merit increases, fail because supervisors are reluctant to use them as they are designed. Instead of being a measure of performance, merit is often disbursed on the basis of nonperformance factors. Consider briefly the example of a foreman we once encountered whose performance was described by his supervisor as "needing improvement." As it turned out, he was given merit anyway because (1) his job involved complex and dirty work, (2) he had one of the toughest work groups to manage, and (3) he would be hard to replace. Under these circumstances, would a supervisor be justified in giving merit? Putting sympathy aside, the circumstances still do not justify the awarding of merit. While a problem is evident, resolving it with merit is not the answer. The awarding of merit is an attempt by the supervisor (1) to create a sense of gratitude within the worker and (2) to motivate him or her to stay on the job. Yet, in effect, the merit award may be telling the worker that current performance is acceptable and improvement (while desired) is not necessary. Is gratitude an effective motivator? Will subordinates feel a moral obligation to pay back a supervisor's blind faith in them? And how will more deserving employees feel about the supervisor's unabashed charity to the less deserving among them?

There is nothing wrong with gratitude. Everyone at one time or another has been grateful to someone for an unexpected, undeserved gift. Occasionally, people will justify the faith others have in them and fulfill the expectations of the benefactor. On the job, however, the gratitude created by undeserved merit is generally not going to result in better performance. Recipients of undeserved rewards may initially feel an obligation to work harder, but with the passage of time, they may also begin to view the unexpected reward as deserved. They begin to recall their performance in a more positive light. More important, a supervisor's generosity might backfire by creating unrealistic expectations about the size of next year's merit, regardless of performance. If this isn't enough, consider the effect of unjust rewards on the more deserving employees. A supervisor who encourages less than adequate performance (which is how some of the better employees might view it) is inviting one of two things. High performers will either lower their own performance standards, doing only what is minimally required, or they will refuse to compromise themselves and will look for employment alternatives outside the organization (where they perceive their efforts will be more equitably rewarded).

> There are problems with gratitude

MONEY AS A MOTIVATOR

Does Money Motivate? Coal miners, steelworkers, and clerical workers all express a desire for more money. Does money reflect a basic need? Does money motivate? And what does it take to make monetary incentives a viable motivational strategy?

SCHOOL'S MERIT-PAY PROGRAM DRAWS GRIPES

Millersville, PA—Merit pay for teachers is becoming a hot national issue, but it's something of an embarrassment for the Penn Manor School District.

Last month, Penn Manor paid $1,000 bonuses to 25 of its 233 teachers. The eight-school district, which has its headquarters in this Susquehanna Valley town, joined the few school systems in the country that tie teacher pay to classroom performance.

The checks distributed here are a significant reward in a community where teachers' salaries average about $20,000 a year and starting pay begins at less than $12,000. Yet, most of the losers and many of the winners aren't happy about the selection process. Penn Manor administrators and school board members still aren't sure whether the payments do more harm than good.

The idea of paying more to good teachers than mediocre ones has intrigued school systems for decades. But the National Commission on Excellence in Education stirred new interest in the subject earlier this year when it suggested that "performance-based" teachers' salaries were one of the ways to push back the "rising tide of mediocrity" threatening U.S. education.

A POLITICAL ISSUE

Merit pay has become a political issue. President Reagan is pushing the idea. And, according to the National Education Association, legislatures in California, Texas, Oklahoma, Tennessee, and Florida have before them proposals for merit pay or higher "master teacher" salaries.

At Penn Manor High School, Barbara Andrew, an innovative English teacher, was a merit pay winner. While gratified to be honored, Mrs. Andrew describes herself as "horrified" by the effect of the merit program on her fellow teachers.

"Teachers are very fragile, dedicated people," Mrs. Andrew wrote in a draft of a letter she intends to send the school board. "They receive very little praise throughout their careers—from students, from parents or from administrators. Thus, to keep on teaching, they must develop their own self-confidence, fed mostly from within. Then, poof! slash! rip! zap! Nearly 90% of the staff are told they don't measure up. Their aura of confidence is shattered."

The Penn Manor board's decision to make public the names of the 25 merit-pay recipients didn't help matters. The daily paper in nearby Lancaster published the names in a page-one story that quoted a Penn Manor school official as hoping "that these people will serve as models" for other teachers.

PERSONAL REBUKES

The report hurt a science teacher who failed to qualify for a bonus, even though his principal regards him as a meritorious teacher. The teacher keeps a carefully mounted copy of the newspaper story in his desk drawer; it's clear from the underlined sentences and paragraphs that he regards his failure to make the bonus list as a personal rebuke. He bitterly recalls that on the day the list was published, his wife and a fellow member of his church choir asked why his name was missing. The science teacher is convinced the questions meant, in effect, "I'm not excellent in my field."

The merit plan also put on the spot the principals and department heads assigned to select the award winners. Penn Manor High, for instance, was allotted only 10 merit awards to distribute among the 45 of its 94 teachers who competed for the bonuses. As a result, many worthy teachers were disappointed, says the school's principal, Robert King.

Even more troublesome to Robert Wyble, head of the high school's science department, was the subjectivity involved in choosing winners. "As department head, I can't tell my teachers, 'This is what you can do to get a merit payment next year,'" he says. The school administration advises losers to sit in on winners' classes and learn for themselves.

The idea of merit pay is bad news to the National Education Association, which represents 70% of the nation's 2.2 million public-school teachers. The NEA regards merit pay as a step backward from fixed-salary schedules based on academic credentials and seniority.

"ENGULFED IN POLITICS"

"Subjective evaluation of classroom competency has been engulfed in the past by personality conflicts, politics and other personal factors," says Don Camron, NEA executive director. Adds Mary Futrell, NEA secretary-treasurer: "Suppose you go into my building and you decide . . . to identify 15% [as meritorious], but when you conduct the evaluation, you determine that 30% meet the standards you set. What do you do with the other people? You don't have the money to give them."

Indeed, the unwillingness or inability of school boards to invest sufficient money in merit pay has contributed to the failure of some such programs, studies show.

Neil Jones, president of the Penn Manor school board and chief proponent of Penn Manor's merit-pay program, isn't certain at this point what the district is getting for its money. What it wanted was to motivate teachers toward excellence. Mr. Jones, a materials-purchasing executive with Armstrong World Industries Inc., insisted on $1,000 payments rather than a smaller amount because a willing teacher "can look at a TV set or summer trip and say, 'That's what the bonus did for me.'"

Now Mr. Jones acknowledges "grave doubts" about whether the local teachers' association would agree to continue the program when its contract with the district runs out in 1985. Says Harry Frey, a high school health and physical-education teacher who is head of the local teachers' association: "The first week after the winners were announced you could have lit a match anywhere and gotten an explosion."

Mr. Frey insists merit pay never will accomplish anything at Penn Manor until the district gets teachers' salaries "up to professional levels." But he suggests distributing a larger number of smaller-sized awards, something school officials are considering. "Meritorious people should all get the same thing," he says, "even if it's only one dollar."

Wall Street Journal, June 16, 1983.

The rate buster

Undoubtedly there are people who seek money for its own sake and use it as a standard for measuring personal achievement. A rate buster is one such person. Many workers are paid on the basis of units produced. The more that is produced, the more money the worker receives. The rate buster is a worker who forgoes social interaction on the job and chooses instead to devote all of his or her efforts toward getting as much work accomplished as possible. For the rate buster, money is a most powerful incentive; it has to be, because the rate buster is often ostracized by co-workers and is the object of ridicule and horseplay.

Symbolic meaning

For most workers, however, money has a symbolic as well as a material meaning. While they may not go to the extremes of the rate buster, money does represent a means to an end. It may provide a means for satisfying an individual's need for security or the more complex needs of power and status. In terms of Maslow's hierarchy, money may serve to satisfy not only a person's more basic drives but some of the higher-level needs as well. What makes money so powerful is the multitude of opportunities it makes available to those who have it, as well as its symbolism in our society. The value of using money as an incentive cannot be ignored. It is both powerful and versatile, and it is as close to being a universal incentive as self-actualization. Yet except for jobs that are linked directly to commissions (e.g., sales), monetary incentive plans are generally ineffective.

Are Merit Increases More Trouble Than They're Worth?

Supervisors frequently complain about their role in the distribution of merit. Their lack of enthusiasm and commitment to the system is evident in such comments as: "I really enjoy what I do except when I have to make merit recommendations. It just seems that no one is satisfied. I expect some hard feelings with my low performers, but even my best guys seem to resent the process because they think they deserved more."

Is it any wonder that merit increases are the subject of jokes—until it is time to give them out; then everyone's attitude turns deadly serious. Employees want to know who received what and how much. While management decides how much is budgeted for merit, it is the supervisor who plays the key role in making, supporting, and implementing the recommendations, as well as justifying to all concerned why a particular worker did (or did not) receive a merit increase.

Merit attempts too much

For many supervisors, merit systems, while they may be widely accepted as a motivational device, are a complete failure in practice. There are too many factors that undermine their effectiveness. Many people wonder why management doesn't do away with them and put the money into cost-of-living adjustments and improved fringe benefit packages instead.

Arguments for abolishing merit pay include: (1) merit pay is not perceived as being related to job performance, (2) performance ratings are seen as biased, (3) trust and openness about merit increases are low, and (4) the amount of merit received is perceived as too insignificant to matter.[7] Employees are generally skeptical about merit. If they don't believe good performance is going to be rewarded, then no amount of merit can act as an incentive. Organizations that have a history of inconsistent merit systems will have to overcome the mistrust that employees naturally have toward a "new" incentive system.

Employees tend to be skeptical

Ironically, supervisors can undermine the perceptions employees have of good performance being rewarded when they, for whatever reason, reward employees for mediocre performance and ignore good performance. Wanting to be liked by their subordinates and not wishing to cause hard feelings are just a few of the excuses we have heard from supervisors.

Rewarding mediocre performance

Sometimes the merit system is inequitable because it is being used by the supervisor to make up for past inequities. It isn't unusual to hear a supervisor say, "The fact is that some of my people are underpaid and need to catch up, so I'm forced to do something or I might lose them. I know I'm undermining the intent, but what else can I do?" For merit systems to be effective, employees' salaries must be fair and competitive both within the organization and in the external labor market. When this is not true and an employee's salary is out of tune with the going wage rate, there is intense pressure on the supervisor to rectify it. If the personnel department is unsympathetic to requests for a salary adjustment, the supervisor is inclined to use whatever means (including monies allocated for merit) to reestablish equity. Subverting the incentive system is often the only way a supervisor can retain key employees. It is a no-win situation created by the organization and economic necessity. It is usually only a stop-gap technique, because there is seldom enough merit money to maintain equity during inflationary periods.

Finally, supervisors often create inequity inadvertently because they lack an approved system for identifying who is deserving and who isn't. In other words, the supervisor must know in explicit terms what is effective performance. It is unfair and unwise to expect a supervisor to implement an incentive system when he or she has not been given adequate training, clear performance standards, and an objective appraisal system.

---

[7] W. Clay Hamner, "How to Ruin Motivation with Pay," *Compensation Review,* 3rd Quarter, 1975.

What Is a Good Merit Increase? If an employee believes she out-performed a co-worker, she will expect the reward to reflect the difference. Should the actual reward be a disappointment, a feeling of inequity will develop. Consider the case of an employee who works for a social services department in a public sector organization that annually budgets 3 to 5 percent for merit increases.

> I make $2,000 per month. If I go all out, I *might* be awarded top merit, which this year amounts to 5 percent. That would bring my base up to $2,100 per month. Now ole Tom, who works with me, doesn't do any more than he has to. He gets his $2,000 and doesn't have any hassles about it. What's more, after taxes, what do I have to show for it? Is the extra 5 percent worth the agony? Frankly, I don't think so.

In effect, two factors are contributing to this employee's reluctance to "go all out." The first is the doubt that his efforts will be recognized and rewarded. The second is his conclusion that, after taxes, the amount received is insignificant.

Typically, money allocated for merit averages from 3 to 7 percent, which may sound like a lot until one considers what the take-home portion actually comes to. How much does it take for merit to be perceived as significant? Compensation specialists suggest that a minimum of 7 percent is needed to have an effect. But the actual amount would obviously vary depending on the particular organization, the strength of the economy, and the expectations of the work force.[8] Trial and error alone can tell.

Adding to the problem of how much is enough is the problem of inconsistency. Management, in an attempt to demonstrate fiscal responsibility, may take a short-term view of incentive systems. Merit support may be generous one year then suddenly dry up the next, leaving employees disappointed and maybe angry with management. Public sector organizations, in particular, are guilty of using merit inconsistently. Elected officials are generous when times are good; but when the economy stalls, merit is usually one of the first items cut. It takes years to develop and fine-tune a monetary incentive system; but it takes only days to destroy it.

STATUS SYMBOLS AS A MOTIVATOR

A second category of motivators that has wide appeal is the use of status symbols. The concept of status refers to how an individual is viewed by others within a group, organization, or community. It is most

Is it significant?

[8] Ibid.

often thought of in terms of the relative standing a group member is perceived to hold among his or her peers. A person of high status will have more prestige, influence, and overall power than a person with low status.

High status can be the result of many different factors. Employees who make more money, for example, tend to have relatively higher status. Whether or not the reasoning is valid, employees who earn more are generally perceived as being worth more as employees. Experience is somewhat related to money; workers with seniority frequently have superior skills and capabilities, traits most co-workers admire. But there are workers with less experience who nevertheless possess certain skills that are valued by co-workers, for example, a young key-punch operator may already be admired as the fastest worker in the group. Working conditions also attest to a person's status. An employee who works in a plush, air-conditioned office and can wear stylish clothes to work possesses a higher status rating than the grease-stained worker on the dingy plant floor. Also, status can be seen in the job position one occupies in the organization's hierarchy. White-collar occupations are viewed by many as having higher status than blue-collar positions. This occurs in spite of the more complex skills that might be required of manual workers or the better pay they may receive.

Examples of high status

Status is communicated through the use of symbols. Common symbols would include the distribution of prized equipment, titles, office trappings, and special privileges. Supervisors frequently have access and some degree of control over equipment and supplies. Take a case where only a limited number of self-correcting typewriters is available. By selectively determining who is issued the better typewriter, the supervisor can influence subordinate performance. Deciding who gets the use of prized equipment or the choicest work station is a subtle method for improving the performance-reward connection.

Examples of status symbols

The granting of titles is another method used to influence employee performance. The title "assistant supervisor," while minor compared to the overall organizational structure, can be a valued and sought-after prize for the typical clerical worker. Giving a title to a worker satisfies the human need to be recognized.

For a status symbol to remain a valid incentive, it must not be granted indiscriminately. If everyone had a title, how important would titles be? Moreover, since only unsatisfied needs motivate, a supervisor needs to be very selective in the awarding of prized status symbols. The supervisor must be willing to make some hard decisions as to which employees will receive them and which employees will not. The consistency and equity with which the symbols are distributed to the better performers will determine the effectiveness of the strategy.

How status symbols work

One might wonder why status symbols are so important to the typical employee. If there should be any doubt as to their importance, just recall from your own experience some of the seemingly trivial incidents that were blown out of proportion. The location of an employee's desk, for example, can lead to an all-out office "war." While it may seem a trivial matter to the supervisor, the positioning of a desk may have a direct bearing on who is deemed to have influence in the workplace.

Status symbols may also provide informal guidelines for determining acceptable or unacceptable behavior. It is only human to seek out situations in which there is certainty and predictability in the environment. Individuals are more comfortable in familiar and predictable settings. Status symbols help make sense of the environment by creating order in confusing situations.

PRAISE AS A MOTIVATOR

Telling employees that everything they do is wonderful will not motivate them. People lose respect for the supervisor who means well but goes overboard with lavish praise for an average accomplishment. The degree of recognition must reflect the difficulty of the accomplishment. Employees need to be able to trust that the supervisor will be honest with them. Most employees have already learned to live with less than constant lavish praise.

Be honest

What's wrong with telling an employee merely that his or her work is "fine" or "meets standards"? Saying more may only reinforce the wrong behavior. If there is still room for improvement, don't use up all your praise before you get there. Leave something special for the superlative performance. For example, "You did a great job on that report. I've not seen anyone in the company do it better," should be spoken only if it's true. Saving the highest praise for special accomplishments helps retain its value and gives employees something to work toward.

Don't take good performance for granted

Common sense suggests that employees need to know where they stand. Unfortunately, it is not uncommon for supervisors to say nothing about an employee's good performance. The philosophy of "management by exception" is evident in some supervisors' practices. In this philosophy, the supervisor says: "I expect a job to be done well—my job is to let you know when you screwed up." The result is an atmosphere that leads to employee defensiveness and hostility.

Some useful guidelines

There are a few hints to keep in mind about the use of praise. First, be specific when recognizing the efforts of others. Sweeping praise, although positive, is too vague for the employee to link to a specific behavior. By linking approval to specific achievement, you encourage the subordinate to do more, identify what you believe to be important, and set the standards for success. This applies to criticism as well—make sure it is the behavior, not the person, that is discussed. Second, don't overpraise; going overboard about a minimal achievement won't fool anyone. On the other hand, don't be too blunt. Focusing on the negative aspects of a worker's performance may not prove worth the effort and may demoralize the worker. Instead, a more strategic approach may lie in building on the subordinate's positive strengths while ignoring (or glancing over) the negative. Finally, avoid "loaded" praise, such as: "The report is great, but wouldn't it be better if. . . ." This technique implies criticism; it conveys to the subordinate that he or she hasn't quite measured up.

Good Intentions, Bad Techniques

Most supervisors would like a contented work force because, deep down, they believe the old cliché, "A happy worker is a productive worker." Supervisors themselves have natural human emotions and want to be appreciated for making the work environment as pleasurable an experience as possible for their subordinates. Therefore, a common but ill-advised strategy for motivating employees is to give them valued rewards whether deserved or not. Praise, merit increases, even promotions, are rewards that are sometimes provided to undeserving workers. Supervisors hope the undeserving employee will reciprocate this act of kindness by producing. Gratitude is certainly a powerful emotion; in too many cases, however, the hoped-for motivation to produce is either insufficient or suppressed by the worker. What frequently happens instead is that the unexpected reward serves only to strengthen the undesired behavior.

How often does this situation occur? A simple examination of any organization would unfortunately suggest that giving undeserved rewards is too frequently the rule rather than the exception. Take, for example, the worker who is continually tardy but even after being reprimanded continues with the tardiness. The fact that tardiness continues suggests the reprimand was insufficient. The worker is probably well aware of the organization's procedures for handling tardiness and knows that it will take months (and an enormous number of infractions) before the organization "gets serious" about the problem. The organization is, in essence, ignoring the infraction, thus giving it tacit approval. Another example is the supervisor who gives his or her subordinates the same

Rewarding the wrong behavior

merit increases because "they're all good," but who in reality doesn't want to incur the wrath of the workers who should have received less. A third example is the slow clerical worker who is paid double time to work overtime on a task that should have been accomplished during regular work hours.

These are just a sampling of the different ways supervisors (and their respective organizations) reinforce the wrong behavior. While their intentions are admirable, their techniques frequently lead to the wrong results. For behavioral change to occur with any degree of effectiveness, rewards must be linked to desired performance.

REWARDING DESIRED PERFORMANCE

Positive reinforcement is the process of giving valued rewards to someone who has just engaged in a desired behavior. The technique is based on the theory of B. F. Skinner [9] and the principle of operant conditioning, which proposes that behavior is a function of its consequences. In other words, people engage in actions that cause desired outcomes to occur.

Positive reinforcement

Some critics claim that the technique is manipulative in that it attempts to control people's behavior and shape them into something they have no desire to become. We believe that organizations have always provided rewards for their better employees and that positive reinforcement is a new name for an old strategy—the "incentive system." Parents, teachers, friends, and coaches, to name just a few, use this technique. Of course, the prevalence of positive reinforcement alone would hardly be sufficient justification for a wholehearted endorsement. But the technique makes good sense. Unlike rats in a maze, people have free will and can choose not to behave in a desirable fashion. But for those employees who want the rewards an organization has to offer, positive reinforcement identifies for them exactly what behavior gets rewarded.

Besides positive reinforcement, a second means for increasing the likelihood of a particular response is through negative reinforcement. Although often confused with punishment, because both use unpleasant stimuli, negative reinforcement differs by encouraging the worker to engage in a specific *desired* behavior. Punishment is applied when an undesired behavior occurs.

Negative reinforcement

Examples of negatively reinforcing situations are found throughout the work environment. If a group of employees stand around gossiping when they should be working, and the supervisor walks by frowning, the group will probably disperse. What happened is simple to explain.

[9] B. F. Skinner, *The Technology of Teaching* (New York: Appleton-Century-Crofts, 1968).

The unpleasantness of the supervisor's frown made the group uncomfortable, and as long as the group stood around the supervisor was going to show displeasure. Consequently, the only way to remove the unpleasantness of the supervisor's frown was to get back to work—the behavior the supervisor wanted. Another example of negative reinforcement is the supervisor who hassles the lazy worker. Nagging is classic negative reinforcement. Until acceptable work is done, the unpleasantness of the nagging will continue. Only doing the job correctly (i.e., desired behavior) will terminate the obnoxious nagging.

Punishment, on the other hand, although effective at reducing undesired behavior, does little to direct the worker into behaviors that would be rewarding. It is not a reinforcer. Furthermore, it tends to have only a temporary effect in repressing nonproductive behavior. Take the employee who continually takes long lunch breaks. A reprimand may indeed result in the employee returning on time, but it may also result in the employee engaging in dysfunctional activities, such as having a co-worker punch the employee's time card. Punishment may reinforce the belief that "The only mistake I made was getting caught." If that isn't enough to dissuade a potential punishment user, think about the other undesirable side effects, such as hostility, reduced productivity, and a desire to "get even."

Punishment

The act of reinforcement is only a *part* of the reinforcement process. How it is scheduled, or administered, is also important. The fastest way to shape desired behavior is to reinforce the behavior every time it occurs, referred to as a *continuous* schedule. Yet this is hardly practical for the supervisor. Watching everything an employee does and then reinforcing every desired act is unrealistic. With several employees to watch over, the task becomes impossible. Perhaps most practical is a *variable* reinforcement schedule. It is based on the same principle that a person uses when playing a slot machine. Every so often, there is a winner. And the unpredictability of the process doesn't seem to bother the gambler. The employee whose behavior is shaped with a variable schedule doesn't know when a reinforcer, such as praise, will occur and will continue performing in the desired direction for a very long time without reinforcement. While nonreinforced behavior will eventually be extinguished, behavior that is shaped with a variable reinforcement schedule is very persistent.

Schedules of reinforcement

IDENTIFYING VALUED REWARDS

The term "rewards" can be defined as meaning "anything the individual takes pleasure from." *Valued rewards*, however, are reinforcers (i.e., rewards) that have been functionally determined to be related to desired outcomes. The distinction is important. It could be a mistake to assume that a particular objective—say, a promotion—that might be personally important to the supervisor will be equally important to a subordinate. Identifying valued rewards is unfortunately no sure thing, as any supervisor will attest.

The following is one model for identifying general categories of valued rewards. It is efficient, reasonably fast, and most important, generally accurate. To simplify the model, the reward structure of the organization is broken down into two categories, extrinsic and intrinsic. The first step involves identifying what rewards are currently offered by the organization and classifying them into the appropriate category (see Table 4.2).

Determine what is available

The second step is to construct a questionnaire that will assess how each employee feels about each of the items identified in the table. It doesn't make much difference if employees respond anonymously or

Survey work groups

TABLE 4.2   Common Reward Strategies

EXAMPLES OF *EXTRINSIC MOTIVATORS*	*EXAMPLES OF* *INTRINSIC MOTIVATORS*
Economic rewards: 　Salary 　Bonus 　Overtime 　Piece rate 　Profit sharing 　Deferred compensation 　Fringe benefits 　Cost of living adjustment	Relevant and meaningful work
	Complete cycles of work
	Decision-making opportunities
	Diverse job experiences
	Goal setting that is realistic and challenging
Promotions	Constructive feedback on goals and work results
Organization-sponsored social functions	Social: 　Opportunity to help people 　Opportunity to develop friend-
Status symbols: 　Titles 　Special equipment 　Office furnishings 　Access opportunities, such as 　　parking privileges	ships
	Esteem: 　Prestige of organization 　Feeling of worth
Working conditions: 　Air conditioning 　Flexible working hours 　Four-day work week	Autonomy: 　Opportunity for independent 　　thought and action 　Feeling of self-fulfillment

not, but the responses should be categorized according to job family (e.g., clerical, technical, maintenance).

It is important at this point to recall that motivation to perform results from unsatisfied needs; therefore, simply identifying what is important to employees is insufficient. It must be determined how much employees are presently satisfied or dissatisfied with each item. To do this, three questions need to be asked, and answers need to be rated. First, How much is there now? Second, How much should there be? If the rating on the second question is greater than the rating on the first, dissatisfaction is assumed to be evident. The third question measures the relative importance of the item to the employee. Employees would be instructed to circle on the scale for each item the number that reflects how they feel. For example:

SALARY THAT I RECEIVE	*MINIMUM*						*MAXIMUM*
(1) How much is there now?	1	2	3	4	5	6	7
(2) How much should there be?	1	2	3	4	5	6	7
(3) How important is it to me?	1	2	3	4	5	6	7

The third step is the administration and scoring of the results. Table 4.3 represents the hypothetical responses of employees of the ABC Organization. Note that security is ranked first in importance. Does this mean that supervisors in the ABC Organization should design motivational strategies in which primary focus is the security needs of the employees? Not necessarily—importance is only *half* of the analysis. The other half is the degree of dissatisfaction employees have with the item. In this case, although security ranks high in importance it is perceived by the employees as only moderately unsatisfactory (it ranks eighth). Keeping in mind that only unsatisfied needs will motivate employees, it becomes quite clear that any effort to reinforce desired performance with a reward that is already abundantly provided will have only marginal results. Furthermore, these efforts may not be cost-effective. Instead, effort would be better spent on providing items that are identified as having the potential of being strong reinforcers. In this example, strong reinforcers include responsibility in the form of greater decision-making opportunities because it was ranked number 1 on dissatisfaction. Any other new strategies would probably be of questionable value in terms of cost-benefit analysis.

While this technique works well for identifying whole groups of potentially strong reinforcers, it is not designed to identify the valued rewards of any single employee. The needs of a particular employee are usually

Determine importance of item *and* dissatisfaction with it

TABLE 4.3 Responses of Employees of the ABC Organization

	RANK ORDER OF IMPORTANCE	RANK ORDER OF DISSATISFACTION *
Security	1	8
Responsibility (i.e., decision-making opportunities)	2	1
Meaningful goals	3	2
Constructive and timely feed-back	4	5
Diverse job experiences and variety	5	3
Social opportunities to interact on the job	6	9
Organization-sponsored social functions	7	4
Indirect economic rewards (e.g., fringes)	8	11
Status symbols	9	10
Promotions	10	7
Complete cycles of work	11	6
Flexible working hours	12	12
Working conditions	13	13

* Dissatisfaction is measured as the difference between "how much there is" and "how much should there be."

identified using a one-on-one technique. What this model does offer is an efficient procedure for empirically verifying where resources are being wasted and what valued rewards are being underutilized.

Job Design Strategies

What can be done to make an employee's job more interesting and worthwhile? Some supervisors look at their subordinates' jobs as fixed and inflexible. They view the job as etched in stone by the job description, meaning there is virtually nothing the supervisor can do to make a boring, repetitive, mechanistic job something that provides intrinsic and deep satisfaction. Although defining jobs so narrowly may result in lower production costs because of the advantages of intensive specialization, it also leads to worker dissatisfaction and dehumanization. Effective job design can ensure against such negative developments by making the job challenging and giving the employee as much discretion as possible. This section discusses some basic strategies for making the job more interesting without making radical and expensive alterations in job structure and content.

JOB ROTATION AND JOB ENLARGEMENT

An effective technique for combating monotony and repetitiveness involves the rotation of workers among various jobs. When technical and/or cost factors prohibit complete or partial redesign of work, the mere rotation of workers is often sufficient to release the frustrations that build up from doing the same job over an extended period of time. It also enhances the supervisor's flexibility in meeting periodic staffing and absenteeism problems, by having workers who are capable of performing more than one job.

Job rotation is used in several large industries. The automotive industry, for example, depends on workers being able to rotate from one assignment to another. For the most part, the change is viewed with anticipation by the affected employees. Rotation may entail working in different groups, thus giving the individual opportunities to make new friends. Rotation is also a way of giving employees a broader outlook on what the organization really does and may be viewed by the supervisor as an excellent training program for breaking in new employees.

Job rotation

Yet in spite of its possibilities as an acceptable motivational device, there are disadvantages to job rotation. For one thing, scheduling can be a problem. Workers must often be willing to come in at odd times; for example, they may be assigned to work the "graveyard shift" one week in five. It is important to remember also that job rotation is not job redesign. If the worker is simply moved to a new task that is equivalent to the old, nothing is solved. The worker may become just as bored and alienated after learning several jobs as she was when she performed only one. Still, it represents a plausible and reasonably effective strategy when job content changes are too expensive to consider.

Job enlargement, on the other hand, is a technique that concentrates on expanding the number of tasks in which a worker is currently involved. It means giving a worker a variety of tasks that demand greater utilization of skills. Job enlargement is designed to relieve boredom by keeping the worker productive. The additional job responsibilities are similar to the current job requirements and are not intended to increase decision-

Job enlargement

making opportunities. The success of this technique has not been overwhelming. Giving a person more work generally creates resentment or hostility and seldom results in increased morale and productivity. However, for the worker who operates best in a challenging environment, an enlarged job may possess a number of motivational properties that can have a positive impact on performance.

JOB ENRICHMENT

An extension of the simplified job rotation and job enlargement techniques is a strategy referred to as job enrichment. Job enrichment concentrates on providing opportunities for achievement, recognition, responsibility, challenge, and personal growth within an existing job. Rather than simply rearranging the task, the emphasis is placed on making the individual want to work harder through the use of intrinsic rewards.

Job enrichment programs are traditionally carried out in three steps.[10] The first step involves achieving the goal of meaningfulness. The best way to comprehend what a meaningful task entails is to examine a job that fails to capture this component. An automotive assembly line worker who is responsible for attaching door handles to truck bodies will seldom perceive the job as meaningful. The degree of skill needed is obviously minimal; thus the individual's skills are not utilized. If asked, "Do you take pride in building trucks?" the worker frequently responds, "I don't build trucks." In fact, he probably has never seen what goes into the complete process. He knows his contribution to the finished product is minuscule. What makes this particularly demoralizing is that he recognizes that anyone can do his job as well as he. Rather than taking pride in the quality of his work, he is often too embarrassed even to talk about his job with strangers or with members of his family. It is as if working on the assembly line diminishes his self-worth.

For a job to be meaningful, it must provide opportunities to develop skills in which a worker can take pride. Meaningfulness results from the time-consuming process of acquiring knowledge and developing talent that someone else doesn't have. Meaningfulness is related to the degree to which each worker is given a complete, natural, or identifiable unit of work. Being aware of how one's efforts fit into the total scheme of things, and believing that one's work is indeed an important contribution to the achievement of the organization's goals, are two major components of job enrichment.

In addition to meaningfulness, an enriched job must contain increased

Meaningfulness

Responsibility

[10] See Hackman and Oldham, "Motivation Through the Design of Work," pp. 250–279.

JOB ENRICHMENT IN ACTION

An example of job enrichment may be illustrated by the experience an industrial relations superintendent had with a group of janitors. When the superintendent was transferred to a new plant, he soon found, much to his amazement, that in addition to his duties, fifteen janitors in plant maintenance reported directly to him. There was no foreman over these men. Upon browsing through the files one day, the superintendent noticed there was a history of complaints about housekeeping around the plant. After talking to others and observing for himself, it took the superintendent little time to confirm the reports. The janitors seemed to be lazy, unreliable, and generally unmotivated.

Determined to do something about the behavior of the janitors, the superintendent called a group meeting of all fifteen men. He opened the meeting by saying that he understood there were a number of housekeeping problems in the plant but confessed that he did not know what to do about them. Since he felt they, as janitors, were experts in the housekeeping area, he asked if together they would help him solve these problems. "Does anyone have a suggestion?" he asked. There was a deadly silence. The superintendent sat down and said nothing; the janitors said nothing. This lasted for almost twenty minutes. Finally one janitor spoke up and related a problem he was having in his area and made a suggestion. Soon others joined in, and suddenly the janitors were involved in a lively discussion while the superintendent listened and jotted down their ideas. At the conclusion of the meeting the suggestions were summarized with tacit acceptance by all, including the superintendent.

After the meeting, the superintendent referred any housekeeping problems to the janitors, individually or as a group. For example, when any cleaning equipment or material salesmen came to the plant the superintendent did not talk to them, the janitors did. In fact, the janitors were given an office where they could talk to salesmen. In addition, regular meetings continued to be held where problems and ideas were discussed.

All of this had a tremendous influence on the behavior of these men. They developed a cohesive productive team that took pride in its work. Even their appearance changed. Once a grubby lot, now they appeared at work in clean, pressed work clothes. All over the plant, people were amazed how clean and well kept everything had become. The superintendent was continually stopped by supervisors in the plant and asked, "What have you done to those lazy, good-for-nothing janitors, given them pep pills?" Even the superintendent could not believe his eyes. It was not uncommon to see one or two janitors running floor tests to see which wax or cleaner did the best job. Since they had to make all the decisions including committing funds for their supplies, they wanted to know which were the best. Such activities, while taking time, did not detract from their work. In fact, these men worked harder and more efficiently than ever before in their lives.

This example illustrates that even at low levels in an organization, people can respond in responsible and productive ways to a work environment in which they are given an opportunity to grow and mature. People begin to satisfy their esteem and self-actualization needs by participating in the planning, organizing, motivating, and controlling of their own tasks.

Paul Hersey and Kenneth Blanchard, *Management of Organizational Behavior*, 3rd ed. (Englewood Cliffs, N.J.: Prentice-Hall, 1977), pp. 70–71.

responsibility. The supervisor must be willing to delegate to the worker decision-making opportunities. Decisions that were formerly made by the supervisor, but which could just as well be made by a competent and willing worker, should be delegated to the worker. Quite often the worker is better acquainted with the problem and in a better position to make accurate decisions regarding a solution. Greater independence and authority in scheduling, designing, and performing work builds employee commitment. From the supervisor's point of view, delegating responsibilities to subordinates permits the superior to spend more time on other critical matters.

Knowledge of results

The desire for feedback is a vital human need. Too frequently, the message conveyed to the worker is perceived as a negative one, fraught with criticism that creates defensiveness in subordinates. Constructive feedback minimizes defensiveness and concentrates on opening lines of communication with the subordinate. How this is done is the subject of a later chapter.

Job enrichment depends on effective two-way communication. Employees need to know where they stand in relation to their work. Specifically, if they are not performing at the required level, they want to know it. They also need to know precisely *what* is expected of them. If they are performing well in some areas, they want the supervisor to be aware of this and to recognize them for their efforts.

IS JOB ENRICHMENT THE ANSWER?

JE: Not for everyone

Despite all the praise bestowed on job enrichment programs, research attesting to its effectiveness is mixed. There is no single strategy that is universally effective in motivating workers. For one thing, the role of individual differences should not be overlooked. Some people do not desire more responsibility or involvement. The primary issues, for many of them, are still wages and job security. Also, job enrichment may disrupt established job relationships and interfere with the satisfaction of social needs. Instead of being welcomed, job enrichment programs are often met with covert or overt resistance.

Is JE cost-effective?

Another argument against job enrichment is the question of practicability. Is enrichment a practical method for motivating the typical employee? The only way this question can be answered is by making a cost-benefit analysis. Undoubtedly, there will be some costs associated with enrichment. The steps needed to form complete, natural, and identifiable units of work may be quite expensive. If the combining of different job tasks, thus creating whole units of work, is all that is needed, then the benefits might outweigh the costs. But when redesign involves technological change, the costs can be astronomical.

What kinds of workers respond positively to job enrichment programs? Certainly one kind is the employee who wants more from the job than just a paycheck. Another is the employee who is ambitious and wants to get ahead. In sum, workers with new ideas, creativity, energy, and talent, and workers who have strong needs to excel, to advance, and to grow in the job are good prospects for successful job enrichment strategies.

In spite of the arguments against job enrichment, the potential for benefits is enormous. Documented evidence is available that job enrichment can improve quality, increase productivity, raise the level of job satisfaction, reduce absenteeism and turnover, and cut the size of the work force.[11] But as this section has pointed out, successful job enrichment is contingent on so many diverse factors that it would be presumptuous to believe that every difficulty can be avoided.

Characteristics of successful JE workers

Goal-Setting Strategies

Goal-setting strategies are the latest in applied motivation theories. Such strategies as management by objectives (MBO), management by results, and objectives-oriented approaches, to mention only a few, are well known. Basically, goal-setting strategies involve a systematic process whereby the supervisor and subordinate discuss and agree upon a set of jointly determined objectives. With proper preparation, each party should be able to present a case for or against each objective. If the system is functioning properly, the final result will be a set of objectives for subordinates that is in keeping with the overall goals of the organization. Moreover, the supervisor will have something concrete upon which to assess the subordinate's performance. Feedback on progress is periodically supplied, enabling the worker to make necessary corrections. Above all, the link between performance and rewards is made explicitly clear to the subordinate, with emphasis on *what* was achieved rather than on *how* it was accomplished or how hard someone tried.

What is MBO?

However, for goal setting to work on a consistent basis, supervisors must be (1) comfortable with the objective-setting process, (2) adept in coaching techniques, and (3) endowed with an abundance of patience.

[11] Anthony Alber, "Job Enrichment for Profit," *Human Resource Management*, vol. 18, no. 1 (Spring 1979), pp. 15–25.

COMMON ERRORS MANAGERS MAKE IN SETTING GOALS*

- Doesn't clarify common objectives for the whole unit.
- Sets goals too low to challenge the individual subordinate.
- Doesn't use prior results as a basis for using intrinsic creativity to find new and unusual combinations.
- Doesn't clearly shape his unit's common objectives to fit those of the larger unit of which he is a part.
- Overloads individuals with patently inappropriate or impossible goals.
- Fails to cluster responsibilities in the most appropriate positions.
- Allows two or more individuals to believe themselves responsible for doing exactly the same things when he knows having one man responsible is better.
- Stress methods of working rather than clarifying individual areas of responsibility.
- Emphasizes tacitly that it is pleasing him rather than achieving the job objective which counts.
- Makes no policies as guides to action, but waits for results and then issues ad hoc judgments in correction.

* Based on a survey of 1,100 managers.

- Doesn't probe to discover what program his subordinate proposes to follow to achieve his goals but accepts every goal uncritically without a plan for its successful achievement.
- Is too reluctant to add his own (or higher management's) known needs to the programs of his subordinates.
- Ignores the very real obstacles that are likely to hinder the subordinate in achieving his goals, including the numerous emergency or routine duties which consume time.
- Ignores the new goals or ideas proposed by his subordinates and imposes only those which he deems suitable.
- Doesn't think through and act upon what he must do to help his subordinates succeed.
- Fails to set intermediate target dates by which to measure his subordinates' progress towards their goals.
- Doesn't introduce new ideas from outside the organization nor does he permit or encourage subordinates to do so, thereby freezing the status quo.
- Fails to permit his subordinates to seize targets of opportunity in lieu of stated objectives that are less important.
- Is rigid about not scrapping previously agreed-upon goals that have subsequently

Goal setting takes time. It will not work overnight. Organizations that are considering goal setting are told to expect a breaking-in period of at least three years.

THE IMPORTANCE OF GOOD OBJECTIVES

Like job enrichment, goal setting has its problems. For one thing, a great deal of employee training is needed to instruct individuals in identifying and writing realistic, challenging, and measurable objectives. A good objective will answer four questions: who? what? when? and how?

proved unfeasible, irrelevant or impossible.
- Doesn't reinforce successful behavior when goals are achieved, or correct unsuccessful behavior when they are missed.

SETTING GOALS TO MEASURE THE UNMEASURABLE

1. It is often necessary to devise measurements of present levels in order to be able to estimate or calculate change from this level.
2. The most reliable measures are the real time or raw data in which the physical objects involved comprise the measures to be used (dollars of sales, tone of output, number of home runs hit).
3. When raw data can't be used, an index or ratio is the next most accurate measure. This is a batting average, a percentage, a fraction, or a ratio.
4. If neither of the above two can be used, a scale may be constructed. Such scales may rate "from 1 to 10," a nominal rating against a checklist of adjectives such as "excellent, fair, poor" or one which describes "better than or worse than" some arbitrary scale. These are useful but less precise than the above.

5. Verbal scales are the least precise but can be extremely useful in identifying present levels and noting real change. Verbs such as "directs, checks, and reports" are indicative of actions to be taken.
6. General descriptions are the least useful, but still have value in establishing benchmarks for change. "A clear, cloudless fall day" is obviously not the same as a "cloudy, foggy misty day" and the two descriptions could be used to state conditions as they exist and conditions as they should be.
7. The statements of measurement should be directed more toward results than toward activity. (Much activity may prove impossible to state in specific terms, whereas results of that activity can be stated.)
8. In stating results sought or defining present levels, effort should be made to find indicative, tangible levels and convert verbal or general descriptions into such tangible scales, ratios or raw measures where possible.
9. If you can't count it, measure it, or describe it, you probably don't know what you want and often can forget about it as a goal.

George S. Odiorne, *Industry Week*, June 8, 1970.

Who is the performer? What is the action expected? When will the action take place and when can results be expected? Finally, how will we know if success is achieved? (what do we look for, and what measures will be used?).

One of the foremost authorities on goal setting, George Odiorne, describes the process itself as worth at least as much as the results achieved. For those who are interested in the details of goal setting, we have included Odiorne's perspectives on the most common mistakes managers make in identifying, implementing, and evaluating objectives. (See accompanying box.) We will continue to address goal setting throughout the book (see Chapter 7), including examples of goals, forms, and procedures.

We would like to share one final thought about objectives. While good objectives are essential, they should not become an obsession to those affected. When an employee's overall performance is judged totally by the number of objectives accomplished, compared to the number missed, the integrity of the system is called into question. Gamesmanship takes over. Employees will then attempt to negotiate easy goals, rather than focusing on more difficult targets that stretch their talents. Good sense must always prevail when it comes to evaluating an employee's overall performance.

GOAL SETTING VERSUS JOB ENRICHMENT

Is goal setting better than job enrichment? First of all, the two approaches are remarkably similar. Both concentrate on satisfying the individual's intrinsic needs. Second, both provide independence to the individual, allowing personal discretion regarding how and when a job is to be performed. Finally, feedback and knowledge of results are encouraged in each strategy. Recognizing that each of us has a fundamental need to know how well we're doing is a major component of any intrinsic reward program.

Both serve a purpose

The emphasis with goal setting is on objectives or targets; the emphasis with job enrichment is on meaningfulness. For individuals with a high need to achieve, setting targets can be a most effective approach. A meaningful task, on the other hand, may or may not contain sufficiently concrete objectives. Instead, emphasis is on making the work interesting, which in turn leads to better performance.

Building on Trust ———————————

Trust is the cornerstone

Throughout this chapter, different motivational strategies have been presented and examined—in some cases modified with the simple purpose of being useful to the supervisor. Yet the cornerstone for any motivation theory is the trust and confidence of subordinates in the supervisor. If confidence in the supervisor is nonexistent, then even the soundest strategy backed by all of the organization's resources is doomed to failure. Employees have to believe in the integrity, maturity, and emotional stability of the supervisor. Anything less diminishes the supervisor's effectiveness as a leader.

Developing trust is a time-consuming process. It begins by treating employees as worthwhile individuals—not simply as social security numbers. Employees take pride when personal interest is shown in them by the supervisor, especially when it seems clear that there are a hundred other pressing matters, each demanding the supervisor's attention. There are times when supervisors become so preoccupied with their concerns that little attention is directed toward employees. It is easy to forget the employee as an individual—one with feelings, emotions, and opinions. Treating the employee as an individual not only helps to build trust, it also helps to raise that person's self-esteem.

Sensitivity and empathy are other key elements when it comes to trying to understand the other person. As a supervisor, you need to make a sincere attempt to understand the employee's point of view before acting. It is particularly helpful to keep a receptive mind. Supervisors who spend most of their time imparting their knowledge to their subordinates obviously can't learn from them.

Empathize

A concerted effort should be made to have subordinates participate in some of the decision-making processes. When given an opportunity, most employees welcome the idea of helping the boss make work-related decisions. If commitment is needed to ensure the success of the decision, then it becomes even more important to bring employees fully into the process.

Foster employee participation

Finally, the supervisor should be ever alert for opportunities that allow subordinates to grow both professionally and individually. It may mean the assignment of increasingly complex and challenging tasks, the opportunity to set up some departmental program, or the chairing of an employee committee. Employee growth and development could be nurtured through a suggestion by the supervisor for the employee to attend a particular training workshop, enroll in a particular college course, or get involved in a specific community project. The bottom line for all of these activities is increased motivation and the broadening of the employee's capacities, thus making him or her a more valuable person to have around.

Create growth opportunities

Earlier, the supervisor's learning to read employees' behavior was discussed. By implication, the opposite also occurs. Employees are constantly observing what the boss is doing, saying, acting, and otherwise treating subordinates, clients, management, and people in general. It makes good sense for a supervisor to improve in those areas that are most readily apparent to subordinates. These areas are:

1. Being *genuine* and *generous* with praise but stern only in private, never punishing an employee in front of others

2. Being *patient* when listening to a colleague or a subordinate
3. Being willing to take the time to get the facts and provide feedback in a *constructive* style; knowing when to use two-way communication and when to depend on one-way communication (i.e., giving commands)
4. Avoiding placing blame, seeking solutions to problems, and concentrating on *conflict resolution* rather than conflict
5. Encouraging *challenging* but attainable objectives for each subordinate
6. Being willing to stick his or her neck out for subordinates when it is right to do so—even at great personal risk.

These are only a few of the characteristics that are needed to build trust and confidence into the supervisor-subordinate relationship. They are characteristics that anyone can acquire over time—and become a better person as a result.

SUMMARY

Understanding motivation theories offers nothing for the supervisor unless he or she can translate them into productive strategies. The purpose of this chapter has been to demonstrate the various ways this can be accomplished. Different methods of motivation have been discussed, including money, status symbols, praise, redesigning tasks, and setting objectives. It was noted that there are many ways, beyond increased monetary compensation, in which supervisors can reward good performance.

In particular, nonmonetary rewards should be considered because the amounts, timing, and form of these rewards can be designed by supervisors in such a way as to achieve maximum results in each situation. Increased recognition, for example, can occur by sharing privileged information, such as departmental plans, with the subordinate. Soliciting input from subordinates when important decisions must be made is yet another strategy for enhancing employee self-esteem.

Increasing development opportunities for employees is not only a sound strategy for meeting today's needs but represents a tool for meeting an organization's future manpower needs. It would include, for example, special one-time assignments, rotating the employee through other positions, sending the employee to training programs, and/or simply including the employee in meetings with management. Other strategies for satisfying subordinates' higher-level needs include job enrichment techniques and giving the subordinate increased responsibility, in the form of challenging and satisfying work assignments.

Nevertheless, not all employees will be "turned on" by these techniques. Some individuals are more concerned about their social needs. For these employees, perhaps informal work groups is a strategy a supervisor can utilize. Since people are essentially "social animals," teamwork and cooperation help to satisfy social needs. Knowing that they "belong" does much for employees, and when the group's goals are aligned with the organization's, everyone wins.

Whatever strategy is used, there are still some basic principles to effective implementation. The process begins by developing a relationship with subordinates that is based on trust. How subordinates feel and what they think about the supervisor's motives determine credibility. A supervisor who is not credible to subordinates is not going to be successful. Once a degree of trust is established, the supervisor should try to get to know each employee well enough to figure out what makes each one tick. Maslow's and Herzberg's theories, for example, provide a useful frame of reference for understanding subordinates' job needs.

Motivation is the key to both employee and organizational success. The challenge of supervisors in the future is to find, create, and administer alternative motivation strategies that more fully utilize the capabilities of the organization's human resources.

PERFECT PIZZERIA

Perfect Pizzeria in Southville, in deep southern Illinois, is the second largest franchise of the chain in the United States. The headquarters is located in Phoenix, Arizona. Although the business is prospering, it has employee and managerial problems.

Each operation has one manager, an assistant manager, and from two to five night managers. The managers of each pizzeria work under an area supervisor. There are no systematic criteria for being a manager or becoming a manager trainee. The franchise has no formalized training period for the manager. No college education is required. The managers for whom the case observer worked during a four-year period were relatively young (ages 24 to 27) and only one had completed college. They came from the ranks of night managers or assistant managers, or both. The night managers were chosen for their ability to perform the duties of the regular employees. The assistant managers worked a two-hour shift during the luncheon period five days a week to gain knowledge about bookkeeping and management. Those becoming managers remained at that level unless they expressed interest in investing in the business.

The employees were mostly college students, with a few high school students performing the less challenging jobs. Since Perfect Pizzeria was located in an area with few job opportunities, it had a relatively easy task filling its employee quotas. All the employees, with the exception of the manager, were employed part time. Consequently, they worked for less than the minimum wage.

The Perfect Pizzeria system is devised so that food and beverage costs and profits are set up according to a percentage. If the percentage of food unsold or damaged in any way is very low, the manager gets a bonus. If the percentage is high, the manager does not receive a bonus; rather, he or she receives only his or her normal salary.

There are many ways in which the percentage can fluctuate. Since the manager cannot be in the store 24 hours a day, some employees make up for their paychecks by helping themselves to the food. When a friend comes in to order a pizza, extra ingredients are put on the friend's pizza. Occasional nibbles by 18 to 20 employees throughout the day at the meal table also raise the percentage figure. An occasional bucket of sauce may be spilled or a pizza accidentally burned. Sometimes the wrong size of pizza may be made.

In the event of an employee mistake or a burned pizza by the oven man, the expense is supposed to come from the individual. Because of peer pressure, the night manager seldom writes up a bill for the erring employee. Instead, the establishment takes the loss and the error goes unnoticed until the end of the month when the inventory is taken. That's when the manager finds out that the percentage is high and that there will be no bonus.

In the present instance, the manager took retaliatory measures. Previously, each employee was entitled to a free pizza, salad, and all the soft drinks he or she could drink for every 6 hours of work. The manager raised this figure from 6 to 12 hours of work. However, the employees had received these 6-hour benefits for a long time. Therefore, they simply took advantage of the situation whenever the manager or the assistant was not in the building. Though the night manager theoretically had complete control of the operation in the evenings, he did not command the respect that the manager or assistant manager did. This was because he received the same pay as the regular employees; he could not reprimand other employees; and he was basically the same age or sometimes even younger than the other employees.

Thus, apathy grew within the pizzeria. There seemed to be a further separation between the manager and his workers, who started out as a closely knit group. The manager made no attempt to alleviate the problem because he felt it would iron itself out. Either the employees that were dissatisfied would quit or they would be content to put up with the new regulations. As it turned out, there was a rash of employee dismissals. The manager had no problem in filling the vacancies with new workers, but the loss of key personnel was costly to the business.

With the large turnover, the manager found he had to spend more time in the building, supervising and sometimes taking the place of inexperienced workers. This was in direct violation of the franchise regulation, which stated that a manager would act as a supervisor and at no time take part in the actual food preparation. Employees were not placed under strict supervision with the manager working alongside them. The operation no longer worked smoothly because of differences between the remaining experienced workers and the manager concerning the way in which a particular function should be performed.

Within a two-month period, the manager was again free to go back to his office and leave his subordinates in charge of the entire operation. During this two-month period, the percentage had returned to the previous low level and the manager received a bonus each month. The manager felt that his problems had been resolved and that conditions would remain the same, since the new personnel had been properly trained.

It didn't take long for the new employees to become influenced by the other employees. Immediately after the manager had returned to his supervisory role, the percentage began to rise. This time the manager took a bolder step. He cut out any benefits that the employees had—no free pizzas, salads, or drinks. With the job market at an even lower ebb than usual, most employees were forced to stay. The appointment of a new area supervisor made it impossible for the manager to "work behind the counter," since the supervisor was centrally located in Southville.

The manager tried still another approach to alleviate the rising percentage problem and maintain his bonus. He placed a notice on the bulletin board, stating that if the percentage remained at a high level, a lie detector test would be given to all employees. All those found guilty of taking or purposefully wasting food or drinks would be immediately terminated. This did not have the desired effect on the employees, because they knew if they were all subjected to the test, all would be found guilty and the manager would have to dismiss all of them. This would leave him in a worse situation than ever.

Even before the following month's percentage was calculated, the manager knew it would be high. He had evidently received information from one of the night managers about the employees' feelings toward the notice. What he did not expect was that the percentage would reach an all-time high. That is the state of affairs at the present time.

1. Considering each of the motivational strategies discussed in this chapter, which one explains what happened at Perfect Pizzeria when the manager restricted the incentives of free food and drink?
2. How might the situation be corrected using the motivational strategies discussed in the chapter?

Lee Neely. This case appears in John E. Dittrich and Robert A Zawacki (eds.), *People and Organizations: Cases in Management and Organizational Behavior* (Plano, Texas: Business Publications, Inc., 1981), pp. 126–128.

DISCUSSION QUESTIONS

1. Why is it important for supervisors to know what people want from work?
2. How can management affect the *degree* to which money is a motivator?
3. Will merit raises be meaningful if they are the same or less than what average performers get just because they are union members? Explain.
4. In job enrichment, which of the concepts (or dimensions) that lead to increased motivation would be easiest to change?
5. How might employee resistance to job enrichment be confronted and resolved?
6. When employees are asked what rewards they want from their job, they tend to respond with extrinsic rewards. Why is this true?
7. Describe how generous extrinsic rewards might tend to overwhelm the intrinsic satisfaction that comes from the work itself. Can you provide some examples?
8. How might a supervisor create a motivating work environment for subordinates who must spend their entire workday on an assembly line producing electric toasters?

REFERENCES

Babb, H., and Kopp, K. "Application of Behavior Modification in the Modern Organization." *Academy of Management Review* 3, no. 2 (April 1978): 291–293.

Campbell, J. P.; Dunnette, M. D.; Lawler, E. E.; and Weick, K. E. *Managerial Behavior, Performance, and Effectiveness.* New York: McGraw-Hill, 1970.

Gellerman, S. W. *The Management of Human Resources.* Hinsdale, Illinois: The Dryden Press, 1976.

Hackman, J. R., and Suttle, J. L. *Improving Life at Work.* Pacific Palisades, California: Goodyear, 1977.

Herzberg, R. *Work and the Nature of Man.* Cleveland, Ohio: The World Publishing Co., 1966.

Herzberg, F. "One More Time: How Do You Motivate Employees?" *Harvard Business Review* 46, no. 1 (1968): 53–62.

Herzberg, F., Mausner, B., and Snyderman, B. *The Motivation to Work.* New York: John Wiley and Sons, Inc., 1959.

House, R. J., and Wigdor, L. A. "Herzberg's Dual-Factor Theory of Job Satisfaction and Motivation: A Review of the Evidence and a Criticism." *Personnel Psychology* 20 (1967): 369–389.

Hulin, C. L., and Blood, M. R. "Job Enlargement, Individual Differences, and Worker Responses." *Psychological Bulletin* 69 (1968): 41–55.

Latham, G. P., and Yukl, G. A. "Assigned Versus Participative Goal-Setting with Educated and Uneducated Wood Workers." *Journal of Applied Psychology* 60 (1975): 299–302.

————. "A Review of Research on the Application of Goal-Setting in Organizations." *Academy of Management Journal* 18 (1975): 824–845.

Lawler, E. E. *Pay and Organizational Effectiveness.* New York: McGraw-Hill, 1971.

————. *Motivation in Work Organizations.* Monterey, Calif.: Brooks/Cole, 1973.

Locke, E. A., "Toward a Theory of Task Motivation and Incentives." *Organizational Behavior and Human Performance* 3 (1968): 157–189.

————. "The Nature and Causes of Job Satisfaction." In *Handbook of Industrial and Organizational Psychology,* edited by M. Dunnette. Chicago: Rand McNally, 1976.

Maslow, Abraham H. "A Theory of Human Motivation." *Psychological Review* 50 (1943): 370–396.

Schneier, C. E. "Behavior Modification in Management: A Review and Critique." *Academy of Management Journal* 17 (September 1974): 541.

Skinner, B. F. *Science and Human Behavior.* New York: Free Press, 1953.

————. *Contingencies of Reinforcement*. New York: Appleton-Century-Crofts, 1969.

Steers, R. M. "Task-Goal Attributes, Need for Achievement, and Supervisory Performance." *Organizational Behavior and Human Performance* 13 (1975): 392–403.

Steers, R., and L. W. Porter. *Motivation and Work Behavior*, 2nd ed. New York: McGraw-Hill, 1979.

Terkel, S. *Working*. New York: Pantheon, 1974.

Vroom, V. *Work and Motivation*. New York: John Wiley and Sons, Inc., 1964.

Wahba, M., and Bridwell, L. G. "Maslow Reconsidered: A Review of Research on the Need Hierarchy Theory." *Organizational Behavior and Human Performance* 15 (1976): 217–240.

CHAPTER 5

THE ABCs OF LEADERSHIP

When the best leaders' work is done the people say: We did it ourselves.

—Lao Tse

Chapter Outline

Defining Leadership
A Brief Look at Leadership Studies
   Trait Theory
   The Behavioral Approach to Leadership
   The Situational Approach to Leadership
   House's Path-Goal Theory
Putting the Theories into Practice
   A Catalog of Leadership Styles
   Putting Your Leadership Style into Practice
   Specific Ingredients of Supervisory Leadership

Objectives

Leadership involves influencing an individual or group toward the accomplishment of certain specified goals and objectives. Leadership is an elusive quality that enables a supervisor to direct and help motivate subordinates to this end. This chapter has two main objectives: (1) to explain the concept of leadership by examining the leadership role of a supervisor and providing a brief summary of what is known about leadership, and (2) to help the supervisor adopt behavior patterns that will enable him or her to become a successful leader. Specifically, in this chapter you will become familiar with:

1. The leadership role of a supervisor
2. The history of leadership studies
3. The situation's effect on leadership style
4. The behavioral approach to leadership
5. Some common leadership behavior patterns
6. Ways of being a successful leader

Major Concepts

Leadership
External duties
Internal duties
Trait theory
Behavioral model of leadership

Situational model of leadership
Path-goal model of leadership
Autocratic leadership
Participative leadership
Instrumental leadership

When I graduated from high school, I took a job with the fire department. I held this job for three years before deciding to go to college. The chief was a very nice guy who frequently joined in chess games, pool, and other activities around the firehouse. We had lots of work to do around the station, even when there was no fire. Such things as cleaning equipment and paperwork had to be done regularly, but the chief pretty much let us decide who would do what, when we would do it, and how.

Basically, he was an easy-going sort, and he rarely used the power of his position around the station. However, when we had a fire, he was a different person. He would always be the first to the scene; he would bellow out orders, directing our attack and cursing anyone who failed to react immediately or correctly. Although his behavior sometimes irked us, we always obeyed his commands. One thing about it, we were the most effective fire-fighting unit in the city.

Adapted from Michael A. Hitt, R. Dennis Middlemist, and Robert L. Mathis, *Effective Management* (St. Paul: West Publishing Company, 1979), p. 277.

Defining Leadership

Generally speaking, supervisors are charged with maintaining and, if possible, improving overall organizational effectiveness and efficiency. These responsibilities are carried out through workers. It is also important that the supervisor ensure some degree of job satisfaction for workers as they carry out their required duties. Supervisors are managers who are involved in the coordination of both human and material resources toward some predefined objectives. *Management*—a more general term—involves planning, controlling, making decisions, and leading. Hence, leadership is an essential part of management. With leadership there is emphasis on the human aspects of the managerial functions. Leadership primarily involves relationships with people; it involves actions

Leadership: an essential part of management

on the part of one person to influence the behavior, attitudes, and opinions of others to accomplish a given task.

Leadership involves an exchange between followers and a leader—an exchange that must carry satisfaction for each of the parties involved. For example, the coach of an athletic team exercises leadership and coaching abilities by leading his team to a championship. The followers, in this case the team members, follow the coach's advice because they receive psychic and, in the case of professional teams, economic rewards. Psychic rewards consist of the fulfillment of personal goals, a sense of achievement, personal popularity, and media focus for the players and the team. Economic rewards may include higher salaries, bonuses for winning, and opportunities for team members to make commercial endorsements. In short, the leader in a workplace situation is one who influences others to perform while simultaneously satisfying workers' individual, group, and professional needs.

The leadership-followers exchange

Factors that determine a leader's style include a supervisor's superior, his or her peers and associates, his or her subordinates or followers, the organizational objectives, policies, office climate, education, background, experience, personality, and the situation or task to be carried out. Figure 5.1 shows that these factors influence the leader and that

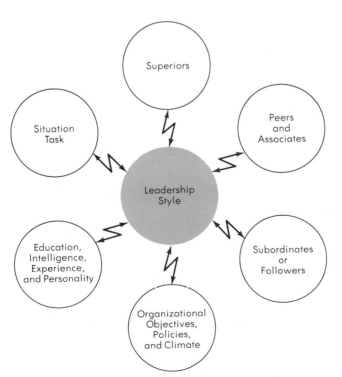

FIGURE 5.1
Factors Affecting a
Leader's Style

the leader influences these factors in return. The results of this two-sided association of factors determines how well the leader carries out his or her job.

Typically, designated leaders—such as directors, foremen, chairpersons, and supervisors—have a positive balance of the official power or influence in an organization. However, this official power may not always result in effective leadership. Official authority is sometimes termed positional authority, and this may not be enough to persuade subordinates to engage effectively in the appropriate activities. A supervisor must build on his or her official power to establish an environment that promotes effective performance.

Supervisors perform two types of duties. External duties are oriented outward from the individual unit or section for which the supervisor has been given control. Examples of external duties are coordinating the work of the unit with other units or obtaining equipment, materials, people, and other resources. A second type of duties are internally oriented. These duties involve such things as handling employee complaints and dealing with unproductive workers. A supervisor must perform a mixture of external and internal activities for a unit to perform at a high level.

Leadership is primarily an internal activity, but it also relates to external activities. The intensity and duration of research on leadership training reflect the view that leadership capability is vital to organizational success. To understand something of the nature of leadership, it is appropriate to review some of the phases that the study of leadership has moved through over a period of years. Figure 5.2 illustrates the various theories and their emphases.

| | Leadership is not positionship |

FIGURE 5.2
A Classification of
Leadership Theories

LEADERSHIP EMPHASIS

THEORY OPERATION		Inherent Leadership Traits of the Individual	Leader Behavior
	Universal Frameworks	The Great Man Theory	A Behavioral Orientation as described in the Michigan and Ohio State studies
	Situational Approaches	Fiedler's Situational Theory	Hersey and Blanchard's Theory House's Path-Goal Theory

A Brief Look at Leadership Studies

TRAIT THEORY

The study of leadership behavior has moved through three distinct periods or phases. The first phase involved a number of studies wherein researchers attempted to determine the traits or qualities of effective leaders. The underlying concept was that effective leadership extends from a leadership ability derived from certain personality traits, either inherited or acquired at an early age, and that all great leaders have these traits in common.

Trait researchers dominated the study of leadership from the beginning of the twentieth century until the end of World War II. Over one hundred studies were done over a fifty-year period with results indicating that leaders tend to be more influential, more original, more adaptable, more reasonable, more popular, and more capable. However, the results were less clear and less conclusive than the above indicates. For example, six studies found that leaders were older than followers, whereas two found that there was no age difference. Because of such inconclusive, contradictory results, around 1949 several researchers discredited the trait theory. Consequently, this approach has been largely neglected in recent years by those involved in leadership research.

Results of trait theory studies inconclusive

THE BEHAVIORAL APPROACH TO LEADERSHIP

When the trait theory fell into disrepute, attention was then directed toward relationships between leader behavior and work performance. A number of research programs were directed toward studying leader behavior. Two of the most popular were carried out at Ohio State University and at the University of Michigan. The Ohio State researchers concentrated on the broad issues of unit effectiveness and the impact of leader behavior on the actions of individual subordinates. The Michigan studies, on the other hand, were concerned more with interactions among leader behaviors, group behaviors, and employee satisfaction and performance.

Two popular studies

The Michigan researchers first studied clerical workers at a large eastern insurance company. Their research disclosed four major factors that influence employee performance and satisfaction:

Major factors influencing performance

1. *Differentiation of the supervisor's role:* The study found that supervisors of effective work groups tend to perform only those functions that lie within the realm of their assigned responsibilities and leave production tasks to their subordinates.
2. *Looseness of supervision:* The study found that supervisors of more effective groups tend to give subordinates greater freedom in determining job performance.
3. *Group relationships:* Although the studies did not establish a specific relationship between morale and productivity, the researchers felt it was probable that group satisfaction affects such things as absenteeism and turnover.
4. *Employee-oriented leadership:* Supervisors of more effective groups were found to be usually more interested in subordinates as individuals than were leaders of less effective groups.

Later studies showed that while these factors held true in general, they were not necessarily applicable to specific situations. In short, their effect was altered by varying the situation. In the beginning, researchers felt that it would be difficult for a supervisor to employ both employee-oriented and production-oriented methods at the same time. However, later work showed that this could be accomplished in some situations. Both the Michigan and the Ohio State studies concluded that a universal (or best) way of leading proved to be very elusive.

THE SITUATIONAL APPROACH TO LEADERSHIP

During the 1950s and early 1960s a number of leadership theories were developed which emphasized that leadership traits and behaviors vary with the situation. This was in effect the beginning of what is now known as the situational approach to leadership. Generally, the factors that are seen as influencing leadership effectiveness include

Factors affecting leadership effectiveness

1. The personality of the leader
2. The performance requirements of the leader and the job requirements of subordinates
3. The attitudes, needs, and expectations of the subordinates
4. The organizational and physical environment of leader and subordinates

There are many situational theories; however, only two of the more popular ones will be discussed here.

Fiedler's Theory. Probably the most completely tested of the situational leadership theories is the one developed by Frederick Fiedler. Fiedler began his studies in 1951 by studying the relationships among the three areas he considered important to leadership.[1] He identifies these areas as (1) the supervisor's interactions with subordinates, (2) subordinates' productivity, and (3) subordinates' morale. From his studies, Fiedler developed a theory of leadership having three situational factors assumed to influence a leader's effectiveness: (1) *leader-member relations:* the degree of confidence subordinates have in their leader; (2) *task structure:* the degree to which employees' jobs are routine versus loosely structured; and (3) *position power:* the power inherent in the leader's position. Position power includes the ability to give rewards and punishments. In addition, it ensues from the support the leader receives from his or her superiors and from the organization in general.

Fiedler suggests that leaders who are directive and leaders who are permissive each manage best in certain types of situations. Instead of saying a leader must adapt his or her style to the situation, Fiedler identifies the type of leader that functions best in a given situation. The point is not whether a leader is a good one or a poor one, but rather whether a leader fits a particular situation. A person may be an effective leader in one situation and not be at all effective in another situation. Fiedler assumes that a supervisor can enhance subordinates' effectiveness if carefully chosen for situations favorable to his or her style. Fiedler offers some practical procedures for improving leader-member relations, structure, and position power:

1. *Leader-member relations:* These relations can be improved by restructuring the leader's subordinates so that the group is more compatible in terms of educational level, technical expertise, and ethnic background. Fiedler points out, however, that this procedure could be extremely difficult in a unionized group, which might assume that this restructuring is a management attempt to weaken the collective bargaining unit.

2. *Task structure:* The task structure can be modified in two directions. First, it can be made more structured by defining jobs in greater detail. Second, it can be made less structured by providing only general directions for the work that must be accomplished. Some workers like a minimal task structure, whereas other workers prefer a detailed and specific task structure.

> **Fiedler stresses three situational factors**

> **Leader should fit situation**

> **Practical procedures**

[1] Fred W. Fiedler, *A Theory of Leadership Effectiveness* (New York: McGraw-Hill, 1967); and Fred W. Fiedler, "The Leadership Game: Matching the Man to the Situation," *Organizational Dynamics* 4 (Winter, 1976), 6–16.

3. *Position power:* This dimension can be strengthened in a number of ways. The supervisor can be given a higher rank in the organization, or he or she can be given more support or greater authority. This modification could be accomplished by simply issuing a memo indicating a rank change and specifying the additional authority the leader now possesses. In addition, the leader's reward power could be increased if the organization delegates to the leader the authority to evaluate the performance of his or her subordinates.

One important facet of Fiedler's theory is that it takes into account the leader's personality as well as the situational variables related to particular workers. This is a major improvement over earlier theories, which failed to recognize that the situation plays a very important part in the effectiveness of a leader.

Hersey and Blanchard's Theory. Hersey and Blanchard's situational leadership theory is based on the theme that there is no one best way to influence people. The theory complements Fiedler because it encourages leaders to *evaluate employees* in determining an effective style. A supervisor's leadership style should depend on the maturity level of the people he or she is attempting to influence. The theory was originally published as a "life cycle theory of leadership," [2] using the basic theme that as the maturity of the followers increases, the appropriate leadership behavior requires adjustments in degree of task and relationship orientation. When children are young, their parents are involved with dressing and feeding them—behavior that is basically task-oriented. As the children get older, they accept greater responsibility for their own behavior, and the parents begin employing more relationship-oriented behavior. Such behavior can also apply in a work situation. If workers are allowed to mature, a changing leadership behavior pattern can be exercised by the supervisor, as shown in Figure 5.3. The figure shows four basic leadership styles: *S1* indicates a need for high task and low relationship behaviors, *S2* indicates a need for high task and high relationship behaviors, *S3* indicates a need for high relationship and low task behaviors, and *S4* indicates a need for low task and low relationship behaviors. Just below the bell-shaped curve of various behaviors is a continuum representing the maturity of the workers; *M1* represents low maturity and *M4* represents high maturity. The bringing together of basic leadership styles and the maturity of the workers makes up the central theme of this situational leadership theory.

Hersey and Blanchard propose that various leadership styles are appro-

Stresses maturity level of followers

---

[2] Paul Hersey and Kenneth H. Blanchard, "Life Cycle Theory of Leadership," *Training and Development Journal*, May 1969, pp. 26–34.

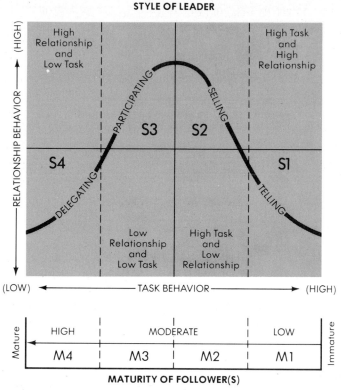

STYLE OF LEADER

FIGURE 5.3
Hersey and
Blanchard's Situational
Leadership Model

Adapted from Paul Hersey and Ken Blanchard, *Management of Organizational Behavior: Utilizing Human Resources,* 4th ed. (Englewood Cliffs, NJ: Prentice-Hall, 1982), p. 152.

priate for each of the maturity levels. In the initial phase where subordinates first join the organization, a high task orientation is necessary because subordinates have to be instructed in their tasks and in organizational rules and procedures (Telling). As subordinates learn their jobs, a task orientation by a supervisor must continue because subordinates are not yet willing and able to accept responsibility. However much a supervisor's trust and support for the employee may have increased, further encouragement is still needed on the part of the supervisor (Selling). In the third phase, the subordinate's ability and motivation have increased and as a result the subordinate seeks greater responsibility. At this point, the supervisor will no longer need to be directive, but he or she must continue to be supportive and considerate in order to encourage the subordinate to seek greater responsibility (Participating). Finally, subordinates become experienced, confident, and self-directing; they are "on their own" and do not need or expect a close relationship with their supervisor. The supervisor can reduce the amount of support and encouragement that he or she has been providing (Delegating). Using the situational leadership theory, supervisors should adjust their leadership behavior through the four styles along the bell-shaped curve in Figure 5.3.

The key to effective leadership, then, is to identify the maturity level of the worker or group the supervisor is trying to influence and then use the appropriate leadership style of telling, selling, participating, or delegating. Maturity consists of ability and willingness. Ability has to do with the worker's knowledge, experience, and ability to perform certain tasks without direction from others. The able employee can work alone without much help from the supervisor. The other dimension of maturity is willingness, which involves confidence and commitment. Willing individuals do not need continual encouragement to do their jobs well.

HOUSE'S PATH-GOAL THEORY

One of the most recent and still evolving approaches to the study of leadership has been presented by Robert J. House. House's path-goal model attempts to provide a better understanding of leader effectiveness by incorporating both the Ohio State approach and Fiedler's theory. According to House, supervisors have at their disposal a number of ways to influence subordinates. The supervisor, for example, can offer rewards and clarify to subordinates what they must do to earn these rewards. In other words, the supervisor can show subordinates the "paths" for reaching the rewards.

The leadership style a supervisor uses will affect the types of rewards the supervisor offers and the subordinates' perceptions of what they must do to earn those rewards. An employee-centered supervisor provides a wide range of rewards to subordinates, such as pay, promotion, support, security, respect, and encouragement. In addition he or she is sensitive to individual differences among subordinates and tailors the rewards to the individual needs and desires of the subordinates. A task-oriented supervisor, on the other hand, sticks to a narrower, less individualized set of rewards. Individuals reporting to a task-oriented supervisor will typically know exactly what performance level is required to obtain salary increases and bonuses.

Expectancy theory

House changes the focus of research by not only analyzing leadership style per se but also its effects on the ways leaders motivate subordinates. House's approach uses expectancy theory, that is, individuals will be motivated to produce only if they perceive that their efforts result in successful performance and desired outcomes. In other words, the style of leadership should be aimed at influencing the motivational level of the subordinates.

House, like Fiedler, recognizes the importance of the situation; but he also analyzes (1) task performance, (2) formal authority, and (3) the primary work group. The ambiguity of the subordinate's task will affect leadership style in a number of ways. For example, an individual who has a structured (unambiguous) job, such as an automobile mechanic, is likely to find an overly directive style unnecessary, since it is clear exactly what needs to be done. However, an individual performing an unstructured (ambiguous) task, such as selling a product, is likely to appreciate some direction, because the direction will clarify to the subordinate what must be done in order to be successful. The organization's formal authority system identifies for subordinates what actions are likely to be met with rewards (exceeding a production quota, for example) and what actions are likely to be met with disapproval (requesting unnecessary overtime). When formal authority is too rigid, the employee-centered supervisor is more motivating, however. When formal authority is lacking, the task-oriented supervisor will let subordinates know what they must do to earn tangible rewards.

The primary work groups can also have an effect on which leadership style is more effective. When the work group is cohesive, the employee-centered supervisor will create an environment that is less motivating because subordinates are deriving satisfaction from the group. In less cohesive groups, an employee-centered supervisor who is supportive and understanding may be more effective.

There are a number of techniques a supervisor (as leader) can employ to improve the motivation of unhappy employees. First, the supervisor can be considerate. Second, the supervisor can encourage employees to believe that they are capable of performing successfully on the job. Third, the supervisor can point out instances where successful performance has resulted in desired rewards. Fourth, the supervisor can change the job expectancies of the employees; job satisfaction may then increase as a result of the change in expectancies.

How to improve motivation

House has pointed out that it is usually the most capable employees who quit when they are dissatisfied. He also points out that a leader can combine consideration and task orientation, and thereby improve morale and employee performance. For Fiedler, this combination did not occur for a leader who is task-oriented or for a leader who is employee-centered.

In summary, House proposes that a number of factors determine leader effectiveness. First, the style of leadership must take into account the motivation of the subordinates. In this sense, House has combined motivation theory with leadership theory. Second, the effectiveness of a particular leadership style is related to its impact on two situational factors—job ambiguity and job satisfaction. Third, a supervisor cannot significantly

Factors determining leadership effectiveness

influence the level of employee performance, especially if there is already a low degree of job ambiguity. Finally a leader can simultaneously influence group morale and employee performance if he or she is both considerate and task-oriented.

Putting the Theories into Practice

A CATALOG OF LEADERSHIP STYLES

Having examined the theories of leadership, it seems appropriate to examine at a practical level some principles by which supervisors can deal effectively with subordinates. At the operational level, supervisors should try to be democratic in their relations with subordinates but at the same time maintain the necessary control within the organization for which they are held responsible. The democratic relationship has come more into focus in recent years. Traditionally, people tend to think of the world as being divided into leaders and followers. In the more modern approach, the leader focuses on the group rather than on a single employee. Researchers have classified this as *group dynamics*, and it appears to be a much better representation of the actual workings of a leader-follower or supervisor-subordinate situation.

Democracy plus control

Group dynamics

When supervisors emerge from training sessions, they are often still unsure as to what path they should follow. There are situations in which they are torn between exerting an autocratic leadership pattern or a somewhat permissive leadership pattern. The point is, supervisors generally are unsure which is the most appropriate way to handle many managerial decision-making situations.

Figure 5.4 shows how leaders can be characterized by three rather distinct behavior patterns. The first is the autocratic or dictatorial type of leader. These individuals seldom give reasons for their orders and are reluctant to accept decisions that run counter to their own opinions. Typically, this type of leader implies that there could be punishment, or that reward could be withheld, if his or her decisions or orders are not carried out in a satisfactory manner. In this behavior pattern (the *telling* approach) the supervisor identifies the problem, chooses a solution, and then dictates to the subordinates what that solution is and what action will be taken. Generally, no consideration is given to subordinates' opinions or suggestions. In this environment, coercion may or may not be used, but it is often implied. A somewhat different version of this

The autocratic leader

Supervisor-Centered Leadership   Employee-Centered Leadership

FIGURE 5.4
Patterns of Leadership

Use of Authority by a Superior

Allowable Freedom for Employees

Autocratic or Dictatorial   Instrumental   Participative or Supportive

Adapted from Robert Tannenbaum and Warren H. Schmidt, "How to Choose a Leadership Pattern," *Harvard Business Review,* March–April 1958, pp. 91–101, and May–June 1973, pp. 162–166. Copyright 1958 by the President and Fellows of Harvard College, all rights reserved.

approach occurs when the supervisor makes a decision and then takes the additional step of persuading his or her subordinates to accept it. The supervisor realizes that there is the possibility of some resistance among the subordinates. By using a *selling* approach, the supervisor tries to reduce their resistance to the proposed alternative.

A second type of leader illustrated in Figure 5.4 is the participative or supportive type of leader. These supervisors are in direct contrast to the autocratic leader. They endeavor to create a social climate in which subordinates will want to do their best. They encourage subordinates to use their own initiative. Such supervisors tend to reject the use of unilateral authority and make every effort to provide recognition of individual rights and dignity. When using this style of leadership, supervisors define the limits and then pass to the group the right to make the decision; however, before doing so, they define the problem to be solved and the boundaries within which the decision must be made.

The participative leader

In another variation of the participative approach, the supervisor permits the group to define the problems as well as make the decisions, within the prescribed limits. It must be noted that this represents an extreme degree of group freedom and is rarely encountered in formal work organizations. The exception might be a research group. In a research group, supervisors impose very few structural limits on the group's activities, and typically those limitations are specified by someone higher up in the organization. In such situations, supervisors participate in the decision-making process with no more authority than any of the subordinates. In this research type of environment, the supervisor is committed in advance to concur with and assist in implementing whatever decision the group makes.

A third type of leader specified in Figure 5.4 is the instrumental leader. Instrumental managers are those who plan, organize, control, and coordinate the activities of their subordinates. Their real ability

The instrumental leader

lies in the fact that they attempt to control the available resources and use them in the most effective way possible. In this type of situation, the supervisor presents his or her ideas and then invites questions from the subordinates. The purpose is so that associates can better understand what the supervisor is trying to accomplish. Question-asking sessions can be characterized as give and take, as they enable a manager and subordinates to explore more fully the implications of a particular decision. The supervisor in this situation can make a tentative decision. However, before the decision is finalized, the proposed solution is presented to the group for its reactions. The final decision does rest with the manager; but group input provides a very important source of information. In this situation, the supervisor presents the problem, gets suggestions, and then makes the decision. The manager's initial role involves identifying the problem. He or she then attempts to get an expanded list of possible solutions through interaction with the group. From the results of this interaction, the manager chooses the solution he or she feels will obtain the best results.

PUTTING YOUR LEADERSHIP STYLE INTO PRACTICE

Leadership style should relate to situation

The types of leadership behavior described earlier represent rather strict definitions of the manner in which leaders may behave in certain situations. The fact remains, however, that supervisors are unsure of which style to apply to a particular situation. In order to gain some insight into leader effectiveness, one must look not only at the leadership style but at a given situation as well. It is important to note that leadership is explained not only in terms of interaction between leader and subordinates; a third dimension must be considered—the work environment. Leadership should always be relative to the situation. Leadership goals should be in tune with group goals and should depend on the nature of the organization. The supervisor must be a member of the group and must share its norms, its objectives, and its aspirations. A supervisor's style, therefore, depends on three factors: (1) the supervisor himself or herself, (2) the subordinates, and (3) the situation.

Values and personality affect leadership style

The Supervisor as Individual. A manager's behavior in any given instance or decision-making situation will be influenced greatly by the many variables operating within his or her own personality. Values definitely affect behavior. Foremost is the feeling that you as supervisor have toward the individuals who are subordinate to you. Should they have a share in making the decisions that affect them? Your behavior as supervisor is also influenced by the relative importance you attach to organizational efficiency, to the personal growth of your subordinates, and to organizational objectives. Another influencing factor is your confidence in your subordinates. This depends on the amount of trust that you have in people generally as well as on your feelings about your subordinates' knowledge and competence with respect to a particular task. A fourth factor is that of your leadership inclinations. Some supervisors seem to function more comfortably and naturally as authoritarian or directive leaders. Others appear to operate more comfortably in a team role where they are continually sharing many of their functions and ideas with their subordinates. A final consideration that affects your leadership style is your feelings of security or insecurity in an uncertain situation. Some supervisors have a greater need for predictability and stability in their work environment and fear losing control of the decision-making process and thereby reducing the predictability of an outcome. An individual who has a great need for security will be reluctant to relinquish control to his or her subordinates.

Another important influence on leadership style is the career state of the individual supervisor. Young supervisors tend to take a proactive stance and tend to stress (1) work priorities, (2) proving their technical confidence, and (3) backing up their subordinates. More mature managers tend to emphasize a more mediative and more personal approach. They tend to relate to subordinates and to stress the use of group decisions more often than do younger supervisors. As managers get older, say over forty, they frequently display a shift towards homeostatic (fatherly and maintenance) concerns. They seem to be increasingly occupied with counseling and training subordinates. One should be cautious, then, in prescribing a uniform style for all supervisors in an organization. Different age groups contribute differently. One cannot assume that all managers have a common set of standards and that certain participative leadership characteristics produce more effective results than do others. Supervisors should realize that application should be in more flexible terms; they must accede to the fact that there are effectively run organizations that have learned to deal with personalized leadership adaptations. The fact is that a young manager is likely to employ participative actions differently than a senior supervisor working on the same type of problem. Good supervisors take into account the career state of other supervisors and the career state of their employees.

Career state affects leadership style

The Subordinates. Subordinates themselves are the second major factor in the leadership process. Like individual supervisors, each employee is influenced by many personality variables. Each has a set of expectations about how the supervisor should act in relation to him or

Subordinates affect leadership style

her. Generally the supervisor can permit subordinates greater freedom if the following essential conditions exist:

1. The subordinates exhibit a relatively high need for independence
2. The subordinates show a readiness to assume responsibility for carrying out the supervisor's decisions
3. There is a relatively high tolerance for ambiguity, some employees preferring to have clear-cut directives, others preferring a greater degree of freedom in determining job performance
4. The subordinates have a sincere interest in problem solving and recognize its importance
5. The subordinates understand and identify with the goals of the organization, tending over time to develop goals that coincide with the organization's
6. The subordinates have the necessary knowledge and experience to deal with problems on a rather independent basis

Each of the above conditions helps to generate a decision-making environment that lends itself more readily to a democratic, facilitative type of leadership environment. When these conditions do not exist, the leader is forced to take a more authoritarian or dictatorial stance to ensure that problems are attacked correctly.

The Situation. The third major factor affecting leadership style involves the situation itself. Sometimes this can be a very powerful determinant. There are certain characteristics of the general situation that affect a manager's behavior. The first of these is the type of organization. Organizations, like individuals, have values and traditions that inevitably influence the behavior of the people who work within them. These values and traditions are communicated to employees in various ways— such as through job descriptions, public statements by senior executives, disciplinary practices, and policy pronouncements. If an organization wants to have dynamic, imaginative, decisive, and persuasive executives, then there must be communication that orients and motivates supervisors in the desired direction. Some organizations put more emphasis on the executive's ability to work effectively with people; others emphasize a production orientation. The way in which a supervisor's environment is defined is likely to push him or her toward one end of the behavior range.

Furthermore, the amount of employee participation is influenced by such variables as the size of the working units, their geographical distribution, and the degree to which inter- and intraorganizational security are required to meet organizational goals. For example, the size of the working unit and the need for keeping plans confidential may make it necessary for supervisors to exercise more control than would otherwise be the case. These factors limit the flexibility of the environment in which the supervisor must function.

A further major set of situational variables affecting leadership relate to time pressures. When the manager is under pressure for an immediate decision, it is more difficult to involve other people. In organizations where there is a constant state of crisis or crash programming, the supervisor is likely to use a high degree of authority and relatively little delegation to subordinates. When time pressures are less intense, it becomes more feasible to involve subordinates in the decision-making process.

Time pressures affect leadership style

Successful supervisors can be characterized neither as solely authoritarian nor as solely permissive. Rather, a successful supervisor is one who is successful in assessing the factors that determine the most appropriate behavior at any given time and then behaving accordingly. A good supervisor is one who possesses both insight and flexibility; one who sees the problems of leadership not as a dilemma but as an opportunity.

SPECIFIC INGREDIENTS OF SUPERVISORY LEADERSHIP

Supervisors usually develop a style whereby they can deal effectively with their particular environment. The ultimate style achieved is generally a result of trial and error and not one deliberately adopted by the individual. The following suggestions are offered for the use of supervisors. Each suggestion can be modified to suit both the individual supervisor and the particular working environment.

Leadership is more process than plan

1. As a supervisor, you should set standards that are in tune with employee needs and abilities as well as organizational goals.
2. When possible, you should determine objectives through working with subordinates on a *participative* basis. It is important for you as a supervisor to convince the employee of the importance of the job. And you must explain to the employee how this particular job fits the overall objectives of the organization. It is very important that you let workers know where their jobs and their performance fit into the overall picture.
3. The supervisor should delegate authority whenever the situation permits.
4. The supervisor should permit the freedom to achieve results. Realistically, the possibility to do this depends on the nature of the employee

Practical suggestions

and the employee's personality. However, where these factors are positive, the supervisor should try to offer this freedom.

5. The supervisor should keep employees informed about their jobs, their performance, and the organization. The supervisor must have the capacity to communicate verbally and, when necessary, in other ways with the employees. Communication is a two-way street, and it is important that lines of communication be kept open to accept subordinate input and to effect a good worker-supervisor relationship.

6. Occasions arise when the supervisor must offer criticism. The primary rule in this area is to make sure that criticism is constructive, not destructive, in nature. Allied with this is the fact that the supervisor should then support the employee in effecting desired change.

7. The supervisor should also set a good example. Employees often seek a model for their behavior on the job, and the supervisor is the closest, the one employees see the most often, and therefore the most logical model in the organization for them to emulate.

8. The supervisor should encourage worker participation when appropriate. Participation is often a function of time and the urgency of the problem. When time is not a constraint, the supervisor should encourage employees to participate in decisions.

9. The supervisor should acknowledge accomplishments and reward them. The supervisor is in the best position to fulfill subordinates' needs for recognition and reward.

10. Besides showing a personal interest in the subordinates, the supervisor's function is to develop an environment of mutual trust and support. Supervisors and subordinates like to feel that they are part of the team, and this team activity comes as a result of trust and support.

11. As a supervisor you should try to be futuristic. That is, you should try to have a grasp on possible future developments. You should be aware of your present environment and be aware of factors that may influence and change the attitudes and efficiency of your employees.

12. Decisiveness is another important asset of a supervisor. Once a decision has been made, the supervisor must ensure that it is workable and proceed to carry it out. The ineffective supervisor is one who worries about whether he or she did, in fact, make the correct decision. Good supervisors do not vacillate once a decision has been made.

13. Supervisors should be predictable. Most employees like to work in an environment where they can anticipate what will happen as a result of their activities. Employees should be able to anticipate

what will result if they continue to exceed organizational expectations.

14. Supervisors should have toughness of mind, that is, the capacity to confront difficult decisions. Some supervisors when faced with having to make a tough decision do not make any decision at all. They feel that no decision is better than the wrong decision. Good supervisors, on the other hand, avoid postponing decision making or passing the buck. They rise to the occasion and handle the problem to the best of their ability.

SUMMARY ▬▬▬▬▬▬▬▬▬▬▬▬▬▬▬▬

Leadership patterns in the work environment evolve from personal expertise, knowledge, and persuasiveness of the leaders involved. In short, specific patterns often develop because of the particular situation at hand. In view of the complexity of factors that determine the relationship between leader behavior and group performance, it is apparent that there is no single recipe for leader effectiveness. There is no universal approach that is applicable in more than a small proportion of situations encountered.

However, knowledge of the leadership process is increasing. It suggests that a contingency or situational view can be used effectively to provide guidelines for leadership behavior that is dependent on the interaction of a number of situational variables.

Typically, good leaders are seen as being helpful, both in setting goals and in structuring or designing a means of achieving these goals. In short, good performance often leads to satisfaction. It is unrealistic to assume that there can be simultaneous attention paid to all dimensions of leadership effectiveness. Some trade-offs are necessary and are bound to occur. An appropriate balance should be maintained according to the situation at hand.

The key to effective leadership is the clarification between leaders and subordinates of job expectations. This must be achieved to set the tone for the entire leader-follower relationship. The very nature of the situational approach involves contingency or alternative styles. A good leader is a good diagnostician. He or she can ascertain the most appropriate leadership style and then employ that style according to the circumstances. The autocratic style may be the most appropriate when it is the expected procedure or necessary procedure. This would be useful in a police or military type of organization. In the event of a fire, for example, the fire chief would not discuss alternative methods of fighting the fire; he would give the order to begin extinguishing the fire and would expect that the order would be carried out immediately.

On the other hand, in situations where time permits, a more democratic approach, which includes a decision-making process and input from subordinates, may be the most effective and the most efficient. The supervisor should be as flexible as possible, gearing his or her style to the specific situation and to the individuals involved.

It is important for supervisors to recognize the complexity of the leader-subordinate relationship. Included in this relationship are human motivations, group dynamics, and organizational climate. The best supervisors seem to have a tolerance for ambiguity and recognize that the more subordinate involvement in the decision-making process, the more likely they will be committed to the decisions that evolve and that they will work to implement them. Supervisors should keep in mind that there are trade-offs in approaches employed in terms of cost and time. The autocratic approach has appeal in terms of tidiness and speed of response; when the situation demands it, it is by far the most appropriate method of leading individuals. On the other hand, when time and flexibility are appropriate, the leader should consider the more participative approaches for leading individuals.

AUTO AND AWNING REFINISHING COMPANY

The Auto and Awning Refinishing Company was established in 1970 to refinish the painted surfaces of automobiles and awnings. The company was founded by Bob Tudor and Arty Grodenski. Bob handled the administrative and sales functions of the business while Arty managed the refinishing shop.

Arty had five men working under him in the shop. Two men worked on preparing the awnings to be painted, and two men worked on preparing the automobiles. The awnings and automobiles were painted by Arty and his assistant. Work was seasonal, and in the spring, summer, and fall the shop was mainly devoted to refinishing awnings. In the winter the shop concentrated its efforts on automobiles.

The five men in the shop worked well together under Arty's supervision. Arty encouraged a congenial atmosphere, allowing the men to participate in deciding who would do what specific task on a given day. For example, if Arty had to go out on the road and pick up a customer's awnings, he would ask if anyone in particular wanted to go. This would break up the routine of the shop, and no one man would be placed in the position of doing the same job day in and day out. Even though each man was given a choice as to what he was going to do in a given day, the men fell into a pattern of having the same two men go on the road while the other three worked in the shop. The men were satisfied, however, because each was doing what he wanted to do.

Work was usually done on schedule with the men taking pride in the way their work was done. This worked out well for Arty, for often he was not able to closely supervise his men; while he was at the shop, he was usually painting inside a closed painting booth. The only time work would back up was at the height of awning refinishing season, when the company did not have the manpower to keep work going on schedule. This would upset Bob Tudor, who believed it was Arty's lackadaisical method of handling the men that caused the work to fall behind schedule.

During the peak of the awning season, Bob confronted Arty concerning the way in which Arty managed the men. Bob argued that Arty should develop a more organized and efficient method for getting the work done. He also said that Arty should discourage the men from so much talking with each other, because this was only wasting time. Arty disagreed; he felt that he would need more men if business continued to grow at the present rate and that his men were already working to capacity. The heated argument continued until Bob insisted that Arty leave the partnership, to be replaced by someone who could get the job done more efficiently. No longer being able to tolerate Bob's interference, Arty left and was replaced by a manager Bob hired away from a competitor.

The new manager, Tom Terser, was quick to take charge in the shop at Auto and Awning Refinishing Company. His first step was to set up work schedules for the upcoming months for road work and work in the shop. Mr. Terser required that the schedule be followed without question. Mr. Terser's next move was to separate the jobs of preparing the awnings and autos for painting into different sections of the building with the men working alone in each section. Mr. Terser also made a point of constantly inspecting the men's work and making sure his men were working.

AUTO AND AWNING REFINISHING COMPANY (Con't.)

With Mr. Terser, Bob Tudor felt certain that more work would be accomplished since less time would be spent on talking and on deciding what each man should be doing. Mr. Tudor also liked the way Mr. Terser took charge of the situation, demanding that the men put forth a greater effort to get more work done while constantly making sure that the men were working.

With an optimistic outlook, Mr. Tudor worked hard to increase sales. At the same time he was facing more customer complaints than ever, especially that the awnings were being returned dented and showing signs of poor-quality workmanship. Also the customers had to wait longer for their awnings to be refinished.

Mr. Tudor returned to the shop to confront Mr. Terser with these problems, only to find one of the men in the shop had quit; Mr. Terser was considering firing one more.

1. Contrast the leadership styles and results of Arty and Mr. Terser.
2. "Leadership is dependent on the voluntary response of those being led." Relate this statement to what happened in the case, both under Arty and Mr. Terser.
3. Compare Arty's and Mr. Terser's leadership from the perspective of Tannenbaum and Schmidt's leadership continuum.
4. Why was Arty a successful leader, while Mr. Terser was not?

Robert M. Fulmer and Theodore T. Herbert, *Exploring New Management,* 3rd ed. (New York: Macmillan, 1982), pp. 216–217.

DISCUSSION QUESTIONS

1. Define the concept of leadership. What characteristics do *you* find appealing in a leader?
2. How can a manager be both task-oriented and people-oriented?
3. Identify three leadership styles. What work situations seem appropriate for each style?
4. What kinds of subordinates would react well to each style of leadership?
5. Identify some organizational characteristics of your college or workplace. What kind of leadership would you expect to be most effective in that environment?
6. Discuss some leadership qualities that are important to *all* supervisors.
7. What is the life cycle perspective on leadership? How does a supervisor's style vary in each of the four phases of the cycle?
8. According to Tannenbaum and Schmidt, what factors influence a supervisor's choice of style?
9. Describe how a chief teller in a bank would use the path-goal approach to supervise tellers.

REFERENCES

Black, Robert R., and Mouton, Susan S. *The Managerial Grid.* Houston: Gulf Publishing, 1964.

Fiedler, Fred E. "Style or Circumstance: The Leadership Enigma." *Psychology Today* (March 1969): 39–45.

Gellerman, Saul. *Managers and Subordinates.* New York: Holt, Rinehart and Winston, 1976.

House, Robert J., and Mitchell, Terrace R. "Path-Goal Theory of Leadership." *Journal of Contemporary Business* (Autumn 1974): 83–89.

KcKenney, J., and Keen, P. "How Managers' Minds Work." *Harvard Business Review* (May–June 1974): 79–90.

PART 3

FEEDBACK AND CONTROL SKILLS

CHAPTER 6

GETTING THE MESSAGE ACROSS

If I've told you once, I've told you a thousand times.

—Anonymous

Chapter Outline

Objectives

Management is communication. Most of a supervisor's day is spent directing, telling, explaining, listening, coaching, counseling, interviewing, and building work relationships. This chapter is designed to help supervisors understand the communication signals of others as well as get their own messages across. Specifically, in this chapter you will become familiar with:

1. The impact communication has on the organization, its members, motivation, and performance
2. The components that go into the making, sending, and receiving of messages
3. The many ways in which communication can become fouled up
4. The important part that nonverbal cues play in the transmission of a message
5. Good listening techniques
6. The part that informal networks play in the communication process
7. The role of communication in improving motivation and performance

Major Concepts

Communication process	Doubletalk
Encoding	Noise
Medium	Active listening
Decoding	The "hidden agenda"
One-way communication	Eye contact
Two-way communication	Personal space
Stereotyping	Active listening
Psychological barriers	The grapevine

THE THREATENING CORRIDOR

Management consultant Scott Myers tells a story that shows how simple yet complex the communication function is. He was called in by a client to suggest ways management might communicate better with its work force. The company, always run along traditional lines, was trying to update itself and its communication practices. Before retaining Myers, management had decided to stress the traditional media methods— more articles in the company paper on corporate objectives and employee benefits, improvement of bulletin board displays, and a new monthly letter from the president.

In his initial talk with the president, Myers learned that the company was about to spend almost $300,000 to install what it saw as the most effective and up-to-date way to transmit messages to employees: closed-circuit television monitors scattered throughout the premises. Myers, dismayed by this news, asked for a short delay of the order until he could size up the situation and make some recommendations. The president reluctantly agreed.

At his next meeting with the president, Myers suggested that he join his people out in the corridor at a coffee bar. The president smiled patiently and said he couldn't do that. Asked why not, he replied that "it simply wasn't done." Top officers all had their coffee in their own offices dispensed from a mahogany cart. They never mingled with other employees during breaks. It would have been bad form and might even constitute an intrusion.

Myers persisted, however, and reluctantly the president agreed to try the radical idea. His first attempt was an abysmal failure. He didn't even know how to work the coffee machine. A bystander, seeing him fumble with coins, walked over and told him the coffee was free (i.e., a company practice). Red-faced, he took the cup in hand and looked for someone to begin a conversation with. No one approached him; employees were clustered in little groups quietly discussing their various concerns and glancing curiously at him. He drank his coffee and walked back to his office.

To Myers he pronounced the experiment a flop—they wouldn't talk to him. Myers told him that the problem was twofold. He made his appearance too formal; instead of wearing his suitcoat, he should have gone out in shirt sleeves. Moreover, the workers weren't used to seeing him in their area. To make this a fair test, Myers urged, he must go back tomorrow. At first the president was emphatic in his refusal to subject himself to such humiliation. Eventually, he agreed to try it one more time, but with his coat off.

This time he got his coffee without incident and screwed up the courage to break into the perimeter of a small gathering. After some conversation about the weather, he asked how things were going and heard some pleasantries from the group indicating that everything was fine.

The following morning, after doing some homework on a current concern of the work force (the opening of a plant in Europe), he raised the subject with a coffee-break group and explained the logic behind the decision. He was surprised to find himself in the middle of an animated discussion about the plant.

The next day and the next the president went out to the corridor for his morning coffee. In time he found himself holding forth on all kinds of company issues with employees, who now felt comfortable enough to air their concerns. The kaffee klatsches were working so well that he asked his senior staff to begin mingling with *their* people at coffee time. He also canceled the TV equipment in favor of the simpler and more effective technique of firsthand, face-to-face communication.

Reprinted by permission of the *Harvard Business Review.* ''The Oldest (and Best) Way to Communicate with Employees,'' by Roger D'Aprix, September–October (1982), pp. 30–32.

Good
communication
skills—a
prerequisite for
success

*I*f there is one single activity that exemplifies the function of a supervisor, it would be communication. This activity is pervasive and vital to the supervisor's success. It is also a complex process. A supervisor's effectiveness cannot be understood or improved without an examination of the communication process.

Supervisors who are effective in getting the work done are usually able communicators. They give clear instructions, are comfortable fielding subordinates' questions, practice active listening, and keep their subordinates informed. Effective communication can lead to greater employee productivity, personal satisfaction, rewarding relationships, and effective problem solving.

Yet, as important as the communication process is, it is probably one of the supervisor's greatest problems. Hasn't everyone, at one time or another, heard the remark, "He knows his stuff, but he just can't get it across." This complaint typifies many supervisors. They may be competent, friendly, and sensitive human beings, but unless they are able to communicate successfully with employees, these good points won't be enough to help them.

Why Bother with Communication?

From an organizational perspective, good communication is important for enhancing coordination across departments, giving employees organizational progress reports, answering employees' complaints and criticisms, letting people know what is expected of them, and publicizing policies, rules, and programs.

From a supervisor's perspective, good communication is important because it conveys the expectations of management and provides the information necessary for getting a job done properly. Identifying standards of performance and giving timely feedback can be accomplished only by supervisors who are communication conscious. A supervisor's ability to motivate subordinates is also dependent on communication skills. As noted in Chapter 4, a supervisor cannot directly affect the subordinate's motives. However, the supervisor can *indirectly* affect those motives by manipulating the environment in which the subordinate exists.

Once the subordinate's motives have been identified, the environment might be altered in a manner that would link desired performance to rewards. But only through communication and observation can the supervisor hope to identify the subordinate's important motives. Good communication, then, is a prerequisite for effective leadership. Supervisors, as leaders, must be able to listen, be supportive, and learn to differ constructively with their subordinates.

Communication is the core of a supervisor's ability to coordinate plans and people to achieve results. It is not just a process; it is a key ingredient in making things happen. Nothing will happen right for the supervisor unless his or her communications are right to begin with.

Anatomy of a Message

When people use the word "communication," they are referring to the whole communication process: a chain of components that form the message being sent. The chain is only as strong as its weakest link. The danger is that a message can be distorted anywhere along the chain by a number of barriers or obstacles. This may make it impossible to complete the communication process.

THE COMMUNICATION PROCESS

Communication is basically a four-step transmission process (see Figure 6.1). First, the sender must *encode* the message. This requires the sender to transform internal thoughts and ideas into a package that can be understood by the intended receiver. Second, a medium must be selected as the vehicle for *transmitting* the message. Selecting the proper medium is not as easy as it sounds. Complex messages should be transmitted using some type of written, oral, or visual medium, or some combination of these, to increase the likelihood of accurate reception.

A four-step process

The third part of the communication process is for the receiver to *decode* the message—that is, translate it into something meaningful to the receiver. There may be any number of potential barriers preventing an accurate translation, some of which will be examined shortly. Finally, there is a need for *feedback* to the sender. Without some indication that the message was not only received but understood correctly, both sender and receiver may experience uncertainty and, for important messages, a certain degree of anxiety.

FIGURE 6.1
The Communication
Process

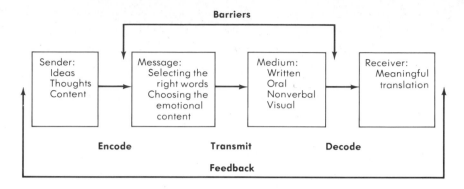

ONE-WAY AND TWO-WAY COMMUNICATION

One-way medium suits routine information

While real communication implies a two-way process, supervisors usually spend more time telling, explaining, or directing their subordinates than they do engaging in a dialogue. Supervisors are often caught up in one-way communication techniques with downward tendencies, in that feedback from the receiver to the sender is not a predominant component. Because time pressures are a constant problem, supervisors tend to resort to faster media, such as memos (a one-way medium), for getting their ideas across. As long as the message is routine and familiar to subordinates (e.g., "Don't forget, I want entertainment expense form 2403 filled out before you leave this afternoon"), receivers will have no trouble understanding the thought that is conveyed, making one-way communication a very efficient device.

One-way messages can't be clarified

Problems occur, however, when there is a new twist or something unfamiliar transmitted within the message. One-way directives make it difficult for receivers to clarify uncertainties (e.g., "I want form 2403 filled out before you leave this afternoon, and this time attach supporting documentation for any unusual reimbursements or you won't get paid"). When there is a need for clarification of the message and feedback channels are inadequate, tension will usually develop. And the discomfort of receivers can lead to all types of behaviors. For example, they may seek clarification from an informal network such as the grapevine. Or they may *assume* what the message means. Naturally, the chances for miscommunication are much higher whenever someone other than the sender attempts to clarify the message (e.g., one worker might "explain" that there is no need to worry about documentation since "we've never needed it before").

Use two-way when message is complex or important

The decision as to whether a communication will be one-way or two-way should never be taken lightly. Typed memos, signs or posters, and rules and policies are examples of one-way communication. Unfortunately, these devices are often overworked or used inappropriately. Supervisors can become too dependent on them. When the message is complex or important, feedback is necessary as a check for the correctness of the information received. One-way media don't provide for this. But two-way communication, if it is to be done properly, takes planning and time—something supervisors are short on most of the time. The supervisor needs to acquire skill with both types of communication, as well as the ability to know when to use one or the other or a combination of the two.

MORE THAN JUST WORDS

To be effective, communicators must be able to see what others see in order to relate and make understood the words they use to describe an idea. Regardless of how skilled the sender is, the message will seldom coincide exactly with the meaning the receiver will attach to it. In effect, every message contains more than just words. Communication has two components: content and feeling. In fact, much of the communication between people involves more than information. And this is especially true of face-to-face communication. Feelings surface in messages because they are filtered through the different experiences that have given meaning to the words used by the sender. Of course the different experiences receivers have might lead to different meanings behind the words. Therefore, the sender must take into consideration such factors as the receiver's education, experience, training, and cultural background when deciding how best to convey his or her message.

Content and feeling

Since a large part of all face-to-face communication involves nonverbal messages (through gesture, facial expression, and the like), it is desirable that supervisors convey nonverbal cues that suggest warmth, respect, concern, equality, and a willingness to listen. It is equally desirable to avoid cues that suggest coolness, superiority, disinterest, and disrespect. It is extremely important to learn positive nonverbal cues because through nonverbal behavior supervisors motivate—or demotivate—their employees. In other words, it is not so much *what* the boss says as *how* the boss behaves that matters to the subordinate.

Actions speak louder than words

WHAT CAN GO WRONG?

Do you think and express yourself clearly? Do you pay attention to the right timing for sending your message? Are the tone of your voice, facial expressions, and gestures supportive of what you're saying? Do you tend to speak to your listener's level of knowledge? Are you comfortable in expressing your feelings? These questions reflect whether or not real communication is occurring. If you fail to answer yes to one or more of these questions, then chances are you're not communicating what you think you are.

Most of the supervisor's time is spent communicating

Studies indicate that supervisors spend anywhere from 75 to 95 percent of their time communicating in one way or another. Such communication may take the form of written or spoken words, gestures, or visual symbols. The many ways it can be done make the transferring of information a dynamic, on-going, and complex process.

A breakdown in communication

Imagine the following scenario: Your boss has just finished talking to his boss. A report that was promised two days ago didn't materialize. Your boss has been chewed out. He's mad and demands to know from you what happened. "Didn't I give you a memo about needing this report a week ago?" he screams. "And didn't I specifically say, 'Please expedite this information to appropriate personnel'? Well then, why didn't you get the report to my boss? Can't you understand the English language?" The problem is that the word "expedite" means "as soon as conveniently possible" to you, whereas to your boss it means "today."

Communication breakdowns such as the one exemplified above happen in every organization. For whenever communication exists, the potential for communication breakdown also exists. The communication process is constantly being threatened by disruptions that may either block or distort intended meanings between a sender and receiver. In effect, communication isn't even occurring unless there is a mutual exchange of facts, thoughts, opinions, and emotions. Simply sending information down a one-way channel without any indication that the *intended* message has been received is not effective communication.

Meanings are in people

Communication involves a lot more than simply picking the right word from the dictionary. It involves the total person. As the saying goes, "meanings are in people, not in words." Words in and of themselves do not convey the total message. They are simply labels for meanings that people attach in unique and individual ways. In fact, words themselves convey just a small portion of the oral message. Therefore, when a supervisor encodes a thought into a message, the words used will reflect the experiences, needs, values, assumptions, and therefore perceptions of the world as seen through the sender's eyes.

Tone of voice, facial expression, and gesture give a whole variety of meanings to even the simplest expressions, as do rate, volume, pitch, and rhythm. Words themselves may have multiple meanings (see the accompanying box). Although words in and of themselves may have very narrow meanings, when combined with feeling from the sender, additional meaning is given to the words.

INTERPRETATIONS OF THE WORD "FIX"

An Englishman visits America and is completely awed by the many ways we use the word "fix." For example:

1. His host asks him how he'd like his drink fixed. He meant *mixed*.
2. His hostess calls to everyone to finish their drinks because dinner is all fixed. She means *prepared*.
3. As he prepares to leave, he discovers that he has a flat tire and calls a repairman who says he'll fix it immediately. He means *repair*.
4. On the way home he is given a ticket for speeding. When he calls his host, he says, "Don't worry, I'll fix it." He means *nullify*.
5. At the office the next day, he comments on the cost of living in America and one of his cohorts says, "It's hard to make ends meet on a fixed income." He means *steady* or *unchanging*.
6. Later, he remarks that he doesn't know what to do with his college diploma. A colleague says, "I'll fix it on the wall for you." He means *attach*.
7. He has an argument with a co-worker. The latter says, "I'll fix you." He means *seek revenge*.
8. Another one of his cohorts remarks that he is in "a fix." He means *condition* or *situation*.
9. He meets a friend at his boarding house who offers to "fix him up" with a girl. You know what that means.

Leslie Rue and Lloyd Byers, *Supervision: Key Link to Productivity* (Homewood, Ill.: Irwin, 1982), p. 85.

What can a supervisor do to minimize message misunderstandings? First, one should become aware of the thoughts and feelings of the individual subordinate. Supervisors are human and therefore fall prey to the human frailty of making quick judgments—positive or negative—about people they meet—and even about people they've known for some time. One tends to stereotype other people by grouping or categorizing them in an attempt to simplify one's world (e.g., "Marleen can't handle stress—I know, because no women have been able to in this unit"). Sex, race, a man's height, physical characteristics, facial expression, and even a handshake may well lead to false first impressions. Getting to know each subordinate and keeping an open mind are two ways supervisors can avoid stereotyping.

Avoid stereotyping people

PSYCHOLOGICAL BARRIERS

Attitudes can inhibit effective communication. For example, everyone can recall situations where it was obvious that input was not wanted. This may have been signaled through nonverbal cues such as closed body position, tone of voice, or reluctance in granting an audience ("I'm

Attitude barrier

rushed; you've got two minutes; make it quick!"). Here the receiver's attitude is blocking or inhibiting two-way communication. In this case, unless the receiver realizes that he or she represents the barrier blocking communication, there is very little the sender can do.

Doubletalk

Attitude is only one kind of psychological barrier that interferes with the communication process. Doubletalk is a tactic supervisors often use to regulate the way their employees behave. Supervisors may resort to doubletalk when they anticipate a negative reaction to an unpleasant request. When bad news has to be conveyed, it may be couched in a positive tone or mixed with encouraging language (see the accompanying box). Subordinates who hear doubletalk from their supervisors over a period of time will begin to lose faith both in the sincerity of the supervisor and in the value of his communication.

Noise

Noise is yet another barrier to effective communication. Noise includes any interference that disrupts the usual flow of ideas between two or more people. It represents an inability to receive the message, rather than a matter of understanding content. Noise can be tangible; for example, static on a telephone line, construction work being done outside the office, or two conversations occurring simultaneously will distract the listener. To handle this type of barrier, simply attempt to remove it or repeat the message. But noise may also be psychological; for example, the supervisor thinking about last night's ballgame may be hearing but not listening to a subordinate's problem.

Information overload

Noise often occurs in the form of information overload. For instance, imagine working at your desk on an important report that's due on your boss's desk before you leave for lunch. A subordinate walks in, and you quickly glance up and acknowledge the person. She asks if she can ask you a question. Again you look up, but you never stop concentrating on your report. You have to ask her to repeat her question, but still you don't follow it all the way. Eventually, you will have to decide whether to ask the person to return later or whether you are willing to disengage yourself from the report you are working on.

Listening is an active mental effort, demanding tremendous concentration. Sometimes when supervisors are really under the gun, they begin to look for shortcuts. One way to save time, they believe, is to listen only for the facts. They make such comments as: "Forget the details—just paint the broad strokes." Consequently, they tend to miss the feeling content of the total message. Of course, when the feeling content is irrelevant, this tactic is understandable and appropriate. However, when it is an integral part of the message and is suppressed, it becomes a barrier. When short of time to listen attentively, you should either ask the subordinate to return later (when you can devote time and effort

WHEN THE BOSS SPEAKS: A GUIDE TO DOUBLETALK

If you're having a hard time understanding the real meaning of some of your boss's words, rest assured that you're not alone. Doubletalk is one of the most troublesome office communication problems.

There are many varieties of doubletalk. Some of the most common you're likely to encounter on the job are:

1. *The humorous warning:* If something you've done is annoying but not terribly serious, your boss may try to bring it to your attention by teasing you about it. For example, he may say with a smile, "Here are the calls I took for you—you're obviously a very popular person." But the hidden message may be: "Why wasn't your phone covered when you were away from your desk?"

2. *Misplaced irritation:* A boss may sidestep what's really making him angry and instead pick on a more obvious but less important slip-up. For instance, he might say, "You were late to arrive at the meeting," when what was really annoying him was the fact that you weren't around beforehand to help him prepare for it.

3. *The coded message:* Rather than being straightforward about a difficult bit of news, a boss may communicate his feelings through innuendos in an attempt to spare your feelings.

4. *The cool tone of voice:* There's no direct criticism, but conversation is less friendly than usual, probably because your boss hasn't decided how to respond to something you did that he doesn't like.

Peggy Schmidt, "When the Boss Speaks: A Guide to Double-talk," *Family Weekly*, October 11, 1981.

to active listening), or you should voluntarily disengage yourself from your current task and focus on the subordinate's needs rather than your own.

Nonverbal Communication: The Hidden Agenda

What is an elaborate code that is written nowhere, known by none, and understood by all? What is it that we are least aware of in ourselves, but most aware of in others? The answer is—nonverbal communication. Facial expression, gesture, tone of voice, posture, eye contact, and use of space are all the result of a person's "hidden agenda" (i.e., the thoughts that are *really* on a person's mind). Unfortunately for most of us, our formal education totally neglects the role that body language (another name for nonverbal communication) has in revealing our hidden agenda.

The importance of body language is seldom discussed in the work arena. Nevertheless, its influence is widespread. In fact, some supervisors

The "hidden agenda"

would credit management success to being able to "read" people accurately. In other words, these supervisors are acutely aware that what people say is not always what they mean.

Nonverbal impact is significant

Undoubtedly, much of our interaction and involvement with others is carried out by nonverbal means. Research shows that between 65 and 90 percent of the meaning we obtain from what others say comes through nonverbal signals.[1] Mehrabrian has devised a formula that attempts to explain the impact, in percentages, of verbal, vocal, and facial dimensions that make up face-to-face communication. The total impact that a message might have is broken down as follows: 7 percent verbal, 38 percent vocal, and 55 percent facial.[2] Most of these nonverbal signals, or cues, are given and received on the subconscious level of human perception. People form countless impressions without ever being aware of having received these nonverbal messages.

It has often been noted that it is not *what* you say, but *how* you say it that counts. Nonverbal communication is the primary means of communicating emotions. Interpreting nonverbal signals should be done with great caution, but usually is not. The problem of misinterpreting such signals often gets us into trouble.

SOME NONVERBAL CUES TO WATCH FOR

Certain occupations require a high level of nonverbal skills. Professional gamblers, for example, depend on nonverbal skills for their livelihood. In fact, any occupation that is predominantly concerned with people utilizes nonverbal skills.

Supervisors especially are in a position where listening to the whole person, and not just to what is said, can bring a high payoff. While some gifted supervisors do have a natural talent for reading people accurately, it takes most supervisors years (and some painful experiences) before they learn how to interpret nonverbal cues correctly. The next few paragraphs describe the "meaning" of different nonverbal cues for many people (but not everyone) in this country.

Eye contact

Probably the single most important factor in a face-to-face discussion between supervisor and subordinate is the degree of eye contact. It can suggest confidence, honesty, and interest—or the opposite of these. The eye acts as a rapid scanner of the other party and can pick up cues more quickly than any other sensory organs. Of course, the eyes may

[1] Albert Mehrabian, "Communication Without Words," *Psychology Today*, September 1968, p. 54.
[2] Ibid., p. 56.

also be read by others, letting them know our emotions, desires, and feelings. In eye contact, each person gathers much nonverbal information about the other. The act of looking itself indicates that the channels of communication are open. In general, a periodic exchange of glances between two individuals suggests that each is interested in what the other has to say. According to Julius Fast, a glance held with a stranger for less than three seconds signals, "You are another human being. I recognize you as such." Anything longer might suggest, "I am interested in you."[3]

Of course, it is wise to remember that eye contact varies depending on culture. Latin Americans and Middle Easterners depend on eye contact much more than Americans; therefore, their "looking times" are longer. Europeans, too, have shorter "looking times"; and the Japanese pay little attention to eye contact at all.[4]

Eye contact varies with culture

The purpose of good eye contact may vary among cultures as well.[5] In Middle Eastern countries, for example, people will stand closer together than in America. One reason is to gauge the size of the other's pupils. The eyes are said to be the window of the soul; and it is true that by noting subtle changes in pupil dilation (have the pupils become larger?) one can detect how the other is responding to a situation.

Even between members of the dominant culture in this country, degree of eye contact is relied upon during the course of a face-to-face discussion for interpreting subtle nonverbal messages. In a discussion between supervisor and subordinate, if one party responds while gazing at the ceiling, it may connote a hidden message. To some, it may suggest to the listener that the other person is lying or is scared to look the listener in the eye. In any case, this action will tend to be interpreted negatively.

The distance between the speakers is another aspect of nonverbal communication that has a significant impact on supervisor-subordinate exchanges. For example, status often determines the distance between two people. A dominant (i.e., aggressive and assertive) individual will frequently intrude upon the submissive (i.e., meek and mild-mannered) individual's personal space. A supervisor may not give a second thought to coming within inches of a subordinate's face to discuss some element of the job; but if a subordinate did that to a supervisor, chances are the atmosphere would become tense and strained. Intrusion into another's personal space may lead to that person feeling frustrated and embarrassed.

Personal space

[3] Julius Fast, *Body Language* (New York: Pocket Books, 1971), p. 37.
[4] Ibid., p. 73.
[5] Ibid., p. 71.

Americans are particularly annoyed and uncomfortable when their personal space is violated. For example, when standing in a crowded line on a bus, most people will automatically observe certain rigid rules of behavior, and by so doing will communicate to their fellow passengers how they feel. They may hold themselves as rigid as possible trying not to touch any part of their neighbor. If they do touch, they will either draw away or tense their muscles in the touched area. This is a form of apology in body language. If, on the other hand, they were to relax into the situation and let their limbs freely and easily touch those of their neighbors, they could be committing a serious social blunder.

Yet there are cultures (e.g., in the Middle East) in which the objective is to move as close as possible to the other party in order to read what the eyes have to communicate. Middle Easterners prefer to talk face-to-face within two feet of each other or less. Americans, on the other hand, generally maintain at least three to five feet of space for business conversations.[6]

Vocal mannerisms are yet another type of nonverbal cue. Such vocalizations as "ah" or "er," or the unnecessary repetition of a word are often indications of anxiety or conflict. When coupled with rapid gestures, these disturbances may be particularly annoying to the listener. On the other hand, when the individual is emphasizing a particular part of the message, he or she will use hands and arms—hoping that this behavior will help to make the point or capture the attention of the listener.

Whether verbally or nonverbally, we communicate all the time. As John Stewart once said, "Like not behaving, not communicating is impossible."

MAKING A GOOD IMPRESSION

Along with eye contact, a prime ingredient for making a good first impression is the handshake. In this society, the handshake is seen as a measure of personality. People tend to react initially to a stranger on the basis of how he or she shakes hands. When the fingers are limp and loose (like wet spaghetti) and the grip is nonexistent, the individual might be perceived as insecure and incapable of handling an anxiety-producing situation. When one's hand is grasped mechanically and pumped up and down in a series of convulsive jerks, the impression it leaves is one of rigidity and determination. On the other hand, people who are always extending the hand (like a politician campaigning for

---

[6] Dan Millar and Frank Millar, *Messages and Myths* (New York: Alfred Publishing Co., 1976), p. 80.

votes) might leave the impression that they have a strong need for acceptance. The ideal handshake, at least in the view of most people in this society, is a simple, firm, dry clasp, with no more than one or two pumps of the hand. The key to handshaking is to meet the expectations of the other person.

In the case of women, first impressions are especially important. In the South, for example, males who hold traditional values are often reluctant to accept females on an equal basis in an organizational environment. The handshake, especially if it fails to meet the firm, dry expectations of the male, can lead to negative first impressions of the female—reinforcing the stereotype of the female as not being able to handle the competitiveness and stress of the "real world."

Women and handshaking

Most women are aware of the importance of a good, firm handshake. But compounding the problem may be their own particular upbringing, in which shaking hands with males was not considered proper. Some women will be reluctant and choose not to engage in handshaking for fear of a rebuff. The thought of extending your hand and having it ignored is certainly a chilling one; thus handshaking for women can be an anxiety-producing experience until they get enough practice to feel comfortable at it.

For those women who are uncomfortable about the handshake, one successful female executive offered the following recommendation:

> A good friend of mine taught me how to shake hands—which is very important in the business world. As a woman, I had formerly practiced what could be described more as a "finger shake." I extended my hand, but in a coy, feminine way. I only used my fingers—as if I were expecting the man to kiss my hand instead of shaking it. My friend's secret, which has given me confidence in handshaking ever since, is to connect the scoop in the hand between thumb and index finger with the equivalent portion of the other person's hand and grasp tightly. It leads to a firm and confident exchange of greetings.[7]

First impressions don't begin and end simply with the handshake. What one wears is considered to reflect how one sees oneself and what type of image one wishes to project to others. A supervisor who wears flannel shirts with the sleeves rolled up in order to display his muscular and oil-stained arms may be trying to project the image of a boss who is tough, masculine, and not afraid to get dirty. Such an image, he believes, will help him to be a more effective supervisor. To him, good

Clothing

---

[7] Dianne Minner.

things seem to happen when he's dressed in this manner. But the clothing that is worn may not succeed in projecting the desired image. If the image the supervisor is trying to project is not compatible with how others perceive him, then it will be rejected.

Personal apparel is an important aspect of nonverbal communication because inferences may be made regarding the status and worth of individuals from what they wear. When you see a man wearing a $500 Brooks Brothers suit, it is generally a safe bet that he is not a college professor. While clothing may not "make the man," it does influence the way in which others perceive him.

Vocal quality

What one says and how one says it can do a lot to make (or break) a good first impression. Good pitch, pace, and tone can make spoken words more dynamic and impressive. Studies indicate that pitch should be kept low because it is the deeper voice that strokes the body. High-pitched tones can be irritating and lacking in authority, besides suggesting an inability to handle stress.

Body language

Finally, good impressions may be enhanced by body language. One can project confidence simply by standing straight, smiling occasionally, and maintaining eye contact. Gesturing is acceptable, because we all do it, and it helps to relieve tension. But don't be extravagant with gestures. In addition, as people grow in confidence, they blink less, have more frequent eye contact, and tend to avoid such gestures as covering the mouth or scratching the nose or head.[8] As a practical matter, one should not talk about oneself too much but should focus instead on the other(s). Saying only a little about oneself suggests interest in the other person.

Listening ═══════════════════════════

ACTIVE LISTENING

Unless subordinates hear and understand what is being said, effective communication cannot take place. While most employees think they are good listeners, few actually are. In fact, people in the United States listen only 25 percent of the time. Listening, for the most part, is taken for granted. People often assume that if they hear a speaker, they are listening. But hearing and listening do not necessarily go hand in hand.

---

[8] Gerard I. Nierenberg and Henry Calero, *How to Read a Person Like a Book* (New York: Pocket Books, 1971).

Listening involves much more than just hearing; it is a difficult and complex process and requires a great deal of practice. Hearing, on the other hand, is a purely physical response; you must hear to listen, but you need not listen to hear. Hearing becomes listening only when what is being transmitted by the sender is understood by the receiver. There is the often-told story of the hostess who remarked while serving canapés to her guests, "Do try one. I've filled them with strychnine." Not a single guest hesitated.

Listening is hard work

Another factor that interferes with listening effectiveness is that early in life most people are taught to be good conversationalists. Never letting a conversation drag is one of our society's basic social objectives. When a conversation among two or more people dies and silence takes over, everyone becomes extremely uncomfortable. The anticipation of this unpleasant occurrence forces many people to ignore what is being said while desperately searching for something to talk about in case the ball is bounced their way.

The need to avoid silence

A good listener, on the other hand, is like a lineman in football. He seldom ever shares in the glory because he doesn't carry the ball. Yet without the lineman's blocking, there wouldn't be any scoring; thus there would be no glory for the ball carriers. Every talker needs a listener. A good listener makes the talker look good and feel good besides. A listener who really listens has powerful appeal—the artistry to make other people feel worthwhile.

Good listeners have social appeal

BAD LISTENING HABITS

Undoubtedly the number one bad habit when listening is failing to pay attention. Of course, this failing may be the result of other bad habits as well. For example, supervisors may not *want* to hear what subordinates have to say. Suppose one of your longtime subordinates is having personal problems with her marriage and it's beginning to affect her job performance. You're at lunch with her, and she brings it up. If you're like most people, you probably don't like to get involved in others' private lives. You might say, "Gee, I'm sorry to hear about that—but these things tend to work themselves out. Let's try the salad today. I hear it's got everything." The message is clear to the subordinate: "Don't bother me with your personal problems."

Not wanting to hear

Bad listening habits may also result from a listener's frame of reference. Some people, when they are listening to certain individuals, know what to expect—or think they do. Suppose you are a new supervisor. Over time you observe the behavior of two subordinates working for you.

Frame of reference

You perceive them as lazy, sloppy, prone to mistakes, and constantly needing attention. You conclude that they are not concerned about making a contribution to the organization, but are only interested in drawing their paychecks. It would not be hard to understand if your communication with these two workers took on a different tone than that with your other subordinates. If, for example, one of the two "lazy" workers tried to explain why something went wrong, your behavior as a supervisor would be different than if one of your "better" employees was trying to explain it. Your impulse might be to shout to the "lazy" worker, "I don't want to hear what happened!"

The average supervisor would tend to infer that the "lazy" worker is trying to avoid responsibility, whereas in the case of the "better" worker, the supervisor would infer that the worker is trying to reach a solution to a problem for which he or she shares responsibility. In other words, expectations about another can influence and even destroy the meaningfulness of the communication. Instead of listening, one prejudges what the speaker has to say.

Preset notions and prejudices

Whether such preset notions are based on personal prejudices or actual past experiences is not the issue. What is at issue is that when listening, you cannot afford to distort or block the message for any reason. If staff meetings have always been a bore, it is easy to dismiss what is said during this week's meeting as unimportant. Good listeners will avoid such a temptation and will concentrate instead on the present issues.

Finding fault

Finding fault with the speaker may lead to missing the point the speaker is trying to make. For example, one of your workers is trying to tell you about a potential problem with some office equipment, but this worker happens to stutter. Will you listen? If you are like most supervisors, you are always in a hurry. There just isn't enough time in the day to do everything. Consequently, patience isn't one of your strong suits. After a few seconds of patiently listening to the worker, you either begin to fake attentiveness or become preoccupied with your own thoughts. People find fault not only with speech disturbances, they may also find fault with the speaker's appearance (tall, short, fat, complexion, etc.) or the speaker's mannerisms (fidgeting, wild gesturing, weak handshake, etc.).

Note taking

One last note on bad listening habits. Some people believe that good note taking will promote good listening. Actually, taking too many notes may detract from your understanding of the message being communicated. A note taker may become so preoccupied with details that the important facts get lost. Taking notes requires time and concentration. Because attention is focused on writing, instead of listening, the message may become garbled. If some type of record is needed later, either because of a bad memory or the need for details, try using a recorder. Remembering detail is fine, but without the important facts the detail will do little good.

WHAT DOES IT TAKE TO BE A GOOD LISTENER?

Being a good listener may be one of the most difficult skills a supervisor must learn. It requires total concentration. It also requires practice and patience. Most of all, it should never be taken for granted. The following are five simple steps for improving your listening effectiveness:

1. Be ready to really listen—sit up straight and make good eye contact.
2. Create a climate, or atmosphere, that is open and allows the other person to speak his or her mind without fear of punishment.
3. Be sensitive—learn to register feelings as well as ideas.
4. Don't be judgmental—hear the other person out before expressing an opinion.
5. Provide feedback to the other person so that he or she knows the message was correctly received—occasionally summarize the thoughts that are conveyed.

Improving listening effectiveness

Listening is an acquired skill. It cannot be developed overnight. But like any journey, it begins with the first step. Learn to control your emotions, otherwise your nonverbal behavior may contradict what you say. Put aside personal judgments and preoccupations about the speaker or his remarks. Instead, put yourself in his shoes and attempt to view the world through his eyes. The ability to empathize with, feel close to, and understand another person is probably the most tested means for bridging the communication gap.

Much of the time we communicate through spoken and written language. But our body movements, eye contact, and facial expressions are frequently more meaningful than any verbal statement. As noted earlier, when we try to hide our feelings and thoughts, our nonverbal behavior still sends out messages. We communicate in spite of ourselves. So try to block out distractions—that presentation to the financial committee scheduled for this afternoon or that argument you had with your spouse this morning. Show that active listening is occurring. Maintaining good eye contact, an occasional positive gesture with the hand, an encouraging nod of the head—these are just a few of the ways that a supervisor can communicate an active listening attitude.

We communicate in spite of ourselves

Minimize interruptions

Being a good listener demands more than simply paying attention. A proper listening environment must be created. For important conversations, probably the best location for listening is a pleasant and comfortable one, for example, a quiet office that is free from distractions. It is critical that interruptions be minimized. While a supervisor isn't always in a position to control the listening environment (e.g., out on the production floor), he or she should be aware of the limits that the environment places on effective communication. Trying to hear someone is next to impossible when heavy machines, equipment, telephones, and people are blaring. When this is the case, don't try to communicate unless it is absolutely necessary. Be patient and try to locate a quiet nook away from the noisy distractions. Above all, avoid screaming what needs to be said over the racket of the workplace.

The Grapevine: Help or Hindrance?

WHY THE GRAPEVINE?

The grapevine is the unofficial, informal network of information that exists within any organization. Whether the supervisor likes it or not, the grapevine is inevitable and practically impossible to eliminate. If management fails to provide workers with the information they need or want, the workers will ultimately establish a grapevine to find the answers they are seeking. Usually the result is information being passed from one worker to another that is distorted, unsubstantiated, and a burden to the supervisor. In the absence of reliable information, the grapevine takes over. To understand how this may happen, consider the case of the distraught dishwasher.

The case of the distraught dishwasher

For fourteen years, a hard working dishwasher washed dishes by hand for the same restaurant. Then one day two suspicious-looking men came in and began taking measurements of his work area. The men stayed for a long time, whispering to each other, measuring, and taking notes, until the restaurant's manager joined them. Thereupon, the three men began talking in hushed tones, deliberately withholding information from the dishwasher. The dishwasher, fearing the loss of his job, told some co-workers that their jobs were in jeopardy. Morale dropped like a bomb. Absenteeism increased, and the quality of service declined. What threatened the dishwasher grew until it threatened the entire restaurant. In reality, the two mysterious gentlemen measuring the dishwasher's work area were making a preliminary analysis of where to put a new automatic dishwasher.

What happened in this case is not that unusual. An employee perceived a threat because management had not been open with him. This resulted in his using the grapevine for his own protection, thereby negatively affecting the morale of all the restaurant's employees.

The above case outlines the basic processes involved in grapevine communication. First, it is directly concerned with the employees' welfare and is often based on unfounded fears. Second, it deals with incomplete information gained through limited and partial observations and conclusions. Third, it often results from a simple case of managerial communications failure. Finally, the rumor that feeds the grapevine starts as a simple speculation or opinion and spreads like a forest fire through the organization. As it is told and retold, the rumor grows in size and scope until it becomes something very different from what it was originally. The nature of rumor is such that it makes people believe that whatever is wrong is worse, of greater magnitude, or of longer duration than is really the case. In general, a story that moves from one telling to another loses many details, and the details that remain are sharpened—relaters of the story tend to extend, explain, and interpret those details to make the story more complete and interesting and to impress the listener. Consequently, "dressing up" a story is common practice.

Grapevines are important to all employees, including supervisors. First, grapevines are directly concerned with the employees' welfare. If management doesn't level with them, workers will find out what the score is for themselves. Who cares if the validity of the information is questionable—after all, some idea of what is going on (whether it is accurate or not) is better than no idea at all. People dislike uncertainty. Therefore, any grapevine information that makes sense, no matter how wild or irrational it may be, is acceptable.

Second, the grapevine satisfies the employees' need to be "in the know," to be a member of a group (formal or informal); and it provides an opportunity to influence, to some extent, the work environment. Being a part of the grapevine may give a worker the feeling he or she knows something that somebody else doesn't. The grapevine provides excitement. The "juicy tidbits" coming through may even present a reason for coming to work when the job itself does not.

Key people in making the grapevine work are referred to as liaisons. Secretaries, for example, are usually excellent liaisons because they are in regular contact with primary sources of information. They also have frequent opportunities to pass along information to their co-workers during coffee breaks and lunch hours.

Processes involved in the grapevine

Management isn't leveling

The need to be in the know

The grapevine is not strictly limited to lower level employees or particular divisions or departments within organizations. It may in fact operate upward, downward, diagonally, or laterally within an organization. Anywhere two or more employees gather and social interaction takes place, the grapevine will exist.

Thus understanding how the grapevine works is the best means for living in harmony with it; complete control is impossible. In the case of the dishwasher, if someone had told him he was merely getting a new machine, which *he* would operate, destructive rumors would not have been encouraged.

THE CARE AND FEEDING OF THE GRAPEVINE

Most supervisors view the grapevine as a rumor factory or worse. Although the grapevine form of communication may be troublesome, it can also be a valuable asset to the supervisor. It is probably the quickest method for conveying information throughout an organization. Some supervisors have learned to use the grapevine effectively when they have important information to relay to employees and little time to do it.

Grapevine fills an information vacuum

Since the grapevine is clearly a permanent part of every organization, the problem facing management is not how to eliminate it but what to do in order to coexist peacefully with it. Most rumors carried by the grapevine are an attempt, however inept, to fill an information vacuum. The spreading of false rumors may be minimized by making all the necessary facts available. After the facts have been released, the spreading of rumors will be greatly diminished. Grapevine communication rapidly loses its effectiveness and its credibility once word is officially out. Giving employees the straight story in simple and easily grasped language as soon as possible prevents gossipy rumors from spreading.

Supervisors must accept the presence of the grapevine because they simply cannot remove it. They cannot fire it or suppress it. Terminating an employee who is the established root of a grapevine network has only a temporary effect, at best. Before long, a new grapevine emerges that is as vigorous as the old network ever was.

Make it work for you

Don't attempt to fight or suppress grapevine communication. Instead, make it work for you if your formal communication network is not functioning properly. For example, when new developments occur and things are about to happen, pass this information along informally to subordinates in addition to making use of company newsletters, organization bulletin boards, public address systems, and other communication media. On an individual level, face-to-face contact is probably the best means of keeping false information from spreading. Keep workers up to date on matters that concern everyone. Remember the company president who spent the coffee break with employees discussing business matters. When employees receive information promptly and clearly, the possibility of it becoming garbled and incomplete along the grapevine is eliminated.

We suggest that while employees do receive a good deal of information through the grapevine, they would prefer to receive it straight from the supervisor. So it is up to the supervisor to see that news of any developments—things that are about to happen or events that have already taken place—is fully and promptly reported to all members of the group who are directly or indirectly affected. This could be accomplished at informal meetings or staff conferences, thus ensuring that everyone receives the news at the same time. Remember that the grapevine flourishes when supervisors are careless about keeping their workers up to date.

Communicating for Improved Performance

Good communication is one key to improving the performance and productivity of the work group. Improved performance begins with identifying what is important to each subordinate. As observed in an earlier chapter, supervisors cannot directly affect what another person values. They can, however, affect the extent to which a subordinate believes that he or she can perform a task and that performance will result in desired rewards.

Employees must possess the self-confidence that they can perform at the required level before they will be motivated to do so. A supervisor can enhance and maintain a subordinate's self-confidence by communicating high expectations (e.g., "Richard, I've seen the report you did for Purchasing; I know you can handle this challenge and do it well"). Recognition from the supervisor is yet another communication technique for building an employee's self-confidence. Recognition is a reward, sought in and of itself, as well as a guidepost in directing desired performance. High expectations plus positive reinforcement in the form of recognition can do wonders in beginning the process of building and maintaining a high level of employee motivation. A supervisor can do

Communicate high expectations plus recognition

all of these things through coaching, counseling, and publicly recognizing good performance.

The motivational process

Studies also show that the communication of a supervisor's support of subordinates' ideas, problems, and concerns has a motivational impact. This motivational process is simple. It begins when the supervisor assumes the subordinate has useful ideas, information, or a point of view to share. The process then moves to the active listening stage: The supervisor anticipates where the conversation is leading, periodically reviews and summarizes the information being discussed, and pays attention to non-verbal behavior for cues that signify strong emotional messages. When specific elements of the discussion are identified as useful, the supervisor builds on them. If follow-up is needed, and in most cases it is, he or she is careful that every promise made to the subordinate is kept. This motivational process can serve the supervisor whenever there is a need to identify subordinates' training needs, conduct coaching sessions, or give performance appraisals.

Be receptive

As simple as the above process appears, there are some hurdles that may need to be overcome. The first is the lack of receptiveness—not being willing to believe that another person has something valuable to contribute. If we objectively examine our behavior in this situation, we have to admit that the first reaction to another's idea is immediately to take the idea apart and show why it won't work. This reaction is evidenced in such remarks as: "Gee, that won't work; we tried it just last month." While there are a multitude of reasons for this tendency (e.g., possessiveness, perceived loss of self-esteem), self-awareness will usually correct it. Knowing that we are prone to being critical of another's ideas and problems is the first step in overcoming such a bias.

Everyone appreciates being listened to. Even when an obviously bad idea is proposed, if it is examined in an objective fashion before being discarded, the experience is not particularly painful. There is almost always something that can be learned and put to use from the comments that the idea generates. The experience becomes painful—and this often occurs—when an idea is rejected early and then is later resurrected successfully by another person, who is given full credit for it. The original initiator of the idea obviously feels rejected and in any future sessions will probably withdraw from active involvement in the group.

Be sensitive

The second hurdle to overcome in communication is a lack of sensitivity. Good supervisors are sensitive to the feelings, thoughts, and problems of their subordinates. Insensitive supervisors hear what the subordinate is saying but don't take the time to listen and make their own feelings known. Just lending an attentive ear, even when there is absolutely nothing the supervisor can do, can help the subordinate live with the problem. Sharing a personal problem with the boss makes the burden seem lighter. When things improve, the subordinate will usually remember the consideration shown by the boss and be more willing to make the "extra effort" that is occasionally needed.

A third communication hurdle is the inability to clarify expectations. Supervisors are often fuzzy about performance standards. Employees are not mind readers, and even if they were, they would often find the supervisor's expectations as fuzzy as their own. The fuzziness stems from the supervisor not knowing exactly what it is he or she wants. And if the supervisor doesn't know, how can the subordinate be expected to know? The starting point in any communication process is to define clearly the purpose of the message—if it is not clear to the sender, then it won't be clear to anyone else.

Clarify expectations

That no two people interpret words and phrases alike is a safe assumption to make. If you want improved performance, avoid an overreliance on metaphors, slang, and figures of speech. When possible, use simple words or phrases, and remember to use as few words as possible to get your message across. The more specific you arc, and the more you illustrate the points you're trying to make, the better your chances of communicating effectively. It might help if you speak more slowly when you really want the message to get across. Occasionally, you might emphasize key words when speaking to subordinates. Words such as "now," "tomorrow," "quickly," and "right" are more effective when reinforced by nonverbal behavior.

Speak clearly, simply

To determine if your message is being understood, occasionally ask questions. It can safely be said that feedback is the most important link in the communication process. And one method of obtaining feedback is to ask questions. These questions should be precise but open-ended (a topic discussed in detail in Chapter 10). You don't want workers responding in yes or no terms because the pressure will then be on them to answer in a manner that protects their self-image. For example, when an employee is asked if she understands the instructions for filling out a purchase order, chances are that she will answer yes whether she understands or not. By asking her to explain the process in her own words will increase the odds for effective communication. Another form of feedback is to ask the worker to repeat the message or reword the message, thus enabling the sender to determine whether communication really took place. Table 6.1 presents some key requirements for good communication. On the basis of your own experience, plus what you have learned in this chapter, can you add to the list?

Ask questions

TABLE 6.1 Key Points to Remember for Effective Communication

1. Keep the message simple.

2. Don't forget; if anything *can* be misunderstood, it *will* be misunderstood.

3. When someone says, "I'll level with you" be cautious—leveling is obviously not that person's customary form of communicating.

4. Don't fiddle around; get to the point as quickly as possible.

5. If *you* don't understand something, don't attempt to communicate it to someone else.

6. Don't talk too long; remember the mind cannot absorb more than the seat can endure.

7. Know what to say before saying it, that is, think before you speak.

8. Don't fake attention; be sensitive.

9. Avoid yielding to distractions and learn to concentrate.

10. Listen to others as you would like to be listened to.

SUMMARY

Effective communication is fundamental to effective supervision. The impact communication has on performance cannot be emphasized enough. A definition of "communication" as "giving orders and answering questions" is too narrow. Communication skills are needed with almost everything a supervisor does.

Developing good communication skills begins with an understanding of the total process. Encoding is the first step. Putting an idea into words that form a meaningful message means, literally, knowing what it is you want to say. Selecting the proper medium and transmitting the message is the second step in the process. In general, supervisors rely on oral and nonverbal (as opposed to written) mediums because of the need for fast and efficient transmissions. The third step in the process is decoding the transmission. The only

way for the sender to know if the message is received as intended is through feedback—the last step in the communication process. Of course, even with the absence of feedback communication can still occur. In fact, for routine and familiar messages a one-way pattern is the preferred choice.

While breakdowns in the communication process can occur at any point, most tend to take place at the decoding step. Unfamiliar vocabulary, doubletalk, intimidation, and negative attitudes are common examples of communication roadblocks. Furthermore when a subordinate is already inundated with information and new information is being directed at him, he can become frustrated and turn the communication process completely off.

Heavy dependence is placed on one-on-one communication techniques because supervisors spend a lot of time counseling, coaching, and interacting with each subordinate. But one-on-one communication is more than words alone. Messages are interpreted within the context of tone of voice, eye contact, facial expressions, and the personal space between sender and receiver. Nonverbal communication patterns are good indicators of what the message really means. Supervisors should learn to read the "whole" person as well as develop skills in using their whole self to project the message they want to send.

Listening also plays a big part, especially active listening. It begins with a self-assessment of biases, stereotypes, and negative judgments that might color the meaning of the sender's message to you. Active listening involves concentrating on what the speaker is saying, making good eye contact, being sup-

portive and sensitive, and building on the comments of the speaker.

Grapevines are an inevitable channel of communication in the organization—even when formal channels of communication are working. The pervasiveness of the grapevine can be traced to the basic employee need to be "in the know." Any attempt to eliminate the grapevine is pointless; it will just surface somewhere else. Instead, the grapevine should be used to the supervisor's advantage. Recognizing that the grapevine is an attempt to fill an information vacuum, the supervisor should continually maintain an open communication channel with one or two subordinates. Giving employees the straight story as soon as it develops and in simple terms is the best technique for controlling it.

GET OFF MY BACK

Joe Toby, director of management services, schedules an appraisal session with Herman Sutherland, a management consultant on his staff.

Joe: As you know, Herman, I've scheduled this meeting with you because I want to talk about certain aspects of your work. And my comments are not all that favorable.

Herman: Since you have formal authority over me, I guess I'll have to go along with the session. Go ahead.

Joe: I'm not a judge reading a verdict to you. This is supposed to be a two-way interchange.

Herman: But you called the meeting, go ahead with your complaints. Particularly any with foundation. I remember once when we were having lunch you told me that you didn't like the fact that I wore a brown knitted suit with a blue shirt. I would put that in the category of unfounded.

Joe: I'm glad you brought up appearance. I think you create a substandard impression to clients because of your appearance. A consultant is supposed to look sharp, particularly at the rates we charge clients. You often create the impression that you cannot afford good clothing. Your pants are baggy. Your ties are unstylish and often food-stained.

Herman: The firm may charge those high rates. But as a junior the money I receive does not allow me to purchase fancy clothing. Besides, I have very little interest in trying to dazzle clients with my clothing. I have heard no complaints from them.

Joe: Nevertheless, I think that your appearance should be more businesslike. Let's talk about something else I have on my list of things in which I would like to see some improvements.

A routine audit of your expense account shows a practice that I think is improper. You charged one client for a Thursday night dinner for three consecutive weeks. Yet your airline ticket receipt shows that you returned home at three in the afternoon. That kind of behavior is unprofessional. How do you explain your charges for these phantom dinners?

Herman: The flight ticket may say 3 P.M. but with our unpredictable weather, the flight could very well be delayed. If I eat at the airport, then my wife won't have to run the risk of preparing a dinner for me that goes to waste. Food is very expensive.

Joe: But how can you eat dinner at 3 P.M. at the airport?

Herman: I consider any meal after one in the afternoon to be dinner.

Joe: Okay for now. I want to comment on your reports to clients. They are much more careless than they should be. I know that you are capable of more meticulous work. I saw an article you prepared for publication that was first rate and professional. Yet on one report you misspelled the name of the client company. That's atrocious.

Herman: A good secretary should have caught that mistake. Besides, I never claimed that I was able to write perfect reports. There are only so many hours in the working day to spend on writing reports.

Joe: Another thing that requires immediate improvement is the appearance of your office. It's a mess. You have the worst-looking office in our branch. In fact, you have the worst-looking office I have ever seen in a CPA or management-consulting office. Why can't you have a well-organized, cool-looking office?

Herman: What's the difference? Clients never visit me in this office. It's just a workplace. Incidentally, Joe, could you do me one favor?

Joe: What's that?

Herman: Get off my back.

1. What communication mistakes has Joe Toby made?
2. What communication barriers are most evident?

3. How might the information Joe wants to convey to Herman be presented constructively?

Derived from Gary Dessler, *Management Fundamentals,* 4th Edition, 1985. Reprinted with permission of Reston Publishing Company, a Prentice-Hall Company, 11480 Sunset Hills Road, Reston, VA 22090.

DISCUSSION QUESTIONS

1. Explain why and how communication is the single most pervasive process for effective supervision.
2. In terms of the communication process described in the chapter, what barriers frequently prevent the message from being decoded? Encoded?
3. Why is it so often said that communication is "more than just words"?
4. Identify some of the more universal nonverbal cues that suggest that "meanings are in people" and not necessarily in what they say.
5. Describe a good listener. Ask a friend to describe your listening tendencies. How much of what your friend perceives about your listening tendencies comes as a surprise to you?
6. Explain how the office grapevine may play a positive role in maintaining morale and productive work habits.

REFERENCES

Alessandra, Anthony, and Wexler, Phillip. *Non-Manipulative Selling.* San Diego, CA: Ashtin Learning Systems, 1977: 33–41.

Alessandra, Anthony; Davis, Jacqueline; and Wexler, Phillip. "Removing Pressure and Still Getting the Sale." *California Real Estate* (January 1977): 44–45.

Barbara, Dominick A. *The Art of Listening.* Springfield, IL: Charles C Thomas, 1958.

Fast, Julius. *Body Language.* New York: Pocket Books, 1971.

Geldard, Frank A. "Body English." *Psychology Today* (December 1968): 42–47.

Goffman, Erving. *The Presentation of Self in Everyday Life.* Garden City, NY: Doubleday, 1959.

Huseman, Richard; Lahif, James; and Hatfield, John. *Interpersonal Communication in Organizations.* Boston: Holbrook Press, 1976.

Longfellow, Layne E. "Body Talk—A Game." *Psychology Today* (October 1979): 45+.

Mehrabian, Albert. "Communication Without Words." *Psychology Today* (September 1968): 53–55.

Nichols, Ralph G. "Do We Know How to Listen? Practical Helps in a Modern Age." *The Speech Teacher* 10 (March 1961): 118–124.

Nierenberg, Gerald I, and Calero, Henry. *How to Read a Person Like a Book.* New York: Pocket Books, 1971.

Rogers, Carl. "Active Listening." In Cohen, Allan R., et al. *Effective Behavior in Organizations.* Homewood, IL: Richard Irwin, 1976: 277–290.

Rogers, Carl, and Roethlisberger, F. J. "Barriers and Gateways to Communication." *Harvard Business Review* 30 (July–August, 1952): 46–52.

Rosenthal, Robert, et al. "Body Talk and Tone of Voice: The Language Without Words." *Psychology Today* (September 1974): 64–68.

Ruben, Brent D., and Budd, Richard W. *Human Communication Handbook.* Rochelle Park, NJ: Hayden Book Company, 1975.

Sathre, Freda S., Olson, Ray W.; and Whitney, Clarissa I. *Let's Talk.* 2d ed. Glenview, IL: Scott, Foresman and Company, 1977.

Stewart, John. *Bridges Not Walls.* 2nd ed. Reading, MA: Addison-Wesley Publishing Company, 1977.

Stewart, John, and D'Angelo, Gary. *Together: Communicating Interpersonally.* Reading, MA: Addison-Wesley Publishing Company, 1975.

Wiener, Morton, and Mehrabian, Albert. *Language Within Language: Immediacy, a Channel in Verbal Communication.* New York: Appleton-Century-Crofts, 1968.

CHAPTER 7

THE "JOY" OF PERFORMANCE APPRAISALS

Four things belong to a judge: to hear courteously, to answer wisely, to consider soberly, and to decide impartially.

—Socrates

Chapter Outline

Objectives

Theoretically, supervisors should view performance appraisal as a valued management tool. Most people think the idea is good; they feel an employee should know where he stands and how he can improve. But practically speaking, too many appraisals are ineffective. The fault may be with the process (e.g., fuzzy or conflicting objectives, ambiguous forms) or the one-on-one skills of the supervisor. This chapter examines the appraisal process. Specifically, in this chapter you will become familiar with:

1. The need for performance appraisals
2. The conflicts that inevitably occur between the supervisor and subordinate regarding the appraisal process
3. The wide range of performance appraisal forms
4. The effective use of a subjective appraisal system

Major Concepts

Performance standards

Graphic rating scales

Ranking techniques

Critical incidents method

MBO

Multiple raters

Pay-for-performance plans

Nonmonetary rewards

THE SUPERVISOR'S DILEMMA

Bill Kirby supervises ten social workers, and his problem is one of them: case worker Mark Garcia. Mark is a nice guy who relates well to his peers and to Bill. During Mark's first six-month appraisal session, he was rated as excellent in working with clients, above average in how he handled himself in court cases, always willing to work overtime if called upon, and actively involved with the community. Bill made it a point to mention how important these areas were and also saw to it that Mark received the maximum merit increase. How could a top case worker like Mark be a problem?

Bill's concern is over the other critical elements of the job, areas in which Mark received only an average rating last period (a rating that Bill now candidly admits was too lenient). The fact of the matter is that Mark has not submitted a court report on time yet (he began his employment about twelve months ago), has not kept his case record dictation up to date, and has not filled out the numerous federal reporting forms required by law. Bill has noticed that Mark's performance in these areas has not improved; it has in fact worsened. As supervisor, he has told Mark that report writing is as much a part of his job responsibilities as community relations. Yet Bill's remarks seem to fall on deaf ears. In fact, during a discussion with Mark about the problem a month ago, Mark said: "Why should I waste my time filling out reports? I do my job, and I do it better than most. I know what counts around here— so why are you hassling me with this paperwork burden?"

Regardless of what Mark thinks, the reporting documents are critical to effective case worker performance, required by law, and need to be made available in advance for use by attorneys. Furthermore, the written documentation of case work must be available as background information for use by others in crisis situations, especially when the case worker is absent or otherwise unavailable. Bill is at the end of his rope, the probation period is almost up for Mark, and Bill is contemplating recommending his termination.

*T*he tongue-in-cheek message of the title of this chapter captures the frustration many supervisors experience when dealing with performance appraisals. Most organizations spend a great deal of time, money, and effort on employee performance appraisal (PA), yet this remains one of the most problematic areas in basic supervision. For most supervisors, performance appraisals are a difficult task. Bill Kirby, for example, attempted to use the PA system to promote gratitude from Mark Garcia, hoping to motivate Mark by giving him a higher rating than he really deserved. The fact that this strategy failed (as it usually will) only serves to point out how distasteful and difficult the appraisal process can be to the supervisor. Repeated failures to produce better performance leave the supervisor with an attitude of indifference concerning employee performance appraisals. A view often expressed in PA seminars is that PA systems are a nuisance, at best a necessary evil— something that is expected of every supervisor but is not a critical part of their job. Some supervisors, however, seem not so much concerned with whether PA is needed but with how it could be done better.

In spite of these negative attitudes, performance appraisals are becoming increasingly important, both for motivating and rewarding improved performance and for documenting personnel decisions. This chapter lays the foundation for developing a useful PA system; Chapters 8 and 9 address the actual appraisal interview and learning to deal with different employee reactions on the job. Since most supervisors are not in a position to design a whole new PA system, we aim to provide some guidance on how to make an existing appraisal system more effective.

Why Bother with PA?

The front-line supervisor typically is overwhelmed by having to do performance appraisals. The amount of time a single PA demands is no small matter. When it is multiplied by the number of subordinates in the work group, it is no wonder that supervisors are reluctant to commit their time to an endeavor in which the payoff is often difficult to gauge.

Top managers take PA for granted

Many top managers do not take the time to explain the "whys and hows" of the PA function to the personnel responsible for the appraisals. This happens because top managers tend to take PA for granted. The need for performance appraisals seems self-evident. But only when management in general and supervisors in particular set themselves to answer such questions as the following will they know how PA can pay off:

1. Why are we spending money on the appraisal process?
2. What are we getting in return?
3. Why should we continue to conduct appraisals at all?

PA is needed for human resource development

Appraisal is a dollars and cents matter. Most successful organizations are willing to spend a large amount of time and money on the development of sophisticated appraisal systems to ensure that adequate talent and manpower will be available to fill both the expected and the unexpected vacancies that inevitably occur. Such large expenditures suggest that organizations are aware that they must plan a program of development for their human resources just as they do for their capital resources (e.g., plant expansion). Simply leaving employee development to chance is too costly and inefficient. Consequently, the PA process serves as the primary mechanism for determining those who require development, those who would profit most from development, and the kinds of development that are needed.

PA: A strategy for motivation

The PA process, furthermore, is an excellent strategy for influencing the motivation of organizational members. Often, appraisal results are directly linked to the employee's pay level and to promotional opportunities. By demonstrating to the employee, in no uncertain terms, that good performance is rewarded, a clear connection can be established between performance and rewards. Thus the basic human question, "What's in it for me?" is unequivocally answered.

Don't forget the law!

Perhaps the most persuasive argument for appraisals is the law. There is an increasing number of court cases involving discrimination in the distribution of such rewards as promotion and training. Since the passing of Title VII of the Civil Rights Act of 1964 and the establishment of the Equal Employment Opportunity Commission (EEOC), a number of changes have occurred in the PA process. Certain legal requirements now make it necessary for organizations to demonstrate that rating forms and ranking procedures are actually related to job performance. Rulings from a number of court cases [1] suggest the following guidelines for designing an effective system:

1. Performance ratings must be job-related rather than based on abstract personality characteristics.
2. Rating systems that are designed from a thorough job analysis hold up better than traditional trait rating systems.
3. The system must provide for intrarater and interrater consistency through proper validation procedures.[2]
4. Forms and instructions should be clear, concise, simply worded, and backed with acceptable validating data.

Needs of PA system

The impact of these legal concerns is to require performance appraisals to be tied as closely as possible to the job itself, hence to reduce subjectivity. But aside from the need to comply with the law, the law's intrusion into the workplace represents a golden opportunity to revamp an existing PA system, enabling a more efficient and effective mechanism to be developed—one that capitalizes on the latent talent at the organization's disposal. From a purely organizational point of view, a thorough and valid PA system with well-trained raters is becoming a necessity rather than a luxury for more larger organizations.[3]

Today, PA is not a luxury but a necessity

Sources of Error

OVERCOMING RESISTANCE TO PA

Performance appraisals are a sensitive matter for supervisors and subordinates alike. One manager told us frankly that whenever he had to pass along to a subordinate a candid statement of the subordinate's strengths and weaknesses, he would inevitably resort to writing a letter. This reflects the uncomfortable feeling many supervisors have toward their participation in the appraisal process.

The cause for most of the negative attitudes subordinates have of

Perspectives vary

[1] See, for example, *Griggs* v. *Duke Power Company*, 401 U.S. 424 (1971); *Moody* v. *Albermarle Paper*, 474 F. 2d 134 (CA-4, 1973); and *Wade* v. *Mississippi Cooperative Extension Service*, 372 F. Supp. 126 (1974).

[2] *Intrarater reliability* means that a rater using the same rating mechanism at different times will produce reasonably similar results; *interrater reliability* means that different raters using the same rating mechanism will produce reasonably similar results.

[3] For the time being, organizations employing fewer than fifteen full-time employees or whose employees work for less than 20 weeks a year are exempt from EEOC investigations.

performance appraisals can be traced to misunderstandings that stem from simple differences in perception. The supervisor's perceptions of an employee's performance is not always the same as the employee's perception of his or her own performance. Human judgment is influenced by all kinds of factors, not the least being attitudes and values. Combined, these factors explain the individual's view of reality. For the most part, differences about "reality" simply reflect differences in people and how they perceive the world. It is important, then, to examine the different perspective that each party has of employee performance, because it is only through such an awareness that negative attitudes can be identified and confronted.

Negative anticipations

The Employee's Perspective. Anyone who has ever had a job can recall times when the boss seemed to focus entirely on one's mistakes. Positive accomplishments were ignored. (Possibly making it worse was the boss's negative tone.) Performance appraisals are not likely to be looked forward to in mistake-centered situations such as this. Not only are all the employee's major violations brought out, but many of the minor ones are highlighted as well. It is only natural for employees to approach an upcoming evaluation with apprehension and skepticism when all they think they will hear is a long list of criticisms.

Nobody likes to be told she is not doing well. But how this is done can make all the difference. If the appraisal appears to the employee to be inconsistent or arbitrary, it will be rejected, the employee will become defensive, and performance may actually decline.

The subordinate's self-esteem needs to be protected

The key to successful appraisal is the employee's self-esteem. Negative feedback *can* be given to employees without damaging their belief in themselves. As long as the supervisor concentrates on specific job performance, minimizes surprises, maintains a balanced and even-handed approach (mentioning good points as well as bad), and seeks the employees' thoughts about their own performance, it is possible to reach a mutual understanding. This does not mean that employees will agree every time with the supervisor's judgment, but the process is likely to minimize employee resistance.

Real communication is a two-way process

"Sit down and I'll show you what you got," says the supervisor. On the surface, this type of opening remark may seem harmless enough. But behind it lurks a supervisor who is either not interested in opening up lines of communication or is simply not aware that such remarks hinder two-way communication. More often than not, however, the problem is not a supervisor's lack of interest in what the employee has to say, but lack of knowledge in using the PA process as a tool for opening up lines of communication.

We are not suggesting that making up your mind about an employee's performance prior to the appraisal is wrong. We are suggesting that being closed-minded to new information can turn off the employee, especially if the rating is less than expected.

Keep an open mind

Why not ask employees ahead of time to assess their own performance, and then compare their self-ratings to your ratings of their performance? It may well be that the employees are harder on themselves than you are. Employees, on the whole, will be honest as long as they believe that being honest will not jeopardize expected rewards. This tactic would actually save time for the supervisor by pinpointing areas of disagreement, in which more discussion time is needed, while by-passing areas in which both parties already have a meeting of minds.

Use self-appraisals when possible

The Supervisor's Perspective. Supervisor resistance to PA is understandable when one considers the uncomfortable and unnatural position that supervisors find themselves in when having to play the role of judge. Nevertheless, like it or not, the passing of judgment is an integral part of every supervisor's job.

Supervisors are uncomfortable with conducting PA for two reasons. First, as a general rule, they don't like to "play God." Second, because of the lack of supervisory orientation, they are unsure in their handling of the interpersonal problems that inevitably occur. Having to judge another person's behavior is, for most supervisors, an unpleasant prospect. When coupled with the possibility that such action may jeopardize the desire to be liked (an instinctive human need), it becomes very difficult to maintain objectivity. Furthermore, the supervisor's lack of training in counseling, coaching, interpersonal relations, and basic feedback skills contributes to the anxiety and general uneasiness that typically accompany the appraisal session. The result is the attitude often expressed by both supervisors and subordinates, "Let's get this distasteful meeting over and get out of here."

Training in PA helps

THE PROBLEM APPRAISAL FORM

When talking to supervisors, one often hears criticisms directed toward the rating forms themselves—specifically, that the forms are subjective, unfair, inconsistent, cumbersome, misleading, and dangerous (when there is too much emphasis on changing personality rather than on changing performance). Some forms appear to emphasize the negative—the mistakes an employee makes—rather than indicating how improvement in performance might be accomplished.

Forms should focus on the positive

Good forms are
job-specific

It is not enough to say, "Look, Joe, you've got to show greater initiative in your group" simply because the form happens to have an item labeled initiative. Such feedback is too vague and abstract, and it almost always triggers hostility (hidden or otherwise) in the subordinate. The better forms include examples of good employee performance, so that the subordinate understands what it will take to get a good rating. If the form fails to mention examples of desired job behaviors, then supervisors should provide these themselves.

What is
"average"?

One of the more obvious drawbacks to PA is the general resistance supervisors have towards rating an employee on the basis of "average," "above average," "outstanding," "needs improvement"—or some other overworked set of adjectives. What is "average" to one supervisor may be "outstanding" to another supervisor. These types of judgments will vary across raters depending on their individual experiences and observations.

One way around the fuzziness of such overworked adjectives is to identify performance standards (i.e., conditions that will exist when a job has been done well). In fact, specific work standards (such as those enumerated in Figure 7.1, for example) provide a benchmark for measuring a subordinate's real performance and can contribute to a productive, high-morale department in the following ways:

The value of
performance
standards

1. Standards make it possible to base merit and salary increases on something more objective than personality traits and general impressions.
2. Standards make it easier for the supervisor to discuss performance with an employee in appraisal sessions. When objective yardsticks are used to measure performance, there is less room for conflict than when subjective, emotionally charged criteria such as personality traits are used.
3. Since performance standards clarify the objectives of a job, the supervisor and the subordinate can agree on tangible improvement goals. Having a measurable goal that the supervisor wants them to reach within a certain period gives subordinates a strong incentive for improvement.
4. Workers who know that their jobs have certain specific standards are always aware of how they are doing. They can rate their own job effectiveness, and their initial improvement in unsatisfactory areas, without waiting for an appraisal from the supervisor.
5. Performance standards enable supervisors to evaluate the whole department realistically. They can spot areas where individual employees need improvement and also areas where steps to improve the whole group are called for.

FIGURE 7.1
Performance Standards: Two Examples

OPERATIONS MANAGER

ACTIVITIES/DUTIES	PURPOSE	STANDARDS
Review and approve budget costs	To be knowledgeable about budget costs and satisfied as to their reasonableness	Satisfactory performance has been attained when the actual costs are within 10 percent of the budget
Review cost reports	To see that cost reports are promptly and properly presented to affected personnel; to be knowledgeable of actual costs as they relate to estimated costs	Satisfactory performance has been attained when I have transmitted cost reports to affected personnel, with appropriate remarks, within two days of when they are placed on my desk
Formulate the divisions' operating plans	To develop a capable, efficient, and economically operating organization utilizing to the maximum the abilities of available personnel	Satisfactory performance has been attained when personnel are operating within 90% of target
See that individual reviews of performance standards are made	To see that the organization's policy regarding this management tool is used	Satisfactory performance has been attained when the standards have been reviewed in writing for those reporting to me by March 15, 1986

CLERK TYPIST

Purpose of this job: To provide clerical support to five training specialists in the Management Training group.

DUTIES AND RESPONSIBILITIES:

1. Receive incoming telephone calls for group; answer questions; refer calls; take messages.

2. Do typing as required for staff members—correspondence, teaching materials, reports, etc.

3. Process class enrollments by received telephone, interoffice memo, or in person; prepare instructors' rosters; telephone participants one day ahead of first class session as a reminder.

4. Maintain group files according to established filing system.

5. Maintain log of all purchase orders initiated by group staff members, including cumulative record of approved charges made against each.

STANDARDS EXPECTED:

1. a. Telephone should be answered after no more than two rings.
    b. Telephone manner should follow that described in the Telephone Courtesy Handbook.
    c. Messages should carry date and time of receipt as well as relevant names, phone numbers, and other information.

2. a. There should be no typographical or spelling errors and no more than three erasures on each finished page of typing.
    b. Typing should be completed by deadlines specified (refer priority conflict to supervisor).

3. a. Deadlines as specified must be met.
    b. Errors in entry or notification should not exceed 2 percent per month.

4. Filing backlog should not exceed one week.

5. a. All entries in log must be made on the same workday received.
    b. Related staff member and/or supervisor should be notified prior to expiration of purchase order or amount of funds authorized.

Appraisals cannot be constructive or accurate when there is uncertainty over what is acceptable or unacceptable performance. Setting standards helps to clarify expectations and minimize the frustrations of not knowing beforehand what it's going to take to succeed. Just going through the process of identifying standards is an eye-opening experience for many supervisors—as well as for subordinates who are invited to participate.

TYPICAL RATING ERRORS

It is imperative that supervisors avoid, as much as possible, evaluating the group on the basis of personal preferences and prejudices. As unnecessary as this warning may seem, it is still a constantly recurring problem. Furthermore, even conscientious supervisors may simply possess inadequate or erroneous information. Consequently, we would like to highlight a few of the more serious rating errors to avoid.

Bias

First, there are the personal biases that everyone has and that inevitably creep into the judgment process. All of us are aware of supervisors who don't like people of a particular nationality or race. Other supervisors have more sophisticated biases, such as a preference for people who wear stylish clothes, don't have facial hair, or are over six feet tall. These biases lead to decisions about a person's worth that are not based on sound judgment.

Similar-to-me comparisons

Some of the bias may appear in the form of similar-to-me comparisons: The supervisor is blind to certain types of defects in others because they are just like his or her own. This is likely to happen the more closely the subordinate resembles the supervisor in attitudes or background. When supervisors tend to rate subordinates higher than they deserve because they find them pleasing in manner and personality, they fall victim to a most common bias—that of flattery. If in doubt, ask yourself whether you are flattered when someone nods his head when you are talking or, even better, makes notes of your comments. If so, and who of us isn't, then ask yourself, Do I subconsciously give better ratings than deserved to this person?

The halo error

The one-asset person

Certain types of bias are commonly referred to as the halo error. The employee's performance is viewed through a filter that shades favorably or unfavorably toward the employee depending on the bias. Giving an employee a bad evaluation because he has done poor work in the distant past is one example of the halo error. The one-asset person is yet another example. The glib talker, the person with nice looks, the person with a degree, the person with the right attitude—these individuals have the advantage of an upward bias when they are evaluated. The error is impossible to eliminate even with the most advanced PA methods. However, forms that emphasize goals and activities, as opposed to traits, do tend to minimize its occurrence.

One error that can be brought under control is the effect of recency. It occurs when the subordinate's outstanding performance the previous week or the previous day is allowed to offset mediocre performance over the previous months. Sometimes called the Santa Claus effect, recency reflects a sudden improvement in employee performance, much like the behavior of kids just prior to Christmas. The best way to control for this error is documentation. Supervisors who have disciplined themselves to note exceptional behavior throughout the rating period seldom fall victim to the recency effect.

Recency (the Santa Claus effect)

Yet another group of rating errors that deserves mention are leniency (giving evaluations that are undeservedly high), strictness (being too hard or too tough), and central tendency errors (the inability to make any decision at all and choosing instead to play it safe by rating the employee down the middle). Each of these errors makes it impossible to separate the good performers from the poor performers. These forms of error also make it difficult to compare ratings from different raters; for example, a good performer who is evaluated by a supervisor who commits errors of central tendency may receive a poorer rating than a poor performer who is rated by a supervisor who commits errors of leniency.

Leniency, strictness, and central tendency

Raters should be particularly aware of being unduly influenced by first impressions. Sometimes supervisors will make sweeping generalizations based on initial encounters with subordinates and tend to retain these impressions even when faced with contrary evidence. In any subsequent contacts with that person, the supervisor is inclined to look for patterns of behavior that seem to support the first impressions and may be unaware of behaviors that contradict them. Somewhat related is the error of guilt by association. Individuals who are not well known are often judged by the company they keep. If they hang out with a frivolous or undisciplined crowd, the chances are their ratings will be lower than they deserve.

First impression effects

Guilt by association

Rating errors can be minimized—but never eliminated—when supervisors are provided proper training in counseling, coaching, and interpersonal skills. It also helps to have an appraisal system that minimizes personality measures and focuses instead on job-related standards of performance. Documentation that is accurate and consistent is yet another means for reducing bias in ratings. Nevertheless, even with all of these precautions, it is important to remember that supervisors are individuals. It would be naive to believe that any two supervisors will agree on the performance of a single employee.

WAYS IN WHICH PA PROCEDURES VARY

An expert in performance appraisal once commented: "Appraisal systems are like religion. If there were one right one, I'm sure we'd all believe in it." There is no such thing as a perfect performance appraisal method. Appraisal systems differ with regard to their stated objectives, the various forms and procedures used, and the amount of subjectivity involved. And their successful execution depends to a very large extent on the sophistication of the training received by those who have to administer them—the supervisors. Undoubtedly, the one thing that all appraisal systems do have in common is their reliance on human judgment. As one noted author has pointed out, "No system can put precision into a process that is inherently imprecise." [4]

Avoid "fuzzies"

Performance Versus Personality.

Appraisals that are composed of broad and abstract criteria ("fuzzies")—such as attitude—are generally referred to as traditional trait ratings. Whether intended or not, trait rating forms put more emphasis on aspects of the employee's personality than on the employee's on-the-job performance. It is hoped, for example, that telling a worker that his or her attitude needs improvement will lead to improvement, and that a "good" attitude will in turn promote good performance. The weaknesses of this approach are apparent. It has no tie-in to specific job performance. In fact, it leads away from discussion of an employee's job responsibilities and focuses instead on reshaping personality. Most important, it creates defensiveness and hostility within the employee, and ultimately has no positive effect on job performance.

Use a combination of traits, activities, and results

Nevertheless, to state that performance alone should be measured is too simplistic. It fails to take into account the essential personal characteristics inherent in the responsibilities of the position being evaluated. For example, such traits as self-confidence, empathy, and firmness combined with flexibility may indeed be necessary traits for the job of supervisor. Traits cannot be ignored. A good form, then, will combine measures of traits, activities, and results.

Keep it simple

Simplicity Versus Complexity.

No matter how sophisticated and expensive a PA system may be, if it is not accepted by the supervisors who have to use it, it will be unproductive. We believe that the better and more successful rating forms are the simpler ones. One organization has an appraisal system that includes nothing more than a few clearly

[4] Richard Ritti, *The Ropes to Skip and the Ropes to Know* (Columbus, Ohio: Grid, 1977), p. 146.

worded major responsibilities for each employee. These responsibilities are identified from position descriptions, which cover the broad on-going functions, and from any added or special tasks that employees are occasionally asked to perform. Performance standards are then identified by asking employees themselves what specific accomplishments indicate "above average" performance, "below average" performance, and so on. Keep in mind, however, that this system is built on sound job descriptions. If job descriptions were out of date or vaguely worded, then the completed process would be meaningless. Certainly this system has its problems, as every PA system does, but it is accepted by both supervisors and subordinates, and it does appear to be working. More sophisticated systems have met with less success.

One drawback about investing in the development of complex rating systems is the amount of time and paperwork required of the supervisor. Keeping the system simple is always a safe path to follow.

Types of Rating Forms

While there are many types of rating forms, the following are the most commonly used and represent variations of the three approaches mentioned earlier—traits, activities, and results. (1) Graphic rating scales have evolved from the trait approach; (2) ranking techniques (these don't fit any of the three approaches but are included because of the pervasiveness of comparative methods in appraisal systems); (3) critical incidents and behaviorally anchored scales are adaptations of the activity-oriented approach; (4) management by objectives (MBO) represents a results-oriented approach.

GRAPHIC RATING SCALES

Graphic rating scales are the oldest and most widespread of the performance rating techniques. Their simplicity is both an advantage and a pitfall. Most organizations prefer them because one form can be used for the whole work force. Furthermore, these scales are relatively easy to develop and use. All that is needed is a series of descriptive qualities that in some manner relate to job performance. The rater then assesses the ratee on the basis of each quality. The intensity of the quality is measured in terms of adjectives, usually covering the range "excellent" to "needs improvement."

When graphic scales include personality characteristics (a common feature), they are referred to as traditional trait rating forms. (See Figure 7.2 for an example of one such form.) Recall that the major problem

Traditional trait rating forms

FIGURE 7.2

Example of a Traditional Trait Rating Form: Appraisal Form Used by the Carter Administration

Work Habits:

1. On the average when does this person:
    arrive at work _____
    leave work _____

2. Pace of Work:
    1 2 3 4 5 6
    slow   fast

3. Level of Effort:
    1 2 3 4 5 6
    below   full
    capacity   capacity

4. Quality of Work:
    1 2 3 4 5 6
    poor   good

5. What is he/she best at? (rank 1–5)
    _____ Conceptualizing
    _____ Planning
    _____ Implementing
    _____ Attending to detail
    _____ Controlling quality

6. Does this person have the skills to do the job he/she was hired to do?
    yes _____
    no _____
    ? _____

7. Would the slot filled by this person be better filled by someone else?
    yes _____
    no _____
    ? _____

Personal Characteristics:

8. How confident is this person? (circle one)
    X X X X X X
    self-   confident   cocky
    doubting

9. How confident are you of this person's judgment?
    1 2 3 4 5 6
    not   very
    confident   confident

10. How mature is this person?
    1 2 3 4 5 6
    immature   mature

11. How flexible is this person?
    1 2 3 4 5 6
    rigid   flexible

FIGURE 7.2   (*continued*)

12. How stable is this person?
         1 2 3 4 5 6
      erratic   steady

13. How frequently does this person come up with new ideas?
         1 2 3 4 5 6
      seldom   often

14. How open is this person to new ideas?
         1 2 3 4 5 6
      closed   open

15. How bright is this person?
         1 2 3 4 5 6
      average   very bright

16. What are this person's special talents?

     1. _____

     _____

     2. _____

     _____

     3. _____

     _____

17. What is this person's range of information?
         1 2 3 4 5 6
      narrow   broad

Interpersonal Relations:

18. How would you characterize this person's impact on other people? (for example, hostile, smooth, aggressive, charming, etc.)

     1. _____

     _____

     2. _____

     _____

     3. _____

     _____

19. How well does this person get along with
     Superiors   1 2 3 4 5 6
     Peers   1 2 3 4 5 6
     Subordinates 1 2 3 4 5 6
     Outsiders   1 2 3 4 5 6
               not well   very well

FIGURE 7.2   (*continued*)

20. In a public setting, how comfortable would you be having this person represent:
    you or your office   1 2 3 4 5 6
    The President   1 2 3 4 5 6
                        uncomfortable   comfortable

21. Rate this person's political skills.
    1 2 3 4 5 6
    naive   savvy

Supervision and Direction:

22. To what extent is this person focused on accomplishing the
    Administration's goals _____ %
    personal goals   _____ %

                                    _____
                                    100 %

23. How capable is this person at working toward implementing a decision with which he/she may not agree?
    1 2 3 4 5 6
    reluctant   eager

24. How well does this person take direction?
    1 2 3 4 5 6
    resists   readily

25. How much supervision does this person need?
    1 2 3 4 5 6
    a lot   little

26. How readily does this person offer to help out by doing that which is not a part of his/her "job"?
    1 2 3 4 5 6
    seldom   often

Summary:

27. Can this person assume more responsibility?
    yes _____
    no _____
    ?   _____

Heroic assumptions

with trait ratings is that they tend not to be linked directly to performance; consequently, they are likely to produce employee defensiveness. Trait proponents believe that by defining the model employee in terms of personality characteristics and then judging an employee in terms of those qualities, the rater can persuade the ratee to reshape his or her personality to fit the ideal mold. Such views, of course, make two heroic assumptions about human nature: (1) that people will change their behavior if only someone points out their flaws and blemishes and (2) that people can change if they want to. Needless to say, both assumptions are overly optimistic.

Graphic rating techniques that incorporate traits need to ensure that each trait is adequately defined and that the rater will not be uncomfortable using it. Figure 7.3 is an example of a trait form that attempts to link traits to actual job behaviors. It represents a significant improvement over the form depicted in Figure 7.2 because the traits are not only adequately defined but contain meaningful descriptions of the kinds of behaviors that reflect effective (or ineffective) performance.

RANKING TECHNIQUES

When the group being rated is small (preferably comprising less than fifteen persons), one appraisal procedure that is quick, simple to perform, and inexpensive is the ranking method. The rater ranks the ratees from best to worst in terms of "value." Ranking techniques are generally characterized by relative comparisons among ratees made on the basis of some global (single) measure of overall effectiveness. Three popular ranking techniques are: (1) straight ranking, (2) alternative ranking, and (3) paired comparison.

For a rater, straight ranking is the most natural of the four techniques. It consists of simply rank-ordering those in the rating group—from the very best performer to the very worst.

Straight ranking

In alternative ranking, the rater's first selection is the best performer, the second selection is the poorest performer, and the third selection is the second best, the fourth selection is the second poorest, and so on. Following the selection of an individual, his or her name is crossed off the list, allowing the rater to concentrate on the remaining selections.

Alternative ranking

In paired comparison, which is a somewhat more time-consuming method, individuals are rated in pairs. The supervisor compares each employee with every other member of the group. The ratee most frequently chosen as the better of a pair is the most valuable. For groups with less than ten members, this technique is quite acceptable and is much favored; but for larger groups, the number of comparisons that must be made makes the method unwieldy and cumbersome.

Paired comparison

Ranking techniques may be appropriate when a supervisor is familiar with the members of the work unit, knowledgeable about the tasks being performed, and able to suppress dislikes, biases, and other rater errors. Obviously, this is not an easy set of conditions to satisfy. The weaknesses of ranking techniques are obvious: (1) the arbitrary designation of an employee's performance as being less than that of another; and (2) the inability to give sufficient and specific feedback to the ratee as to how

FIGURE 7.3

Example of a Trait Form That Links Traits to Job Behavior

EMPLOYEE PERFORMANCE EVALUATION
(NON-EXEMPT PERSONNEL)

NAME	DEPARTMENT	PERIOD COVERED FROM TO
JOB TITLE	SUPERVISOR	DATE REVIEWED

SECTION I ANALYTICAL CHARACTERISTICS

(Place an X in the appropriate box)   PART A—WORK

1. QUALITY OF WORK (Accuracy) (Adequacy)	Work requires considerable checking; amount of rework high; lacks accuracy, clarity, and/or adequacy.	Requires general checking; results accomplished with minimal rework; work is accurate & adequate.	Consistently turns out work of the highest quality; all work is accurate, adequate & efficient.
2. QUANTITY OF WORK	Produces a minimal amount of acceptable work; works exceptionally slowly as compared to co-workers; does not complete work on time.	Produces amount of work meeting job requirements; completes assigned work on time.	Does an exceptional amount of work; consistently produces more than co-workers; completes assignments ahead of schedule.

PART B—PERFORMANCE

3. APPLICATION OF KNOWLEDGE (Understanding) (Adaptability)	Does not understand principles, methods, or procedures; applies knowledge only after repeated explanation; adapts slowly to new situations.	Understands principles, methods, & procedures, applying knowledge to routine assignments; adapts readily to new situations.	Easily applies principles, methods, & procedures to complex assignments; adapts quickly to new situations.
4. PLANNING AND ORGANIZATION	Needs assistance in developing an approach & method on routine assignments; generally unorganized.	Plans & organizes adequately; steps are logical & efficient; normally does not require assistance in developing approach.	Develops sound & suitable plans; logically integrates steps & component parts into an effective unit; understands inter-relationsihps & over-all scope.
5. DEPENDABILITY (Supervision) (Accomplishing objectives) (Meeting schedules)	Needs close supervision even after a reasonable amount of time has been allotted to learn the job; unreliable; experiences difficulty in accomplishing objectives & in meeting schedules.	Requires general supervision; reliable & conscientious; accomplishes objectives & meets schedules.	Merits complete confidence on assignments, requires minimal supervision; accomplishes objectives efficiently & often finishes ahead of schedule.

FIGURE 7.3 *(continued)*

PART C—PERSONAL CHARACTERISTICS

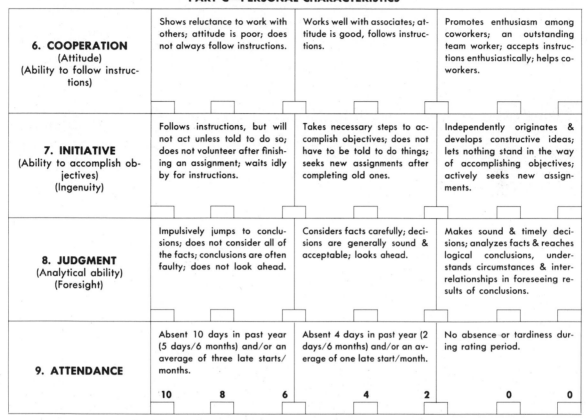

6. COOPERATION (Attitude) (Ability to follow instructions)	Shows reluctance to work with others; attitude is poor; does not always follow instructions.	Works well with associates; attitude is good, follows instructions.	Promotes enthusiasm among coworkers; an outstanding team worker; accepts instructions enthusiastically; helps coworkers.
7. INITIATIVE (Ability to accomplish objectives) (Ingenuity)	Follows instructions, but will not act unless told to do so; does not volunteer after finishing an assignment; waits idly by for instructions.	Takes necessary steps to accomplish objectives; does not have to be told to do things; seeks new assignments after completing old ones.	Independently originates & develops constructive ideas; lets nothing stand in the way of accomplishing objectives; actively seeks new assignments.
8. JUDGMENT (Analytical ability) (Foresight)	Impulsively jumps to conclusions; does not consider all of the facts; conclusions are often faulty; does not look ahead.	Considers facts carefully; decisions are generally sound & acceptable; looks ahead.	Makes sound & timely decisions; analyzes facts & reaches logical conclusions, understands circumstances & interrelationships in foreseeing results of conclusions.
9. ATTENDANCE	Absent 10 days in past year (5 days/6 months) and/or an average of three late starts/months. 10 8 6	Absent 4 days in past year (2 days/6 months) and/or an average of one late start/month. 4 2	No absence or tardiness during rating period. 0 0

he or she might improve. Add to this the possibility that ranking techniques may be illegal in the future because of the inability of users to provide supporting evidence that the results are reliable and valid. We do not recommend ranking techniques because they add little to employee development.

THE CRITICAL INCIDENTS METHOD

The critical incidents method is a method of appraisal radically different from any discussed so far. With this method, the supervisor keeps for each subordinate a written record of exceptional behavior, whether positive or negative. This enables a running tab to be kept on job performance, recorded in a timely and relevant manner. Studies for the General Electric Company have suggested that supervisors are inclined to rate a subordi-

Pros and cons of the critical incidents method

nate on the most recent performance, rather than over a complete appraisal period.[5] The critical incidents method is useful in countering this tendency. It also provides good documentation and feedback to the subordinate that is timely, specific, and job-related. Consequently, employee defensiveness is minimized. The major difficulties of the critical incidents method are: (1) deciding which incidents deserve recording, (2) finding the time to write it all down, and (3) avoiding the tendency to record only the negative incidents.

BARS

A variation of the critical incidents method is a technique usually referred to as behaviorally anchored rating scales (BARS), which is increasingly favored by organizations. BARS is an attempt to develop a rating scale that focuses on job content, job behaviors, and employee goals. Figure 7.4 is an example of a BARS form with a single performance dimension.

In this method, the rater measures the ratee on each performance dimension. Generally, there are between four and seven dimensions for each ratee, covering such job areas as knowledge and judgment, interpersonal skills, and technical skills. Each performance dimension could have anywhere from four to ten behavioral incidents anchored to the horizontal scale. In the example, there are nine behavioral incidents to the interpersonal skills dimension. The behavioral incidents range from examples of highly effective interpersonal skills (9 on the scale) to highly ineffective behaviors (1 on the scale). After reviewing the list of incidents, the rater will designate a point on the scale that best summarizes the ratee's interpersonal skills performance. This is repeated for each of the performance dimensions. Since the designated points are quantifiable, the performance dimensions can be summed for each ratee and used as a basis for making comparisons across different employees.

Limitations of BARS

BARS does appear to provide feedback that is specific and job-related. Moreover, the method appears to adhere to legal requirements because it reduces rating errors. But the method also has its limitations. One major disadvantage is the expense involved. Even though no outside consultants are needed, a significant amount of time is required for the developmental procedure. Another limitation of the method is the necessity that there be at least fifteen employees who perform reasonably similar tasks. Obviously, such a restriction limits the use of BARS to jobs that are well-known and routine—tasks that are usually found at the lower levels of the organization's structure.

---

[5] Herbert H. Meyer, Emanuel Kay, and John R. P. French, "Split Roles in Performance Appraisal," *Harvard Business Review*, January–February, 1965, pp. 123–129.

FIGURE 7.4

Example of a Behaviorally Anchored Rating Scale for Sales Managers

Performance Dimension: Interpersonal Skills

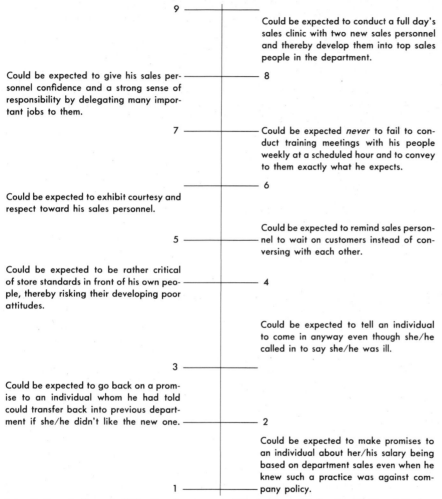

9 —

Could be expected to conduct a full day's sales clinic with two new sales personnel and thereby develop them into top sales people in the department.

Could be expected to give his sales per- — 8
sonnel confidence and a strong sense of responsibility by delegating many impor- tant jobs to them.

7 — Could be expected *never* to fail to conduct training meetings with his people weekly at a scheduled hour and to convey to them exactly what he expects.

6

Could be expected to exhibit courtesy and respect toward his sales personnel.

5 — Could be expected to remind sales person- nel to wait on customers instead of conversing with each other.

Could be expected to be rather critical of store standards in front of his own peo- — 4
ple, thereby risking their developing poor attitudes.

Could be expected to tell an individual to come in anyway even though she/he called in to say she/he was ill.

3 —

Could be expected to go back on a prom- ise to an individual whom he had told could transfer back into previous depart- ment if she/he didn't like the new one. — 2

Could be expected to make promises to an individual about her/his salary being based on department sales even when he knew such a practice was against com-
1 — pany policy.

John P. Campbell, et al., "The Development and Evaluation of Behaviorally Based Rating Scales," *Journal of Applied Psychology* 57 (February 1973), p. 17. Copyright © 1973 by the American Psychological Association. Reprinted by permission of the author.

MANAGEMENT BY OBJECTIVES

Management by objectives (MBO) is an alternative form of evaluating that represents a change in focus from conventional rating and compara- tive procedures. Basically, MBO involves the supervisor and subordinate *jointly* identifying common goals—goals that are acceptable to the organi-

MBO is a philosophy of management

FIGURE 7.5
An Example of MBO

NORTHERN ARIZONA COUNCIL OF GOVERNMENTS
PERFORMANCE PLANNING AND EVALUATION REPORT

NAME __Michelle Carrell__

POSITION __Personnel Technician II__

PERIOD FROM __Jan. 1, 1986__ TO __June 30, 1986__

TYPE OF EVALUATION: Regular
Midprobationary [x]
Probationary
Other (specify)

OVERALL PERFORMANCE EVALUATION RATING

1 Unsatisfactory ☐
2 Needs improvement [x]
3 Achieved results expected ☐
4 Exceeded results expected ☐

RECOMMENDATIONS

Permanent status   Yes ☐   No ☐
Not applicable ☐

Merits increase ☐
Does not merit increase [x]
Not applicable ☐

I. RESPONSIBILITIES	STANDARDS FOR RESULTS EXPECTED	1	2	3	4	EVALUATION OF RESULTS ACHIEVED
(1) Assist in the employee selection process, specifically: a) Design a telephone reference check form that is valid and legal b) Make pre-employment inquiries of all applicants who meet minimum qualifications c) Test and score applicants d) Interview applicants e) Determine top three candidates	(1) a) Telephone reference check form satisfies the organization's legal office and the Personnel Manager b) 90% of the references are contacted c) Applicants tested are asked to fill out a brief questionnaire that measures: test administration, sensitivity of test given to the needs of the applicant, & ability to communicate test instructions. Standard performance is 80% satisfaction. d) Interviewing skills are evaluated by co-workers who participate in the interview process. e) Departmental supervisors will determine the quality of the top 3 applicants.	x	x x x		 x	(1) a) Two questions were viewed as illegal and had to be omitted. b) Carrell contacted over 95% of the references c) Applicants tested generally viewed Carrell as insensitive, threatening, and noncommunicative. d) Co-workers who participated in the interview process with Carrell believed her questions were not well planned and even bordered on the verge of illegality. e) Departmental supervisors were not unhappy with the recommendations made by Carrell

PLANNING

EMPLOYEE:
Michelle Carrell 7/6/86
Signature   Date

SUPERVISOR:
[signature] 7/6/86
Signature   Date

EVALUATION

SUPERVISOR:
Rates increase ☐   Does not rate increase [x]

EMPLOYEE:
Agrees [x] Disagrees ☐
Disagrees and requests review ☐

DIVISION CHIEF:
(if applicable)
Rates increase ☐   Does not rate increase ☐

EXECUTIVE DIRECTOR:
Approves ☐ Disapproves ☐ Other ☐

Signature _____ Date _____

Signature _____ Date _____

Signature _____ Date _____

Signature _____ Date _____

zation's mission and the individual's needs—for the year or for some other appropriate length of time. These goals are worded in personalized specifics, stating exactly what is to be accomplished. However, it should be noted that MBO is more than an evaluation technique; it is a philosophy of management. It is a commitment by the manager to involve subordinates in the work by identifying challenging goals.

The effective introduction of an MBO program takes a great deal of time and effort and requires top management commitment and participation. Because organizations do not operate in a vacuum, the objective-setting mechanism needs continuous monitoring and revisions. This is especially true for the nonprofit sector of this society, where the organization or agency faces constant reshuffling of priorities due to changes in funding sources and political interference. When output is measured in terms of profit or goods produced, objective standards are relatively easy to set. In nonprofit or service industries, arriving at objective criteria that can be measured quantitatively is another matter. Nevertheless, objectives can be determined with a little creativity on the part of the supervisor and subordinate. While the standards in such settings as social work may not be as precise as those for sales personnel, adequate standards that make it possible to assess how well a given job is being performed can be established (see Figure 7.5 for an example of MBO in a public sector organization).

The effectiveness of an MBO approach to PA lies in the ability of the supervisor to define (with the subordinate) each individual's major areas of responsibility in terms of the results expected, and to use these measures as a guide for operating the unit and assessing the contribution of each of its members. On completion of the appraisal period, the supervisor and subordinate jointly discuss the activities and the results. The focus is on the steps leading up to goal accomplishment rather than on accomplishment itself, because emphasis on results alone tends to generate a defensive posture on the part of the employee toward the rater.

Ideal for identifying expectations

Aspects of Appraisal

MAKING A SUBJECTIVE FORM WORK

The greatest failure of most rating forms is their failure to cover the job. If the forms don't provide an adequate frame of reference for the rater, then it is unlikely that critical behaviors will be discussed with the subordinate. The supervisor can improve the usefulness of the form

Translate "fuzzies" into specific job behaviors

by translating the items into specific job behaviors. This at least provides common ground and a point of departure for constructive dialogue. However, should an approach such as this be needed, one warning is in order: Saving critical comments about performance for the annual review can be demoralizing for the subordinate. It is best to balance the comments with constructive remarks and/or to institute informal progress reviews throughout the year.

Occasionally, managers will decide to give verbal support and emphasis to performance factors that do not appear on the appraisal form. However, such support seldom improves employee performance in the long run. The following account represents one such occurrence:

> The plant accident rate had been increasing and so had accident insurance premiums. In an all-out effort to reduce the high rate, top management got together with the first-line supervisors to push accident prevention and employee safety programs. Weekly discussions of the topic were conducted with employees. Posters were hung all over the plant and a continuous supply of films was brought in and shown. A drop in preventable accidents did occur. However, six months following the intensive safety program, the rate again had increased to its prior level.

If a job behavior is important, it should be on the rating form

The comment of one employee in the plant makes clear why the safety program ultimately failed: "If safety is so important, why isn't it on the performance evaluation form. Since it isn't, why exert any sweat in accident prevention when my efforts are ignored instead of being rewarded?" The message is clear: Workers will strive for performance success when their accomplishments are recognized and rewarded. If a particular job behavior is really important, as is the case with safety, then it should be included somewhere on the form.

Identify basic responsibilities

One way to improve subjective forms might be to identify the employee's major responsibilities and from this list determine the standards against which performance will be measured. In many cases, supervisors find it useful to let subordinates suggest or help develop appropriate standards. Letting them participate in the process helps them understand what is expected. Effective appraisals are based, in part, on the clear definition of expectations.

Avoid relying on your memory

Effective appraisals also depend on good documentation. Taking a little extra time to sit down and record what has been observed at the time it occurs will actually save time later. Trying to reconstruct events just prior to the appraisal interview or *during* the interview itself, when the subordinate might question the accuracy of your memory, is not recommended. Remembering details that may have occurred months ago is an almost impossible task.

Many supervisors have found that keeping an "incidents file" is quite helpful when trying to reconstruct the employee's past performance. However, there are problems that should be mentioned. Do not fall into the habit of recording only mistakes or instances of inept performance. Such negative documentation can only be perceived by employees as threatening. It is important to balance the bad with the good whenever possible in order to maintain credibility with the employee. A useful file will note the date, an objective account of what happened, and what the supervisor did to remedy or reinforce the employee's particular behavior (see Figure 7.6 for sample entries in an incidents file).

Good documentation focuses attention where it belongs—on the employee's job performance. When the supervisor sits down with the employee to discuss his or her performance, instead of a conversation that is aimlessly wandering or one that inevitably ends in dispute, the discussion can be directed toward specific job occurrences. Attention can be given to how performance might be improved as well as to how performance was commendable or deficient in the past.

> **Keep an "incidents file"**

> **Good documentation helps direct discussion of performance**

FIGURE 7.6
Sample Entries in an Incidents File

Michelle Carrell, Personnel Technician II

3/3   Carrell designed the reference check form and immediately began using it before it was approved by our legal staff. Subsequently two questions on the form were identified that could get us into trouble with the EEOC. Carrell immediately removed the questions and agreed that, in the future, she would exercise more patience before implementing such a sensitive process.

4/23   Carrell's reports indicate that over 95% of the applicants' references were contacted during the past two weeks. I complimented her on doing the work of two.

5/10   Reports from tested applicants suggest that Carrell's demeanor while administering our tests borders on rudeness. Specifically, comments that were made include:
— "She's insensitive"
— "She's pushy"
— "She's aloof and arrogant"

I discussed this with her this morning and reminded her about the importance of creating a test environment that is supportive, friendly, and nonthreatening. She said she would attend an evening class at the college on nonverbal communication to help her improve in this area. I said we would pay for it.

6/15   Carrell mentioned that she enrolled in the class and is really getting something out of it. I asked her to let me know when she completed the course so I could reschedule her back into test administration (also I would then put a request for reimbursement through the appropriate channels).

HOW OFTEN SHOULD APPRAISALS BE DONE?

Doesn't have to be a once-a-year event

How often do employees need feedback?

Minimize surprises

Focus on the future

The dilemma: Honesty versus desire for rewards

When most of us think about PA, we think of the once-a-year event in which we sit down with the subordinate and discuss job performance. Outside the paperwork hassle there is really no reason why a PA could not take place twice or four times a year. In fact, more frequent appraisals permit an averaging to occur that tends to de-emphasize the importance of any single appraisal.[6] There are other reasons, too, for considering more infrequent appraisals.

The first reason is that PA is a feedback device, and since every employee needs feedback, it is beneficial to design a PA system so that it gives the employee maximum feedback as often as possible. One study went so far as to recommend day-to-day informal progress reviews.[7] In effect, the emphasis of day-to-day coaching is on employee development rather than on judgmental decisions. The typical once-a-year PA does not usually lend itself to employee development, both because of its infrequency and because of its thrust from a judgmental point of view (i.e., salary and promotion decisions). Also, saving up problems for discussion during the annual review is not practical. Maintaining a dialogue throughout the year minimizes the number of surprises that occur at the annual session. Day-to-day reviews should not be interpreted as spending valuable time every workday talking with employees about their jobs. But when problems do occur, they can be confronted in timely fashion, well before they have a chance to affect everyone negatively.

A second reason for having frequent appraisals concerns the tendency for annual reviews to overemphasize the past rather than looking to the future. Of course there is nothing wrong with examining the past— how else would we determine who is deserving of merit and other rewards? But with rewards in the offing, it becomes extremely difficult to get the employee to open up and discuss job performance, since the discussion itself might reveal new information that could jeopardize those rewards. It is an organizational fact of life that when an employee has to choose between an honest but negative self-evaluation and an opportunity to look good to attain a reward, he or she will usually choose the latter. Some theorists go so far as to suggest having two separate yearly reviews, with one focusing on rewards and the other on employee development.[8] The suggestion points up how important and difficult it is to strive for an honest dialogue between supervisor and subordinate.

[6] Richard Henderson, *Performance Appraisal: Theory to Practice* (Reston, Va.: Reston, 1980), pp. 181–182.

[7] Meyer, Kay, and French, "Split Roles in Performance Appraisal."

[8] L. Porter, E. Lawler, and J. Hackman, *Behavior in Organizations* (New York: McGraw-Hill, 1975), p. 234.

IS THE SUPERVISOR THE ONLY ONE
WHO CAN EVALUATE THE GROUP?

While the usual practice in most organizations is that evaluations are the responsibility of the supervisor, that doesn't mean the supervisor cannot solicit or use the observations of others. Co-workers, for example, may be more familiar with some aspect of the subordinate's performance than the supervisor. In service-type organizations, such as a hospital, patients may be in a better position to judge some elements of a nurse's performance than the nurse's immediate superior. Department chairpersons at some universities are evaluated by the professors within the department, in effect giving the subordinates responsibility for evaluating their bosses. Finally, in one organization where employees worked alone, self-appraisals were allowed that proved quite valid.[9]

Maybe the best strategy is to gather as much information as possible about the ratee's performance from relevant others. By including such sources as the employee himself or herself, co-workers of the employee, subordinates reporting to the employee, and customers or clients of the employee's work unit, a judgment based on multiple observations can be made. Obviously the supervisor cannot ask just anyone—such as a customer—what he or she thinks of an employee's performance. Proven integrity and objectivity are necessary qualities of the people whose opinions are sought.

> When possible, use multiple raters

APPRAISAL AND REWARDS

What Should the Supervisor Say About Compensation?

Some organizations don't want the supervisor saying anything at all to the employee about co-workers' salaries. Essentially these organizations believe that pay secrecy prevents dissatisfaction with pay. It seems ironic that research suggests otherwise. One study found that in organizations in which pay secrecy was practiced, employees perceived co-workers' salaries to be higher than they actually were.[10] Nevertheless, a policy of openness is not always the best policy. Organizations that attempt to use money as a motivator and who practice openness had better be sure that money is indeed awarded to the best performers. Compensation inequities are quickly noticed and will lead to more problems than a pay secrecy policy could ever bring.

> Openness versus secrecy

[9] G. A. Bassett and Herbert H. Meyer, "Performance Appraisal Based on Self-Review," *Personnel Psychology* 21 (1968), pp. 421–430.

[10] Edward E. Lawler, *Pay and Organizational Effectiveness* (New York: McGraw-Hill, 1971), p. 133.

Avoid making promises

On the whole, organizations today are moving toward a philosophy of openness regarding compensation matters. As far as performance appraisals are concerned, however, it is probably best for supervisors not to make promises that may not be kept later. This would include promising raises of specific amounts. All that needs to be said to the employee at the end of the appraisal is that "salary action will be recommended on the basis of your performance and your position in the salary range."

Monetary Incentives and Performance Appraisals.

Monetary incentives are controversial. The public as well as many chief executive officers are intrigued with the idea of linking pay to performance. But those who are expected to implement such "pay-for-performance" plans insist that they do not and cannot work.

Pay-for-performance plans work on a simple principle: The better the performance, the better the reward. They assume that money is the primary factor in creating the motivation to work more productively. In some organizations the plan means bringing marginal employees up to the level where standards are fully met; to most organizations, it means giving various levels of monetary incentives to employees who fully meet standards. In a few public sector organizations, it means holding merely good performers to the midpoint of the pay range until they excel in performance. It also means not rewarding nonproductive employees—and hardly anyone disagrees with this.

Yet in spite of the logic favoring the idea, pay-for-performance plans seldom succeed. There are several arguments against monetary incentive systems (in the accompanying box, one articulate supervisor mentions a few). The one we will focus on is the tendency of such plans to overwhelm the employee's intrinsic motivation—motivation that comes from the work itself.

Extrinsic rewards can overwhelm intrinsic motivators

Tangible reinforcers, such as money, are extrinsic rewards and work effectively when used wisely and sparingly. Too much of an extrinsic reward, however, can erase a person's commitment to perform effectively and thoroughly. Supervisors must realize that subordinates do not always want more money or bonuses—in fact, "the added extrinsic motivation tends, under many conditions, to cancel the old intrinsic motivation." [11] Take Bob, for example, who works as a volunteer for the local United Way Agency. He is offered a salary by the agency's trustees to continue what he once was doing for free. It doesn't take long before Bob loses interest in working for the agency and quits. His motive was the need to make a contribution to his community. Getting paid distracted from

---

[11] Harold J. Leavitt, *Managerial Psychology* (Chicago: University of Chicago Press, 1978), p. 23.

ONE SUPERVISOR'S OPINION ABOUT LINKING MONETARY INCENTIVES TO PERFORMANCE APPRAISALS

"The experience that I have had covers a lot of years and a lot of different organizations. Throughout it all, I have seen no single pay-for-performance plan succeed with the hourly worker. There's a half-life which varies as people learn how to beat the appraisal system. I really can't think of a performance appraisal system, regardless of its objectivity, that has proven effective in linking monetary incentives to performance. The difficulty lies with the standards that are used and the application of those standards among all the supervisors who have to give the ratings. It's been my experience that it is difficult enough to get supervisors simply to rate perfor-

mance—if to do nothing else but talk to employees—and when we add other factors in there, such as money, then the task becomes a great deal more difficult. Supervisors start to play political games just so they can get their fair share of the compensation budget.

Don't misunderstand me. I fully buy into the idea of pay for performance. I think the concept is good—I have tried it a number of times myself—but the practice, in spite of the best training, is so fraught with political infighting, fuzzy standards, and negative attitudes that it is extremely difficult to carry out."

the intrinsic satisfaction he once received. The same process is at work with Sue, a commercial artist, who is considered by her boss to possess masterly skills in graphic design. When her boss adopts a pay-for-performance plan, whereby Sue receives a small bonus for each drawing, the quality of her work starts to suffer, although the number of completed drawings increases. Her boss's strategy has probably backfired. (We say "probably" because we can only assume that quality was at least as important as quantity in this instance.)

Experience in designing effective reward systems teaches that only a careful combination of both extrinsic and intrinsic rewards will promote motivation and improved performance. Granted that money and other extrinsic rewards must be minimally adequate to attract and retain good people; but at a certain point intrinsic rewards, such as self-fulfillment and a sense of achievement, become more important—or at least equally important. For motivation to occur over the long run, supervisors should learn to use a complementary mix of extrinsic rewards (e.g., money and recognition) while always striving to tap the inherent worth of the task as a source of intrinsic motivation.[12]

[12] For the reader who would like to learn more about this concept, we recommend Thomas J. Peters and Robert H. Waterman, Jr., *In Search of Excellence* (New York: Harper & Row, 1982), pp. 70–71.

NONMONETARY REWARDS

Money and getting more of it seems to be on the minds of almost every working person. Labor unions are always asking for more, the government always wants more, so it is only logical to expect employees always to be talking about what their cost-of-living and merit raises will be next year. As a supervisor, this is one area you don't have a lot of control over (although you may make salary recommendations). What supervisors do have control over are the nonmonetary rewards. Unlike merit raises, nonmonetary rewards are almost completely controlled by the supervisor.

Recognition

Recognition, for example, is one nonmonetary reward that can be given to the employee whenever the supervisor feels it would be most appropriate and have the greatest impact. Sharing privileged information with the employee, such as about new expansion plans, is one way of showing recognition. Seeking the employee's opinion when important decisions have to be made is another.

Increased responsibility

A second nonmonetary reward is increasing the level of an employee's responsibility. Many people covet the more challenging work assignments that come with increased responsibility. Increasing the employee's opportunities to make more challenging decisions is an aspect of this type of reward.

Employee development

A third nonmonetary reward involves employee development. Giving special one-time assignments, rotating the employee through different jobs, and sending the employee to training programs are viable ways for rewarding good performance.

One thing nonmonetary rewards have going for them is that they can be given to the employee immediately after the desired performance is noticed by the supervisor. This strengthens the employee's perception that good performance is indeed valued and rewarded. It also reduces the clamor for more money.

SUMMARY ══════════════════════════

Why supervisors are uncomfortable about conducting PA is not difficult to understand. When the system itself is vague and full of abstractions and generalizations, the supervisor will tend to avoid becoming involved, much less give it full support. Furthermore, if appraisals are an expected part of a supervi-sor's job but no adequate explanation is given as to how the results are to be used, supervisors will minimize the importance of appraisals. Finally, because PA involves the giving of con-structive feedback to a subordinate, a talent most bosses don't intuitively possess and a technique for which most organizations don't provide adequate training, supervisors are uncomfortable with the one-on-one appraisal interview.

Subordinates have misgivings about appraisals, especially if they anticipate criticism that tears down their self-esteem. This may lead to defensiveness and little likelihood of wanting to improve.

Some PA systems require supervisors to make woefully subjective judgments about what is being appraised—for example, by requiring rating of an employee's attitude. Supervisors certainly form opinions about such broad and abstract employee attributes as attitude, loyalty, creativity, dependability, initiative, and judgment; but to ask them to evaluate these attributes is equivalent to asking them to be practicing psychologists. And although supervisors will make these evaluations when required to do so, it is unfair of the organization to ask them to defend those ratings.

A related problem has been the overemphasis on putting together a PA system that is complete, sophisticated, valid, and fail-safe. Often systems are so elaborate and cumbersome that supervisors resist (with good reason) management's attempt to implement them. Filling out periodic evaluation forms can be a supervisor's biggest headache.

There are a wide variety of appraisal mechanisms available, ranging from the traditional graphic scales to results-oriented systems. Each has its own merits and limitations, but as yet there is no such thing as a perfect performance appraisal system. The critical factor in determining the optimal appraisal system for an organization is the degree of trust prevalent. The more supportive the organization is of the employee, the more subjective the rating system can be and still maintain some degree of effectiveness.

Weak or subjective forms can be effectively used if the supervisor is willing to take time to translate the "fuzzies" into specific and meaningful job behaviors. Being able to tell an employee, for example, what "attitude" means, as well as define how job performance relates to attitude, can make all the difference. Good documentation, however, is the basis for making subjective evaluation systems work.

Finally, supervisors should concentrate on linking nonmonetary rewards to good performance. Talking about compensation can create more problems than it solves, so it is usually best to discuss monetary issues separately from employee development. Monetary incentives, while popular, are difficult to implement and administer. Where they are possible, pay-for-performance plans need to be part of a more comprehensive reward system. Specific nonmonetary rewards such as greater responsibility, recognition, and employee development make the total reward system appealing to almost everyone. It is worth remembering, too, that supervisors have more control over nonmonetary rewards than they do over salary matters.

IS THERE A BETTER WAY?

Mike Miller was not very fond of personnel rating systems. He had always felt, too keenly perhaps, that the evaluations he made of an individual's performance could dramatically, and sometimes drastically, affect the man's entire career. This was a little too close to omnipotence to suit Mike. Still, it was that time again and, since there wasn't any use in delaying the unpleasant chore past Friday's deadline, Mike got out the 15 rating sheets and started to work.

He had barely gotten started when Pat Parsons, one of the new managers from another department, knocked on his door and asked for a few minutes of time. Noting that Mike was working on the evaluation forms, Pat commented upon the coincidence since this was why he had come to talk. It developed that Pat had no previous experience in rating people and was seeking advice how to proceed.

Mike found himself in a quandary. He knew what he did and how he went about the task, but he was not at all sure that his approach was the best possible. He wanted to help Pat but was reluctant to give advice about a matter in which he truly lacked confidence in his own actions.

As might be expected, Mike temporized, while he gathered his thoughts, by talking about the company's policy statements concerning evaluations. Those written statements expressed the philosophical bases for having personnel evaluations, gave some general guidance regarding completion of the rating forms, and established the reporting and reviewing dates.

Pat listened quietly until Mike finished and then stated that, while this was all well and good, he needed to know specifically how Mike really approached the actual rating of each of his men. Seeing that there was no avoiding the issue, Mike briefly described his procedure as:

1. Comparing the individual's output in terms of what is expected of him.
2. Evaluating the individual's knowledge of his job.
3. Ascertaining how the person relates to his fellow workers and his superior.
4. Estimating his future potential.

Mike stated that this framework permitted him to establish an overall impression of the worker's value to the organization and, from that, he proceeded to record the individual markings required on the form. Mike said that he rarely made any extra written remarks, although it was permissible to do so. Mike concluded his remarks by saying that he mentally ranked his subordinates in an order-of-precedence list and then checked to see that the evaluation ratings came out correctly. If not, he made some adjustments in the ratings.

In response to Pat's question as to whether Mike kept a running record of his subordinates' performance during the rating period, Mike stated that he used to do so but had not found it helped too much, so he stopped. Mike explained that he considered progress, which was best shown in recent performance, to be a better rating basis than trying to "average-out" a full rating period's activity.

The next question was really a difficult one for Mike to answer. Specifically, Pat wanted to know whether Mike gave much thought to morale factors in making his markings. After talking about the matter for some minutes, Mike finally admitted that he did consider morale to a great extent.

Mike also was asked if he knew how other supervisors marked, and if he tried to keep in line with the other raters. Mike admitted he had some general idea, but no specific knowledge, of how other people rated their subordinates. Mike expressed the hope that he rated as highly as others did, since he didn't want his good men to suffer because of a difference in raters. Mike admitted that he leaned a little toward the "high side" of the sheet just to be sure of this but defended this action by saying he had some top-notch people in his branch. Mike gave as an example the fact that one of his subordinates, who was the fastest man with figures Mike had ever seen, always received an outstanding rating. After all, as Mike noted, if he was the best "figures man" in the division, no one should be able to get a better rating.

The next question was concerned with the factors Mike considered in assessing a subordinate's potential. Mike said that he considered, basically, the promotability of the employee. If a man was qualified to be promoted—i.e., trained, had sufficient time in grade, and was a good man—then his potential was good. If he wasn't ready for promotion for some reason, then his potential was obviously limited, at this time. Mike stated that he had found it necessary to use this approach in order to be consistent in his rating. He explained that he found it impossible to say that a man had good potential but that he wasn't good enough to be promoted.

Pat's final question was to ask Mike how he handled the counseling interview sessions required by agency policy. Mike said that he had encountered no real problems. You simply told the outstanding employees they were doing a fine job, which they already knew, and advised them to keep up the good work. The few average subordinates were advised that they had done a good job and to keep on improving their performance. Mike did admit that, on two occasions, he had given marginal ratings to employees. In both cases, he told the employees that their work was passable but not as good as they could do if they applied themselves. Both men left the company for other jobs within a few months of the counseling session. Mike was of the opinion that their performance potential was so poor that they and the company were better off for their departure.

Pat thanked Mike for his assistance and advice and returned to his office.

1. What type of rating system is Mike ultimately using on his subordinates? Could Mike defend his ratings to the subordinates' satisfaction?
2. What rating errors is Mike committing? How might these errors be minimized?
3. Explain how measuring subordinate performance in terms of morale might lead to subordinate confusion and, possibly, resentment.
4. Are Mike's objectives for performance appraisal realistic? Can he accomplish evaluation, counseling, and development during a single appraisal meeting? How might Mike go about accomplishing all of these things?

Source: William D. Heier, Arizona State University. This case appears in John E. Dittrich and Robert A. Zawacki (eds.), *People and Organizations: Cases in Management and Organizational Behavior*, (Dallas, Texas: Business Publications, Inc., 1981), pp. 278–279.

DISCUSSION QUESTIONS

1. Why are appraisals necessary?
2. It has been said that supervisors are reluctant to conduct performance appraisals. Why might this be the case?
3. Explain what might happen if your performance appraisal system was strictly MBO, and the only thing that mattered was whether you achieved a specific set of measurable goals.
4. Explain what might happen if your organization's appraisal system was completely centered on such items as loyalty, attitude, and dependability.
5. How can inconsistency across raters be minimized?
6. Is it more important to emphasize results at the expense of activities (processes) or vice versa? Explain.
7. Some organizations have spent literally thousands of dollars on the development of sophisticated performance mechanisms (forms and techniques) and yet the overall performance results are not much better than before the new system was installed. What reasons might cause such failures?
8. What is the most common and difficult error that raters have to deal with?
9. Assume that the organization for which you work is very supportive of the employee. What appraisal system would be effective and not too expensive to implement?

REFERENCES

Beer, Michael, and Ruh, Robert A. "Employee Growth Through Performance Management." *Harvard Business Review* (July–August 1976): 59–66.

Colby, John D., and Wallace, Ronald L. "Performance Appraisal: Help or Hindrance to Employee Productivity?" *The Personnel Administrator* (October 1975): 39–49.

How to Review and Evaluate Employee Performance. Chicago: The Dartnell Corp., 1976.

Levinson, Harry. "Appraisal of What Performance?" *Harvard Business Review.* July–August 1975: 30–46.

McGregor, Douglas. "An Uneasy Look at Performance Appraisal." *Harvard Business Review* (May–June 1957): 89–94.

Meyer, Herbert E. "The Science of Telling Executives How They're Doing." *Fortune* (January 1974): 102–112.

Meyer, Herbert H.; Kay, Emanuel; and French, John R. P., Jr. "Split Roles in Performance Appraisal." *Harvard Business Review* (January–February 1965): 123–129.

Millard, Cheadle W.; Luthans, Fred; and Ottemann, Robert L. "A New Breakthrough for Performance Appraisal." *Business Horizons* (August 1976): 66–73.

Oberg, Winston. "Make Performance Appraisal Relevant." *Harvard Business Review* (January–February 1972): 61–67.

Reider, George A. "Performance Review—A Mixed Bag." *Harvard Business Review* (July–August 1973): 61–67.

Schrader, Albert W. "Let's Abolish the Annual Performance Review." *Management of Personnel Quarterly* (Fall 1969): 20–28.

Williams, M. R. *Performance Appraisal in Management.* London: Heinemann Ltd., 1972.

CHAPTER 8

APPRAISAL INTERVIEWING: DEVELOPING ONE-ON-ONE FEEDBACK SKILLS

If you can't say anything nice, don't say anything at all.

—Somebody's Mother

Chapter Outline

Objectives

Understanding the appraisal process is the first step in giving constructive feedback. The second step is developing one-on-one feedback skills. This step is absolutely critical for managing and improving performance on a day-to-day basis. Specifically, in this chapter you will become familiar with:

1. The characteristics of effective appraisal interviews
2. The benefits of good feedback skills
3. How to plan for the appraisal session
4. Three different methods for giving constructive feedback
5. The means for resolving disagreement and conflict

Major Concepts ————————————

Leniency   Self-appraisal
Feedback   Tell-and-sell
Scorekeeper   Tell-and-listen
Coach   Problem solving
Counselor   Perception sharing
Performance standards   Trust
Specific objectives

WHERE DO I BEGIN?

When Andy Thompson knocked on his boss's office door, he was invited in and asked to take a seat. Andy was a first-line shipping manager for the Turnkey Lock Company, a medium-size manufacturer of home security systems located in Willmette, Illinois. He came to Turnkey a year ago, after graduating from Northwestern University with a major in organizational behavior. Andy declined an offer of coffee from his boss, Frank Mayfield, as he didn't want anything to upset an already queasy stomach. This was Andy's first performance evaluation, and he was noticeably nervous about the meeting with Frank. Frank sensed Andy's high anxiety and tried to put him at ease with an off-color joke—a tactic Frank often used with all his subordinates. After chuckling at his own punchline, Frank began:

"Andy, as you know, the purpose of our meeting this morning is to review your performance for the past year. I'm sure you've seen the form we use, so I won't bore you with explanations. Since we're both pretty busy, I'll try to get this over as quickly as possible. Let me begin by highlighting the important points of the form and how you've done.

"First, the 'quantity of work' has been OK. You and your group have always met the production targets assigned to you. Also, the quality hasn't been too bad either. In fact, except for that screw-up in shipping out the wrong order, I don't recall any real problems in quality.

"The next area is attitude. I gave you a high rating on this. You're never late or absent, and you always seem to be willing to stay late on short notice. I've also heard from reliable sources in other departments that you're easy to work with.

"While you have generally been a pretty good supervisor, there is *one* thing I want you to work on. Your leadership style is too soft and too 'marshmellowy' for the kind of people who work on the loading dock. They're a tough group and need to be supervised closely and with authority. Don't be afraid to crack the whip, because if you don't, they'll eat you alive. Other than that, I see no problems.

"So, if you don't have any questions, I'm going to give you an overall rating of satisfactory and recommend that you receive some merit."

Andy was numb. Sure he had questions. For example, what about some of the other items on the form, such as "responsibility," "initiative," and "problem solving skill"? And why didn't Frank mention the time Andy gave up his weekend at the lake as a favor to Frank because a rush order had to get out by Monday morning? And what did Frank mean when he said Andy's leadership style is too "marshmellowy"? "Where do I even begin?" Andy wondered. But as the moments passed, so did his courage. "No sir, I don't have any questions."

The interview between supervisor and subordinate is the most crucial element in a performance appraisal system. It is also, as organizations—profit and nonprofit, large and small—readily admit, the weakest. Supervisors candidly state they feel ineffective in handling one-on-one feedback sessions. Even with the best intentions, they often make a situation worse with the appraisal interview.

Appraisal sessions often have negative effects on subordinates—even good performers. They can walk away from an appraisal just as discouraged as anyone else. Ironically, low performers can actually leave the interview relatively unscathed and seemingly unaware that performance improvements are imperative. This situation can occur because the supervisor's approach to the good and poor performer is inconsistent. In a thirty-minute appraisal interview with the good performer, for example, the supervisor will typically spend only five to ten minutes on the strong points of the subordinate's performance—generally relying on broad statements of praise. Negative remarks often represent the largest amount of time and dialogue, producing a negative effect, despite the employee's overall good rating. Paradoxically, poor performers are handled much more delicately. With them, the interview will tend to be longer; any criticism is usually mild and unthreatening; and criticism will often be sandwiched between positive opening remarks and an uplifting "You can do it" speech at the end. Low performers, all too frequently, leave the appraisal meeting without ever realizing that they need to improve.

The problem is due, in part, to the supervisor's lack of training in appraisal skills. Too much emphasis is placed on amateur psychology. Supervisors, for example, assume that good performers can take criticism. However, the unpleasant task of raking the poor performer over the coals is approached with caution and is often not done at all. Supervisors need to learn practical and proven appraisal techniques that teach them how to give constructive criticism. This chapter will focus on how the feedback skills of a supervisor might be developed.

Overview of a ━━━━━━━━━━━━━━
Feedback System

The development of effective appraisal skills cannot occur overnight. The supervisor's desire to develop a better interview technique is not enough. An improved technique takes time, commitment, and above all, practice. It begins with the supervisor collecting as much pertinent and factual information as possible regarding the subordinate's performance. The supervisor must also have the desire and skills to listen, ask probing questions, clarify, review, empathize, and above all, maintain control of emotional situations.

PA interview is a feedback device

There is a universal desire to know how well we are doing and what others think of us. The appraisal interview is the feedback mechanism for giving the employee this important information. Without it, employees inevitably end up floundering around and misdirecting their efforts.

PA is a control device

Performance appraisals are control devices. Good appraisal systems identify the job behaviors that lead to effective performance, thus enabling the employee to be rewarded. Good appraisal systems also identify job behaviors that should be terminated. The combination of feedback and control, applied constructively, will provide the employee with direction and purpose. On the whole, people dislike uncertainty and prefer a predictable work environment. Performance feedback on a continuous basis can provide a predictable work environment.

An appraisal system that enables the supervisor to document performance (effective or ineffective) is required. Such a system will give the supervisor greater confidence and competence in preparing and conducting the appraisal interview. If the face-to-face session is to be effective, two factors must be present. First, there must be adequate documentation—to ensure that the feedback is accepted by the subordinate. The previous chapter noted the different types of appraisal methods, but having a good rating system is not sufficient in itself. It must be delivered well, which takes proper preparation. Second, the supervisor must have good communication skills. This means the ability and readiness to listen as well as to speak. He or she must direct the interview in a way that is neither too overbearing nor too informal. Most important, the supervisor must be able to pass along negative or unpleasant information to the subordinate in a constructive fashion.

> Good records plus good delivery

> Good communication skills

WHY APPRAISAL SESSIONS ARE INEFFECTIVE

Most people, in anticipating an event they perceive to be unpleasant, will avoid thinking about it. But such a reaction prevents them from making adequate preparation and thus serves only to bring about what they dreaded in the first place—an unpleasant experience. Again, it is the phenomenon of the self-fulfilling prophecy: If you think an event or activity is going to be disastrous, then chances are that it will indeed be as bad as you had anticipated—or worse.[1]

> The self-fulfilling prophecy

Proper preparation is essential to effective interviewing. Careful thought concerning the purpose of the interview, the proper topics to be covered, the types of questions that should be asked, and other relevant matters should never be left to chance. Don't just throw out a few ideas off the top of your head. Such tactics are usually a waste of time and effort. Planning in advance the topics to be covered is not easy; but the effort is worthwhile, and it usually becomes easier with experience.

> Don't leave it to chance

Another reason appraisals may not be fully effective is that emotions frequently get out of control. Loss of emotional control can completely negate the purpose of the interview. When emotions arise, a cool head is required to maintain composure and direction. Realistically, supervisors should expect occasional verbal abuse. But expecting it and handling it are two separate matters. The latter involves a degree of maturity and understanding that training seldom provides. When an employee becomes angry, for example, let him have his say. Afterward, try to

> Learn to control the situation

[1] For a more thorough understanding of the self-fulfilling prophecy see J. Sterling Livingston, "Pygmalion in Management," *Harvard Business Review*, July–August 1969, or Robert Rosenthal, "The Pygmalion Effect Lives," *Psychology Today*, September 1973.

find out the cause. Your sincerity will seldom go unnoticed. Over time, the patience you acquire will defuse many explosive situations.

WHY BOTHER TO DEVELOP FEEDBACK SKILLS?

Is it worth a supervisor's time and effort to learn feedback skills? Some argue that since performance appraisal is done only once or twice a year, the time and effort needed to develop adequate skills are hardly worthwhile. But this is short-sighted thinking. The skills needed for effective feedback will also be useful in the day-to-day interpersonal activities of the supervisor.

Why good feedback skills are needed

Good feedback skills can provide a number of benefits. Asking subordinates their ideas during the interview (or almost any time) encourages participation. And employee participation is the first step in attaining commitment. Having something personal at stake, such as an implemented suggestion, often results in more effort by subordinates to complete the project successfully. Good feedback skills are also necessary to set realistic and challenging objectives.

The creation of a supportive and nonthreatening relationship may also result from good feedback skills. A helpful and constructive attitude by the supervisor defuses confrontations over performance problems and minimizes threats to the subordinate's self-esteem. In this kind of environment the subordinate is less likely to hide mistakes or avoid the supervisor when there is a problem too big for the subordinate to handle.

WHAT'S WRONG WITH BEING LENIENT?

Leniency

Giving a worker a higher rating than he or she deserved is called leniency. It has the effect of grouping everyone together and not distinguishing effective performance from ineffective. It is a double-edged sword, in that the good worker goes unrewarded and the poor worker is not provided the opportunity to improve. It occurs when supervisors have inadequate interpersonal skills, a lack of self-confidence, a high need to be liked, and/or a poorly documented appraisal system.

Leniency affects morale

For the short run, leniency appears to make everyone happy (except top management), but this is deceptive. Sooner or later co-workers will hear about the employee who didn't really deserve merit but received some anyway. Usually (although not always) the effect leniency has on morale is negative. Employees who receive merit and are deserving of it become demotivated. Receiving merit (as well as other rewards) implies recognition for above average performance; but when almost everyone begins receiving merit, it becomes nothing more than a glorified cost-of-living adjustment.

Not only does leniency have a harmful effect on the group's morale, it really doesn't do the undeserving employee much good either. She is led into the belief that she is doing better than average work, and she then tends to rationalize that maybe she really did deserve the reward. Some supervisors back themselves, and top management, into a corner by giving undeserved merit one year and the next year attempting to terminate the worker. Understandably, the worker has a hard time trying to reconcile a meritorious rating one year and termination the next. In union settings, management is almost always forced into backing down on termination. In nonunion settings, it is becoming more common to hear of terminated workers taking the case to court.

Undeserved rewards

HOW TO RECOGNIZE THE AVERAGE EMPLOYEE

Some supervisors are prone to extremes. They either go too far by giving almost everyone merit, or they become miserly and give it out as if it were coming out of their own pockets. For the average employee it means either feast or famine—supervisors are too generous or they provide no recognition whatsoever.

Some of the most experienced supervisors still find it hard to discuss employee performance with the average worker. During the appraisal interview, supervisors sometimes slip into using such overworked adjectives as "good," "very good," "very satisfactory," and "excellent." Yet trying to emphasize the positive side of the employee's performance may lead to trouble. The supervisor may merely mislead the worker with these generous adjectives into believing that his or her overall performance falls within the meritorious range. When told that the overall rating is only satisfactory, the employee begins to show signs of resentment.

Emphasizing the positive can backfire

At the other extreme are supervisors who are uncomfortable about praising any aspect of the employee's performance. Employees complain, "The only time my supervisor talks to me about the job is when I screw up!" Certainly there are times when formal criticism is necessary. But continually dwelling on the negative gives the employee the perception that his or her good work is unimportant.

But don't be entirely negative, either

Discussing performance with the average worker demands at least as much preparation as with the poor or outstanding worker. Careful thought is needed in developing a dialogue that does not create unrealistic expectations about either rewards or punishments. The dialogue should emphasize what is expected in terms of the subordinate's performance. If possible, goals should be set that encourage the employee to strive even harder, stressing the connection between specific accomplishments and meritorious rating. There is nothing wrong in recognizing an employ-

Don't create unrealistic expectations

ee's strengths as long as it is done within the context of future performance.

In sum, the key to recognizing the average performer is no different
than recognizing any other performer. The focus should be on performance—not personality. Do not fall prey to using those overworked
adjectives; discuss the performance in specific and candid language. Recognize the employee's strengths in terms of a base on which improvement
is not only possible but expected. Demonstrate your sincerity in wanting
to help by offering assistance when unusual problems are encountered.
And always answer these questions for the worker: How am I doing?
And where do I go from here?

THE SUPERVISOR'S DILEMMA

Not surprisingly, many supervisors believe they are paid for what they
do—for the responsibility they carry and for managing others. But this
is not entirely accurate. A supervisor is rewarded for what *subordinates*
accomplish. The point is that the supervisor needs subordinates more
than they need the supervisor. Since your reward as supervisor will be
based on their performance, you should do everything possible to create
working relationships conducive to successful performance.

Scorekeeper

Certainly this does not mean giving up the role of scorekeeper. If
organizations are to be managed effectively and efficiently, someone must
make judgments as to the quality of employee performance. As a supervisor, you cannot divorce yourself from this role. It is a responsibility
you must accept, however reluctantly.

TABLE 8.1   The Primary Roles of a Supervisor

---

1. Scorekeeper
    —Keep tabs on performance
    —Allocate rewards
    —Make unpopular decisions

2. Coach
    —Help subordinates learn the right way to do a job
    —Encourage them
    —Correct less than satisfactory performance

3. Counselor
    —Help subordinates make important decisions
    —Listen to their side of a story and maintain an open mind
    —Provide resources when subordinates have problems that they and the
      supervisor together cannot solve

On the other hand, if you want to correct performance that you have judged to be unsatisfactory, you must also be able to assume other roles as well—those of coach and counselor. This is the supervisor's dilemma. You must be capable of playing three roles: scorekeeper, coach, and counselor (see Table 8.1). Convincingly playing the role of a scorekeeper is easier than counseling. Nevertheless, the position of supervisor does provide a natural base for counseling. The dilemma occurs when the supervisor attempts to carry out all of these functions at the same time.

> Coach and counselor

Preparing for the Appraisal Interview

Good appraisal interviews do not just happen. They result from diligent preparation and knowing how to use such interviewing tools as job description, performance standards, specific objectives, and an incidents file (see Table 8.2).

TABLE 8.2 Tools for Building a Good Performance Appraisal Interview

1. Job description	An item-by-item list of principal duties, responsibilities, and accountability
2. Performance standards	The conditions that will exist when a job is well done; to establish performance standards: a. Determine what's to be done b. Determine how results can be measured
3. Specific objectives	Targets—mutually established by employer and employee—that are realistic, stretching, measurable, and achievable within a given length of time
4. Incidents file	A clear and specific record of both positive and negative happenings, to aid the recall of good and bad performance; entries should be recorded and discussed at the time of happening
5. Questions on which to base the appraisal	a. What results do you want to achieve from the appraisal? b. What contribution is the employee making? c. Is the employee working toward his/her potential? d. What training does the employee need?

Set the stage

Proper planning includes scheduling a time well in advance and locating a place that is free of interruptions. Scheduling during the middle of the morning or afternoon is usually better because it is then that people are most alert. Telephone interruptions are particularly annoying, so either remove the receiver from the phone, have calls rerouted, or find a conference room away from such distractions. Arrange not to be interrupted. Plan to devote enough time so that rushing through the issues is unnecessary. Figure 8.1 outlines the steps in preparing for a performance appraisal interview.

Self Appraisal

Although some organizations do not ask subordinates to prepare ahead, it is usually in their own best interests for employees to spend some time organizing their own thoughts on the issues. Ask subordinates to evaluate their own performance and to bring to the interview whatever materials or information they may need. But mention that you will share your perceptions of their performance with them only at the designated time, not before. Self-appraisal is recommended because it requires subordinates to collect their thoughts and review the rating period, resulting in a two-way discussion rather than a monologue by the supervisor.

Explain the process

To build confidence, indicate to subordinates prior to the interview the purpose of the session and how it will be conducted, and make clear that they will be free to express their opinions openly. Be positive and enthusiastic about the session. Emphasize your desire to create even better working relationships. The more subordinates understand about the interview, the more comfortable they will be in preparing for it.

As a supervisor, your preparation requires greater diligence and forethought than the subordinate's. The following are some specific guidelines to follow in preparing for a feedback session:

Preparation for a feedback session

1. Define the objectives of the interview (e.g., counseling as opposed to compensation) and the desired outcomes.
2. Determine the interview style that will work best; formulate questions to get the subordinate talking and to find out how things are going.
3. Formulate your ratings, being as specific about job performance as possible.
4. Gather documentation that will substantiate your assessment of the subordinate's performance.
5. Practice empathy; put yourself in the subordinate's place: How is he or she likely to react? How would you react? Can defensiveness be minimized?
6. Before assuming you have all of the facts, take time to double-check with others. Remember the only view you have is your own, and that may not be entirely accurate.

FIGURE 8.1

Steps in Planning for a Performance Appraisal Interview

PERFORMANCE APPRAISAL CHECKLIST

1. Do I have the TOOLS I need for the appraisal?

    ☐ Job description   ☐ Incidents file
    ☐ Performance standards   ☐ Rating form
    ☐ Specific objectives

2. What CHANGES do I want to accomplish in the employee?

    Attitude _____

    Productivity _____

    Effectiveness _____

3. GOALS (During the appraisal write at least one sentence on how to meet these goals):

    a. Increase rapport with the employee. _____

        _____

    b. Fully communicate what is expected of him/her on the job. _____

        _____

    c. Increase the employee's understanding of how his/her job is important in relation to the whole organization.

        _____

    d. Review (together with employee) the job description, performance standards, and objectives, and discuss whether the employee is working within the guidelines stated in these documents. Do they need to be updated or changed? _____

        _____

    e. Establish what change in direction (if any) the employee must make to meet his/her job description and objectives. _____

        _____

4. What attitudes and beliefs do I hold about the employee's personality, appearance, interests, and work habits and methods? Am I letting my biases affect my view of him/her?

5. Schedule the appraisal interview several days in advance—beginning time, ending time, place. If at all possible, make sure it is convenient for him/her.

6. Inform the employee what will be expected of him/her and how you would like him/her to prepare for the interview (e.g., a self-evaluation of his/her performance based on the job description, objectives, responsibilities, agreed upon projects, and relevant materials or information).

Be sure to ANSWER these three questions for the employee:
1. How am I doing?
2. Where do I go from here?
3. What are my most outstanding skills and abilities?

7. Condition yourself to listen—one way this can be done is to remain open to new inputs.

Evaluate your own attitudes

Preparing for a feedback session also requires that you ask yourself some pertinent, realistic questions. Have I formed any opinions about the "worth" of this employee? Does one particular aspect of his behavior or personality influence my overall perception of his performance? Am I letting our out-of-the-office relationship affect my judgment? Being honest with oneself about personal feelings and biases is a critical part in preparing for a useful appraisal session. Recognizing that you may be favoring one subordinate over another does not doom your chances for success. It only points up the need for increased objectivity.

Methods of ———————————————
Appraisal Interviewing

A foremost authority on appraisal interviewing, Norman R. F. Maier, defined three basic interview styles: tell-and-sell, tell-and-listen, and the problem-solving approach.[2] The sheer volume of literature on problem solving suggests it is the best approach. But it is important to look at the other two methods in order to be aware of their applicability. As you read these, ask yourself: Is this *my* natural style? Do I really want to stay with this style? What must I do to change to a more productive approach?

TELL-AND-SELL

Simply stated, tell-and-sell involves informing the subordinate what must be changed and how it shall be done. This method works only when there is high trust and credibility between supervisor and subordinate. It is also necessary that the subordinate have the desire and the skills to change.

Demands both judge and helper roles

The difficulty in using this approach is that supervisors must play two roles. One role is similar to that of a concerned parent—as an all-knowing authority figure. The second role is that of helper or "good guy." But it is difficult to combine these two quite different roles. It requires the supervisor to be both judge and confidant. Whatever success occurs is usually due to the ability of the supervisor to persuade the

[2] Norman R. F. Maier, *The Appraisal Interview: Three Basic Approaches* (La Jolla, Calif.: University Associates, 1976).

employee to change in the desired direction (the "sell" part of the approach).

When change is arbitrarily imposed, however, it usually meets strong resistance. Tell-and-sell is a one-sided transaction; it lacks subordinate input. Few explanations are given. The subordinate often feels threatened in such situations. In an effort to reduce the effects of this feeling of threat, the subordinate will attempt face-saving measures. He will try anything to reduce the appearance of lacking ability. Although the subordinate may choose to hide his negative feelings for the present, over time the frustration can build and create a potentially explosive situation. Resentment directed against the supervisor is frequently the outcome.

"Telling" may build resentment

There are a few instances in which the tell-and-sell method might work effectively. One such instance would be the young worker who is impressionable and more than willing to accept the opinions and direction of an older, experienced supervisor. Another instance is one in which a supervisor is considered by subordinates to be an expert on the topic he or she is trying to sell. Such expertise is often sufficient when attempting to convince others. All things considered, however, the tell-and-sell method fails more often than it succeeds. It is just not very conducive to developing two-way communication.

When tell-and-sell might work

TELL-AND-LISTEN

Maier's second method of appraisal interviewing is tell-and-listen. Recall that tell-and-sell's chief disadvantage is the assumption that a high level of trust exists. With tell-and-listen, the importance of this assumption is somewhat lessened. As the title implies, the first part of the interview is the same. The supervisor tells the subordinate what is wrong and what should be done to correct it.

In the second part of the interview, however, the supervisor takes the time to listen. The hope is that the subordinate will use this as an opportunity to release frustrations that are blocking improved performance, that by giving the subordinate a chance to express whatever misgivings he is experiencing, resistance to change will be reduced. Once anxieties are released, the subordinate will supposedly be ready to listen to suggested remedial measures and more willing to change in the desired direction.

Attempts to release anxieties

Before attempting this method, consider some pros and cons. On the positive side, by taking the time to *listen*, you may learn about aspects of the subordinate's job never before known. External factors that have been interfering with successful performance may come to light. Other deficiencies inherent in the job itself (lack of appropriate training or poor feedback processes) may be discovered.

Prepare yourself for abuse

However, before any positive results occur, you as supervisor may well be the recipient of verbal abuse. If this should occur, the session could degenerate into an all-out confrontation. In order to minimize the possibility of creating even greater resistance in the subordinate, you should be prepared. Assuming that tempers cool after a while, a second difficulty may yet occur. Because the plan of action is still the supervisor's, the subordinate may feel he has little at stake should it fail. Since tell-and-listen does not draw on the strengths and ideas of the subordinate, it usually results in little or no acceptance of the supervisor's recommendations. When a positive change does occur, it is likely to be of only short duration.

THE PROBLEM-SOLVING APPROACH

In a sense, the problem-solving approach is not a formal performance evaluation at all. This method has just one objective—that of changing behavior. This aim is accomplished by concentrating the interview on the employee's capacity to grow and develop with the job. It looks to the future as well as dwelling on the past.

Emphasis is on solving problems

The method ignores numerous other objectives often assumed in traditional appraisal systems. Compensation decisions, for example, are not the intent, nor are disciplinary actions considered. This method does not subscribe to the passing of judgment on the worker. It does not tell the employee how management has appraised her past performance. Instead, the problem-solving method helps the employee to examine her own performance and behavior. It is hoped that self-review will allow the employee to reflect more honestly on past behaviors and provide a personal plan for improvement.

The basis for such high expectations is simple: There is a reduction in anxiety and in the need for face-saving behaviors, because the interview is not a confrontation and is not intended to be threatening.

Relies on self-diagnosis

Since the primary purpose of this method is the development of the employee, it emphasizes the use of self-examination. The employee, by admitting that a problem exists and suggesting a means for correcting it, also accepts the obligation of living up to whatever commitments are made. With other methods of appraisal interviewing, the employee is prone to take a defensive attitude. The primary concern becomes the defense of previous performance, and little thought is given to improvements in future performance.

The skills a supervisor needs are much more complex with problem solving than with other methods. Perhaps this is the reason that other methods are more widely used. Certainly this approach is personally demanding. Any time lines of communication are cleared, a supervisor becomes more vulnerable because his or her motives and actions are open to scrutiny. Fear of failure may cause a supervisor to limit the conversation to a one-way dialogue in order to escape possible public criticism of his or her own alleged deficiencies. For supervisors who are normally dominant and aggressive, this difficulty can be a major obstacle.

> **Supervisor is more vulnerable**

Developing Problem-Solving Skills. The basic skill the supervisor must have in problem solving is the skill of listening. The emphasis of the approach is on encouraging the employee to identify the problems. Both the supervisor and the subordinate must be open to new information, even when some of it flies in the face of old assumptions. The supervisor accomplishes the role of helper by discussing job behavior rather than personality improvement. Comparison of the following two statements will demonstrate the weakness in discussing personality development:

1. "Abner, your attitude regarding the transfer of Pete (a co-worker) suggests you disapproved of my judgment. I think you need to improve your attitude if you want to get ahead here."
2. "Abner, I've noticed a definite decline in your productivity over the past two weeks. In fact, since Pete was transferred, your output has dropped 23 percent. I wonder if there is any way we can correct the drop?"

The first statement implies that a judgment has been made about Abner's attitude. The boss has already diagnosed the cause of the problem. Whether the diagnosis is correct is almost irrelevant at this point. What is relevant is that the boss has ordered Abner to do something about his attitude. But what is attitude? And how can Abner improve it? The boss considers this issue to be Abner's problem. Abner, if he is like most of us, will become defensive. No one appreciates hearing comments that reflect negatively on oneself. More important, the inability of the boss to translate an abstract concept, such as attitude, into specific situational examples makes correction unlikely. The subordinate needs a plan for improvement that defines exactly the type of job behavior expected.

> **First statement is judgmental and abstract**

Second statement keeps an open mind, shares responsibility

The second example, in contrast, begins with a statement of fact. Performance has declined by 23 percent. And no assumptions are made about the cause for the drop in production. This is important. Even when the supervisor has a fairly sound idea of the reason for the problem, she refrains from making a diagnosis. She wants the subordinate to identify the cause. The likelihood of the subordinate being willing to change is much greater when he, and not the supervisor, identifies the cause. Notice, too, that the boss in the second statement presented the problem as one of mutual responsibility. It isn't Abner's problem, it is "our problem." Sharing responsibility for a subordinate's problems helps to produce an atmosphere of mutual interest, creativity, and trust.

A limitation of this method is that the supervisor is often not sufficiently skilled to steer the discussion in a nondirective fashion. Too often, a supervisor will become impatient with the slow progress and inject his or her own diagnosis and remedy instead of remaining neutral. Then again, there are those subordinates who react negatively to this seemingly unstructured and permissive interview. They are more comfortable being told what to do and how to do it.

Nevertheless, if your intention is to do everything you can to help your subordinates do their very best, then this approach is for you. The problem-solving method is the most complex style of appraisal counseling and requires a great deal of time, effort, and practice. But it is the most effective in correcting performance deficiencies.

WHICH METHOD IS BEST?

Decide on the purpose before you choose a style

Three basically different approaches to appraisal interviewing have been presented. Which method is best? The answer really depends on the reason for the interview. Trying to accomplish more than one objective within a single interview might, in some cases, lead to failure with the whole interview. Linking discussions of merit to agreement on job problems, for example, is almost impossible to do because the employee will tend to deny there are problems (or argue that they are "just minor") if he feels that admitting their existence will jeopardize his merit increase. Consequently, you must know what you want to achieve from the interview before you can choose the most effective interview method.

If the primary objective of the interview is to communicate evaluation and rewards, then the tell-and-sell method is appropriate. It may also be used as a means for letting an employee know what he needs to do to improve. It does demand, however, considerable skill from the supervisor—the ability to persuade the employee to change in the desired direction.

Should a supervisor perceive a high amount of resistance from the subordinate prior to the interview, then an alternative method is tell-and-listen. After an initial evaluation of the employee's performance by the supervisor, the employee is encouraged to relate his personal feelings. Although it will not always work, the opportunity to say what's really on one's mind is often too good to pass up. Unloading on the supervisor may reveal problems that are correctable—but not always. Sometimes the supervisor will be open-minded enough to alter her views in light of the employee's responses; at other times the supervisor will choose to ignore what is said. The danger lies in the supervisor taking an employee's remarks defensively—thus leading to a complete breakdown in communications.

When the purpose of the interview is employee development and not to pass judgment on the quality of an employee's past performance through rating or ranking, then the supervisor should consider the problem-solving approach. This method is designed for counseling the employee about job-related problems. Instead of playing a scorekeeper role, the supervisor acts as a helper—listening, reflecting ideas and feelings, and asking pertinent questions. The focus is on developing a plan for improvement—a plan that is based on employee commitment. We recommend this method because it keeps the lines of communication open between worker and management. But when the formal evaluation interview is taking place, the problem-solving method fails to tell an employee where he stands.

The choice of method does not have to be an either-or one. There is nothing wrong with mixing interview styles. There may be times, for example, when the supervisor suspects that a worker is covering-up a great deal of resentment. The supervisor decides to go initially with a tell-and-listen style so as to clear the lines of communication. After this has been accomplished, he may then move to a problem-solving approach in order to develop a plan for improvement to which the worker will feel committed.

Figure 8.2 represents a combination of the best of the tell-and-sell and problem-solving styles. The objective is to develop and agree on a program for improving employee performance. It gives the employee feedback as to where she stands, yet seeks her ideas and recommendations for future improvements. Discussions regarding merit increases are not incorporated into the framework but are held separately so that the issue of money does not detract from the real purpose of the interview.

> Why not use the best of each?

FIGURE 8.2
The Appraisal
Interview: A
Combination of the
Tell-and-Sell and
Problem-Solving
Methods

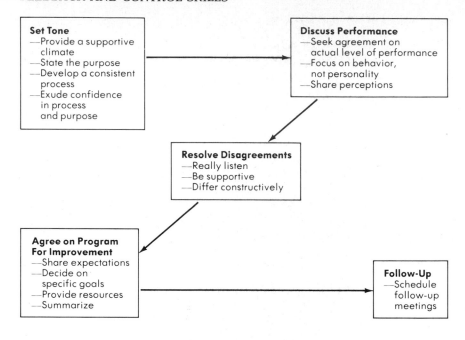

Conducting the ━━━━━━━━
Appraisal Interview

If possible, review the appraisal with a trusted colleague or your boss. A second opinion can be helpful. If opinions differ, reconcile the differences, at least to yourself, before meeting with the subordinate. Above all, do not proceed while your thoughts are still unclear or muddled. If you are not confident about your evaluation of the employee, you can't realistically expect to obtain his or her acceptance.

If the interview is to focus on the improvement of future performance, then you must be willing to follow up on promises made. Are you prepared to make a commitment? Sometimes the supervisor, in an effort to terminate an unpleasant interview, will make promises that she does not intend to fulfill. Such hypocrisy makes the interview a mere formality, to be forgotten as soon as it is concluded. The supervisor must be ready to demonstrate her sincerity. Her word must be her bond.

Other aspects of interviewing that should not be left to chance are "breaking the ice," or the choice of opening remarks (although only one part of the total process, an untimely comment may have disastrous consequences), and what is said without saying anything (nonverbal messages can be a denial of what is said verbally). Finally, not knowing how to handle serious differences of opinions can result in heated arguments that might have long-range ramifications.

BE CAREFUL WITH OPENING REMARKS

It is essential that the supervisor and subordinate get off to a good start. Opening remarks can make or break the whole discussion. Gear your approach to the individual. Assess the temperament of the subordinate. Does the person lack self-confidence? If so, plan to accentuate the positive aspects of his performance. This confidence-building strategy is necessary if deeper problems are going to be resolved.

Build confidence

Although seemingly at odds with building confidence, being forthright and truthful is another recommended strategy. Developing a relationship that is based on sincerity depends on truthfulness. Avoid the mistaken idea that it is best to gloss over deficiencies in the subordinate's performance. Let the employee know exactly where she stands, but in doing so, be tactful and considerate of her feelings. Put yourself in her shoes and ask yourself how you would want this problem brought up and handled.

Be truthful but considerate

Creating a climate that is supportive and nonthreatening to the subordinate is not an easy task. It becomes especially difficult when a performance problem occurs suddenly and must be corrected quickly. There is no time for small talk. In this instance, opening remarks can be misleading and damaging to the overall tone and direction of the conversation. The following is an example of introductory dialogue that could appear hypocritical:

> Glad you could drop by, Joan. By the way you've sure been doing a bang-up job lately. [Pause] But there is a problem you need to take care of.

The supervisor, without considering the consequences, has led the employee into a false sense of security. The employee's ego is inflated by the first part of the opening statement only to be deflated a moment later. The employee is put on the defensive, and the good intentions of the supervisor to create a comfortable atmosphere have only made the situation worse.

Avoid false build-ups

Another common, but dangerous, opening to an interview is to dangle a reward in front of the subordinate. The strategy is simple—by providing an incentive, it is hoped that desired results will occur. For example,

> Joan, you know there will be an opening for a supervisor soon, and you'll be a candidate. However, before I can recommend you, there's a problem that needs to be corrected.

Undoubtedly, the supervisor will succeed in getting the full attention of the subordinate. But will the problem be corrected? It all depends on whose problem it is. If the subordinate is the cause of the problem and desires the promotion, then she will probably do what is necessary to correct the deficiency. But if the problem stems from an external factor, something that is outside the control of the subordinate, the chance of it being solved is remote. The desire to be promoted will probably outweigh the desire for a constructive dialogue with the supervisor—particularly if the subordinate believes the supervisor is part of the problem. If this is the case, the employee will not be inclined to be candid in discussing the problem for fear of jeopardizing the promotion.

Don't mix rewards and development

Mixing rewards with development during an appraisal interview increases the chance of conflict. Developing honest dialogue becomes more difficult. In any case, even though a reward such as money or promotion is not specifically offered, the employee probably knows that the result of the interview is likely to determine future rewards.

Create a comfortable atmosphere

With practice, good opening remarks can help set the stage for developing a comfortable atmosphere. They should include a statement that the interview is important, and that the employee's work (not her personality) is the focus of the discussion. For example, one way to open up the discussion is

> Joan, I've been looking forward to this talk [and you should mean it] because it gives me a chance to find out how it's going with you and your work.

If the purpose of the interview is to discuss a particular problem that has been occurring, then a different type of opening remark might be in order:

But say what you mean

> Joan, I'm uncomfortable about the purpose of this discussion. As you probably know, there is a real problem I've got to deal with in your area. I've called you in so that maybe the two of us can put our heads together and get at the cause.

Supervisors should not be afraid to express their discomfort about some aspect of a forthcoming interview. It indicates the true reason as to why the supervisor's nonverbal cues suggest discomfort—rather than forcing the subordinate to rely on speculation.

Thus opening remarks need to be considered with care. They must be thought out and geared to the individual to be interviewed and to the topics to be discussed. A clumsy remark can jeopardize the entire interview.

WATCH WHAT YOU DO AS WELL AS WHAT YOU SAY

What you say is not the only thing that matters. Your actions can, in fact, negate what you say. When a supervisor tells a subordinate she is glad to see him but does not look him in the eye when she speaks, a contradiction in meaning occurs. The verbal message conveys a greeting, but the nonverbal message suggests otherwise. Which message is ultimately conveyed? Studies indicate that the majority of people perceive the nonverbal message to be the true one.[3]

Be consistent

Nonverbal signals can also be used for prompting elaboration on sensitive issues. Both the nod of the head and the artful use of silence can induce further discussion.

But eye contact and nodding are only a part of the nonverbal "language." Recall from an earlier chapter that posture, facial expression, tone of voice, and personal space are other meaningful communication devices.

STARTING THE DISCUSSION AND SHARING PERCEPTIONS [4]

After breaking the ice, the next step is for the supervisor to create a positive (if not enthusiastic) impression that the interview is important and not just something that management wants done. This is where planning pays off. Start by explaining to the subordinate the purpose of the interview—that the focus is performance (not personality)—what the ground rules will be (what is permissible conduct), how the interview will proceed, and how the results will be used. A good warm-up does all of these. It reduces the anxiety that normally occurs when a person first walks into an appraisal interview.

The warm-up

When the subordinate seems sufficiently aware of what is going on, the sensible thing is to ask her to lead off. Specifically, a supervisor might begin by asking, "How are things going in your area? What is going well, and what do you think you might improve?" Another way of doing this is to ask the subordinate to rate her own performance.

Have the subordinate lead off

Inviting the subordinate to lead off may stimulate her to open up and discuss sensitive issues. Waiting until after the supervisor presents his own views may inhibit the subordinate from saying what is really on her mind. In effect, this strategy involves perception sharing and is

[3] Albert Mehrabian, "Communication Without Words," *Psychology Today*, September 1968, p. 55.

[4] This section draws on Michael Beer, "Performance Appraisal: Dilemmas and Possibilities," *Organizational Dynamics* (Winter 1981), pp. 24–36; and Dartnell, *How to Review and Evaluate Employee Performance.*

Be specific

an excellent device for putting the supervisor into the shoes of the subordinate (i.e., empathizing).

When it is time for the supervisor to share his perceptions, he must do more than simply tell the employee, "You need to improve." Comments regarding perceptions must be directed at specific instances, supported by adequate documentation, and linked to any bad effects the behavior might have had on the subordinate's co-workers or on the supervisor's performance. Be able to reconstruct precisely what happened, what was said, and what was done. Under no circumstances should you cast aspersions or criticize the subordinate's integrity or general character because of poor performance. Instead, focus the interview on the event, the behavior, and the outcome.

The major problem in opening up lines of communication with the subordinate is defensiveness. Defensiveness will occur whenever either party—the subordinate or the supervisor—hears unpleasant information that begins to take on personal overtones. When one party begins to feel threatened—whether from the tone, the discussion, or the body language of the other—the intended message becomes garbled or lost. Defensiveness presents a major obstacle that only the most skilled interviewers can overcome. Table 8.3 identifies some useful rules for communicating satisfaction and dissatisfaction.

TABLE 8.3   Some Communication Rules

To Communicate Satisfaction:

Give praise where praise is due, but do not overdo it. Too much praise makes the subordinate suspect the supervisor's motives.

Reinforce successful practices or behavior. Be specific.

To Communicate Dissatisfaction

Criticize the performance, not the person.

Try not to threaten the individual. Rather than "You did a terrible job," say, "I was disappointed with the result on this project."

Through questioning, attempt to identify why the problem occurred: "Can you shed some light on why we weren't able to accomplish this objective?"

Focus on elements of the job over which the person has control.

Cite specific reasons why performance is not satisfactory.

Be constructive by indicating that you feel performance can be improved.

Be sure to reinforce improved performance when it occurs.

While prevention is easier than cure, it is still hard work. For one thing it demands that the supervisor *really* listen to what the subordinate has to say. It is not sufficient just to provide the sense that listening is taking place. The supervisor must be capable of picking out key points and building on them. Paraphrasing and summarizing are occasionally helpful, by sustaining the purpose and direction of the interview.

Really listen

Sometimes the subordinate will refer to some negative aspect of the supervisor's behavior. When the tables are turned, there is a temptation to become embroiled in petty remarks that lead away from the purpose of the discussion (i.e., the subordinate's job performance). The supervisor cannot afford to be overly sensitive to negative remarks from the subordinate. Stay in control of the situation and in control of your emotions. When things do seem to get out of hand, it is time to pause and collect your thoughts or even reschedule the interview for a later time.

Don't be overly sensitive

REACHING AGREEMENT ON AN OVERALL RATING

It is possible for the boss and the employee to agree on overall performance. The process does not have to become sidetracked on some minor difference of opinion. The major requirement for consensus is that both supervisor and subordinate be aware of what is expected in terms of job performance.

The agreement will usually begin after the subordinate has had a chance to give the boss his side of the story. The supervisor can then respond by focusing first on individual areas of performance where there is agreement, especially about areas of high performance, and then pinpointing areas where there is disagreement. This strategy not only saves time, it also starts the process out on a positive note. To provide greater meaning, mention a few examples of good performance, including the event, actual behavior, and positive outcomes.

Start with areas of agreement

When agreement is reached on mediocre or poor performance, the two—supervisor and subordinate—can immediately begin identifying why it occurred and what can be done to improve it. A technique for analyzing the cause of poor performance is presented in the next chapter.

When disagreement over level of performance is apparent, don't lose patience. Stay in control and do not deviate from the game plan. Go back over the performance with the subordinate and have him explain just what happened. Compare what was expected with what occurred. Provide examples of the poor performance, again including the event, behavior, and outcome. Indicate what type of behavior should have occurred.

Handling disagreement

When individual performance areas have been discussed and specific ratings agreed on, it should not be difficult to reach agreement on an overall rating.

DEVELOPING A PLAN FOR IMPROVEMENT

Participation + involvement = commitment

There is a temptation, at this point, for the supervisor to make recommendations as to what the employee might specifically do to improve. Before succumbing to this temptation, give the employee a chance to identify a strategy for improvement. Commitment to improve is very much a function of participation and involvement in the process. While some direction from the supervisor is probably desirable, don't go overboard; for example, "Joe, you need to keep your office door closed and quit inviting your co-workers in to chit-chat if you want a higher rating in time management."

Build on strengths

Whenever possible, try to build on strengths instead of dwelling on weaknesses. It is easier for the employee to improve when he is confident that improvement is possible; for example, "Joe, you've always been able to get the work out, as past evaluations show; what can we do to get it back up to your high standards?" This strategy presents the problem as a two-way concern, minimizes defensiveness, and opens the door for a constructive solution.

Be prepared to follow up on promises

Be willing to support, both morally and tangibly, the subordinate's drive to improve. If it means more meetings and discussions, then make a concerted effort to follow up. If it means getting someone from another department (e.g., data processing) off your subordinate's back, then intercede on his behalf. Your efforts will not go unnoticed even if the situation fails to improve.

Have employee sign the appraisal form

At the close of the appraisal interview, it is suggested that the supervisor have the subordinate sign the form indicating that the session did occur. While it is important that any disagreements be put down in writing, the major purpose for the signature is to provide a record that the subordinate has seen and understood the completed appraisal form.

HANDLING CONFLICT

Maintain objectivity

Recall that one of the most difficult interviewing skills a supervisor must learn is handling serious differences of opinion. When emotions start to run high, tempers flare, and the discussion turns into a major confrontation, the supervisor needs to be at her best. She must stay with the topic and resist the temptation to bring herself down to the level of the attacking party. Instead of engaging in a game of tit for tat, objectivity must be maintained by concentrating energies on the issues.

Verbal jabs, even though offered in a friendly, humorous manner, often degenerate into piercing attacks. Once the supervisor becomes distracted from the topic, it is almost impossible to return. When this happens, the supervisor might as well terminate the interview and try again when cooler heads prevail.

The supervisor cannot allow her emotions to gain control and cannot afford to lose perspective on her approach to the interview. If a subordinate makes a biting, sarcastic, or disrespectful remark, she must ignore it. The moment this type of remark is acknowledged is the moment the conversation becomes destructive to both parties. Remember, the purpose of the discussion is not to engage in verbal sparrings but to engage in constructive dialogue. When that is not possible, it is best to reexamine the alternatives and make another attempt later.

Ignore negative remarks

When performance problems exist, the surest way to effect a valid and reliable analysis is a one-on-one interview. To be effective, however, both parties must analyze the performance and the reasons for it. When one party, usually the supervisor, evaluates the unsatisfactory behavior of another, there will always be the problem of acceptance. Will the subordinate accept the evaluation as valid? Will the subordinate change and perform in the direction requested by the supervisor? The answer to both these questions depends largely upon the level of trust between the two parties. High levels of trust ensure that the judgment of the supervisor will not be threatening to the subordinate. Otherwise, the supervisor's decisions might be questioned and viewed with suspicion.

Develop trust

If trust is so important to subordinate acceptance, how might it be developed? The answer is simple—it begins by improving the lines of communication between supervisor and subordinate. Accomplishing this task, however, is easier said than done. Trust is built on the consistent and fair treatment of people. If you try to understand their problems, recognize their concerns, and guide them in resolving their problems, then you are beginning to build trust.

SUMMARY

Trying to evaluate an employee's past performance, to correct performance deficiencies, to motivate the employee to improve, and then discussing compensation matters, all in one appraisal interview, is not uncommon. It also explains why so little is actually accomplished and why negative attitudes about appraisals are so pervasive.

Appraisals can be a positive experience for both supervisors and subordinates. All it takes is a clear definition of what is expected, a two-way discussion, balance in presenting both the negative and the positive aspects of job performance, and attention to how performance can be improved.

There are at least two problem areas to overcome if supervisors are to be adept in giving constructive feedback. The first is that, unless skillfully conducted, the feedback session may be an unpleasant experience for both the supervisor and the subordinate, and the subordinate may lose whatever incentive he or she might have had to improve. Second, simply hoping for and expecting a good feedback session is hardly enough—there must be adequate planning and preparation if the supervisor is going to improve the odds for a successful interview. Although it should never be left to chance, the interview session frequently is. Supervisors are prone to putting off performing unpleasant tasks, especially appraisal interviews. Instead of waiting to "bounce around" a few ideas from the top of their heads, both supervisor and subordinate need to plan the topics to be covered and the results to be achieved. With practice, the whole process becomes easier and more productive.

Like an engineer building a skyscraper, supervisors have to be adept at building good appraisals. Some of the tools discussed in the chapter include: a job description, performance standards, specific objectives, and an incidents file. When combined, these tools can create a series of questions that give supervisors a purpose and direction during the appraisal interview.

The interview itself can follow one of three styles, or elements of each may be combined to create a customized interview approach. When the purposes are to pass judgment and persuade the employee to do the job the supervisor's way, the tell-and-sell approach is quite adequate. It is also fast and keeps the supervisor in complete control. However, it is probably the least effective approach when used to change an employee's poor performance because it tends to generate subordinate defensiveness and hostility.

When two-way communication between boss and subordinate is strained, one method for improving it is the tell-and-listen approach. After giving the subordinate an appraisal of the problem, the supervisor asks the subordinate to be candid about his or her perceptions. Ideally, the subordinate's remarks will focus on the problem, and together the two people can begin to solve it. Too often, the subordinate's remarks do not address the real problem or may, instead, be directed at the supervisor, possibly leading to hurt feelings and further deterioration in performance. It is a risky method.

The problem-solving method is the most time consuming and demanding of the supervisor. The objective, however, is quite different from tell-and-sell and tell-and-listen. The emphasis is on employee development. Judgment is minimized because the supervisor deliberately avoids identifying what he or she thinks is the cause of the problem. Open-ended questions are directed at the subordinate so that the subordinate recognizes the cause of the problem himself or herself.

Choosing the best method is only part of the planning process. The interviewer must employ sound communication skills. Opening remarks that are less than truthful, false build-ups, mixing rewards and threats, and insincere nonverbal messages are blunders that can destroy the subordinate's confidence in the supervisor and the interview.

A skillful appraisal interview may compensate for many deficiencies in the organization's performance evaluation system. The reverse, of course, may also occur—that is, the inability of supervisors to give useful feedback can destroy the effectiveness of a sophisticated appraisal system. The development of face-to-face feedback skills is much too important to be left to chance.

THE NEW SUPERVISOR

Terry Miller is anxious. Today is the day she is scheduled to meet with Judy Johnson, a nurse on Terry's floor, and discuss Judy's performance for the past fiscal year. Terry has been the supervisor for Judy's group for six months, having been a nurse on this same floor prior to her promotion. Normally, with her familiarity with the job, a discussion of nurse performance with a subordinate would not be an uncomfortable situation, but this is different. Judy is the nurse Terry beat out for the supervisor's job.

Prior to the promotion, the two had been friends. Since the promotion, a degree of formality has stood between the two women. Compounding the problem, Judy's performance has deteriorated to the point where Terry must do something for her old friend—but what? One alternative for easing the situation is just to overlook Judy's most recent performance and recommend her for a top increase. Such a strategy, hopefully, would make Judy feel better and might even stimulate her productivity. A second alternative is to confront Judy with her drop in performance, recommend her for only a moderate increase, and hope that the situation improves.

Terry is becoming increasingly uneasy about this whole situation as Judy appears at the door for her review. Terry still has not made up her mind concerning the best way to handle Judy. Terry has, in fact, avoided even thinking about the upcoming "confrontation." After only a minute or two into the encounter, Terry's nervousness is quite evident—to the point of communicating discomfort to Judy. The uneasiness being experienced by both begins to take its toll. Defensiveness begins to show in the subordinate. Barriers to communication begin to appear. Terry's opening remarks, which were intended to ease the tension, do nothing; in fact they lead to greater discomfort for Judy. One thing leads to another. Minor disagreements become outright arguments that degenerate into personal attacks. Finally, Judy stamps out yelling that either she must be transferred or she quits.

1. Why did the appraisal interview go so badly? Could anything have been done to prevent it?
2. Of Terry's two alternatives, which had the more merit? Could you add a third alternative?
3. How can Terry get better results from the reviews with the rest of her people?

DISCUSSION QUESTIONS

1. Why are appraisal sessions often ineffective?
2. Why might supervisors tend to be lenient in giving out rewards to most of their subordinates?
3. Steve, one of your average employees, has just walked into your office for his annual performance review. You and Steve have always had a friendly social relationship. Describe how you would handle this interview.
4. When would an employee self-appraisal be beneficial, and when would it create additional problems?
5. Much has been said of the tell-and-sell method for conducting an appraisal interview. Describe the different situations in which tell-and-sell might be the most appropriate strategy.
6. What is the biggest drawback of the tell-and-listen method of appraisal interviewing? Why?
7. Why is there so much emphasis on self-diagnosis with the problem-solving method of interviewing?
8. During the interview, the supervisor is often tempted to dangle rewards to get an employee to improve; yet when resistance is met, the supervisor changes tactics and begins to suggest that if improvement isn't forthcoming, some type of sanction or punishment (e.g., no promotion, possibly termination) will result. What is wrong with this strategy?
9. Why is it important for the supervisor to develop an effective warm-up approach prior to the discussion of an employee's performance? What constitutes a good warm-up approach?
10. Develop a strategy for handling serious differences of opinion between supervisor and subordinate regarding overall level of performance.

REFERENCES

Beer, Michael, and Ruh, Robert. "Employee Growth Through Performance Management." *Harvard Business Review* (July–August 1976): 59–66.

Beer, Michael. "Performance Appraisal: Dilemmas and Possibilities." *Organizational Dynamics* (Winter 1981): 24–36.

Kearney, W. J. "Improving Work Performance Through Appraisal." *Human Resource Management* (Summer 1978): 15–23.

McGregor, Douglas. "An Uneasy Look at Performance Appraisal." *Harvard Business Review* 50 (5), 1972: 133–138.

Maier, Norman R. F. *The Appraisal Interview: Three Basic Approaches.* La Jolla, Calif.: University Associates, 1976.

Meyer, Herbert H. "The Annual Performance Review Discussion—Making It Constructive." *Personnel Journal* (October 1977): 508–511.

Winstanley, N. B. "Performance Appraisals and Management Development: A Systems Approach." *Conference Board Record* 13 (March 1976): 55–59.

CHAPTER 9

THE PROBLEM EMPLOYEE AND THE EMPLOYEE WITH PROBLEMS

What puzzles me is how he's gotten four weeks behind in his work when he's only been here two days.

—AN ANONYMOUS SUPERVISOR

Chapter Outline

Coaching
    Preparing for a Coaching Session
    What Makes a Winning Coach?
Analyzing Performance Problems
    The Intuitive Process
    The Systematic Process
The Employee with Problems
    The Supervisor's Responsibility
    Knowing Where to Draw the Line
    Employee Assistance Programs
Career Counseling Discussions
Communicating Criticism
Discipline
    Progressive Discipline
    Factors to Consider Before Taking Disciplinary Action
    The Nonrule Violation
    Evaluating the Disciplinary System
    Documentation: The Whys, Whens, and Hows

Objectives

A big part of every supervisor's job is to solve problems. Whether the problems are the result of the work setting or are brought to the work setting by the employee, they cannot be ignored when they begin to interfere with job performance. Specifically, in this chapter the reader will become familiar with:

1. The coaching process
2. Analyzing performance problems
3. The supervisor's responsibility in helping the employee with problems
4. Career counseling discussions
5. How to communicate negative feedback
6. The progressive disciplinary process

Major Concepts

Coaching
Modeling
Intuition
Problem awareness
Feedback deficiency
Ability deficiency
"Want-to" problems
Employee assistance programs
Career counseling

Negative feedback
Progressive discipline
Oral reprimand
Written warning
Suspension
Discharge
Nonrule violation
Documentation

A CASE OF SEXUAL HARASSMENT

A Colorado Department of Highways engineer was suspended for two weeks without pay and demoted with a salary loss of $355 a month for sexual harassment of his secretary and other women in his office.

The engineer lost his appeal of the disciplinary action, which was taken after his secretary complained about his remarks and conduct, including "licking his lips and moaning and groaning as she walked by," according to the decision rendered by State Personnel Board Hearing Officer Harriet Moskovit.

According to the decision:

The engineer's secretary said that he told her he liked the way she looked in pants ("You sure fill them out," he is accused of saying); offered to come to her house and put suntan lotion on her body when she remarked once that she planned to sunbathe; commented on a pair of red pants she wore, telling her that wearing red meant she was "horny"; ran his hand up her leg on one occasion; and once, when she was sick, offered to come to her house and "rub Vicks on her."

Another woman in the office complained that the man would make personal comments to her when she went by such as, "You look good enough to eat today."

Another female employee said he used "suggestive hand motions as if he were grabbing (his secretary's) backside behind her back."

The engineer replied that his secretary complained about his behavior to avoid the consequences of a substandard performance evaluation. He said his comments to her were in jest or meant as compliments and had no sexual connotations. He denied having touched her suggestively. He said he had sought no sexual favors from her.

He responded that he licked his lips because he had "extensive restorative plastic surgery" in 1964 and his lips chap badly. He moaned and groaned often, he said, because he had developed "bleeding ulcers" from work stress and was in pain.

He admitted telling one of the women that she looked "yummy," but said it meant only that her appearance was pleasing and had no sexual overtones.

In her ruling, Moskovit found:

The engineer had made no requests for sexual favors nor given his secretary a substandard evaluation because she rejected his advances. But he had violated federal rules which bar "verbal conduct of a sexual nature" which had the effect of "creating an intimidating, hostile, or offensive working environment" for his secretary and other women in the office.

"[His secretary] and the other women witnesses were reasonably offended by complainant's conduct. . . . He reasonably should have been aware that conduct which might not be offensive at a cocktail party, where an offended individual could walk away, might well be offensive in the work place. . . . He reasonably should have known that repeated references to or gestures about women employees' breasts and backsides and to the way their clothing showed off those breasts and backsides might be objectionable to some women employees. . . .

"He reasonably should have known that comments suggesting a desire to see a woman in the nude (wanting to rub Vicks or suntan oil on her or wanting to see her suntan lines) or references to her sexual propensities—(red means you're horny or 'on the make') might make a woman worker uncomfortable."

The engineer, a 16-year employee with the highway department, had worked his way up by continual promotions. His performance evaluations had always been standard, above standard, or outstanding. He had received special commendations for his innovative work and was considered a hard worker and a tough taskmaster, doing outstanding work in his field.

Therefore, he "is held to a higher standard than the ordinary reasonable man. He is judged according to behavior which may reasonably be expected of a well-educated, experienced professional in a supervisory position in state service."

The engineer took a 10 percent pay cut, from grade 89, $3,818 a month, to grade 85, $3,463 a month.

Reprinted from "Man Suspended, Demoted for Harassment of Secretary," *Silver and Gold Record,* December 15, 1983, p. 7.

A big part of every supervisor's job is to solve problems. While many problems pertain to technical and scheduling areas, at least as many relate to people. The latter are the focus of this chapter. Most of a supervisor's people problems stem from a discrepancy between what subordinates actually do and what management wants them to do—that is, they are performance problems. And performance problems are difficult to solve. A big part of the difficulty stems from the supervisor's inability to analyze the problem accurately before recommending a solution.

There are several reasons why supervisors have trouble accurately pinpointing the cause of performance problems. First, there is a natural tendency for people to find a reason for everything they observe—but not necessarily the right reason. Having found a reason, they are not likely to change it even when new information contradicts it. Moreover, some people tend to attribute the problem behavior to the individual rather than to the environment. A nurse who drops a tray of medicine will be chastised if it is viewed as caused by her clumsiness when in fact it may have been caused by a slippery floor. Status is one factor that strongly influences this *attribution process*. High-status people are perceived to be more responsible than low-status people. That is, good intentions are more likely to be attributed to high-status actors than to low-status actors.[1] In effect, our biases or assumptions about people tend to cloud our objectivity when it comes to identifying the true cause of inadequate performance.

Second, management has conditioned its people (through various training programs and policies) to believe that the cause and the solution of a performance problem are almost always to be found in the individual.[2] For example, supervisors frequently assume that the root of people problems lies in subordinate motivation. However, a performance problem may occur because of inadequate feedback, poorly defined job standards, external interference, or a poor fit between the job and subordinate. Simply urging the employee to try harder is not productive. What the supervisor has defined as the problem may not be the problem at all; it may ultimately turn out to be only a symptom of the problem.

This chapter presents a framework for examining performance problems that goes beyond mere intuition and minimizes biases and assump-

---

[1] Joseph Reitz, *Behavior in Organizations*, rev. ed. (Homewood, Ill.: Irwin, 1981), pp. 105–106.

[2] Geary A. Rummler, "Human Performance Problems and Their Solutions," *Human Resource Management*, vol. 19, no. 3 (Winter 1972), p. 2.

tions about people. The process begins when the supervisor has identified a problem and moves to a determination of its cause. Coaching techniques are discussed and a systematic set of guidelines provided that will help the supervisor remedy the problem.

Of course, not all performance problems can be effectively dealt with by the supervisor. Problems that arise because employees have serious personal problems that affect their own or co-workers' performance are difficult if not impossible for the supervisor to solve. The employee's problem may even require the help of an outside professional (e.g., a psychiatrist). It is impossible to know where to draw the line between solvable and unsolvable problems because each person is unique. Nevertheless, there is no mystery to how supervisors find solutions to problems of human performance. Often an employee who is defined by the supervisor as a problem is merely behaving under a set of perceptions that differs from that of management. Therefore, the supervisor who is best at identifying and analyzing the nature of the problem will also be the most successful at solving it. This chapter discusses the supervisor's role in dealing with the sensitive area of employees' personal problems.

Other areas discussed include career counseling, communicating criticism, and discipline. The theme appearing throughout this chapter is the supervisor's need to be able to manage employees' performance through discussions with them. To bring all of this together, a job performance discussion guide is provided at the end of the chapter. The guide summarizes the basic components involved in the various ways supervisors communicate with employees about job performance.

Coaching

Simply stated, coaching is a process whereby subordinates are motivated to learn new job techniques or to improve current job performance. Coaching is not verbally patting an employee on the back, giving advice, formal training, or even discipline. It is guidance, assistance, or instruction aimed at specific performance deficiencies. Unfortunately, typical coaching inducements, such as, "Come on Joe, I know you can do better," are often not effective in solving performance problems. People need constructive feedback about their performance that will help them zero in on the problem. And who knows, maybe the problem is not the subordinate's but rather something that is completely out of his or her control.

What coaching is

Three essential
components

The coaching techniques used today are more refined and sophisticated than those used in the past. A good coach must do more than merely stimulate a subordinate; he or she must know feedback techniques and when to use them. But feedback is only one of three essential components in coaching. The second is complete familiarity with the subordinate's job. A football coach, for instance, has to know as much about the intricacies and details of the quarterback's job as the quarterback himself. That doesn't mean the coach has to be as good at performing the task as the subordinate, although some are. But the supervisor does need to know the hidden complexities of the task, what skills are essential, and how each job fits into the larger picture of the unit or subunit. The third component is knowing the subordinate well enough to have some insight into what makes him tick.

Coaching concentrates on helping subordinates learn the correct principles and skills of a task, removing obstacles that prevent subordinate success, and giving constructive and timely feedback when circumstances allow.

PREPARING FOR A COACHING SESSION

Focus on the
problem

Maintain
employee's self-
esteem

Establish trust

Limit the number of
issues

A coaching session is based on certain fundamental principles. First, the focus of the discussion is the problem, not the person. If the discussion does not center on the problem itself, the subordinate may feel that he is under personal attack. The conversation should be directed at the specific behavior, incidents, or events that have led to the supervisor's concern. Second, it is absolutely essential to maintain the subordinate's self-esteem. People with high self-esteem are more productive and creative. They contribute more. Finally, because the supervisor's effectiveness depends on the degree of his or her influence over the subordinate, every effort should be made to create and maintain a supportive climate. This climate is directly related to the level of trust that exists within the relationship. Seldom can one be influential when a cold, hostile relationship exists.

The coaching session itself should be scheduled and conducted according to a plan, and the plan should be relevant and timely. A session should be scheduled as soon as a problem develops, not weeks or months later. In addition, the number of topics or problems on the agenda should be kept to a minimum. If more than two problem areas are considered, the session could turn into a lengthy and demoralizing encounter for the subordinate. Also, a session that is limited to only a single issue has focus. If more than two issues need to be examined, additional coaching sessions should be planned. If at all possible, the subordinate should be encouraged to solve the problem or identify a realistic solution himself rather than being told, "Here's what you need to do." This strategy should benefit the subordinate in two ways: First, he accepts "ownership" of the solution, and this acceptance gives him more reason for seeing that the problem is resolved; second, it tends to promote greater self-confidence and ability within the subordinate.

WHAT MAKES A WINNING COACH?

Like the directors of athletic teams, supervisors can learn to be winning coaches. But being a winner requires the mastery of four skills: (1) making insightful observations, (2) asking perceptive questions, (3) active listening, and (4) modeling the correct behavior. The first three are interpersonal skills; the fourth emphasizes the importance of being a good model for the employee to copy.

The first skill requires a basic familiarity with the subordinate's job—*how* the subordinate performs critical activities and what key results are achieved. Being an insightful observer will help to get beneath the surface of a problem. By observing subordinates perform their jobs, the supervisor can sometimes identify deficiencies before they turn into major problems. Insightful observers will know how to evaluate what they see and how to correct the deficiencies.

Insightful observation

Observation alone, however, is seldom enough. A good coach must ask the right questions, weed out irrelevant information, and reformulate certain questions when the original ones fail to elicit an appropriate response. Simply asking why until the right answer comes up can result in a conversation that goes around in circles. Instead of "fishing for anything," the coach should begin with a plan in which each question builds on the previous response. Probing questions are particularly useful. They can open up new avenues of exploration, stimulate insight and understanding, and ultimately lead to the generation of acceptable alternatives.

Asking the right questions

A good question, of course, is only half of the question-answer process. The other half depends on active listening. This skill involves much more than just letting the subordinate talk aimlessly. Active listening is achieved by paying attention and responding to the other's feelings and ideas, not interrupting or debating. It includes picking out meaningful verbal and nonverbal cues. It also includes empathizing (looking at the situation from the subordinate's perspective). Occasionally summarizing the content and reflecting back on the overall tone and direction of the conversation reaffirm the focus of the session. When active listening occurs, better questions are asked and better answers result.

Active listening

Being a good model

Finally, a good coach must also be a good model. That is, he or she must be able to provide a correct demonstration of the desired behavior. The importance of valid examples or demonstrations cannot be overemphasized. If a picture is worth a thousand words, then a good example must be equivalent to an entire textbook. Some subordinates may never have seen a good example, because of their newness on the job or not having experienced co-workers around. Thus a good demonstration may show them what is realistically expected. Examples of desired behavior may be observed in the normal course of events or they may be set up specifically for coaching purposes. In either case, it is important to tell subordinates what they are going to learn and what to look for. After the demonstration is over, subordinates should be asked to comment on what they saw and what they learned.

Providing practice opportunities

For modeling to be truly effective, it must be accompanied by practice opportunities. Practice is required to perfect any skill. It builds the skill itself as well as the employee's confidence to try the skill on the job. And subordinates must feel comfortable with new behavior before it can become an accepted and normal course of their actions. Yet contrary to the old saying, practice does not make perfect—at least not by itself. In the words of Vince Lombardi, "Only perfect practice makes perfect." Making practice perfect takes constructive feedback—letting subordinates know when success has been attained or where improvement is still needed.

Analyzing Performance Problems

Identifying the source of performance problems is a significant part of the coaching process. While many supervisors use an intuitive process (sometimes referred to as a "gut level feeling"), most will rely on a more systematic technique.

THE INTUITIVE PROCESS

Supervisors who depend entirely on intuition to identify the cause of a performance problem are depending on their expertise. If they really are as good as they think, everything may work out. However, the subordinate may not be willing to work with the supervisor in attempting to define the problem (much less a solution), particularly if the supervisor lacks credibility with the subordinate. And in such cases, real improvements are unlikely.

Intuition alone is only as good as the person using it. How much bad diagnosis, wasted effort, and unneeded expense are incurred before supervisors gain adequate experience in accurately identifying both the cause and solution of a problem? Most supervisors will concede that it takes years, and countless mistakes, to refine their diagnostic techniques.

THE SYSTEMATIC PROCESS

A systematic procedure offers the supervisor a logical, consistent, and efficient set of guidelines that gets at the source of the problem quickly and accurately. Is intuition in conflict with a systematic approach, then? The answer to this question is: not at all—the two complement each other quite well. Intuition that is based on years of experience, observation, and judgment can make a systematic approach more valid and viable.

> Intuition + systematic approach = correct diagnosis

The following sequence (see Figure 9.1) is a systematic process for diagnosing the cause of unsatisfactory performance.[3] It is suggested that the sequence be strictly followed. Any deviance from it may result in an inaccurate diagnosis of the cause of the performance problem. Rather than simply assuming that motivation is the problem and recommending corrective action on the basis of that assumption, following this approach permits a logical examination of other possible reasons for poor performance. After all, attempting to apply solutions to nonexistent problems is not likely to benefit the organization.

Step 1: Is There a Problem? In initiating a systematic interview, the supervisor must first assess whether the subordinate is aware that a problem exists. Unless the subordinate admits the existence of a problem, the supervisor may be able to do little to improve the situation. Simply *telling* the subordinate he or she has a problem is an invitation to resistance and defensiveness. Rather than working together to determine the cause, the interview turns into an open confrontation between two adversaries.

> Identify the discrepancy

A problem may exist whenever there appears to be a discrepancy in behavior between what is expected and what actually occurs. But however obvious the problem may be to the supervisor, it may not be apparent to the subordinate. This situation poses the first major hurdle in coaching. As long as the subordinate is unaware of a problem or chooses to believe that the problem is not serious, then there is little hope of solving it.

---

[3] Ibid., pp. 2–10.

FIGURE 9.1
Key Questions to Ask
During Coaching
Sessions

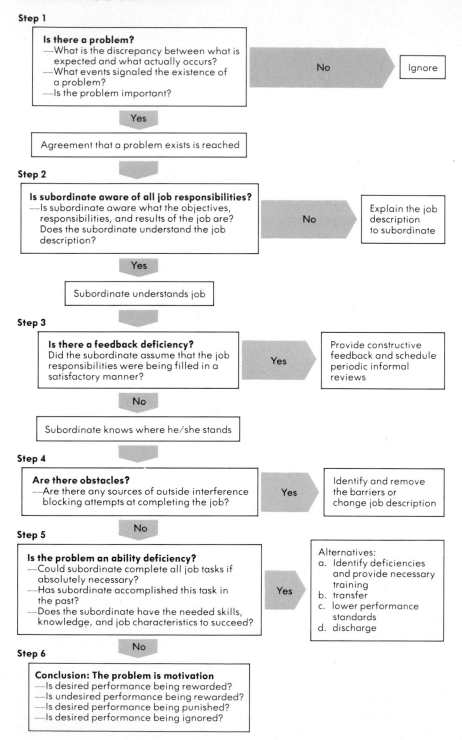

Step 1

Is there a problem?
—What is the discrepancy between what is
expected and what actually occurs?
—What events signaled the existence of
a problem?
—Is the problem important?

No → Ignore

Yes

Agreement that a problem exists is reached

Step 2

Is subordinate aware of all job responsibilities?
—Is subordinate aware what the objectives,
responsibilities, and results of the job are?
Does the subordinate understand the job
description?

No → Explain the job
description
to subordinate

Yes

Subordinate understands job

Step 3

Is there a feedback deficiency?
Did the subordinate assume that the job
responsibilities were being filled in a
satisfactory manner?

Yes → Provide constructive
feedback and schedule
periodic informal
reviews

No

Subordinate knows where he/she stands

Step 4

Are there obstacles?
—Are there any sources of outside interference
blocking attempts at completing the job?

Yes → Identify and remove
the barriers or
change job description

No

Step 5

Is the problem an ability deficiency?
—Could subordinate complete all job tasks if
absolutely necessary?
—Has subordinate accomplished this task in
the past?
—Does the subordinate have the needed skills,
knowledge, and job characteristics to succeed?

Yes → Alternatives:
a. Identify deficiencies
and provide necessary
training
b. transfer
c. lower performance
standards
d. discharge

No

Step 6

Conclusion: The problem is motivation
—Is desired performance being rewarded?
—Is undesired performance being rewarded?
—Is desired performance being punished?
—Is desired performance being ignored?

Problem awareness may be lacking for many different reasons. Some people are simply not aware that their actions, however innocent, add to the burden of others. For example, a receptionist who consistently takes an extra ten minutes for lunch fails to realize that someone has to be there to receive incoming calls, whether it is a co-worker or the supervisor. Before this behavior will change, the subordinate must be convinced that the problem, if uncorrected, will jeopardize future rewards and/or job security. Consequently, before constructive dialogue can occur in a coaching session, the subordinate must perceive the outcome as beneficial to his future. Otherwise he may feel threatened by the supervisor and engage in self-protective behavior.

How serious is it?

People deny problems because they fear that admitting to them may lead to loss of face and a drop in self-esteem. Thus employees who have trouble coping with a performance problem may choose one of the following strategies. The employee may deny that there is a problem. This might be accomplished by disputing the facts or by rearranging them in such a way as to make the evidence appear less damaging. This tactic often works, at least in the short term. Most people are short-term thinkers, so deferring a problem until later seems a plausible strategy. In addition, persistent denial may be convincing enough to forestall permanently recognition of the need to change the problem behavior.

Denial

When facts and documentation are so clear-cut that denial becomes impossible, the employee may resort to hiding the problem (e.g., the alcoholic who uses a breath freshener) or justifying it by lessening its significance (e.g., "But I was only five minutes late!"). Another tactic employees may use (and one that supervisors have difficulty resolving) is finger pointing—by spreading the blame to co-worker(s) who "got away with it" and thereby making it difficult to single out one person. It is only natural that employees will try to utilize coping strategies when they feel threatened.

Finger pointing

Having an employee admit that a performance discrepancy exists may be the most difficult hurdle to overcome. Repeated efforts may be required to succeed in having him or her admit the presence of a problem. Supervisors must have adequate documentation—including actual observations, specific dates the problem was observed, and frequency of occurrence. Reliance on hearsay should be kept to a minimum and should never be the primary source of evidence.

Above all, when identifying to the subordinate a particular performance discrepancy, be specific. Don't couch the problem in generalities. Instead, refer to actual behaviors. It helps when job performance standards are specific (i.e., what to do, how well to do it), measurable (i.e., how will the employee know the standard is met), and communicated to all employees. When performance is shown to be unacceptable in relation to standards, the chances are better for having the subordinate admit that a problem does indeed exist.

Step 2: Is the Subordinate Aware of All Job Responsibilities?

The next step is to verify that the subordinate is sufficiently aware of his or her exact duties, responsibilities, and objectives. Many employees believe they are doing a competent job when in fact they are not meeting the supervisor's standards. If the subordinate is not aware of what she is expected to do, how can she be held accountable for not doing it? When this is the case, part of the blame must certainly fall on the shoulders of the immediate supervisor. It may be that the job description is out of date and in need of revision, and that the supervisor has simply assumed the employee was aware of this.

Not knowing *what* is supposed to be done is only part of the problem. Often, not knowing *when* something is to be done is the real source of the problem. Knowing the expected time of completion is just as important as understanding the task itself. In addition to what and when, the subordinate may not be aware of *how* the result of her efforts, the finished product, is to appear. In other words, the only thing she may know with certainty is what activities are involved. The expected end result of these activities may not have been described to her. Besides identifying duties and responsibilities, the supervisor should identify key result areas. Let the employee know the standards you expect her to achieve. If possible, illustrate—with a clear example—what acceptable results would look like.

The conclusion that a lack of awareness exists suggests that more time should be spent on identifying key job responsibilities, time frames, and result areas, and communicating this information to the employees who will be held accountable. It also suggests that performance improvement is not dependent on the creation of a new motivational strategy.

Step 3: Is There a Feedback Deficiency?

Feedback deficiencies are a common problem in almost every type of organization. Most employees aren't even aware that there is a feedback deficiency until the annual appraisal interview, when they are asked to account for a problem situation that may have occurred months earlier. This deficiency can also be irritating to management. In many cases, timely and relevant feedback from the supervisor to the subordinate about performance deviations could have prevented minor problems from growing into major

Check out the whats, whens, and hows

crises. Moreover, waiting for the annual appraisal makes correcting the deficiency more difficult.

Occasionally, a supervisor will *ask* the subordinate how he thinks he is doing. If he indicates he is doing fine but the supervisor knows otherwise, then chances are that a feedback deficiency exists. As long as the subordinate believes he is performing at the desired level, it won't occur to him to do anything different. To verify that a deficiency is the problem, the supervisor could ask the subordinate to describe his performance. The supervisor should strive for specificity by asking him to describe exactly what he does. There may be a real difference between what he perceives the job to be and what is actually expected of him.

One very effective method of minimizing feedback deficiency is to hold informal progress reviews. Rather than waiting for a formal meeting with the subordinate to clear up a problem, why not schedule periodic feedback sessions? Informal sessions may not only identify a problem before it can cause any serious consequences, it may also create a deeper understanding between supervisor and subordinate. This type of interpersonal "preventive maintenance" diminishes the possibility of surprises occurring during the annual and more formal appraisal sessions.

Feedback, of course, implies a two-way process—a true exchange of views. Too often the supervisor does all (or most) of the talking, which places too great a burden on the subordinate to listen. If an absence of two-way communication is the problem, then clearing the communication lines may be all that is needed. Instead of sending the employee off to some expensive training program, the supervisor should exercise patience and wait to see if the problem clears up by itself after communication channels have been cleared.

Step 4: Are There Obstacles?

One of the most frustrating experiences a conscientious worker may encounter is having someone or something interfere in the performance of her duties. The frustration is further compounded if the boss then blames the worker for the problem when there is absolutely nothing she can do to prevent it. Even greater frustration follows when the employee is forced into a situation of having to explain her "failure." There are times when the supervisor must be made aware of external forces beyond the subordinate's control that are presenting obstacles to productivity.

Outside interference may come from the other departments, co-workers, customers, external regulating agencies, even from the supervisor. If external blockages exist and cannot be removed, both supervisor and subordinate will have to learn to live with them. Often, however, when

> Is the employee aware of the performance deficiency?

> Hold informal reviews

> Remove obstacles if possible

the supervisor's help is enlisted, external factors that were perceived by the subordinate as impossible to overcome prove to be not nearly so formidable.

So before assuming that a problem is due to lack of ability or motivation, it is important to investigate the possibility of external factors being the cause. The supervisor should then make every attempt to remove the obstacle, even if it is the brain child of top management. If this is impossible, perhaps the job description and performance standards can be modified to reflect the subordinate's job more realistically.

Step 5: Is the Problem an Ability Deficiency?

If the supervisor has determined that the subordinate knows what her job is and knows that she is not doing it, and if nothing is preventing her from getting it done, two possible explanations for inadequate performance still exist: lack of ability and/or motivation. Step 5 looks at the first of these possibilities.

Assessing the presence of ability is not difficult. Has the subordinate accomplished this task in the past? Does she have the necessary skills, knowledge, and job characteristics to succeed? Assuming for the moment that the subordinate's past performance demonstrates beyond question that ability is lacking, what alternatives are there? Four realistic solutions deserve consideration. The first is retraining. If the supervisor's analysis suggests an absence of technical knowledge, then classroom training might be appropriate. If, however, the problem is an absence of basic skills, on-the-job training would probably be more effective. The second alternative would be to reassign the subordinate out of the present job and into a task that more clearly fits her capabilities. If neither of the first two alternatives is feasible, a third possibility is to refit the job to the employee. By accepting the situation as it stands and lowering performance standards to realistic levels, you have redesigned the job. The final and most drastic alternative is release. In most cases, the discharge choice is not desirable and should be used only as a last resort.

What if the assessment of past ability does not prove one way or another that the subordinate is competent or incompetent? If this is the case, a more direct approach may be necessary. Be careful, however, of confronting the subordinate with such direct questions as, "Can you do the job?" or "Do you understand what it takes to get the job done?" The pressure will be on her to answer yes. Answering in any other way might jeopardize her self-worth and result in loss of face. Consequently, a more subtle and indirect approach is usually needed—which requires solid preparation and effective communication skills (see page

Four Rs—retrain, reassign, redesign, release

505). For most supervisors, the time invested in developing these skills is well worth it.

Step 6: Conclusion: The Problem Is Motivation.

After exploring each of the five previous steps and concluding that they are not the cause of current performance deficiencies, it is logical to assume that the cause lies in a lack of motivation. Of the six possible causes for substandard performance, motivation is the most difficult to deal with. It therefore requires a great deal of thought and effort on the part of the supervisor. Attempting to ascertain why a subordinate does not want to cooperate is a ticklish problem. Nevertheless, unless you have decided to discharge the employee, the only reasonable alternative is to remotivate him. To do this, an understanding of motivational techniques is helpful.

For high motivation to be present, the employee must believe that he *has* the ability to perform to acceptable standards and that meeting those standards *will* lead to valued rewards. If neither of these conditions exists, the motivation to perform may be lacking. Having already determined (in Step 5) that the employee does have the ability to perform acceptably, the lack of motivation is most likely the result of an inconsistent performance-reward relationship or a perceived negative outcome.

"Want-to" problems

To determine which of the two may be the culprit, ask the subordinate what he expects from his job and how important it is to him to perform to the best of his ability. For example, the organization or the supervisor may be inconsistent or arbitrary in the distribution of rewards, resulting in a low performance-reward perception. Or it may be that the employee fears that some undesirable outcome (e.g., loss of friends) may result from a valued outcome (e.g., promotion).

A second approach to consider involves the use of reinforcement techniques. Recall that reinforcement is based on the notion that people behave in a specified manner because the consequences are pleasant. When a subordinate stops performing desired behaviors, it is usually because he obtains greater pleasure from undesired behaviors. Applying reinforcement techniques to "want-to" problems is not difficult. Begin by asking the subordinate what satisfactions or rewards he receives for doing a good job. Then ask him what satisfactions or rewards he gives up by doing a poor job. In addition, you as supervisor should consider if the subordinate is being rewarded for poor performance or if he is being punished in some fashion for good performance. For example, a supervisor who depends almost entirely on her best worker to handle the tough, unpleasant problems while giving the easy assignments to others (because she feels she can't depend on them) may be creating

Is nonperformance rewarding?

a serious motivation problem. The high-performing employee may begin to perceive the tough assignments not as a challenge but as a punishment.

Undoubtedly, motivation problems are the most difficult to solve. The solution process involves examining the consequences to the subordinate of his or her performance. Once these consequences have been identified as positive, negative, or nonexistent, a plan should be designed that will encourage the desired behavior. Follow-up sessions should be scheduled to assess whether there is improvement or not. If there is no improvement, you can assume that negative consequences are still operating on the subordinate from somewhere inside or outside the organization. While you may have some influence over consequences that are internally related, external consequences are almost entirely out of your control. When motivational strategies fail, there remain for the supervisor only such unpleasant possibilities as disciplinary actions.

The Employee with Problems

It is inevitable that supervisors will encounter employees whose outside personal problems affect their job performance. Unfortunately, when these problems begin to spill over into the job, something has to be done about it. The person who must initially confront employees about the effects of their problems on job performance is the supervisor. What is the supervisor's responsibility? Where does a supervisor draw the line and recommend outside experts? What organizational resources are available for assisting the supervisor in attempting to solve an employee's personal problems? These are the questions we shall be considering in this section.

THE SUPERVISOR'S RESPONSIBILITY

Not so long ago, it seemed easy to tell employees to leave their personal troubles at home. But in today's environment, it is unrealistic to think people can so readily turn on and off problems that deeply affect them. Coping with personal problems is usually a private matter. When it begins to affect performance on the job, however, it becomes a concern of the immediate supervisor.

The supervisor's role begins when there is a negative change in the subordinate's performance. It may take the form of a sudden and unexplained drop in productivity or an increase in accidents or errors. However, the change may be more subtle, such as erratic behavior, argumenta-

Watch for unexplained downturns in performance

tive outbursts, leaving early, tardiness, or an overall increase in irresponsibility. When the behavior is first detected, it should be noted, recorded, and documented by an observer, preferably the supervisor. Secondhand reports should be minimized. Once it is concluded that self-improvement is not going to occur without intervention, it becomes the supervisor's responsibility to sit down and confront the employee with the problem. It is important that threats not be made and that the focus of the dialogue be on the performance, not the person. Simple as this sounds, telling employees the truth about a downturn in performance is an unpleasant task and is therefore often avoided.

Even more difficult is determining the source of the problem. This is a precarious task, even for professionals. For the ill-equipped and untrained supervisor, it is an almost impossible task. The cause of personal problems is virtually unlimited. (Typically encountered sources of employee problems are identified in Table 9.1.) Supervisors should attempt counseling only when professionally qualified to do so. Otherwise, they should refer employees to experts whenever possible. Larger organizations usually provide their employees with programs that focus on specific problems (e.g., alcoholism, drug abuse, or stress). When organizational assistance is not possible, recommend outside public agencies that specialize in providing low-cost human services (e.g., Alcoholics Anonymous).

Refer employees to experts

TABLE 9.1 Typically Encountered Sources of Personal Problems

Family-related problems
  * Family crises (divorce, death, major illness, drugs)
  * Separation from family
  * Family pressures that conflict with job demands

Physical and emotional disorders
  * Physical disorders that affect job performance (muscular, sensory, handicaps, drugs, alcohol)
  * Emotional problems (anxiety, depression, anger, neurosis, psychosis)

Societal effects
  * Employee's values conflict with organization's and/or supervisor's expectations and job demands
  * Litigation (bankruptcy, lawsuits pending)

Job-related problems
  * Work group pressures (social ostracism, conflict with standards, lack of group cohesiveness)
  * Work itself (excessive danger, poor work conditions, undesirable geographic location)
  * Career frustrations (a sense of job immobility, a plateaued career)

Obviously, a knowledge of available services in the community and surrounding region will prove useful to the supervisor.

KNOWING WHERE TO DRAW THE LINE

Continued poor
performance is
unacceptable

While supervisors have a responsibility to their subordinates, there are limits to how far they should go toward involving themselves in their employees' personal lives. This is especially true if the employee perceives the supervisor's concern as an intrusion of privacy. Nonetheless, the supervisor can assist employees. When an employee has any of the following problems, it is usually wise to refer him or her to professional counseling: psychiatric disturbances, drug or alcohol abuse, legal trouble, marital or other family difficulties. For problems such as these, the supervisor should attempt no more than (1) to bring performance downturns to the employee's attention, (2) to provide guidance and assistance in helping the employee seek professional help, and (3) to outline clearly the consequences of continued unsatisfactory performance.

The last point is crucial. Unless an employee clearly understands how the continued unacceptable behavior is going to affect the future negatively, there may be no motivation to improve. A worker with a drinking problem, for example, will usually be reluctant to admit it, much less solve it, until the supervisor clearly outlines the negative consequences of the continued behavior. When the cause of the problem is outside the employee's control, such as legal troubles, the supervisor's role gets sticky. Most supervisors feel a moral obligation to accept the employee's poor performance for a temporary period of time. However, if there isn't any indication that performance is going to improve, you have an obligation to the organization to remedy the problem and bring performance back up to acceptable standards. At this point you could reassign the person to a less demanding job, but this is unlikely. Chances are you will have to release the individual either for a temporary period of time (until the problem is resolved) or, perhaps, permanently.

One key to success is to help the employee recognize and admit there is a problem. Many organizations are improving their handling of this difficult dilemma through the creation of special programs that are specifically designed to help troubled employees.

EMPLOYEE ASSISTANCE PROGRAMS

In general, organizations are becoming increasingly concerned about the effects of alcoholism, drug abuse, and stress on employee production. This concern often takes the form of an employee assistance program

(EAP). While EAPs vary from organization to organization, they do have a number of common characteristics.[4]

First, EAPs share a common philosophy. Instead of taking a punitive approach to troubled employees (e.g., "You either get this problem licked by Friday or you can pick up your paycheck on Monday"), EAPs adopt a supportive approach. When an employee comes to work, for example, he or she is accepted warts and all—the organization accepts the worker as a whole person. Second, most EAPs offer programs that help employees learn to handle special problems. Programs that encourage physical fitness, for example, are designed to give employees a means for reducing stress. Third, EAPs tend to bring people with professional counseling and medical expertise into the organization. Knowing that experts are readily available to handle the sensitive problems of troubled employees is a confidence builder for the supervisor because it will make him or her less hesitant about confronting such unpleasant problems as alcoholism.

When an EAP is available, the supervisor's role is greatly simplified. (Figure 9.2 outlines the role of the supervisor in such cases.) In essence, EAPs are designed to help workers help themselves before disciplinary action becomes necessary. Studies have shown that one out of every twelve employees might face personal problems that could adversely affect job performance,[5] and EAPs appear to offer a realistic means of salvaging troubled employees. In the words of one union president, "Many people who would have gone down the drain are [now] good, reliable employees . . . and are leading happy, useful lives."[6]

> Characteristics of EAPs

Career Counseling Discussions

Not all personal problems demand professional assistance. When employees' troubles are job-related, there are a few things the supervisor can do to help solve the problem. Intense pressures from the work group, the work itself, and career frustrations are three categories of job-related problems that may be effectively tackled by the supervisor. Career counseling, in particular, is a need that is felt from time to time by most employees.

[4] Robert W. Hollman, "Beyond Contemporary Employee Assistance Programs," *Personnel Administrator*, vol. 26, no. 9 (September 1981), pp. 36–42.

[5] Edwin Busch, Jr., "Developing an Employee Assistance Program," *Personnel Journal*, vol. 60, no. 9 (September 1981), pp. 708–711.

[6] R. F. Rothbauer, quoted in ibid., p. 711.

FIGURE 9.2
The Supervisor's Role
When There Is an
Employee Assistance
Program

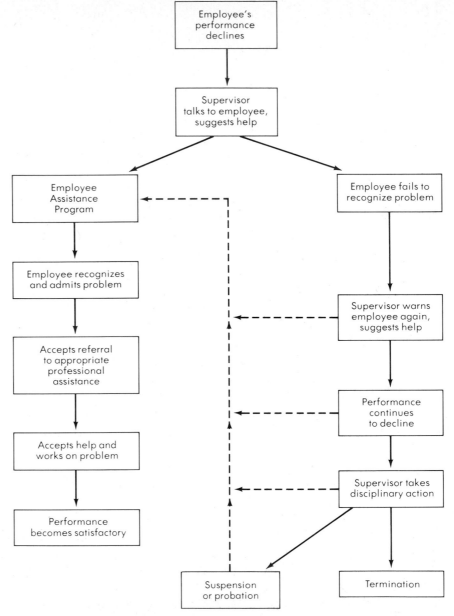

Edwin J. Busch, Jr., "Developing an Employee Assistance Program," *Personnel Journal*, vol. 60, no. 9 (September 1981), p. 709.

Career counseling is a process that maps out for the employee a development plan that attempts to match the employee's needs, abilities, and goals with current or future organizational opportunities. Effective counseling, much like coaching, requires active listening skills, perceptive questions, and the skills of an astute observer. Unlike coaching, counseling does not involve the supervisor in openly diagnosing the employees' problems or recommending a specific solution. The underlying assumption in counseling is that people work out problems themselves. A counselor is not a judge or evaluator. Instead, the counselor's role is simply that of a helper whose objective is to stimulate, facilitate, and guide the employee in making important decisions or learning to cope with difficult situations.

Let the employee work out the problem

Supervisors probably have more impact on a subordinate's career development than any other person. But supervisors are often reluctant to get involved in career discussions because (1) they lack the necessary skills, and (2) there are few rewards for engaging in the development process. The latter point is important; in many organizations supervisors feel that career counseling and development is an unrewarded activity, besides being demanding in terms of their time. But career counseling often is rewarded; one large organization, for example, has a policy that supervisors can be considered for promotion once they demonstrate that at least one subordinate is ready for promotion.

Why supervisors are reluctant career counselors

In order to be good career counselors, supervisors need to know (1) the subordinate's strengths and weaknesses, (2) the requirements of positions the subordinate is considering, (3) the organization's anticipated manpower needs, and (4) the training and development options open to the subordinate.

What the supervisor needs to know

Subordinates, too, have responsibilities when it comes to career planning. They must understand (1) their abilities, (2) what they like and dislike about their jobs, (3) their long-term aspirations, and (4) the kind of commitment (e.g., of time and energy) that is needed to fulfill those aspirations.

Career counseling itself can occur on any number of occasions. It may begin as early as the employment interview, or it can take place during day-to-day supervisor-subordinate exchanges. The more the supervisor knows about the subordinate, the more valid the process becomes.

A significant part of the career counseling process is for the supervisor to be honest with the subordinate. One should never make career promises or commitments that cannot be kept. When employees have unrealistically high aspirations, one should tell them so. Realistic objective feedback about weaknesses is just as important to an employee as praise and encouragement.

Communicating Criticism ━━━━━━━━

In addition to the coaching and counseling activities already discussed, other types of one-on-one communication between supervisor and subordinate are required. In the course of day-to-day activities, feedback—both positive and negative—is an integral part of the job. Since praise (i.e., positive feedback) has already been discussed (Chapter 4), communicating dissatisfaction must also be addressed.

Negative feedback should have a positive purpose

Negative feedback is necessary because it identifies areas where improvements are desired, and it specifies how these improvements can be made. Keep in mind that the purpose of communicating dissatisfaction must always be to improve employee performance. It is advisable to examine one's motivation for passing along unpleasant information. When the purpose is simply to "unload" on the subordinate, bear in mind that the results may be negative as well.

Negative feedback can be made more tolerable to the employee (1) when there is adequate documentation citing specific and recent examples that reflect the problem, (2) when positive expectations are expressed that performance can be improved, and (3) when the action or performance itself—not the person—is the focus of the criticism. These guidelines will work only when the subordinate has an open mind and when he or she can be realistically expected to do something about the problem in the first place.

Discipline ━━━━━━━━

Progressive discipline

Most people interpret discipline as a punishment that is used to eliminate undesired behavior. However, a small but growing percentage of people view discipline in a different light. They believe that instead of using threats, a disciplinary approach should concentrate on dealing with the employee as an adult who must solve a problem. Unfortunately, because employees often do not respond to positive and supportive work environments, a system of progressive penalties is needed to ensure acceptable performance. This system is called progressive, or positive, discipline.[7] It has been found that when disputes are subjected to arbitration, arbitrators are generally supportive of the progressive discipline approach.[8] However, this approach is applicable only for less serious offenses. Serious

[7] Richard Grote, *Positive Discipline* (New York: McGraw-Hill, 1979).
[8] One study, conducted by the American Management Association, reports that 26.4 percent of arbitration cases deal with discipline or discharge. See P. Pigors and C. Myers, *Personnel Administration* (New York: McGraw-Hill, 1980), p. 301.

violations—such as theft, assault, or accepting bribes—are actions that cannot be tolerated in any organization. A person committing such a violation is usually subject to immediate discharge.

PROGRESSIVE DISCIPLINE

The progressive discipline procedure will generally follow a sequence of penalties, with each successive penalty having a greater degree of severity. The steps in the sequence are (1) the oral reprimand, (2) the written warning, (3) suspension, and (4) discharge.

The Oral Reprimand. When an employee breaks a rule the first time, an oral reprimand is given. The oral reprimand consists of clearly informing the employee that misconduct has occurred and that a repeat of the action could result in further disciplinary action. Before the problem has a chance to reoccur, the supervisor should attempt to identify its cause. The coaching technique described in Figure 9.1 gives the supervisor a framework for getting at the cause of a performance problem. The primary concern at this stage is to correct the problem, not to punish the employee.

Clearly informative, nonpunitive

The Written Warning. If a disciplinary problem reaches the point where oral warnings do not seem to be effective, then a notice should be written to the employee and a copy put in the employee's file. After writing the warning, the supervisor should ask herself: "If a new supervisor were coming into the department and read the warning notice, how well would he or she understand the problem relating to the employee's discipline record?" If the answer is, "Very well," then an effective memo has been written.

A written warning could contain the following key elements:

Key elements

1. A statement of the problem. This may include a brief history of events leading up to the problem, but the objective here is to state exactly which rule has been violated.
2. The consequences of continued deviant behavior; that is, what is going to happen to the employee if he or she continues to violate the rules.
3. The employee's commitment. Has the employee made a commitment to improve the situation?
4. A description of any follow-up action to be taken. This would include the action that should be taken by the supervisor and the employee after a reasonable period of time.

Tone

Another important element of the written warning is its tone. The notice should be clear, concise, and nonpunitive. Finally, and probably most important, the notice should have a constructive orientation. The overall approach to discipline is to create an environment in which the employee will once again become a contributing member of the organization.

Shock effect

Suspension. Probably the most controversial step in the progressive discipline sequence is suspension. If oral reprimands and written warnings have not impressed the problem employee, it may be necessary to suspend her temporarily to make her aware of the seriousness of her situation. Suspension will usually involve a period of one to seven working days. Critics claim that some employees do not view suspension as a penalty and that a few employees may even look forward to a suspension as a respite from the stress of the work arena. Furthermore, a suspension may be more of a burden on the supervisor than on the employee because of scheduling problems and production delays resulting from the personnel shortage. The value of suspension usually comes from the shock to the employee of coming so dangerously close to being discharged. It also has the effect of creating a socially embarrassing situation—when friends, family, and co-workers begin asking questions about the employee's absence from work.

Is it fair?

Discharge. When all less severe disciplinary actions have failed, the supervisor must consider the alternative of discharge. A supervisor must ask at this point, "Is it fair to fire this person, considering the way others have been treated for doing the same thing?" For the answer to be yes, management must be uniform in the application of company or organization rules. To aid in the discharge decision, the following questions should be considered:

1. Did the employee have prior warning that the continued behavior would result in discharge?
2. Have other employees who have performed equivalently or worse also been discharged?
3. Was this employee given the same number of warnings as other employees in similar circumstances?
4. Does the punishment fit the act and the employee's record with the organization?

If the supervisor can answer yes to all four of the above questions, then discharge is the appropriate action.

It is very important that a discharge decision be supported by good documentation. Although probationary employees can generally be fired without much explanation, such action may lead to a discrimination complaint. Therefore, documentation of the sequence of events leading up to a discharge—whether of a probationary employee or a long-term employee—is important. This is especially true for long-term employees. To discharge an employee with seniority requires a series of consistent and well-documented job evaluations over a considerable period of time. A well-documented file for just the last few months of the individual's employment is not sufficient.

> **Be able to defend a discharge decision**

When an employee has been discharged, the supervisor should make a point of being involved in his or her last workday. If possible she should schedule an exit interview. This interview should be pleasant, but not apologetic, and should review the reasons for the discharge. This is not the time to pull any punches or to be overly sympathetic to the employee. Many supervisors are reluctant to be candid because they feel that what they say may be used against them later. At the least, the supervisor should give the employee any information about the termination of benefits, being as helpful as possible. As the conversation winds down, she should end on a positive note—by recognizing the employee's strong points—and express confidence that the employee will find suitable employment elsewhere.

FACTORS TO CONSIDER BEFORE TAKING DISCIPLINARY ACTION

What violations necessitate disciplinary action? Unfortunately, no set of rules or regulations is so precise that it covers every conceivable situation. However, it can be said that some problems are more serious than others. Supervisors need to exercise good judgment when analyzing potentially serious problems. Many organizations divide problem seriousness into three categories. The first category covers violation of a major rule and would include acts that seriously threaten the operation of the organization or the safety of its employees. This category of offense normally results in discharge of the problem employee. A second category concerns problems that are somewhat less severe but are still considered serious. Some of these include

> **Three categories of offenses**

Deliberately faulty workmanship
Gross negligence of property
Drinking on the job
Chronic absenteeism and tardiness

Insubordination
Gambling on the premises
Dishonesty

For this category of offenses, the disciplinary process will usually begin with a written warning. The third category consists of lesser types of offenses such as discourtesy to customers. These offenses can usually be handled by a timely oral reprimand.

Guidelines for administering discipline

Administering discipline is never a pleasurable task. By following certain guidelines, however, the supervisor can make this challenge less objectionable and more effective. First, the work rules must be reasonable. Secondly, the rules must be known to the employee. Obviously, rules that are not known or cannot be adhered to by the average employee are not an effective set of work rules. When dealing with work rule violations, there must be substantial proof of the rule violations. Furthermore, the burden of proof rests on management.

A third guideline for the administration of disciplinary cases is that administration of the rules must be consistent. One employee should not be singled out and disciplined any differently from other employees. In short, supervisors must not be arbitrary or capricious in the administration of discipline. When unions are involved, the disciplinary process becomes very legalistic, but that does not mean discipline is impossible. What it does mean is that documentation recording actual events, offenses, and consequences must be provided. Mitigating circumstances, such as seniority and provocation, is a fourth factor that must be considered. When insubordination occurs, for example, and extenuating circumstances are involved, the circumstances may require a reduction in the penalty.

A fifth factor is the past conduct record of the employee. Is the current problem just emerging, or is it related to a previous problem? A supervisor should be familiar with the organization's policies regarding different offenses. Some organizations have separate policies for various classes of violations. For example, an employee who is orally reprimanded for being tardy and later commits an entirely different offense (e.g., screams at a customer) may receive a second oral reprimand instead of a written warning.

A final factor is the period of time that has lapsed since the employee's last violation. If an employee has gone some predetermined period of time without a reoccurrence of the violation, the slate should probably be wiped clean. If performance improves, the employee is told that the disciplinary action has become "inactive." Adequate documentation relating to this fact is included in the employee's personnel file. Richard Grote recommends the following time frames: [9]

Step 1: Oral reminder, which becomes inactive after three months
Step 2: Written reminder, which becomes inactive after six months
Step 3: Suspension, which becomes inactive after twelve months

Although the above guidelines are helpful, the supervisor should remember that each case must be determined on its own merits. No two cases are exactly the same. Even when two employees commit the same offense, there is usually enough difference in the situation or in the work records of the violators to justify some distinction in the penalties given out. The best the supervisor can hope to achieve is a disciplinary process that is perceived by employees as fair and just.

THE NONRULE VIOLATION

There will always be disciplinary problems that do not fall clearly into any infraction category but where some type of corrective action should nevertheless be applied. Take, for example, the supervisor who hears complaints from customers about his service representative. It seems the employee enjoys telling customers off-color jokes. The employee's reaction when confronted with the problem is, "I didn't mean anything by it. It was just a joke. Some people just don't have a sense of humor." Instead of making threats—such as, "Joe, you'd better tone down those tactless jokes"—a problem orientation is recommended. For instance, "Joe, our customers are sensitive about your jokes. Can we be a bit more diplomatic around customers?" Preaching, lecturing, finger pointing, even sympathizing are not nearly as effective as people would like to believe. The biggest problem for supervisors who use any of these approaches is that employees tend to react to the discussion on a personal level instead of on a professional level. As a result, bigger problems are created.

Taking a problem approach, on the other hand, will minimize an employee's fear and increase his sense of personal control over whatever problem exists. It conveys a positive expectation that the problem is solvable. It also creates a climate that encourages more options for solving the problem, so employees are more comfortable making suggestions. Most of all, active participation by the employee improves the chance

Adopt a problem approach

---

[9] Grote, *Positive Discipline*, p. 133.

that a viable solution will not only be identified but be willingly accepted and a commitment made to it by the person most responsible for remedying the problem.

EVALUATING THE DISCIPLINARY SYSTEM

Over the past twenty years, an increasing number of laws and court actions intended to protect employees from discriminatory or arbitrary treatment have arisen. Organizations are constantly undergoing self-examination to determine the defensibility of their internal rules and policies. Are the rules and policies reasonably defined and well publicized? Do supervisors and subordinates understand the rules? Is due process available to all employees? Is adequate documentation collected and maintained?

Occasionally review the relevancy of rules

While it is the personnel department's responsibility to examine the rules and policies periodically in order to assess their legality as well as their contribution to the organization's goals, the supervisor, too, should occasionally assess each rule's worth and effectiveness. After all, supervisors have a big stake in the process; they are key figures in identifying and correcting misconduct before problem situations get out of control. But to be effective, supervisors must themselves know the whys and wherefores behind the rules, as well as where to go for information and guidance. And they must have confidence that management will back them if the going gets rough.

Be on the lookout for bad rules

What is a bad rule? If there appears to be an excessive number of exceptions to a rule or it is not making a contribution to objectives, then the rule should be eliminated from the organization's policy. When the supervisor requests clarification of a specific rule and receives such answers as, "It's our policy" or "We have always done it that way," then management should carefully analyze the rule itself. Some other typical responses include, "I don't have time to explain it to you; just do it." Or the one that a new employee frequently hears, "Don't make waves." Another common response is, "You wouldn't really understand, so let's not discuss it anyway." When these or similar responses are voiced regarding some rule currently being enforced by management, it is the supervisor's duty to clear the air with personnel about the rule's utility and purpose. The rule may need updating.

From an organizational point of view, discipline takes the form of a control system for ensuring sensible behavior. It involves a way of communicating standards as well as monitoring job performance. Unfortunately, outdated rules and penalties are seldom evaluated until an arbitrator or a negative ruling in court points out some flaw in the policy. For example, a rule regarding company dress codes was overruled by an arbitrator because the clothes an employee wore had nothing to do with performance (see Table 9.2). It makes sense to update rules and policies periodically; and the update process should begin with the supervisor.

TABLE 9.2   What Arbitrators and Courts Won't Accept

It is unlawful to discriminate because of race, color, sex, age, religion, national origin, ancestry, and in most states, physical handicap. Disciplinary actions are often thrown out by government arbitrators or others involved with disciplinary problems when the case includes any of the following elements:

Pregnancy: Pregnancy is considered to be a temporary condition. It is not an illness. A supervisor cannot merely assume that a pregnant woman is not able to perform certain job functions. Hence it is unlawful to discharge an employee who is pregnant unless termination is recommended by a physician.

Dress: Maintaining certain dress standards for a given working environment is permissible; however, employers must be sure dress standards are established for sound reasons and not for reasons of discrimination. For example, some people cover their heads for religious reasons, and as long as it does not affect their job performance, it should not be viewed as a violation of dress standards.

Language: This is a very touchy area. For example, it is unlawful to discipline an employee because a customer complains of his or her accent. To do so would amount to national origin or ancestry discrimination, and it is not a cause for disciplinary action. It may also be unlawful to discipline an employee for not reading English, unless reading English is a job-related ability. Ethnic and racial insults fall within the language area. A supervisor may imply insults if he or she is sarcastic or belittling of other races or cultures. Such behavior is considered discriminatory.

Reprisal: It is unlawful to punish an employee for filing a discrimination complaint. This is so even if the complaint is without merit.

Arrests: The supervisor should not assume that an arrest is an indication of guilt. If the incident leading to arrest is job-related, action may be required. However, it is important to establish the connection firmly before any action is taken.

Falsifying an application form: This is another area that is difficult to interpret. For example, not being truthful about being a diabetic could be viewed as a nonviolation under the laws regulating discrimination against physical handicap. It is up to the employer in such cases to prove that the falsification is job-related.

Insubordination: When the supervisor issues an order and the subordinate's response is a direct refusal to obey, some would consider this an act of insubordination and a cause for discharge. Yet if the employee is discharged and appeals to an arbitrator or the courts, a problem could arise because of poor documentation of the events leading up to and including discharge. The employee may also charge unfair treatment as a result of the incident.

DOCUMENTATION: THE WHYS, WHENS, AND HOWS

Said the supervisor: "You can't fire anyone here. It's like working under civil service restrictions." What had happened was that an employee who had been a persistent problem since he was hired was finally brought on the carpet for insubordination. The supervisor wanted the employee terminated; but because the employee was a union member, a hearing was needed to comply with the labor contract. The hearing lasted two hours. At the conclusion, the supervisor's recommendation was overruled. As it turned out, a look at the employee's folder revealed no warning notices, no negative performance evaluations, and no record of unsatisfactory performance. The supervisor who yelled and screamed that the employee was often late, often absent, surly, and insubordinate could not offer one shred of evidence to support these claims.

Documentation is the foundation

As this incident points up, documentation is the foundation for an effective disciplinary system. But it is also a versatile supervisory tool. While it is viewed primarily as a recordkeeping and protection procedure, documentation can (1) aid in improving employee performance and (2) indicate to the employee management's concern with continued poor performance.

All kinds of excuses are put forward by supervisors as to why they don't document: "It takes time"; "I have more important things to do." Sometimes management is guilty—by not stressing the importance of good documentation and not rewarding supervisors for taking the time to build documentation files. However, the single most significant reason for failing to document is, as one supervisor put it, "No one ever told me the why, when, and how of documenting."

Two types of documentation

Documentation is the written record of observed performance, performance effectiveness, and observed events and circumstances concerning performance. The information can serve a multitude of purposes (see Table 9.3)—such as providing a basis for performance appraisals, coaching, career counseling, evidence in litigation, or simply serving as a mental note or reminder. Documentation can be of two types: anecdotal and formal. Anecdotal documentation consists of the supervisor's own notes regarding the factual events that occur on the job. Such notes are usually informal, and they are kept strictly confidential by the supervisor. The law will generally allow a supervisor to maintain his or her private files for one year. After that period, they must either be destroyed or be included in the personnel records, which are available to each employee. Formal documentation consists of such things as the written warning in a disciplinary matter or special commendations, and it is part of the employee's personnel file. Whether informal or formal, documentation should be written in a way that would satisfy an unbiased reader.

TABLE 9.3   Situations When
Documentation May Be Necessary

Local procedures that require documentation
Performance observations
   Performance itself
   Circumstances
   Effectiveness
Informal job discussions
Formal job discussions
   Appraisals
   Grievances
   Meetings
Salary change recommendations
Planning and monitoring
Problem solving
Departmental programs and progress reports
Specific requests for a permanent record
Equal Employment and Opportunity
Safety
Interactions with customers
Incidents that may affect your group
Telephone conversations
Requests from supervisor
Career counseling a subordinate
Self-development

The supervisor should include the following information: who is involved, date and time of incident, a brief statement of what happened, and location. Here is an example of an anecdotal documentation:

Employee's name: Bob Williams
Date: 10–24–84
Topic discussed: Tardiness
  Scheduled arrival time 8:00 A.M.; arrived 8:14 A.M.
Comments: Bob said his car was being repaired, and he had to catch a ride
in. He agrees he didn't plan for this contingency. We both agreed
that he should either make other arrangements to get to work
on time or get prior approval for being absent. Bob said he would
be more thoughtful in the future.

A written warning would include more information because it involves more serious allegations and a copy must be given to the employee. In addition to the above elements, it would include a specific description of the problem, implications, prior record, prior conversations, expected solutions, disciplinary action taken, consequences if misconduct continues, and a scheduled follow-up conference date.

Proper documentation is absolutely critical in supervision. Because taking corrective action is an integral part of the job, and a most unpleasant part at that, supervisors need to have their facts together. Depending on memory for dates, events, and factual circumstances is generally unreliable and unsatisfactory, especially in disciplinary matters. In addition, documentation is becoming the key source of evidence in job-related litigation, since management, not the employee, has been saddled with bearing the burden of proof.

Obviously there are many different kinds of performance discussions. The tone of the discussions will vary depending on the purpose, the degree of trust, and the use or nonuse of threats. In order to bring closure to a complex topic we present in Table 9.4 a job performance discussion guide. For each of the different kinds of performance discussions, a process is described that outlines the manner, purpose, and structure the interview might follow.

TABLE 9.4   Job Performance Discussion Guide

INTERVIEW TO STRENGTHEN DESIRED PERFORMANCE

1. Prepare for the meeting

2. Give your input
   State specific performance; relate to current standards
   Recognize the parts of the job that are being performed well
   New employees need more frequent encouragement than seasoned workers

3. Ask for suggestions and/or solutions (if appropriate)
   Would anything have made the job easier?

COACHING INTERVIEW

1. Prepare for the meeting

2. Give your input
   State specific performance; relate to current standards
   Provide documentation (if appropriate)

3. Ask for employee input
   Observe employee's behavior
   Listen to employee
   Ask leading questions
   Restate employee's remarks in your own words

4. Clarify and discuss
   Have employee identify the problem
   Does employee recognize need for change?

TABLE 9.4   (*continued*)

5. Identify cause
    Assess employee's job knowledge, skills, and responsibilities
    Check for a feedback deficiency
    Are there external obstacles preventing performance?
    Is employee ability a problem?
    Is motivation lacking?

6. Offer your suggestions and/or solutions (if appropriate)
    Instruct, advise, or demonstrate expected performance
    Have employee verbalize or demonstrate expected performance

7. Reach an agreement on what specific things the employee is going to do
    to eliminate problem
    Develop action plan
    Set a date for a future meeting to review progress

CAREER COUNSELING INTERVIEW

1. Prepare for the meeting

2. State purpose and expected outcomes

3. Give your input
    Discuss organizational opportunities available to employee
    Emphasize your desire that this be a forward-looking discussion

4. Ask for employee input
    Examine past job experience, skills, and education
    Assess employee's desire for upward, lateral, or downward job moves
    Assess employee's willingness to relocate
    Assess future job directions—technical, line, or staff management

5. Clarify and discuss
    Use active listening
    Ask leading questions
    Establish long- and short-range goals (i.e., career aspirations)
    Discuss past performance appraisals in light of the presence or absence of
    certain abilities that are never tested in the present job
    Look for evidence from sources off the job (e.g., extracurricular activities
    or accomplishments)
    Discuss assessment center reports, if available
    Discuss performance on the current job—is the employee stretched?

6. Offer your suggestions
    Identify development objectives
    Create development plan—temporary assignments, job relations, enlarge-
    ment, or job enrichment possibilities
    Determine educational objectives—specific correspondence courses, or night
    classes at the local college
    Recommend training needs and programs (both in-house and external)
    Emphasize that these plans must not interfere with current job responsibilities

7. Commit the plan to writing and set date for a future meeting to review
    career progress

TABLE 9.4 *(continued)*

PERFORMANCE APPRAISAL INTERVIEW

1. Prepare for the meeting

2. State purpose and anticipated improved performance
   Establish a supportive tone
   Clarify that the focus is on the employee's performance, not personality
   Explain the process the interview will follow
   Share your conviction that the interview is important

3. Perception sharing (either party can go first)
   Discuss performance
   Seek agreement on actual level of performance
   Cover each of the employee's major areas of responsibilities
   Do not dwell on poor performance
   Cite examples of good performance early in the discussion

4. Discuss overall rating
   Give reasons for rating
   Assess employee's reaction

5. Clarify and discuss overall performance
   Identify strengths, weaknesses, and circumstances that led to current performance
   Concentrate on no more than two or three weaknesses at most

6. Reach agreement or understanding
   Share expectations
   Decide on specific goals and action plan
   Provide resources
   Change standards you can change
   Resolve standards you cannot change

7. Summarize

DISCIPLINARY ACTION INTERVIEW

1. Preparation for the meeting
   Arrange to hold the meeting in private
   Secure the necessary facts related to misconduct
   Obtain verifiable information and supporting documentation
   If requested, the employee is entitled to union representation

2. State purpose and express hope for a mutual understanding
   What was the violation; when did it occur?
   What is the past record of the employee?
   Was the employee previously reprimanded for the same or similar offense?
   Ask if you have all the facts

3. Give your input
   Discuss any previous counseling or reprimands
   Discuss previous actions taken by you or another supervisor

TABLE 9.4 (*continued*)

4. Ask employee for input
    Does the employee deny the violation? Why
    Are there any mitigating circumstances?

5. Clarify and discuss
    Was the investigation fair and objective?
    What action was taken in similar cases?
    Does the penalty fit the action?

6. Inform the employee of the disciplinary decision
    Comply with all contractual requirements, such as notification and formal documentation
    Should you clear the penalty with your boss or personnel department?
    Move quickly but not hastily
    Keep your eye on the goal of the process: to correct improper behavior and to salvage the employee

7. Discuss follow-up
    Develop a plan to meet and discuss future performance
    Provide counseling if needed

SUMMARY

If the supervisor cannot communicate well and control the direction of a job performance discussion, all the knowledge in the world will have little efficacy in improving the performance of subordinates. While there are many common characteristics to different types of job performance discussions, there are also important distinctions. Before jumping into a supervisor-subordinate discussion, you should clarify the purpose and basis for the meeting and determine what materials, documentation, records, or policies will be needed during the interview. As a supervisor, you should ask yourself, "Why am I conducting this interview, and what do I hope to achieve?" If your answer is vague, then the outcome will probably be fuzzy as well. Of course, the basis of any job performance discussion is the employee's actual performance compared to expected organizational standards. Thus it is important that the supervisor be able to specify *what* the employee is doing, *what* the standards for this behavior are, *what* the employee needs to do to improve, and in some cases, *how* improvement is to be achieved.

Because techniques and processes employed during a supervisor-subordinate discussion vary depending on the purpose of the interview, this chapter includes a job performance discussion guide (pp. 272–275) that identifies the major steps as well as some key components for each of the different types of discussion mentioned in this chapter and the preceding one.

The chapter also presents a systematic approach to identifying the cause of performance problems. Essentially the approach involves investigating communication and feedback deficiencies, external obstacles, ability deficiencies, and motivation. It is important to consider motivation as the possible source of the performance problem only after other possibilities have been eliminated.

Everyone has personal problems. But when an employee's problems begin to affect job performance, the supervisor has to take action. While there is not a great deal the supervisor can do, he or she should provide a minimum of counseling, as well as patience and understanding. If your organization has an employee assistance center, find out what it offers in terms of programs and professional counseling and see that the employee makes contact. If the problem continues to affect job performance after counseling services have been exhausted, stronger action is probably warranted.

This chapter concludes with the topic of progressive discipline. The penalties, each more severe than the preceding one, begin with an oral reprimand, move to written warning, and conclude with suspension. Discharge is technically not a part of the disciplinary sequence. Written documentation is absolutely essential for progressive discipline to be administered effectively and for the discipline to hold up under litigation. It is important that supervisors develop the self-discipline to record objectively job-related events that could conceivably have disciplinary significance later. Finally, work rules should be periodically reviewed, updated, and discarded (when out of step with the purpose of the organization). Equally important, they should be publicized and fairly administered by the supervisor.

BACK OFF, BIG MOUTH

Carl Schmidt was the new night-shift manager in the warehouse of the Cascade Packing Company. When he saw the pile of broken boxes that had fallen off the end of an unattended conveyor belt, he felt a sudden rush of anger.

"Hey, where'd they go?" he yelled out without thinking. The workers at the other end of the line looked up emotionless, and the machine operator turned off the line.

"Where's John and Ricardo?" Carl asked again as he headed toward the lunchroom. The other workers whispered to each other and then left their positions for an early break.

When Carl entered the lunchroom and saw John and Ricardo sitting at a table and smoking, he was very upset.

"What are you doing in here?" he demanded. "Don't you know where you're supposed to be?"

"We thought the label machine would be down until break time so we came in here," John explained. He could see how upset Carl was. "We only left fifteen minutes early."

"Well, it wasn't down until break time, it was only down for five minutes, and now there's a whole pile of broken boxes out there that you were supposed to stack." Carl was sure that they had no idea how much their error had cost the company.

John mumbled something about cleaning it up and started to leave. Carl felt like there was more he wanted to say so he faced Ricardo and continued his harangue. Suddenly Ricardo felt picked on. Quickly he stood up, put his hands on Carl's chest, and shoved him backwards.

"Back off, big mouth!" he shouted.

Being shoved and called a big mouth added insult to Carl's angry feelings. He responded by telling Ricardo that he was fired. At Carl's insistence, Ricardo gathered his things from his locker and left.

A brief description of the incident reached the personnel office the next morning. Later that day Ricardo and a friend came to visit the personnel director. They asked several troublesome questions.

1. What was the reason for the firing?
2. Why was one person fired and nothing done to the other person?
3. Does a supervisor have the authority to fire an employee on the spot?
4. Why was only the minority employee disciplined?

From Cherrington, David J., *Personnel Management: The Management of Human Resources.* © 1983 Wm. C. Brown Publishers, Dubuque, Iowa. All rights reserved. Reprinted by permission.

DISCUSSION QUESTIONS

1. How does coaching differ from counseling and disciplining?
2. Describe the skills a winning athletic coach must have, and compare them to the coaching skills of an effective supervisor.
3. What are the dangers of "butting in," even in a friendly way, when a subordinate begins to have personal problems at home that affect his or her job performance? Where does a supervisor draw the line?
4. Why is it so important to have the employee identify the cause of the problem as well as a set of possible solutions?
5. Explain how you would tell a subordinate who has been late for work three days in a row because of her child's illness that she is going to be suspended for one day without pay.
6. Why should a supervisor be careful to make a written record of a spoken warning on a first offense?
7. Your company has just hired several "hard-core unemployables" as part of a public service agreement with the community. One member of this group has been assigned to your work group. His initial performance seemed to be acceptable, but lately you have noticed a sudden and negative change. Explain how you would meet with the individual and discuss the problem. What kind of preparation is necessary?

REFERENCES

Belohlav, James, and Popp, Paul. "Making Employee Discipline Work." *The Personnel Administrator* 23, no. 3 (March 1978): 22–24.

Booker, Gene. "Behavioral Aspects of Disciplinary Action." *Personnel Journal* 48, no. 7 (July 1969): 525–529.

Cross, Gary. "How to Overcome Defensive Communications." *Personnel Journal* 57, no. 8 (August 1978): 441–443.

Duff, C. V. "Discipline: Laying Down the Law Productivity." *Industry Week* 189 (May 17, 1976): 51–52.

Hollman, Robert W. "Beyond Contemporary Employee Assistance Programs." *The Personnel Administrator* 26, no. 9 (September 1981): 36–42.

Huberman, J. "Discipline Without Punishment." *Harvard Business Review* (July–August 1975): 6–8.

McCarthy, J. J. *Why Managers Fail.* New York: McGraw-Hill Company, 1978.

Miner, J. B. "The Management of Ineffective Performance." In *Handbook of Industrial and Organizational Psychology,* edited by M. D. Dunnette. Chicago: Rand McNally, 1976.

Oberle, R. "Administering Disciplinary Actions." *Personnel Journal,* no. 1 (January 1978): 30.

Roethlisberger, F. J. "The Foreman: Master and Victim of Double-Talk." *Harvard Business Review* 23, no. 3 (Spring 1945): 283–298.

Wilson, Thomas. "Making Negative Feedback Work." *Personnel Journal* 57, no. 12 (December 1978): 680–681.

PART 4

SPECIAL CHALLENGES

CHAPTER 10

THE EMPLOYEE SELECTION CHALLENGE

Many individuals have, like uncut diamonds,
shining qualities beneath a rough exterior.

—JUVENAL

Chapter Outline

The Selection Process
The Supervisor's Role
Employment and the Law
   Unfair Employment Practices
   Equal Employment Opportunity (EEO)
   Equal Pay and Age Discrimination Practices
   Executive Orders and Other EEO Regulations
   The Search for Truth—Polygraphs in Employment
   Employee Safety and Health
Analyzing the Job
   The Job Description
   The Job Specification
Interpreting the Completed Application Form
The Employment Interview
   Planning the Interview
   The Art of Questioning
   Conducting the Interview
The Selection Decision

Objectives

As members of management's front line, supervisors play a key role in selecting new members for their work group. This chapter is designed to provide a working knowledge of sound selection procedures and techniques. Specifically, in this chapter you will become familiar with:

1. The supervisor's role in the selection process
2. The government regulations that impact on the selection process
3. Some practical techniques for analyzing jobs
4. Areas on completed application forms that need to be examined
5. Guidelines for preinterview planning
6. The employment interviewing skills needed by the supervisor

Major Concepts

Selection

Discrimination

Equal Employment Opportunity
  Commission (EEOC)

Title VII of the Civil Rights Act
  of 1964

BFOQ

Equal Pay Act of 1963

Age Discrimination Act of 1967

Comparable worth

Executive Order 11246

Executive Order 11375

Office of Federal Contract
  Compliance (OFCC)

Rehabilitation Act of 1973

Vietnam Era Readjustment Act of 1974

Worker's compensation laws

Occupational Safety and Health
  Administration (OSHA)

Job analysis

Polygraph

Job description

Job specification

Application form

Unstructured interview

Structured interview

Directive question

Open-ended question

Reflective question

Hypothetical question

Employment interview

CONFESSIONS OF AN EMPLOYMENT INTERVIEWER

Bill Gilroy is an interviewer for a Vancouver, Canada, pulp and paper plant. He is occasionally asked to interview hundreds of applicants over a short period of time. What follows is his candid description of the questions he or his supervisors ask of each applicant. While many of these questions would be illegal in this country (and would certainly result in costly litigation), the reasoning behind them is worth sharing.

Each of Bill's interviews ordinarily lasted twenty to thirty minutes, unless, as Bill said, "a man was frightened, reticent, or opposed." Before the actual interview started, each man was assured that he did not have to answer any questions he did not want to. Bill felt, however, that any man who did not want to answer all questions directly was leaving himself open to indirect questioning to determine the necessary information.

"In the interview," Bill said, "I look for quite a few things, as you can see from the [interview] form. The main thing the questions bring out is a man's stability, and as far as his personal compatibility goes, I get a good idea of that by the way he conducts himself in the interview, and then of course there's the thirty day probationary period on the job.

"A man has to prove himself in the interview. If the man is obviously trying to gain sympathy from me, say by telling me about his aches and pains, I usually don't want him. This type of thing will carry over to the job. One question I think is pretty important is the one, 'When did you have your last drink?' Typically a man will hesitate a moment, and then remember the beer he had a few nights ago, and then he might mention the drink he had at his birthday party, or something like that. But when a man says, 'I had my last drink at 2 o'clock on such and such a day and year,' watch out! The man, 99 out of 100 times, is, or was, a confirmed alcoholic. Any man that can tell you to the minute the last time he had a drink is the worst risk from the alcoholic point of view.

"I deliberately hired two alcoholics not long ago. When they're sober, they'll work twice as hard as anyone around them—to punish themselves. You can't put them on the line, because when they're out there will be a hole. Maintenance, stores, etc., are O.K. for this type. One of the two I hired had been a major league pitcher, and had owned his own furniture manufacturing outfit. I thought he'd be able to transfer his knowledge, but he couldn't do it; the job was too broad for him.

"Another thing I definitely look for is the man who is accident-prone. That's the only way I can think of saying it, but I don't like the expression. I check on health, car accidents, and the last accident on their former jobs. Of course a man with too many accidents tries to hide it, but it usually always comes out.

"I also look for a smooth domestic life. It's almost a prerequisite. I like to see a good healthy home life too. For one thing, with poor health in the family, a man usually needs extra money—so moonlighting is a problem.

"We have some fringe benefits, but don't forget this plant is still growing and right now we can't afford to commit ourselves more to these expenditures. Take our wage spread—from a base rate of $3.75 up to $7.85. That $3.75 might be a little low, but we deliberately tried to start low in anticipation of union demands.

"Notice the questions about an applicant's financial situation. You'd be surprised how many people come in here and tell me about the farm their father left them, from which they might be earning $18,000 a year. It's not hard to predict that these people aren't going to be the steadiest workers in the world. They just aren't hungry. On the other hand, we can't take people who are too hungry, with too many mouths to feed. As I mentioned before, you can't support six or seven kids in Vancouver on monthly wages of $650, which is what he would make starting with us.

"Single girls on their own are especially bad. It's typical of them to say, in answer to my questions as to how much they need a month, 'Oh, I can live on $400 a month.' Then when I ask them about the payments on the coat they're wearing, and their car, rent, and so on, they'll say, 'Oh, gosh, guess I can't live on that!' Eventually, they realize it will be tough for them to live on the wages that we pay.

"The important thing is to keep the plant operating efficiently," Bill concluded, "and if it is not operating, all this red tape and all records are meaningless. We are attempting to keep it going as efficiently as possible. The plant is the be-all and end-all."

*T*rying to ascertain talent in others isn't easy. And it is, unfortunately, a task that few do well. For some, the process is largely intuitive (i.e., playing hunches). Yet, it doesn't have to be purely a gamble. Some talent hunters minimize the risk by sifting through all kinds of information, and they end up making informed decisions. Employee selection involves talent hunting, in that a prediction has to be made as to whether an outside applicant (or a candidate for promotion) is suited for a particular job. There are a number of selection tools that improve the accuracy of hiring decisions. Nevertheless, even with the best of these tools, it is impossible and unrealistic to predict with 100 percent accuracy who should or should not be hired.

The purpose of this chapter is to give supervisors a working knowledge of good employee selection techniques. Supervisors are becoming increasingly involved in the hiring decision because it is the supervisor who must work with the outcome of the selection process. A bad hiring decision hurts everyone in the company. (Many companies acknowledge this fact by investing large amounts of money, time, and skilled personnel in the selection process.) But in particular, it hurts the supervisor and the mismatched employee. Therefore, this chapter is aimed at those areas in the selection process that involve the direct efforts of supervisors. Making good hiring decisions is undoubtedly one of the supervisor's most serious and pressing challenges.

The Selection Process

While there are an incredible number of selection procedures, most firms—whether large or small, manufacturing or service, profit or public sector—tend to choose from the list presented in Table 10.1. Sometimes items are lumped together under broad categories. For example, job

Selection procedures

TABLE 10.1   Typical Selection Procedures Used in Hiring

SELECTION PROCEDURES	*PERCENTAGE OF COMPANIES THAT USE THESE PROCEDURES*
Reference/record check	97
Unstructured interview	81
Skill tests/work samples	75
Medical examination	52
Structured interview	47
Investigation by outside agency	26
Job knowledge test	22
Mental ability test	20
Weighted application blank	11
Personality test	9
Assessment center	6
Physical abilities test	6
Polygraph test/written honesty test	6
Other	3

Survey of 437 companies conducted by the Bureau of National Affairs, May 1983.

knowledge and mental and physical abilities tests are all aspects of the individual's ability.

The importance of sequencing selection procedures

Building a selection process is relatively simple. Companies choose a battery of selection procedures to be used for making hiring decisions. They then sequence the procedures in such a way that each step efficiently screens out those who are most obviously unqualified to meet the job requirements (as shown in Figure 10.1). While a particular company might not sequence the procedures in the order depicted in Figure 10.1, most companies will.

Each of the procedures is designed to gather new information about the applicant—that is, information that was previously unknown to the company. Furthermore, it might be noted that each succeeding step

FIGURE 10.1
The Selection Process

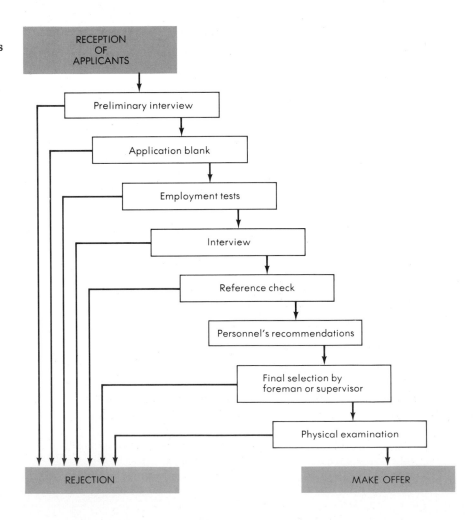

becomes more expensive for the company (e.g., thorough background checks and physical tests tend to run into a lot of money). This is the incentive for designing a process that eliminates unqualified applicants as soon as possible. It also explains why application forms and preliminary screening interviews are almost always the first steps in the selection process.

The Supervisor's Role

The supervisor's role in the selection process is growing—even to the point where supervisors are making the actual hiring decision. This is not to say that the personnel department's role is declining, it is just a reflection of the increasing importance being accorded to the supervisor's position in the organization. The personnel department must still be responsible for many of the steps in the selection process, because it has the resources and staff specialists to recruit and screen out large numbers of unqualified applicants. Their primary task is to reduce the field of applicants to a manageable size, perhaps as few as three or four, after which the supervisor interviews each of the finalists. While the actual hiring decision may be a middle or top management responsibility, more often it is the immediate supervisor's recommendation that carries the greatest weight. After all, it is the supervisor who will be accountable for the new employee's performance. Furthermore, it will be the supervisor's task to train, motivate, and evaluate this person.

Why the supervisor gets involved

While an applicant's performance during each phase of the selection process is recorded and analyzed by personnel staff specialists, it is the immediate supervisor who is most often responsible for conducting and evaluating the employment interview. This claim is supported by a Bureau of National Affairs (BNA) study of the responses of over four hundred personnel executives from all sectors of the economy.[1] Among other things, it found that as many as 87 percent of the survey respondents believe the supervisor plays the major role in conducting unstructured employment interviews (see Table 10.2). It also found that supervisors are involved in the administration of job knowledge and physical abilities tests—though to a lesser extent. Reviewing completed application forms and the results of reference checks may also be a part of the supervisor's job description. Supervisors, however, do not play a significant role in

How the supervisor is involved

---

[1] The study was conducted by the Bureau of National Affairs, Washington, D.C., and was based on responses from 437 personnel managers selected randomly from among the members of the American Society for Personnel Administration.

TABLE 10.2 Individual(s) Responsible for Evaluating Applicant Qualifications, by Selection Technique

	NUMBER OF RESPONDING COMPANIES	PERCENTAGE OF COMPANIES						
		PERSONNEL DEPARTMENT	HIRING SUPER-VISOR	OTHER DEPART-MENT OR MANAGER	PRIVATE CONSULT-ANT	MEDICAL PROFES-SIONAL	PANEL/ COMMIT-TEE	OTHER
Background information								
Reference/record checks	(421)	93%	29%	2%	*	—	1%	1%
Weighted application blank	(45)	91	38	4	—	—	4	—
Investigation by outside agency	(85)	75	18	8	6	—	—	7
Interviews								
Unstructured	(328)	83	87	5	—	—	—	2
Structured	(194)	81	61	7	1	—	7	2
Ability testing								
Skill performance test/work sample	(288)	86	25	2	1	1	*	1
Mental ability test	(71)	73	20	4	8	—	—	8
Job knowledge test	(79)	71	42	4	4	—	—	1
Physical abilities test	(22)	50	41	9	—	5	—	—
Assessment center	(24)	67	13	8	13	—	—	17
Other screening								
Medical examination	(185)	63	7	1	—	32	—	5
Polygraph test/written hon-esty test	(25)	40	16	24	32	—	—	4
Personality test	(33)	64	27	6	24	—	—	9

Note: Percentages are based on the number of companies that responded for each selection procedure.
* Less than 0.5 percent.

applicant tests that are conducted away from the actual work environment.

Employment and the Law

Although supervision has never been thought of as simple, it certainly has been considered by many as well defined. Planning work schedules, coordinating projects, handling crises, and evaluating employee performance are just a few of the duties that traditional supervision involves. While these duties continue to be the major part of supervision, the supervisor's world has become more complex. The contemporary supervisor must now spend time understanding and abiding by hundreds of federal and state regulations.

A good part of the laws and regulations that can affect a supervisor's job involve protecting the employee (or job applicant) from unfair employment practices and unsafe work conditions. Don't be misled into believing that compliance is easy. Asking an illegal question of a job applicant, for example, can open the door to formal complaints of discrimination and result in years of expensive litigation. Nor is ignorance of a specific law accepted by the courts as justification for one's actions. The courts expect all laws to be adhered to, the complex as well as the obvious.

Knowledge of employment regulations is essential

UNFAIR EMPLOYMENT PRACTICES

Discrimination can occur at any point in the selection process. How the job posting is worded and advertised, the types of questions asked on the application form, and the conduct of the interview itself are particularly open to complaints of discrimination, whether intended or not. Consider the case of the military wife who sought employment as a store manager—a job she had held for some years in another part of the country. After several turndowns, one interviewer finally told her that his company had a policy of not hiring military wives because of their high turnover rate. How did the interviewer know the woman was a military dependent? Simple. She was asked on the application form what her spouse's occupation was. Since she didn't know her legal rights under Title VII of the Civil Rights Act of 1964, she missed out on a job offer—and more. Had she known what her rights were, she could have sued the company for discrimination, as one woman did, and won. The courts awarded the litigant back pay, compensation for lost promotions, and a job with the company.

Beware of discriminatory practices

In addition to the risk of being convicted of discrimination by the courts, asking such questions is ethically and morally wrong. Everyone should have the same opportunity to succeed (or fail). Supervisors should be on the alert for practices that tend to favor one group over another, even when the practice seems harmless and well intentioned—for example, asking a female applicant who will care for her children.

EQUAL EMPLOYMENT OPPORTUNITY (EEO)

BFOQ and the EEOC

Perhaps the single most significant piece of legislation ever passed, Title VII of the Civil Rights Act of 1964, as amended in 1972, prohibits discrimination in employment on the basis of race, color, religion, sex, or national origin. Title VII regulations are applicable to state and local government agencies, universities, and private employers who have fifteen or more employees working for more than twenty calendar weeks per year. Any deviation from the provisions outlined in this act must be fully supported with evidence from the employer that the practice in question is related to a bona fide occupational qualification (BFOQ). Enforcement of EEO regulations is the responsibility of the Equal Employment Opportunity Commission (EEOC).

Good intentions, by themselves, are not sufficient. Courts have taken a de facto approach to complaints of discrimination, and they continue to do so. What this means is that company practices that tend to give preferential treatment to whites, whether intentional or not, are subject to investigation by the EEOC or some other regulatory agency. Not only is discrimination assumed, but the full burden of proving otherwise falls directly on the employer—not the government. It is the employer's responsibility to defend the practice and prove that it is a legitimate business necessity. If, for example, the company is a law enforcement agency that has historically hired applicants who are at least five feet eight inches tall, it had better be ready to provide evidence that the requirement is, indeed, a BFOQ.

EQUAL PAY AND AGE DISCRIMINATION PRACTICES

Equal pay for equal work

While Title VII of the Civil Rights Act is undoubtedly broad in scope, it certainly is not the only government regulation that supervisors need to be aware of. The Equal Pay Act of 1963 requires most employers to provide equal pay for equal work. If a woman is performing essentially the same duties and responsibilities as a man, then under this law she has a legal right to demand equivalent wages. Although this law prohibits employers from paying members of one sex less than members of the other sex for performing equal work, neither this law nor Title VII prohibit an employer from paying unequal wages for jobs that are comparable but not substantially equal. This latter issue is referred to as the comparable worth controversy, and it has become one of the hot issues of the decade.

Comparable worth is more than equal pay for equal work. Comparable worth recognizes that equal pay should reflect work of equal value. The controversy centers on the issues of whether the employer should be legally required to evaluate the worth of every job according to a common set of standards. It argues that numerous job areas that have historically been dominated by females (e.g., teaching, nursing, and clerical work) pay significantly less than male-dominated professions. For example, a nurse, who is highly skilled and educated and is responsible for the well-being of her patients, is often paid less than a maintenance worker. The issue is not whether the maintenance worker makes too much; the issue is the gap between the two groups. While the courts have yet to resolve this issue, it is not going to fade away. The implications are enormous. Among other things, it would involve the wholesale reevaluation of an employer's pay structure—a task that not even progressive judicial systems are quite ready to tackle.

| Comparable worth |

In addition to regulations on pay discrimination, there is a law that protects employees between the ages of forty and seventy from discrimination in hiring, job assignment, promotion, termination, or any other aspect of the employment process. The Age Discrimination in Employment Act of 1967 (as amended in 1978) is enforced by the EEOC. Typical of the complaints the EEOC might handle under this law is the withholding of employee retirement benefits from discharged senior employees.

| Age discrimination |

EXECUTIVE ORDERS AND OTHER EEO REGULATIONS

Presidents Kennedy and Nixon issued Executive Orders 11246 and 11375, respectively, which further regulate the employment practices of any employer who desires to do business with the federal government. These orders require federal contractors to take affirmative action with regard to the hiring and promotion of minorities and female employees.

| Executive orders and the OFCC |

The formulation and publicizing of hiring and promotion goals, aggressive recruiting of minorities, and special training for the disadvantaged are the types of strategies expected of federal contractors and subcontractors who have contracts over $10,000 and fifty or more employees. The Office of Federal Contract Compliance (OFCC), the enforcement agency, requires these contractors to file annual summaries of their affirmative action progress. Employers that do not comply with these orders may face termination or cancellation of contracts or may be barred from future contracts.

Local and regional regulations

In addition, many states and municipalities have passed laws that prohibit employment discrimination (as well as laws that protect the employee's health). When state laws are tougher than federal, the state laws are given precedence. Otherwise, the EEOC retains jurisdiction over complaints brought to one of its offices.

Employing the veteran or handicapped worker

Because employment discrimination can occur in so many different ways, the task of describing in any kind of detail each of the specific regulations is beyond the scope of this book. Yet, there are two acts, involving protection of the handicapped and the veteran, that are worth mentioning. The Rehabilitation Act of 1973 and the Vietnam Era Veterans Readjustment Act of 1974 require employers to recognize the special needs of particular segments of society and to take positive action to employ and promote their well-being. To the supervisor, these acts may mean redesigning a clerical task so that an applicant who is restricted to a wheelchair could still carry out the basic duties of the job. Or it may mean spending a little extra time training an employee who is mentally impaired.

THE SEARCH FOR TRUTH—POLYGRAPHS IN EMPLOYMENT

Although supervisors as a general rule would not be expected to administer polygraph examinations to applicants, they might be expected to be aware of its role in the employment process. Furthermore, many organizations are using polygraphs to examine current employees (including supervisors) for particular incidents of theft or wrongdoing. While there has been a dramatic increase in their use, polygraphs, nonetheless, continue to be surrounded by controversy.

Ancient methods

The search for truth is nothing new. In ancient times all kinds of devious, and often painful, methods were used to try to detect whether or not someone was telling the truth.[2] One Oriental custom involved feeding a mouthful of rice to someone suspected of a crime. If the

---

[2] Eugene Block, *Lie Detectors: Their History and Use* (New York: McKay, 1977), pp. 12–15.

suspect could not quickly and easily spit out the rice during questioning, the suspect was presumed guilty. As outlandish as it may sound, there is at least some medical support for the fact that fear and tension usually inhibit the creation of saliva. Similarly, in years gone by, the British required a suspect to chew and try to swallow a "trial slice" of dry bread. If the accused was unable to choke down the dry bread, he was pronounced guilty. Both these examples are based on the same principle as the modern polygraph—that physiological changes accompany extreme stress.

Today, the equipment for lie detection measures three human responses: (1) respiration, (2) blood pressure and pulse rate, and (3) galvanic skin response (or the flow of electric current across the skin as a measurement of perspiration). The presumption is that when a subject is deceptive, one or more of these measurements will change. When enough questions are asked, a pattern of change is recognizable and is repeated whenever the subject lies.

What lie detectors measure

Polygraphs have been most widely accepted as a means for deterring theft, for uncovering information about a specific incident such as theft, and for screening present and potential employees for such undesirable characteristics as dishonesty, alcoholism, drug use, and sexual deviation. They are also used to verify information on application forms. While traditional methods such as psychological testing and background investigations can be used, they tend to be more costly than the polygraph—which might run anywhere from $25 to $75 per subject.[3]

Uses of polygraphs

Although polygraphs have many limitations, their use does present some advantages. Some people are so convinced that the machine will be able to ascertain the truth that they don't attempt to lie. Also, companies that require periodic polygraph examinations of current employees have noticed substantial savings from reduced theft.[4]

Despite the increasing use of polygraphs, they have not been given much credibility by the courts. In fact, most courts will refuse to admit the results of polygraph tests, on the grounds that the techniques are not generally accepted by the scientific community.[5] However, some judges are willing to accept lie detector results when all parties have agreed to the tests prior to their administration.[6] In the employment

Courts are skeptical of polygraphs

---

[3] "Now a Furor over Lie Detectors in Business," *U.S. News & World Report,* March 8, 1976, p. 70.

[4] G. M. Wilson, "Corporate Detectors Come Under Fire," *Business Week,* January 13, 1983, pp. 88–89.

[5] C. B. Craver, "Inquisitorial Processes in Private Employment," *Cornell Law Review,* 63 (1977), p. 33.

[6] Block, *Lie Detectors,* p. 27.

context, no state prohibits the use of polygraph tests, but some states do have restrictions.[7] However, the licensing of professional polygraph examiners is only loosely controlled in some states. Fortunately, this is changing, with most states toughening the certification process.

EMPLOYEE SAFETY AND HEALTH

Job safety and workmen's compensation

The federal government isn't always the first to pass and enforce legislation that affects the workplace. As long ago as 1910, the state of New York passed a law that provided some degree of protection for workers injured while on the job. Today, all employers are required by federal and state laws to provide lost wages and medical expenses to injured employees—as long as the injury is job-related—regardless of who is responsible for the accident. Employers protect themselves from this risk by purchasing insurance or, if they are large enough, through self-insurance.

The cost of worker's compensation insurance can be substantial. Occasionally employers will encourage their supervisors to push job safety practices. Stressing safety not only reduces insurance premiums, it tends to raise the morale of the work force. This occurs because safety incentive programs are attractive to the typical employee. One large manufacturer

[7] Thirty-three states now either restrict the use of polygraph tests in employment situations, require competency-based licensing of polygraph examiners, or both. States regulating the use include: Alaska (ALASKA STAT. § 23.10.037 (1972)); California (CAL. LAB. CODE § 432.2 (West 1971)); Connecticut (CONN. GEN. STAT. § 31–51g (1977)); Delaware (DEL. CODE ANN. tit. 19, § 704 (1979)); Hawaii (HAWAII REV. STAT. §§ 378–21 to –22 (1976)); Idaho (IDAHO CODE §§ 44–903 to –904 (1977)); Maine (ME. REV. STAT. ANN. tit. 32, § 7166 (Cum. Supp. 1980)); Maryland (MD. ANN. CODE an. 100, § 95 (1979); Massachusetts (MASS. GEN. LAWS ANN. ch. 149, § 19B (West Cum. Supp. 1981)); Michigan (MICH. COMP. LAWS § 37.2205(a) (Supp. 1981)); Montana (MONT. REV. CODES ANN. § 41–119 (Cum. Supp. 1977)); New Jersey (N.J. STAT. ANN. § 2A:170–90.1 (West 1971)); Oregon (OR. REV. STAT. §§ 659.225 to –227 (1979)); Pennsylvania (18 PA. CONS. STAT. ANN. § 7321 (Purdon 1973)); Rhode Island (R.I. GEN. LAWS §§ 28–6.1–1 to –2 (1979)); Washington (WASH. REV. CODE §§ 49.44.120–.130 (Cum. Supp. 1981).

States requiring licensing of polygraph examiners include: Alabama (ALA. CODE tit. 34, §§ 25–1 to –36 (1977 & Supp. 1981)); Arizona (ARIZ. REV. STAT. ANN. §§ 32.2701–.2715 (1976 & Cum. Supp. 1981)); Arkansas (ARK. STAT. ANN. §§ 71–2201 to –2225 (1979)); Florida (FLA. STAT. ANN. §§ 493.561–.569 (West 1981)); Georgia (GA. CODE §§ 84–5001 to 5016 (1975)); Illinois (ILL. REV. STAT. ch. 111, §§ 2401 to 2432 (1978 & Cum. Supp. 1981) (An act to provide for licensing and regulating detection and deception examiners, and to make an appropriation in connection therewith, at § 1)); Kentucky (KY. REV. STAT. §§ 329.010–.990 (1977 & Cum. Supp. 1981)); Maine (ME. REV. STAT. ANN. tit. 32, §§ 7151–7169 (Cum. Supp. 1981)); Michigan (MICH. COMP. LAWS §§ 338.1701–.1729 (1970 & Supp. 1981)); Mississippi (MISS. CODE ANN. §§ 73–29–1 to –47 (1973)); Nevada (NEV. REV. STAT. §§ 648.005–.210 (1979)); New Mexico (N.M. STAT. ANN. §§ 67–31A–1 to –11 (1974)); North Carolina (N.C. GEN. STAT. §§ 66.49.1–.8 (1975)); North Dakota (N.D. CENT. CODE §§ 43–31–01 to –17 (1978 & Supp. 1979)); Oklahoma (OKLA. STAT. tit. 59 §§ 1451–1476 (West Cum. Supp. 1980)); Oregon (OR. REV. STAT. §§ 703.050–.140 (1979)); South Carolina (S.C. CODE §§ 40–53–10 to –250 (1976 & Supp. 1980)); Utah (UTAH CODE ANN. §§ 34–37–1 to –14 (1974 & Supp. 1979)); Vermont (VT. STAT. ANN. tit. 26, §§ 2901–2910 (Supp. 1981)); Virginia (VA. CODE §§ 54–916 to –922 (1978)).

lowered its premiums substantially by giving $25 gift certificates to every employee who made it through the year without an employee-caused accident. While over 95 percent of the work force received these certificates, representing a large dollar outlay, the scheme still resulted in huge savings for the manufacturer.

Experienced supervisors will tell you that if voluntary safety programs don't work, you can bet that before long some OSHA inspector will visit. A powerful government agency, the Occupational Safety and Health Administration is directly responsible for establishing health and safety standards in the workplace and enforcing them. Established in 1970, the agency will make on-site inspections on the basis of complaints by employees or the agency's own suspicions. Their inspectors conduct safety checks, establish safety standards, issue citations, and levy fines for unsafe working conditions.

OSHA and its influence

The supervisor is involved in the work of OSHA in many ways. For one thing, the agency expects employees to be educated in safe work procedures. Some of the things OSHA inspectors look for when they review an organization's safety programs is the number of training sessions teaching accident prevention made available to employees. They may also examine how employee safety performance is evaluated—that is, the extent to which safety performance is a part of the employee's formal performance appraisal. Record keeping is yet another way in which the supervisor is involved. Records must be kept of the number of accidents and injuries, and what happened and how it happened; these records are subject to review by OSHA inspectors.

Analyzing the Job

One of the most unexciting tasks a supervisor is called on to perform is job analysis. But tedious as job analysis may appear, its benefits make it well worthwhile. Although usually the responsibility of the personnel department, job analysis cannot be thoroughly and accurately completed without input from both the incumbent employee as well as the employee's immediate supervisor. The supervisor's role in the process might range from simply reviewing the job analyst's recommendations to actually generating a detailed list of the duties expected from the incumbent.

The first part of the process—the job description—involves clarifying the duties and responsibilities of the job itself. The second half—the job specification—involves identifying the essential qualifications of the successful job holder.

A two-part process

THE JOB DESCRIPTION

Enforcement agencies, such as the EEOC, encourage employers to write job descriptions that are based on systematic examinations of what employees actually do. A large percentage of discrimination complaints come from disgruntled employees who argue that what they actually do is quite different from what their job descriptions say they are required to do. Organizations that select, reward, and promote employees on the basis of vague and subjective job descriptions are inviting lawsuits—in particular, from members of the protected classes (e.g., women and minorities). Moreover, if the job is not clearly defined, then the likelihood of there being realistic performance standards is not good.

The process of compiling a job description begins by answering the question: What needs to be done? Quite often there is merit in asking the subordinate to answer this question and then comparing the subordinate's description with your own. The experience can be a real eyeopener to the supervisor.

Itemize job responsibilities

Suppose that you decide to analyze your own job as supervisor of a typing pool with twelve clerical employees. The first thing that comes to mind is your responsibility for checking the progress of each of the employees at various times throughout the workday. Giving directions on the many special projects that come into the pool is another basic duty. Giving constructive feedback at appropriate times also takes a lot of your time. It isn't long before you have jotted down a dozen basic responsibilities. Upon reexamining this list you conclude that you need to be more specific in defining the exact duties. For example, checking work progress really involves seeing that papers and reports coming into the pool are out three hours later. It also means ensuring that the work is proofread by someone other than the person who originally typed it. Following any corrections, the report has to be recorded on a daily log of project activities and placed in the out-going file.

Compare results and identify differing perceptions

At this point, it might be interesting to compare your description of the job with that of your immediate supervisor. How closely in agreement are the two of you on the basic responsibilities, results, and special goals and projects that your job contains? Disagreements are not uncommon, particularly in terms of priorities.

Sharing perceptions of job priorities may point up areas of misunderstanding and confusion. A task a subordinate believed to be a top priority, such as meeting deadlines, might be viewed by the boss as less critical than the number of errors. Only when these differences are identified can clarification actually begin.

THE JOB SPECIFICATION

Presumably, the fact that you are already a supervisor in our hypothetical example means that you have the necessary qualifications. However, if you were told to go out and hire a replacement, what would you look for? What personal characteristics are really necessary (not simply desirable) for performing effectively as supervisor of twelve clerical employees?

You might initially conclude that no one has the combination of personality, knowledge, and skills that you have. And you are right. Everyone is different. What makes one person successful and another a failure will never be completely known. Nevertheless, you eventually reach the conclusion that there are indeed others who probably could handle your job as well as you. But what characteristics would they need to have?

A commonly used method for classifying critical performance characteristics is to look for (1) specific knowledge and skill requirements and (2) critical personal characteristics. As supervisor of a typing pool, you recognize that knowledge of word-processing equipment, including an understanding of microcomputers, is essential. Knowledge of overall departmental operations is also needed—in particular, an awareness of specific policies, procedures, and rules. Furthermore, there are certain supervisory principles and techniques—such as coaching, counseling, and disciplining—that are essential to managing a staff of twelve people. Other characteristics that you believe to be a must include the ability to schedule work, motivate the staff, train subordinates, and delegate authority; a talent for leadership; and oral and written communication skills.

Identify essential skills or knowledge

Identifying critical personal characteristics, on the other hand, is tricky. As a supervisor, you recognize that there are a number of qualities that your replacement should have. He or she should be loyal, truthful, friendly, and so on. But after contemplating you wisely decide that attempting to measure these traits in others would be next to impossible. Gradually you begin to narrow down the list of traits to personal qualities that really make a difference in supervisory performance. Your final list includes patience, an ability to handle pressure, and perseverance.

Identify essential personal characteristics

The end product could now be called a job specification. It represents the type of person who would have a good chance of succeeding in the clerical supervisor's job. When combined with the job description, the two together provide an excellent source for recruiting and selecting job applicants. In fact, supervisors who are actively involved in the selection process should make it a point to take an active role in the analysis

Analysis and selection are complementary functions

of subordinates' jobs. The two functions, job analysis and selection, complement each other. A good analysis leads to a better understanding of the job and to a better selection decision.

Interpreting the Completed ————————
Application Form

The next time the personnel department passes out a stack of completed application forms (or a pile of resumes) and asks you to "look 'em over," don't take the assignment lightly. A common practice is to leaf through the stack, not looking for anything in particular, and hope that someone's application will reach out and grab your attention. By falling into this mode you are allowing yourself to be influenced by the packaging and appearance of the application forms rather than by their content. Don't be fooled by appearances. Study the forms by looking for specific items and information.

Compare applicant's qualifications with the job requirements

Generally speaking, the application form is a most efficient screening tool (see Figure 10.2 for an example). Forms can be reviewed rapidly because they contain standardized types of information. Suppose you are recruiting someone for the position of clerk/receptionist. On the basis of the job posting (see Figure 10.3), you conclude that the job holder should possess communication skills, have one to two years of office experience, be bondable, and be able to type fifty to sixty words per minute. It would not take long to check out a stack of completed application forms and eliminate those applicants who do not possess the basic qualifications. The primary purpose of the application form, then, is to find out if there are any obvious reasons for not hiring the applicant. Besides serving this screening purpose, the application form can also indicate areas that should be checked out later through references or during the interview itself.

If you believe that one of the best predictors of what an applicant will do in the future is what the applicant has done in the past, then study the form. What has the applicant actually been doing with his life? This means tracing his progress—schools, jobs, hobbies—looking for evidence of diligence, accomplishments, knowledge, and skills.

Don't ignore omissions

Don't fall prey to simply looking at the information presented—look for omissions as well. While some omissions may be the result of carelessness or forgetfulness, there is also the possibility that they may be deliberate. If there are gaps in the dates (between school and job or between jobs) that are not explained, check them out. If there have been frequent job changes, check that out. Illnesses or times away from work need to be pinpointed, particularly if the applicant has a history of changing jobs.

Sometimes certain personality traits are evident from the manner in which the application form has been filled out or the resume has been compiled. Spelling or grammatical errors suggest that the applicant tends to do slipshod work. If the instructions on the form are not followed, then this in itself may suggest something. On the other hand, the application form may suggest that the person tends to complete projects that are undertaken, for example, finishing college or completing an apprenticeship program. This is an indicator of perseverance and diligence. Being thorough in pinpointing discrepancies must be accompanied by reasonableness as well as a sense of ethics. If some item appears suspicious but background checks turn up nothing of significance, then the applicant should be given the benefit of the doubt.

Knowing what to look for can make the application form a time saver when interviewing job candidates. The questions asked of each applicant should add to the information already known so that a more complete picture of the person is available. This means that a good interview demands preinterview planning—the next step in the selection process.

> Try to "see through" the application form

The Employment Interview

PLANNING THE INTERVIEW

Would you buy a used car without crawling under it—or paying someone else to crawl under it—in order to see what you are buying? Since your applicant may cost you a whole lot more than a used car, you needn't feel like an intruder when taking a close look at what she is trying to sell—herself. The interview may be your last chance, before the hiring decision is made, to get any questions answered. Although there is usually a probationary period, during which bad selection decisions can be corrected, that process is often messy and unpleasant—not to mention costly—for the typical supervisor.

The fact is, a good hiring interview won't just happen—it takes planning. Unfortunately, the majority of supervisors do not spend enough time planning, or they don't plan because they don't know how. They are the ones who typically think of all kinds of good questions to ask— ten minutes after the interview is over.

> Interview planning pays off

FIGURE 10.2
Sample Employment
Application

EMPLOYMENT APPLICATION

AN EQUAL OPPORTUNITY EMPLOYEE M/F.

This application will be kept active for 60 days only unless updated. A copy of this form is available upon request.

PLEASE ANSWER AND PRINT ALL QUESTIONS YOURSELF. DO NOT TYPEWRITE.

Position(s) Applied for | Referred By | Employment Desired (check one) □ Regular □ Part-Time □ Temporary | If applied with us before, state When Where | Today's Date

If employed by us before give dates
From
To
Job Title | Department | Reason(s) for leaving

PERSONAL DATA
Last Name | First Name | Middle Name | Street Address | City | State | Zip Code

Phone Number ( ) | Date of Birth | Social Security Number | Do you have the legal right to obtain permanent employment in the U.S.? □ U.S. Citizenship □ Permanent Resident Status □ Other

Number of years lived in _____ years

JOB INTEREST
All Jobs are Available to Qualified Candidates of either Sex
Type of work desired: □ Clerical □ Indoor □ Mechanical □ Outdoor □ Technical □ Either □ Other

Distance from your present home that you are willing to travel to work: □ 5 miles □ 20 miles □ 10 miles □ Over 20 miles □ 15 miles □ Free to relocate

Typing Speed _____ wpm
Shorthand Speed _____ wpm

Are you willing to work Overtime? □ yes □ no Nights? □ yes □ no | Weekends and Holidays? □ yes □ no | Shifts and Rotating Shifts □ yes □ no | Do you have a valid Driver's License? □ yes □ no | D.L. Number | Driver's License? | Expiration Date

Number of moving traffic violations over the past three (3) years | How many traffic accidents have you had in the past three (3) years for which you were responsible?

Driver's license ever suspended, revoked or put on probation? □ yes □ no
If yes, please give details below:

Have you ever been convicted of a criminal offense? Are you currently out on bail or on your own recognizance pending trial? (Report all cases except minor traffic violations, sealed or juvenile convictions.) □ yes □ no If yes, complete form

Have you ever been convicted of driving under the influence of alcohol or drugs? □ yes □ no
If so, state the number of times and dates of convictions.

EDUCATION AND SKILLS
Name of High School | City | State | Graduate □ yes □ no | Circle Grade Average D C B A | Major Subjects | | Dates Attended From To

Name of College | City | State | Degree | D C B A | Major Subjects | Units Completed | From To

Name of College | City | State | Degree | D C B A | Major Subjects | Units Completed | From To

Are you now attending school? □ yes □ no □ part-time □ full-time
What courses are you taking? □ Academic □ Business □ General □ Vocational

List any other courses, studies of training:

List any school activities, offices held, scholarships, honors, etc. (Omit organizations whose names indicate the race, creed or national origin of their members.)

List any additional special hobbies, skills, vocational training, registrations, licenses, etc.

(OVER)

Use Space Below for any other experiences, skills, or qualifications which you feel would especially fit you for work with the Company

List Below Three Character References Who Are Not Relatives or Previous Employers

Name	Address	Business or Home Telephone	Position

Will You Work Any Assigned Shift? _____ Will You Work Overtime? _____ Rate of pay expected $ _____ Approximately how many days work did you miss last year? _____

INDICATE NUMBER OF MONTHS EXPERIENCE IN ANY OF THE FOLLOWING:

MACHINE SHOP:	ENGINEERING:	Bookkeeping Machine	Testing
Lathe, Engine	Transformer	OFFICE:	Harnessing
Lathe, Turret	Electrical	Shorthand (WPM)	Circuit Boards
Milling Machine	Mechanical	Typing (WPM)	Tool Crib
Drill Press, Radial	Design	MAINTENANCE:	Receiving
Drill Press, Upright	Drafting, Layout	Electrical	Shipping
Grinder, Internal	Servo Design	Painter	Stock
Sheet Metal Mech.		Carpentry	Fork Lift Driver
	EXPERIENCED IN:	Helper	
Chucker		ACCOUNTING:	ABILITY TO:
General Mach.	Hydraulics	Posting	Read Blueprints
Punch Press	Stress Analysis	Receptionist	Read Micrometers
Experimental Machinist	Electronics	General	Read Gages
Assembly, Mechanical	Mechanisms	Cost	Production Control
Assembly, Instrument	Mechanical-Electrical	Billing	MISCELLANEOUS:
Inspector, Receiving	Actuators	Bookkeeping	Expediting
Inspector, Precision	Bond Pass Filters	Payroll	Solderer
	Low Pass Filters	Accounts Receivable	Winder-Capacitor
	Noise Filters	Accounts Payable	Winder-Toroidal
	Systems Design	Purchasing	Make Machine Set-Ups
	Instruments	Switchboard	Sharpen Tools
		Filing	
		10 Key By Touch	

IMPORTANT: This application must be signed. A false statement or concealment of facts may disqualify you, or result in discharge if discovered at any time after you have been hired. Your employment and its continuance is subject to your passing a physical examination, presenting satisfactory proof of citizenship, signing the patent agreement covering improvements in the company's machines, methods, or products, and agreeing to abide by the company rules of conduct and safety. Investigation of statement made by you on this application and investigation of your references and employment record must meet with our requirements. Your signature on this application authorizes us to make such an investigation.

Applicant's Signature _____ Date _____

(Do not write in this space)	ASSIGNMENT DATA	(Do not write in this space)	INTERVIEWER'S COMMENTS:
Job Classification:	Supervisor	Division	1st Review Date	Company Obligation
Payroll Rate:	per hour ☐ week ☐ month ☐		
Starting Date Time	Shift Dept.		
Physical Exam Time	Date Approved by:		INTERVIEWER

FIGURE 10.3
Sample Job Posting

Position Title: Clerk/Receptionist   University division: Business

Reports to: Assistant Dean   University department: Adult Education

Summary: Responsible for coordinating and directing the daily work and activities of three registration assistants; receiving fees and processing Adult Education applications; and performing a variety of receptionist and clerical duties for the central office staff.

Duties and responsibilities:

1. Processes registration applications including the receipt of a large amount of funds, matching registration requests against available space, endorsing checks and forwarding funds to the Accounting Office.

2. Screens telephone calls; replies to routine inquiries; receives staff and visitors.

3. Maintains current file for Wilson Project; prepares master schedule of classes for Departmental review.

4. Assists in the distribution of instructor packets; assists in drafting Department Bulletin.

5. Composes and types routine correspondence and maintains correspondence files.

6. Processes and routes Department mail.

7. Performs other duties as assigned.

Skills: Must be able to type 50–60 wpm.

Experience: One to two years general clerical activities.

Education: High School Diploma or equivalent.

_____

Approved

| The unstructured interview |

Choosing the Type of Interview. There are essentially two different types of employment interviews. The most common is the unstructured interview. Its popularity stems from the apparent ease that comes from not planning in advance the course the interview will take. All it takes is a few general questions to get it started. Classic questions such as, "Tell me about yourself?" are designed to prod the applicant into talking about things that reflect his or her personality.

The danger of the unstructured interview, however, is that it allows the applicant to take control of the situation. She may stray from the relevant topics, or she may choose to comment only on her areas of strength. The key to conducting the interview effectively is to listen for clues. Subtle nonverbal signals (e.g., nodding, eye contact) combined with brief statements from you (e.g., "Go on, tell me more") encourage the applicant to continue. Positive results tend to occur when the applicant begins to sense that you are trustworthy. By establishing a nonthreatening environment and good rapport, you increase the chance that the applicant will reveal some of her secrets. And these secrets may prove useful for making a hiring decision.

Employment interviews may, of course, be tightly structured. The interviewer may have a list of questions as well as a list of an applicant's possible responses. The sequence of questions on the list is strictly followed while the answers are recorded for analysis at a later time.

Provided the questions are valid to begin with, the structured interview has one major advantage over the unstructured interview. Consistency across applicants is much improved. If each applicant is asked exactly the same things, no applicant can legitimately complain that he or she was unfairly treated—at least during the interview. However, few interviews are structured as they should be. In addition, structured interviews fail to allow the applicant the chance to qualify, explain, or elaborate on an answer. Thus opportunities to collect valuable information about the applicant may be lost. Good applicants may become discouraged or resentful—and they may be tempted to take their talents elsewhere.

The structured interview

The two types of interviews discussed represent extremes. Combining the best of each type of interview is probably the safest approach to follow. This type of interview is referred to as semistructured. However, the key to making the semistructured interview an effective selection device is, again, planning.

Do Your Homework. Lack of adequate planning is obvious when the questions that are asked halfway through the interview focus on topics that have no bearing on the job (e.g., identifying common acquaintances, discussing the weather). A cagey, perceptive applicant (not necessarily the best) may even seize this kind of opportunity to control the direction of the interview. Standard interview questions may also reflect a lack of planning. For example, an applicant would have to be naive not to have a standard answer ready to the inquiry, "Tell us a little about yourself."

Preinterview planning means doing your homework before meeting the applicant. It begins with studying the job description, particularly the exact duties you expect a subordinate to perform. Second, look over the job specification (which usually appears at the bottom of the job description) with an eye toward the critical personal characteristics that can make the difference (e.g., high energy level). Then, match the completed application form (or the resume) against the specification. What kind of match is it? Are there any gaps in the applicant's employment

Match application form against job specification

history? Write down the questions that come to you so that you don't forget them.

Having identified areas that need to be discussed during the interview is only half of your homework. The other half is choosing the right types of questions. If the questions aren't worded correctly, the applicant may misunderstand what is being asked, or the applicant may digress on some irrelevant issue, often leaving you too little time to backtrack with a follow-up question. Yet these problems are minor compared to those that arise when the applicant believes the question asked is illegal.

Questions You Must Not Ask. As far as the courts are concerned, the employment interview is one of the two or three truly critical points in the selection process that are susceptible to bias and discrimination— the others being the application form and psychological testing. Too often, the questions that are asked of the applicant have no real bearing on achieving job success. That is, the questions are not job-related.

Remember legal liability when interviewing

Age, arrests, number of children, and height are a few of the areas that courts have ruled as generally illegal preemployment inquiries. Table 10.3 identifies more comprehensively questions that are unacceptable and those that are acceptable—whether they occur on the application form or during the interview.

As constraining as these prohibitions may seem, there is still a great deal of room for asking insightful questions. Even questions that could be considered discriminatory by the applicant may still be asked if they are proven to be job-related (i.e., BFOQ). Asking about gender on the application form, for example, is a BFOQ for jobs that require certain physical characteristics held by only one sex, such as a fashion model. Keep in mind, however, that race is never a BFOQ.

Although the list of proper and improper preemployment inquiries contained in Table 10.3 is fairly comprehensive, the laws governing preemployment questions are continually changing. The best rule of thumb to use regarding the legality of a particular question is: When in doubt, don't ask it. And as with any other personnel problem, if a question about the legality of an inquiry does arise, contact the personnel department for a ruling.

THE ART OF QUESTIONING

Directive questions

Like good communication, good questions don't just happen. Certain types of questions will lead to certain types of answers. A question that is designed to elicit a specific answer is called a directive question. Examples of directive questions include: asking an applicant what kind of salary he needs, what likes or dislikes he has about work, what he wants to be doing five years from now. When an interviewer asks a directive question, it is because he or she is looking for a piece of specific information.

Directive questions should take up only a small part of the interview. Since the general purpose is to encourage, stimulate, and probe the applicant, the majority of questions should be developed in such a way that they cannot be answered in brief yes or no terms. Open-ended questions are often used to draw the applicant out—in the hope that new information and perspectives will be revealed. Often, they are used relatively early in the interview, with the idea that they will lead to useful directive questioning later. The following are some examples of open-ended questions: How do you feel about working with other employees? How do you get along with people you dislike?

Open-ended questions

It frequently happens that during the course of answering an open-ended question, the applicant will say something that the interviewer wants to pick up on. Rather than interrupting, the interviewer should wait until the applicant is finished, at which time he or she may repeat or rephrase something that was said. Questions asked with the intent of getting the applicant to clarify an earlier remark or to elaborate further on it are known as reflective questions. Their effectiveness depends largely on active listening. The interviewer cannot be thinking about the next question but must concentrate on paying attention (and making a few notes on significant responses).

Reflective questions

Yet another way the interview can be conducted involves asking questions that pose hypothetical problems for the applicant. If you were interviewing a prospect for the clerk/receptionist position, for example, a good question might be:

> Suppose there are two people waiting to see your boss when an irate supplier walks in screaming that his car is being towed away. What would you do?

Hypothetical questions

This type of question can provide insight about the applicant in several ways. First, a level of knowledge about a job-related function can be demonstrated. Second, hypothetical questions show how fast the applicant can think on his feet. Third, the stress created by the question might reveal some interesting clues to the applicant's personality.

Whatever the type of question selected, it is a good rule to keep it simple. Don't run on to the point that the applicant has continually to ask you to repeat it, and don't use words or phrases that are not familiar to the applicant (and for that matter, not natural to the interviewer). Finally, while stress may be a planned part of the interview,

TABLE 10.3   Preemployment Inquiries—Proper and Improper

SUBJECT	PROPER PREEMPLOYMENT INQUIRIES	IMPROPER PREEMPLOYMENT INQUIRIES
Name	Have you ever worked for this company under a different name?	Former name of an applicant whose name has been changed by court order or otherwise.
	Have you ever been convicted of a crime under another name?	Maiden name of a married female applicant.
	Other names under which the applicant has worked. (Needed in order to check educational or employment records or references, if it is standard practice to check such references.)	Specific questions about the name that would reveal applicant's lineage, ancestry, or national origin.
Address and duration of residence	Inquiry into place and length of current and previous addresses.	Specific inquiry into foreign addresses that would indicate national origin.
	How long a resident of this state or city.	Length of residence in the United States.
	Place and duration of previous residences in the United States.	Do you own your own home? Rent? Board? etc.
Sex and marital status	Inquiry as to marital or family status is permissible only if the employer can show that (a) only persons of a particular marital status can perform the job or (b) consideration of marital status does not have the practical effect of denying equal job opportunity to women or men. Inquiry may be made as to whether an applicant has family responsibilities that will interfere with specified job requirements, such as traveling, working unusual hours, etc.	Inquiry as to marital or family status if not based on bona fide occupational qualifications (BFOQ). Sex of applicant. Dependents of applicant. Maiden name of applicant.
Birthplace	Can you, after employment, submit a birth certificate or other proof of U.S. citizenship?	Birthplace of applicant. Birthplace of applicant's parents, spouse, or other relatives. Requirement that applicant submit birth certificate, naturalization, or baptismal record. Any other inquiry into national origin.
Age	If a minor, applicant may be required to state age and submit proof thereof in the form of a certificate of age or work permit.	Requirement that applicant produce proof of age in the form of a birth certificate or baptismal record. Requirement that applicant state age or date of birth.
	Applicant may be told that hire is subject to disclosure and verification of age at time of going on payroll.	

Table 10.3 (Cont'd)

SUBJECT	PROPER PREEMPLOYMENT INQUIRIES	IMPROPER PREEMPLOYMENT INQUIRIES
Religion/creed	An applicant may be told "This is a six-day job. We work Monday through Saturday." An applicant may be advised concerning normal hours and days of work required by the job, to avoid possible conflict with religious convictions or other personal commitments.	Whether an applicant for employment regularly attends a house of worship. Name of priest, rabbi, or minister. Applicants may not be told that employees are required to work on religious holidays that are observed as days of complete prayer by members of their specific faith. Employer must make "reasonable" accommodations.
Race/color or physical features	General distinguishing physical characteristics such as scars, etc.	Complexion, color of skin, or other questions directly or indirectly indicating race or color. Color of applicant's skin, eyes, hair, etc.
Height		Any inquiry into height of applicant, except where it is a BFOQ.
Photograph	May be required *after* hiring for identification purposes.	Requirement that applicant affix a photograph to the application form. Requirement of photograph after interview but before hiring.
Citizenship	Are you in the country on a visa that would not permit you to work here?* Requirement that applicant state whether he or she has ever been interned or arrested as an enemy alien. (See Birthplace)	Of what country are you a citizen? Whether applicant, applicant's parents, or applicant's spouse are naturalized or native-born U.S. citizens. Date when applicant or parents or spouse acquired U.S. citizenship. Requirement that applicant produce naturalization papers or first papers. Whether applicant's parents or spouse are U.S. citizens. Any and all inquiries into whether applicant is now or intends to become a U.S. citizen or any other inquiry related to the aspect of citizenship.*

Table 10.3 (Cont'd)

SUBJECT	PROPER PREEMPLOYMENT INQUIRIES	IMPROPER PREEMPLOYMENT INQUIRIES
National origin/ancestry and languages	Languages that applicant reads, speaks, or writes fluently. (very shaky BFOQ—probably best after hire)	Language commonly used by applicant or in applicant's home. Mother tongue.
		How applicant acquired ability to read, write, or speak a foreign language.
		Date of arrival in U.S. or port of entry; how long a resident of U.S.
		Nationality of applicant's parents or spouse; maiden name of applicant's wife or mother.
		Any inquiry into place of birth of applicant or of applicant's parents, grandparents, or spouse.
Workdays and shifts	Statement by employer of regular days, hours, or shift to be worked.	Any inquiry into willingness to work on particular religious holidays.
	Inquiry into willingness to work required work schedule.	
Education	Inquiry into the academic, vocational, or professional education of an applicant and schools attended.†	Any inquiry asking specifically the nationality or racial or religious affiliation of applicant's school.
Experience	Inquiry into countries applicant has visited.	
Character, arrests, and convictions	Have you ever been *convicted* of any crime? If so, when, where, and disposition of case.	Number and kinds of arrests of an applicant.
	Inquiry into character of applicant.	
Relatives	If applicant is a minor, name and address of parents or guardians.	For other than minor applicant, name and/or address of any relative.
		Maiden name of the wife of a male applicant or maiden name of the mother of a male or female applicant.
		What dependents have you? OFCC
		Names of applicant's relatives already employed by this company or by any competitor. OFCC

Table 10.3 (Cont'd)

SUBJECT	PROPER PREEMPLOYMENT INQUIRIES	IMPROPER PREEMPLOYMENT INQUIRIES
Bankruptcy	Must be BFOQ.	
Garnishments	Inquiry permissible if applicant has access to money.	
Military experience	Whether applicant has received any notice to report for duty in the armed forces.	Applicant's general military experience.
	Military experience of applicant in the armed forces of the United States.	National Guard or Reserve units of applicant.
		Applicant's whereabouts in 1914–1918, 1941–1945, and 1950–53.
	Rank attained? Which branch of service? Military discharge papers will be required *after* hire.	Dates and condition of discharge.
Notice in case of emergency	Name and address of person to be notified in case of accident or emergency will be required *after* hire.	Name and address of relative to be notified in case of accident or emergency.
Organizations	Inquiry into organization memberships, excluding any organization the name or character of which indicates the race, creed, color, religion, or national origin of its members.	List all clubs, social fraternities, societies, lodges, or organizations to which the applicant belongs, other than professional, trade, or service organizations.
	Offices held, if any.	

* Discrimination against aliens does not have the effect of discrimination against national origin (*Farah v. Cecilia Espinoza*, 414 U.S. 86, 92 [1973]).

* *Dept. of Labor and Industry v. Cruz, N.J.* (1965).

† BFOQ-oriented (*Griggs v. Duke Power*).

there is seldom a need to inject much more than is already present. Thus it helps to ask questions in a conversational tone and to minimize the number of loaded (or negative) questions.

CONDUCTING THE INTERVIEW

Make the applicant feel at ease

It is commonly accepted that for most people, the employment interview is an anxiety-producing situation. The applicant can be expected to be nervous and tense. While nervousness is natural, it is to the applicant's advantage to bring it under control as soon as possible. Otherwise, the interviewer might reasonably conclude that this person is not capable of handling stressful situations. But it is also to the benefit of the interviewer (and to the organization) to see the applicant at her best, so it's important to help her relax as soon as possible.

Making the applicant feel at ease is called establishing rapport. It begins when the interviewer introduces himself or herself. A pleasant smile, a warm greeting, and a relaxing handshake are some of the ways to get off on the right foot. Some interviewers might share a humorous personal story with the applicant. (But a minimum amount of small talk is usually appreciated, even by the most seasoned applicant.) The idea is to put the applicant at ease so that she will feel free later to discuss those personal aspects that can make the interview a useful selection tool.

Recognize the pitfalls of losing control

Controlling the Interview. Being in control is something most of us strive to achieve. Therefore, it shouldn't come as a surprise to be reminded that the person being questioned, if presented with the opportunity, would like to direct the tone and topics of the interview. This minimizes the risk that a personality flaw or some deficiency in experience will surface, and it increases the likelihood of being offered a job. Simply knowing this can happen is not enough, because some of the more able applicants may be more clever than you. Being prepared with good questions is one way to keep the interview on track.

At the other extreme is the interviewer who is so much in control that he or she monopolizes the conversation. Interviewers who have the tendency to tell the applicant all about their own personal and professional achievements are victims of their own egos. They may even be playing into the hands of some perceptive applicants—who can then, in subtle ways, turn the tables on the interviewer. Such applicants may answer a question with a question, or compliment the interviewer with such seemingly innocent remarks as "That's interesting," thus encouraging the interviewer to digress.

Maintaining direction (and control) is not really difficult. Qualified applicants appreciate an opportunity to share and clarify their experiences, skills, and goals.

In order to get maximum mileage from the interview, one should follow a plan. It might begin with a list of topics to be discussed—for example: work experience; job progress; qualifications or training; relationships with co-workers, subordinates, and supervisors; reasons for leaving previous jobs; and earnings progress. It is usually wise to begin with an open-ended question for each of these topics, such as: "Joan, I see by your application form that you've worked as a financial analyst for a brokerage firm. Tell me about it." As the interview progresses, move from general discussion to questions that seek specific types of information—for example, "Joan, to what extent have you worked with spread sheet software programs like the Lotus 1-2-3?"

Control begins with good planning

While there is no limit to the number of good questions that might be asked, Table 10.4 presents a list of questions that tend to be used frequently. These questions touch on three areas. Can the applicant do the job? Will the job motivate the applicant? And is there a real opportunity for the applicant to be successful—not only on the job but with the organization? Keep in mind that while it is important to learn about the applicant's personality, temperament, and communication skills, the overall tone of the questions must still be job-related and legal.

Occasionally, organizations will design interview rating forms. These forms (Figure 10.4 is an example) typically contain detailed descriptions of the job characteristics, skills, traits, and knowledge that are considered essential to the successful performance of a job. Interviewers, usually in groups of three to five, will question the applicants on each of the items identified on the rating form. Following the interview, they will score the applicant and then compare their scores to check for interviewer reliability. This approach is considered most acceptable by the EEOC and the judicial systems, because each applicant is asked more or less the same job-related questions.

Confronting the Problem Applicant. Most interviews go smoothly, but occasionally you might encounter a "problem applicant." One type of problem is the applicant who won't stop talking, can't say anything positive about anyone or anything, or is evasive and simply refuses to answer a pertinent question.

There are two strategies available for dealing with the nonstop talker. The first is to let him talk while subtly nudging him in directions that

The nonstop talker

TABLE 10.4 Some Good Interview Questions

Tell me about yourself . . .

What were the circumstances concerning your leaving your previous job?

Would you mind expanding on those aspects of your schooling (or job) that you found to be most satisfying?

Did you finance part of your own education? Doing what type work?

You mentioned that you enjoyed your last job. What type of people were you working with? What type of supervisor?

What experience have you had with . . .

Why do you think the company should hire you?

How long have you been planning for this kind of work?

How did you happen to go to work for them (previous employer)?

What do you expect from the company that hires you?

What are some things you wish to avoid in your next job?

What has accounted for your progress (grades, awards)?

What is your greatest strength? Weakness?

How would you describe yourself?

What do you plan to be doing five years from now? What are your long-range goals? Short-range?

How does this job relate to your plans?

Do you consider yourself a self-starter? Why?

What assignments don't you like?

What would you do if your supervisor made a decision that you strongly disagreed with?

pertain to the job. If you can see that the talker is oblivious to these subtle nudges, then move to the second strategy, the direct approach. Simply interrupt the applicant. Hurt feelings must take a back seat to making the best possible hiring decision.

The nontalker   A completely different type of problem is the nontalker. The nontalker may just be nervous and shy. If it becomes clear that rapport is present and yet the applicant is still not really saying anything, then try to find his emotional "hot buttons." These are value-laden issues that almost everyone has an opinion about. Topics that are good discussion starters are: welfare, the decline of the family unit, lazy workers, worker loyalty, the feminist movement, and so on. Occasionally, an applicant will agree with whatever the interviewer says—hoping to get on his or her good

FIGURE 10.4
Interview Rating Form

Position: _____

Candidate: _____

Qualifications: (Please rate each candidate by placing a check under the appropriate number to determine weight of response.)

Job Knowledge   1   2   3   4   5

(Weight description)

5 points   Excellent: Demonstrates comprehensive knowledge of practices and procedures in specialty and broad knowledge of all major functions. Demonstrates ability to apply specialized knowledge to a wide variety of commonplace and unusual situations.

4 points   Very good

3 points   Good

2 points   Acceptable: Demonstrates broad knowledge of practices and procedures in specialty and general knowledge of most major functions. Demonstrates ability to apply specialized knowledge to a variety of commonplace and some unusual situations.

1 point   Poor: Demonstrates a limited knowledge of practices and procedures in specialty and lacks familiarity of other major functions. Fails to demonstrate ability to apply knowledge to other than routine situations.

Administrative Skills   1   2   3   4   5

(Weight description)

5 points   Excellent: Demonstrates thorough knowledge of management practices and techniques necessary to plan, direct, organize, and follow through with complex workload. Ability to understand, interpret, and follow complex or technical operating procedures. Ability to set priorities, coordinate, and schedule tasks or anticipated problems. Ability to meet a predefined goal with a prescribed timetable. Makes effective use of the chain of command. Ability to forecast future needs.

4 points   Very good

3 points   Good

2 points   Acceptable: Demonstrates general knowledge of management practices and techniques. Ability to understand and follow standard operating procedures. Ability to set priorities, coordinate, and schedule tasks or events so as to maintain efficiency. Understands the chain of command.

1 point   Poor: Lacks knowledge of management practices and techniques. Lacks ability to plan, direct, and organize workload. Unable to set priorities, coordinate, and schedule tasks and events. Unable to maintain efficiency.

SUBTOTAL SCORE _____

Supervisory Skills   1   2   3   4   5

5 points   Excellent: Demonstrates thorough knowledge of actions and behavior necessary to plan, direct, and supervise the work of others. Demonstrates support and concern for growth and development of subordinates. Able to assess capabilities and skills of staff in order to optimize utilization of

Figure 10.4 (Cont'd)

staff. Demonstrates willingness and ability to delegate; evaluates and follows up on the results of delegated assignments; follows through on decisions and keeps subordinates informed of new developments. Able to take actions that may cause negative reactions from staff.

4 points Very good

3 points Good

2 points Acceptable: Demonstrates general knowledge of actions and behavior necessary to plan, direct, and supervise the work of others. Recognizes importance of developing subordinates. Attempts to assess capabilities and skills of staff to optimize utilization of personnel. Understands importance of delegation.

1 point Poor: Demonstrates limited knowledge of actions and behavior necessary to plan, direct, and supervise the work of others. Lacks concern for development of employees. Cannot delegate.

Attitude, Manner, and Self-Expression   1   2   3   4   5
                                                  ___   ___   ___   ___   ___

5 points Excellent: Diplomatic, exceptionally well-poised, adjusts exceptionally well to situations, exceptionally warm and sincere, advances discussion with little guidance, excellent use of word and sentence structure, precise and exact enunciation; voice is very pleasing and well-modulated.

4 points Very good

3 points Good

2 points Acceptable: tactful, considerate, convincing, generally poised, controlled, cooperative, answers freely, proper use of vocabulary and grammar, readily understandable.

1 point Poor: Flippant, overbearing, belligerent, very timid, withdrawn, lacking in control, unresponsive, uncommunicative, mumbles badly, very indistinct, voice is very monotonous.

SUBTOTAL SCORE _____

Oral Communication   1   2   3   4   5
                                                  ___   ___   ___   ___   ___

5 points Excellent: Speaks clearly and understandably. Demonstrates mastery of vocabulary and grammar. Responses are brief, to the point, and logically organized. Can assess understanding of listeners and modifies responses to that level when explaining technical matters. Advances discussion with little guidance. Is able to persuade verbally, summarize and justify effectively. Is able to listen attentively to others' opinions and ideas.

4 points Very good

3 points Good

2 points Acceptable: Properly uses vocabulary and grammar. Responses are relative to subject and understandable. Attempts to explain technical matters at listeners' level of understanding.

1 point Poor: Consistently uses improper vocabulary and grammar. Responses are incoherent, rambling, unresponsive. Explains technical matters by talking down to listeners, intentionally above their level of understanding or with excessive jargon.

Problem Solving   1   2   3   4   5
                                                  ___   ___   ___   ___   ___

5 points Excellent: Demonstrates ability to integrate, recall, and categorize information, see similarities and differences, separate important from unimportant information, and identify basic idea or problem. Able to identify causes of a problem. Breaks complex problems into elements that can

Figure 10.4 (Cont'd)

be analyzed separately. Recognizes when more information is needed as well as being able to research and obtain necessary information through a variety of methods. Demonstrates the ability to develop different solutions to problems, realizing possible results or impact of actions before acting. Ability to make decisions with incomplete information and in pressure situations.

4 points   Very good

3 points   Good

2 points   Acceptable: Demonstrates ability to integrate information, separate important from unimportant information, and identify basic idea or problem. Able to recognize when more information is necessary. Considers more than one solution and possible impact before acting.

1 point   Poor: Has difficulty in properly identifying problems. Considers only one solution without considering its possible impact.

SUBTOTAL SCORE _____

Judgment, Decision-Making Ability   1   2   3   4   5

5 points   Excellent: Unusually perceptive; fully understands implications of questions; carefully and quickly examines and correctly analyzes all aspects of the problem and decides on a proper course of action.

4 points   Very good

3 points   Good

2 points   Acceptable: Grasps intent of question; answers logically related to question; answers given without delay; has examined more than one alternative and decides on a proper course of action.

1 point   Poor: Misunderstands; slow to understand the obvious; requires frequent leading questions; confused; illogical, answers not pertinent to questions. Unable to decide on a proper course of action.

Interactive Skills   1   2   3   4   5

5 points   Excellent: Demonstrates the ability to interact with people of various backgrounds, without eliciting negative or hurt feelings. Ability to consider and adjust to the needs and concerns of others, understanding of the emotions and motives of others and how they will react in different situations. Ability to deal appropriately with hostile individuals or hostility, maintaining control.

4 points   Very good

3 points   Good

2 points   Acceptable: Demonstrates the ability to interact with people of various backgrounds. Demonstrates ability to adjust to the needs and concerns of others. Attempts to understand the emotions and motives of others. Ability to deal with hostile individuals and situations. Demonstrates some understanding of public relations responsibilities and is capable of maintaining satisfactory business relationship.

1 point   Poor: Lacks ability to interact with people of various backgrounds. Demonstrates little ability to adjust to the needs and concerns of others. Lacks understanding of emotions or motives of others. Unable to deal appropriately with hostile individuals or situations, actions tend to escalate the situation. Demonstrates little understanding of the public relations responsibilities of this position. Tends to think only in terms of authority of position and enforcing rules, laws, regulations.

SUBTOTAL SCORE _____

Figure 10.4 (Cont'd)

Overall Suitability for Position	3	6	9	12	15

15 points I recommend this applicant without reservation as an excellent prospect for the position.

12 points On the whole, I would recommend this applicant as a good prospect for the position.

9 points I have some reservations, but I feel he/she has a reasonable chance of success in the position.

6 points I have substantial doubts about the applicant.

3 points I feel the applicant is unsuited for the position.

Additional Comments

Please describe any notable abilities, interests, skills, training, or experience of the applicant related directly to the position.

Please describe any reservations you have or potential weaknesses you see in the applicant.

Total Score _____

_____

Signature of Interviewer   Date

side—so it may become necessary for the interviewer to push opposing opinions in a believable way. Nontalkers, once they open up on one issue, will usually continue to be more communicative when answering later questions.

The negative applicant

The problem of the negative applicant can be a truly unpleasant experience for the interviewer. There isn't a whole lot one can do to change the negative attitude of some people without shutting down the interview process altogether. Listening may be the interviewer's only effective strategy. But even that is often not enough. If the hostility continues, writing off the interview becomes the only sound decision.

The evasive applicant

Yet another type of problem is the evasive applicant. Most applicants will give detailed responses to questions that cast them in a good light. Thus when applicants tend to give evasive answers, chances are they are trying to hide something. If the question is important and needs a clear, precise answer, don't give up. File the touchy area away in your mind with the idea of asking again later. The applicant may change her mind about answering, or you may pick up something that suggests why the evasiveness occurred. In either case, you will leave the interview better informed about the applicant.

Winding Up the Interview. Terminating the interview involves more than just saying, "Thank you for coming in." The applicant has spent an important portion of her time preparing for the interview and meeting with you, and perhaps with several other interviewers. She deserves to know where she stands in the selection process as soon as possible. Of course, an interviewer is not usually prepared, nor expected, to make on-the-spot selection decisions about an applicant—unless the applicant is obviously not qualified. But it is considerate to tell the applicant when she might expect to hear from you. Perhaps you might call the applicant later (the following day) to inform her of her status as well as to check on her continued interest in being hired by the company. At the conclusion of the interview, stand up, shake hands, and escort the applicant to her next scheduled appointment in the organization.

The Selection Decision

The time has come. A selection decision has to be made from the final list of applicants—usually a list of no more than three. While others (e.g., staff and line personnel) may play a part in this process, it is your voice (i.e., the immediate supervisor's) that will carry the greatest weight. You want to be objective and, above all, fair. So you deliberately play down the intangibles because they tend to be subjective and hard to defend.

You begin by reevaluating each piece of information on each applicant that has been collected. You start with the applicant's resume, again checking past work experiences and qualifications. Telephone reference checks provide support for the experiences listed on the resume. As far as knockout factors are concerned (e.g., lack of skill or knowledge), there are none. The check has also turned up the information that the applicant is well liked by her former boss as well as by her co-workers (see Figure 10.5 for an example of a telephone reference check).

Carefully evaluate available information

While the questions you asked in the interview were tough, you thought she handled them well. She answered clearly and honestly. She even stuck to her guns and held her point of view when you deliberately pushed an opposing point of view. You conclude that this applicant "sticks to her convictions"—a personality trait you believe is essential to the job in question.

Pulling all of this information together, you might ask yourself one final time: "Am I being unduly influenced by the applicant's personality or appearance?" If the answer is yes, you may want to double-check for any inconsistencies. One way to check for inconsistencies is to com-

FIGURE 10.5
Telephone Reference Check

Name of Applicant _____ Date _____

Name of Company _____ City/State/Zip _____ Telephone No. _____

Person Contacted (Supervisor) _____ Position: _____

1. What was the nature of his/her work? _____

_____ Checks _____ Doesn't Check _____

2. How many people did he/she supervise? _____

3. Any responsibility for management decisions and policy formulation? _____

_____

4. (If Salesman) What type of selling did he/she do? What type of trade did he/she call on? _____

_____ Checks _____ Doesn't Check _____

5. When did he/she work for you? (Dates of employment and previous positions in the company) From: Yr. _____

Mo. _____ To: Yr. _____ Mo. _____ Checks _____ Doesn't Check _____

Were his/her previous references checked? Yes _____ No _____. Were they satisfactory?   Yes _____ No _____

6. How were his/her results compared with others?   Excellent _____ Average _____ Poor _____

7. Did he/she work hard?   Industrious _____ Enough to get by _____ Below Average _____

8. How was his/her attendance on the job?   Excellent _____ Some days lost _____ Below Av. _____

9. How did he/she get along with others?   Very well _____ Fair _____ Poor _____

10. Did he/she have any financial or domestic difficulties that you know of which interfered with his/her work?
No _____ Yes _____

(Comments) _____

_____

11. Any bad drinking or gambling habits?   No _____ Yes _____ (Comments) _____

_____

12. He/she says his/her earnings were $ _____ when he/she left.   Checks _____ Doesn't Check _____

And of this amount $ _____ was in salary.   Checks _____ Doesn't Check _____

$ _____ was in commission.   Checks _____ Doesn't Check _____

13. Why did he/she leave your company? _____

Reason Agrees _____ Doesn't Agree _____ (If doesn't agree) _____

_____

Figure 10.5 (Cont'd)

14. What would you say were his/her strong points? _____

_____

15. What would you say were his/her weak points? _____

_____

16. Would you re-employ him/her if you had an opening?   Yes _____ No _____ (If no, why not) _____

_____

_____

17. Is there anything else you'd like to tell me that might help in forming an accurate estimate of Mr./Ms. _____

qualifications? (Comments) _____

_____

18. From your experience with this person what can we do to help him/her improve his/her performance? _____

_____

SUMMARY: Good Reference _____

                Some Reservation _____

                Definitely Open to Question _____

COMMENTS: _____

_____

_____

_____

_____

_____

_____

                                        CHECK MADE BY: _____

pare your findings with those of another interviewer (perhaps personnel). Ultimately, however, a decision is made to offer the applicant a job if she can pass a physical examination given by one of the company's physicians.

There is one final note to this process. Supervisors should maintain complete records of the significant events, questions, answers, and observations that occurred during the hiring process. They could prove useful

Keep good records

in at least two ways. First, if one of the rejected applicants believes he or she was discriminated against somewhere in the hiring process, the records may help to prove otherwise. Second, sometime down the road (maybe six months to a year), it would make sense for the supervisor to compare the new employee's performance to the data that were used to select her. Was the application form completely correct? Does the employee possess the skills, knowledge, and critical personal characteristics that the selection process suggested? And most important, could the selection process be improved? History does not have to repeat itself. Supervisors will inevitably make some bad selection decisions. Effective supervisors, however, will learn from their hiring mistakes.

SUMMARY

Supervisors should take an active role in the selection process. Their degree of activity may range from informally reviewing completed application forms to making the hiring decision. Whatever role the supervisor follows, however, one thing is essential. The supervisor must understand the legalities that influence the employment process as well as the legalities that affect employee safety and health. This translates into practices that treat applicants and employees with consistency and fairness, regardless of their race, sex, religion, age, and national origin.

The role of job analysis is critical to making good selection decisions. Employment laws emphasize the need for thorough and accurate job descriptions and job specifications. Furthermore, a sound job analysis provides the employment interviewer (often the supervisor) with a basis for asking job-related questions and improving the validity of the selection process.

Employment interviewing was discussed in depth because it is the one part of the selection process in which supervisors tend to play the deciding role. Planning the interview was emphasized as well as the kinds of questions that should never be asked. In addition, the characteristics of interview questions were presented, including the use of open-ended and reflective questions. Finally, the employment interview itself was discussed. Hints on how to greet the applicant, control the interview, handle the problem applicant, and terminate the interview were provided.

PROMOTING THE BEST QUALIFIED

The Burrito Barn Company has twenty-eight fast-food outlets located in the Southwest. Most of the company's employees are young people still in school who work part-time at the minimum wage rate. Each spring some of the part-time employees are promoted to full-time employees. They receive significantly higher pay and assume supervisory responsibilities. The promotions are decided by each outlet manager, who recommends two or three of the "best qualified" part-time employees for training to be team supervisors. The training is provided by Alberto Mendiola, the manager of outlet operations for the company, who designed the training program and presents it himself.

Marie Ortega, the personnel manager, has been very impressed with the results of Alberto's two-day supervisor training course, and she has appreciated his initiative in organizing it and presenting it. This year, however, there is a problem. After the promotions were announced, three Asian employees came to Marie to ask why they were not on the list. They noted that of the seventy-three part-time employees who are being promoted, almost 80 percent are Hispanic and none of them are Asian. Yet only 45 percent of the part-time workers are Hispanic whereas 20 percent are Asian. The three employees told Marie they had already contacted the EEOC and been told that their complaint is legitimate.

When Marie questioned Alberto about the promotion decisions, he justified them by saying that the managers had been instructed to select the "best qualified." He also reminded her that each employee is evaluated on the company's performance evaluation form and that it is not discriminatory to base promotion decisions on performance.

The performance evaluation form is a simple graphic rating scale that measures work habits, attitude, appearance, punctuality, and overall performance. To learn how effectively the form is being used, Marie called some of the outlet managers. She was dismayed to learn that the form is used in only about half the outlets and that even where it is used the managers generally do not refer to it before deciding who to recommend for promotion. The managers said they do not need to look at this data to decide who is best qualified. Marie also talked to some of the employees who were being promoted and became even further disturbed when they said that their managers could not have recommended their promotions based on performance because their managers did not work with them and therefore had little opportunity to observe their performances.

1. When the EEOC contacts Marie, how can she justify the company's promotion system?
2. Is the system really fair?
3. Is the performance evaluation process satisfactory?
4. What does Marie need to change?

DISCUSSION QUESTIONS

1. Why should supervisors be concerned with the selection process when it is typically the responsibility of the personnel department?

2. Why is a knowledge of legal issues surrounding hiring and employment practices essential for supervisors?

3. What is the difference between a job description and a job specification? What is the significance of each?

4. How is the application form most useful?

5. What are the three most commonly used interview techniques and the advantages/disadvantages of each?

6. Identify and give the purpose of the types of interview questions most commonly used.

7. What is meant by controlling and winding up with regard to the interviewing process?

8. Identify three kinds of problem applicants and strategies to deal with each.

REFERENCES

Arvey, R. E. *Fairness in Selecting Employees.* Reading, Mass.: Addison-Wesley, 1979.

Arvey, R. E., and Campion, James E. "The Employment Interview: A Summary and Review of Recent Literature." *Personnel Psychology* 35, no. 2 (Summer 1982): 281–322.

Byham, W. C. "Common Selection Procedures Can Be Overcome." *Personnel Administrator* (August 1978): 42–47.

Cawsey, T. F. "Why Line Managers Don't Listen to Their Personnel Department." *Personnel* (January/February 1980): 11–20.

Ghorpade, Jai, and Atchison, Thomas. "The Concept of Job Analysis: A Review and Some Suggestions." *Public Personnel Management,* no. 3 (1980): 134–137.

Government Manual: Office of Federal Contract Compliance. "Revised Order No. 4." 36 *Federal Register* 23, no. 152(1971). See 41 C.R.F. 60–2.11 for guidelines regarding race and sex.

Government Manual: U.S. Department of Labor, Employment Standards Administration. *Discrimination in Employment Act of 1967: A Report Covering Activities Under the Act in 1974,* January 31, 1975.

Higgins, James M. "A Manager's Guide to the Equal Employment Opportunity Laws." *Personnel Journal* 55 (August 1976): 406.

Nag, Amal. "Slipping Back: Recession Threatens to Erode Job Gains of Women and Minorities." *Wall Street Journal* (January 7, 1980): 1, 14.

Peres, Richard. *Dealing with Employment Discrimination.* New York: McGraw-Hill, 1978.

Smith, L. "Equal Opportunity Rules Are Getting Tougher." *Fortune* (June 19, 1978): 152.

Witkin, Arthur A. "Commonly Overlooked Dimensions of Employee Selection." *Personnel Journal* 59 (July 1980): 571–574.

CHAPTER 11

TRAINING WINNERS

To rise from a zero
To big Campus Hero,
To answer these questions you'll strive:
  Where am I going,
    How shall I get there, and
    How will I know I've arrived?

WILLIAM BARBER

Chapter Outline

Training—Placing the Responsibility
    Training Usually Has Low Priority
    The Supervisor's Essential Role in Training
Learning
    Learning Principles
    Developing a Learning Climate
Welcome to the Club: Orientation
    Breaking In the New Employee
    General Orientation
    Social Orientation
Training Decisions
    Deciding If Training Is Needed
    Choosing the Right Technique

Objectives

For the contemporary supervisor, training subordinates is a major responsibility. Although training is often conducted by specialists, the most effective transfer of training back to the job occurs when the supervisor uses his or her ability to reinforce what is taught—be it knowledge, skills, or new attitudes. Specifically, in this chapter you will become familiar with:

1. The need to recognize that training is an important supervisory responsibility
2. The basic principles of adult learning
3. The need for a well-planned and systematic orientation program
4. The techniques for identifying training needs among subordinates and for recognizing when training is not the solution
5. The various training techniques available to the supervisor and how to gain employee commitment to training

Major Concepts

Operant learning	Socialization
Social learning	Hazing
Adult learning	Performance gap
Learning principles	Off-the-job training
Practice	Vestibule training
Learning climate	Formal classroom instruction
Empathy	On-the-job training
General orientation	Transfer of learning
Social orientation	Job rotation

WHEN A SUPERVISOR WON'T TEACH

It was going to be Mort's first day on the job, and he was nervous. Thoughts such as "What's my new boss like?" "Are the people friendly?" and "Will I be able to do the job?" went through Mort's head during his drive to work. When Mort arrived, the receptionist guided him into the back shop area and introduced him to Mr. Willaby, the supervisor. After a casual greeting, Mr. Willaby proceeded to take Mort to the drill press which was to be his work station for the time being. Mr. Willaby briefly explained how the machine worked, sampled two pieces, and left Mort on his own to do the job. After about ten minutes, for some unknown reason, the drill bit on the press broke. Mort timidly asked Mr. Willaby for another drill bit and attempted to explain what had happened. Without a word, Mr. Willaby replaced the broken bit and went on his way. Mort continued to have problems with breaking drill bits that morning, and each time Mr. Willaby replaced the parts without comment. Finally, after a fourth drill bit had broken, Mr. Willaby lost his temper, figured Mort was no good for the job, and fired him immediately. After Mort had left the shop, other drill press operators looked over the machine and found a defective part that was causing the drill bits to break. Even the most experienced drill press operator was unable to operate the machine without breaking drill bits. The final result of this incident was a fired employee, a shutdown drill press, and costly production time lost.

While students, especially those paying for their own education, seem to understand the importance of good teaching, one has reason to be skeptical about the importance given this area by "real world" bosses—those denizens of the "Get to work," "Tails up, noses down, and full speed ahead" school of front-line management.

There are, of course, employees who will take their fate into their own hands and learn—formally or informally—what they need to know to do their jobs. They seem to be in the minority, however, making up just a small percentage of the work force. Most people wait for the organization to fulfill its obligation to train them.

Training—Placing the Responsibility

Is the organization, be it a department or the company as a whole, responsible for the individual's job knowledge and development? The answer is yes, at least to the extent that employees become proficient in learning to do what is expected of them. With regard to employee development, many organizations seem to be less concerned. So how shall we know that our new employees are being trained properly? Why, as every front office knows, the supervisor will take care of that. "The supervisor is a good worker," the front office says. "She'll see that her people are trained."

In reality, the supervisor with a reputation for being a hard worker is more likely to be concerned with maintaining schedules and meeting goals and quotas than with becoming a good trainer.

When expecting a supervisor to train subordinates, the assumption is normally made that the supervisor will be an effective teacher. Some supervisors, of course, are excellent trainers. By and large, however, supervisors spend a minimum of time planning and conducting training. Part of this dilemma stems from not knowing how to train, what kind of training is needed, or how people learn. This shouldn't be surprising since employees who are promoted into supervision are usually selected on the basis of their technical knowledge rather than their interpersonal skills. Consequently, supervisors who fall into this mode are more comfortable *doing* rather than training.

> Management assumes employees are trained by supervisors

TRAINING USUALLY HAS A LOW PRIORITY

Training is one of those fuzzy responsibilities that supervisors are expected to carry out but are seldom rewarded for, there being no concrete way the task can be measured. Because there are already so many roles the typical supervisor has to fill—participant in meetings, interviewer, parent at work, coach, counselor, order giver, administrator, and teacher—priorities have to be established. And unfortunately, teacher is usually at the bottom of the list.

Take the case of John H. John graduated from the state university as an honors student and member of Phi Beta Kappa. He taught education courses at a community college for a few years before joining the state government as an auditor. "Brilliant," "ambitious," and "enthusiastic" were adjectives used to describe John. Then he became a supervisor in the taxation division, where he supervised thirty auditors and twenty-six clerical people. John was a hard worker, but when it came to training, he went to sleep. He went to sleep when new hires had problems. He went to sleep when they asked questions. Did John train any of his people to handle taxpayers' complaints? Of course not. Could John instruct? Probably—after all, he had been a "brilliant" educator at one time. Did John want to train? "Of course," said John. "Just let me know what they want taught." And he promptly went back to sleep.

Training is often delegated

Is John typical of supervisors today? In the *degree* of his indifference, certainly not. Yet maybe John's attitude about training simply reflects what many supervisors believe. Training subordinates is generally perceived to include showing how a machine is to be turned on, where to feed in the raw materials, where the bathroom is, when to take breaks, what safety procedures are important, and how many widgets they are expected to produce. The smart supervisors soon figure out that any one of the experienced employees can do most of this "training"; thus delegating these time-consuming duties is a fairly common practice. As one supervisor commented, "Delegating these chores allows me time for more important things; besides, talking to folks, especially in groups, was never one of my strengths to begin with." Fear of speaking to groups exists with many supervisors. Yet this excuse for not training is only one of several. Table 11.1 identifies a variety of reasons why supervisors might fail to commit themselves to the training role.

THE SUPERVISOR'S ESSENTIAL ROLE IN TRAINING

Employees will often receive training from a number of different sources in the course of their organizational careers. In-house training may be

TABLE 11.1   Supervisors' Objections to Training and Developing Subordinates

Training subordinates has a low priority for me and for my own boss.

There are too many other areas to be responsible for—besides it's a staff responsibility.

Training takes too much time.

What if I give bad advice? I can't predict the future.

I hate to train a replacement.

Employee development means "promotion," and frankly, there aren't any promotions to be offered at this time.

This employee is approaching retirement anyway.

You've heard of the Peter Principle—well this guy has reached his level of incompetence.

Nobody has told me how to train.

I don't like addressing groups.

My people are already trained.

provided through the personnel department, academic training may be made available to them from a local college or university, or they may attend a professional conference at some more distant location. Some training programs yield results that benefit the organization as well as the trainees; others aren't worth the cost of the handouts. When the training isn't effective, it is usually for one or more of the following reasons: Training content is not meaningful or pertinent; there is no opportunity to practice or rehearse what is taught; trainees are not motivated to learn because of their lack of active involvement; trainees don't perceive any tangible payoff from the effort it takes to learn.

The likelihood that these obstacles exist is surprisingly high when the training is conducted away from the job and/or the training is conducted by an instructor who has little knowledge of the trainees' duties and tasks. This is the strongest argument in support of the supervisor as trainer. When training is conducted by the immediate supervisor, it carries an enormous amount of effectiveness and relevance—factors that an outside expert cannot easily provide. This is not necessarily an indictment of outside experts. In fact, they do serve a useful purpose and have resulted in numerous positive effects on performance and morale. However, the immediate supervisor is of necessity a trainer, by reason of his or her relationship with subordinates.

Supervisor's familiarity with assigned tasks

It pays to have well-trained people

Maintaining well-trained subordinates should be a primary responsibility of any supervisor. Given that supervisors are themselves evaluated on the basis of the accomplishments of their work units, the importance of having well-trained people should be crystal clear. But too often this logic needs to be spelled out to supervisors by the front office. In particular, the supervisor's personal involvement in the training process is absolutely essential if there is going to be any transfer of learning back to the job.

Scope of the training function

The scope of the supervisor's training responsibilities includes making sure that new employees are properly inducted into the work unit and are provided with the critical survival skills needed to make a successful transition into the organization. Supervisors are also expected to assist experienced employees when it comes to fine-tuning already established skills and keep the old hands up to date on the technical and informational aspects of their jobs. While both of these training functions will be briefly examined, the more fundamental concept of learning needs to be immediately addressed.

Learning

Expecting a supervisor to orient new subordinates, teach required skills, choose the method that best captures the interest of the trainee, and a host of other training procedures demands at least some knowledge of how people learn. In the case of adult learning, we are referring to a relatively permanent change in behavior that occurs as a result of experience or practice. Two major theories have been developed to explain how this process occurs—operant learning and social learning; and while there are differences, the one important commonality is that both depend heavily on positive reinforcement.

Operant learning

Operant learning is based on the principle that people behave in ways that lead to positive consequences or to the avoidance of pain or displeasure. For example, a new worker who places his finger incorrectly under a punch press is not likely to do it again. On the other hand, when that same employee meets standards for the first time and his co-workers take him out to celebrate after work, chances of a repeat performance are good. The key to operant learning is a consequence (positive or negative) that is immediate and certain to occur.

Social learning

A second useful theory, social learning, can best be described as learning through observation. Watching how a co-worker successfully handles a complex task, listening to an accompanying explanation, maybe practicing a time or two, and possibly making revisions based on the comments of the co-worker—these represent the essence of social learning. It is an excellent technique for learning complex skills, because traditional methods such as lectures, discussions, and films do not actively involve the learner, whereas social learning demands trainee involvement.

Any training the supervisor provides should be based on the principles of learning proposed by both operant and social learning theories. Both theories identify the conditions that make learning possible, both help in the design of better instructional methods, and both suggest a common set of principles for learning.

LEARNING PRINCIPLES

People differ, and because of their differences they learn in a variety of ways. Some people are fast learners of skills. Others take longer to acquire even a minimum level of proficiency. Some people have a positive outlook and attitude when it comes to learning; others appear to have a lackadaisical or even negative attitude toward instruction. For the trainee to be motivated to learn, he or she must perceive the content of the instruction to be relevant. The principle to keep constantly in mind is that training must be meaningful to the learner. It is unrealistic to expect success with a trainee, even one who is blessed with a repertoire of instructional retention capabilities, when the training doesn't fit the trainee. Moreover, one must accept the fact that 100 percent success cannot always be expected, even with good training.

Training must fit the trainee

A second principle is that the consequences of learning must be positive and be seen as beneficial to the trainee. It is not realistic to expect trainees to learn for learning's sake. Learning is not adequate reward in itself. While learning will provide the trainee with a sense of accomplishment over the long run, some form of extrinsic reinforcement is still essential. Furthermore, reinforcement should occur as soon as possible after a trainee takes a step in the right direction. People will exert tremendous efforts to learn and will become active participants in training when they believe they will be rewarded for doing so.

Reinforcement and active participation

Which groups learn faster, adults or children? If you think adults learn faster, you're wrong. Adults are slower learners, in part because of established beliefs, attitudes, values, and habits acquired over the years.[1] The longer a particular behavior has been practiced and reinforced, the more reluctant people are to change it. There is more than a particle of truth in the old saying, "You can't teach an old dog new

Adults learn differently than children

[1] Ron Zemke and Susan Zemke, "30 Things We Know for Sure About Adult Learning," *Training/HRD Journal*, June 1981, pp. 45–52.

tricks." Often, the only way a trainee can learn new skills is by first unlearning old habits. This may sound like an impossible barrier for the supervisor to overcome; but techniques such as breaking down the task into small units is one way to begin the learning process. When the first steps to learning are relatively easy and nonthreatening, the adult learner will gain confidence. Increasing the learning dosage at a gradual rate, rather than overwhelming the learner with complex details, is always a good procedure to follow.

Only perfect practice makes perfect

"Practice makes perfect" is also appropriate when describing training with the adult in mind. It is a basic principle of learning. Numerous studies consistently demonstrate that when people are encouraged to practice what they have learned as soon as they have learned it, their retention is much higher.[2] When not provided an opportunity to practice or to become actively involved in the learning process, trainees will forget most of what they have learned. But practice alone is meaningless. Following through on the Vince Lombardi credo that only perfect practice makes perfect, trainees need help in "practicing perfectly"—that is they need accurate and timely feedback that lets them know when they have succeeded and how their performance could be improved.

While each of these principles is certainly important, they will not individually or collectively guarantee trainee learning. All learning is completely under the control of the learner. The supervisor as trainer can only offer data, situations, or events that provide possibilities for the learner to acquire new skills, knowledge, or attitudes. The supervisor can only provide a learning climate—it is the trainee who learns. But creating a climate conducive to learning is well worth the effort.

DEVELOPING A LEARNING CLIMATE

Learning climate

Just as individuals have distinct personalities, each organization has a unique atmosphere. The degree to which the organization encourages psychological growth and professional development is strongly influenced by the organization's learning climate. Specifically, the degree to which favorable and stimulating learning attitudes are encouraged by top management, the extent of trust between workers and their supervisor, and the presence of a system that maintains and nurtures the employee's self-esteem are critical components of an effective learning environment.

[2] Craig Schneier, "Training and Development Programs: What Learning Theory and Research Have to Offer," *Personnel Journal*, April 1974, pp. 288–293.

And the burden for creating such an environment often falls heaviest on the employee's immediate supervisor.

It is the supervisor who has the greatest influence on the employee's feelings toward his or her task, toward other members of the work group, and toward the total organization. Since the supervisor strongly influences the work behavior of new employees, this influence must coincide with the objectives of the organization. Specific behaviors that are emphasized during training sessions and that are expected to carry over to the job must be positively reinforced by and modeled by the supervisor; otherwise, the training will not be effective. The supervisor's behaviors can in fact reduce the chances for learning to occur. For example, employee safety programs attempt to provide workers with an appreciation of safe work habits; however, supervisors whose own work habits run counter to the content taught in the program undermine the trainee's safety efforts— and those of the organization as a whole. Supervisors whose words say one thing and their actions another convey a double message. Inevitably, the actions speak louder than the words.

> **The supervisor's influence on learning.**

Most individuals have a natural desire to learn, but this desire may be stifled when the atmosphere is not conducive to learning. Thus it is necessary for management to create a learning climate on the job that will enhance the acquisition of new behaviors, and it is important that such a climate be created early in the training program. This is the supervisor's responsibility when he or she is doing the training.

The following are some guidelines for creating a motivating learning climate:

> **Guidelines**

1. Establish the relevance of the training to the job requirements.
2. Point out personal benefits to be gained from accomplishing the learning.
3. Provide feedback to the trainee that is constructive and nonthreatening.
4. Provide opportunities to practice the skills or tasks taught.

These guidelines are elaborated on in the paragraphs that follow.

When the need for knowledge becomes obvious because of work demands, most employees want to learn and are willing to learn. But training usually occurs before the need is obvious to employees. Therefore, employees need to be made aware of the connection between what they must know to do their jobs and what they are going to be asked to learn. Establishing relevance is thus the first step for motivating the trainee.

> **Establish relevance**

Identify training benefits

Provide feedback

But protect employees' self-esteem

Provide practice opportunities

In addition, specific benefits need to be identified, and employees successfully completing a training program should receive these benefits. Rewards may be either external (provided by the supervisor or the organization) or internal (perceived by the individual). External benefits, for example, might include pay increments, promotion, increased security, or increased job status, recognition, and additional job responsibility. Internal benefits are more powerful and long lasting because they relate to higher-order needs (i.e., self-actualization and self-esteem). They might include personal growth and a sense of achievement, and the self-satisfaction that comes from learning to do a job better.

The feedback channel lets a trainee know what progress is being made toward attaining the identified reward. Feedback can come from the supervisor or from the trainer—if they are not one and the same person. Feedback needs to be provided periodically (more frequently for unsatisfactory performers) and constructively throughout the learning process. It is just as important to tell trainees when they're doing a bad job as when they are doing the job right. This will get them back on the right track quickly as well as clear up any misconceptions they may have. However, criticism should always focus on the problem, not the person. Sometimes the best supervisory intentions are misunderstood by trainees, and they feel threatened because feedback seems too personal. One of the most priceless of human attributes is self-esteem, and a supervisor can minimize damage to this frail attribute by focusing on specific behaviors, incidents, or events that cause concern, rather than focusing on the trainee's personality.

Supporting desired behaviors with favorable responses is the responsibility of both the trainer and the supervisor. If at all possible, find something about the trainee's performance that suggests personal accomplishment or improvement. Don't dwell solely on poor performance; instead, positively reinforce behaviors that should be repeated.

Finally, when the training objective involves behavioral change, it is important to provide trainees with practice opportunities. Practice is the heart of skill acquisition and retention. Watching someone else perform complex maneuvers does not build sufficient skills. It is practice that builds the skill itself, along with the trainee's confidence to try out the newly learned behavior in the real world or on the job. Some of the most effective training programs include a step-by-step guide to achievement, thus enabling trainees to experience success through rehearsal of on-the-job behaviors in the classroom. This builds trainee confidence so the skill will be put into practical application with the least amount of fear on returning to the job.

Welcome to the Club: Orientation

Do you remember when you started your first job? Weren't you a bit shaky, nervous, or downright scared? Didn't the strangeness and uncertainty of the new job, new co-workers, and a new supervisor threaten your self-confidence? These anxieties are not uncommon among new hires.

BREAKING IN THE NEW EMPLOYEE

Fear of the unknown can be an anxiety-producing psychological state. In fact, it is a tactic that is systematically planned and encouraged in some organizations to shape up the new hires' behavior more quickly. The Marines, for example, use boot camp to mold new recruits into cohesive units that can move into action on a moment's notice. A less extreme example is the supervisor who recalls how tough his own initiation period was and chooses to perpetuate this tradition. In the words of one old supervisor, "After all, it worked on me. Why shouldn't I use it on them?" The assumption behind this tactic is that one way to build team spirit and camaraderie is to socialize new hires into the system through mild forms of harassment, hazing, rites, and rituals. Once successfully socialized into the system, it is hoped the new hires will continue to uphold the traditions, values, and culture of the organization or unit to which he or she is assigned.[3]

High-stress orientation programs

For the military and law enforcement agencies, high-stress orientation programs serve a useful purpose. However, for other types of organizations, the drawbacks are numerous. First, too much anxiety leads to a decrease in learning speed and can inhibit performance. In fact, the fear of failure can become a self-fulfilling prophecy for some new employees. Second, some new employees will refuse to play along during what they perceive to be a "phony" initiation process and instead will choose to exit the organization. Given the contemporary values of most young employees, it is not surprising that many of them are unwilling to undergo what they perceive as an attempt to subvert their individualism, and even their personality, simply to "join the team." In response, many organizations are adopting a more humane approach to orienting new hires.

Today's youth resist high-stress orientation

[3] For the reader who wishes to learn more about the process of employee socialization, we again recommend the amusing and informative work of Richard Ritti and G. Ray Funkhouser, *The Ropes to Skip and the Ropes to Know,* 2nd ed. (Columbus, Ohio: Grid, 1982).

TABLE 11.2   Concerns of Supervisor and New Employee

SUPERVISOR	*NEW EMPLOYEE*
1. Can this person do the job?	1. What exactly is my job?
2. Will this person fit in, be accepted?	2. What does it take to get ahead?
3. What kind of work ethic does this person have?	3. Is my boss fair?
4. Is this person dependable?	4. Will my boss like me?
5. Is this person a team player and loyal?	5. Will I like my boss?
6. What makes this person tick?	6. Will my co-workers accept me?
7. How important are money and security to this person?	7. What kind of organization do I work for?
8. Does this person have a strong need to achieve?	8. What are the unwritten rules around here?

Indeed, it is becoming fairly common for organizations to spend more money, take more time, and put more thought into the orientation process for new employees. A carefully designed program can alleviate anxiety, create positive work values, reduce start-up costs and turnover, and save the time of supervisors and co-workers.

Benefits of empathizing

One of the more popular and successful orientation processes centers around the practice of empathy. It begins by soliciting information from veteran employees regarding their experiences, concerns, fears, anxieties, and recollections of their first few weeks on the job. Recollections might include such comments as, "My supervisor didn't rush through explaining my new job but actually walked me through it, giving me time to ask questions" or "My supervisor overwhelmed me with detail—there was absolutely no way I was going to remember that component P-471 wouldn't work when placed at anything other than at a 246 degree position on the circuitry board."

Get to know the new hire

Empathy helps supervisors understand where the new employee is coming from, the anxieties of being a stranger, and the questions that need to be answered. Table 11.2 highlights some of the concerns that affect the supervisor and the new hire during the orientation period. It might be noted that during this period the supervisor has a golden opportunity to get to know the new hire, and more important, to begin identifying the person's most important needs and wants. New employees are just about the most anxious-to-please people any supervisor could ever hope to encounter. They want to do a good job and to make a good first impression. Part of their anxiety stems from the fear of being perceived as a failure or a mistake in the hiring process. Most new employees will readily open up, unlike many experienced employees, and they are more willing to confide to the supervisor what their plans include, what their immediate goals are, and what most concerns them regarding the new job. Their willingness to trust their new boss is an opportunity that should not be wasted.

GENERAL ORIENTATION

Many potentially talented people have been lost during their initial months on the job because of an inadequate orientation program. On the other hand, when such a program is properly conducted, it can have a positive influence on job expectations, job satisfaction, and job performance.

A good orientation program starts by pointing out to the new hire what seasoned employees take for granted—the basic bits and pieces of information that everyone needs to know in order to survive in the organization. Table 11.3 identifies the typical content of a general orientation program and includes questions that are on every new employee's mind. What time do I start? When do breaks occur? Where can I

> Don't take survival for granted

TABLE 11.3   General Orientation Topics and Their Content

TOPICS	CONTENT	TOPICS	CONTENT

Company overview	Welcoming speech
	History of company
	Current growth trends, goals, priorities, and problems
	Long-range plans
	Operating budget and financial situation
	Organization's structure and branch relationship
	Organizational chain of command and facts on key management staff
	Service to community
		Employee benefits	Holidays
			Vacation
			Insurance
			  Group health
			  Disability
			  Workers' Compensation
			  Life
			  Medical-dental
			Leave
			  Illness—personal or family
			  Military or jury duty
			  Bereavement
			  Maternity

Table 11.3   (Cont'd)

TOPICS	CONTENT	TOPICS	CONTENT
Review of company policies and procedures	Employee classifications Working conditions and regulations Salary structure Review of terms and conditions of employment Promotions and assignments Performance expectations and probationary period Late arrival or sickness Supervision and performance evaluation Termination of employment Personnel records Communication channels	Employee-employer relations and labor unions	Employee responsibilities and rights Management responsibilities and rights Shop stewards relations Reprimands and discipline Grievance procedures Safety equipment Cleanliness and sanitation Handling of rumors
		Safety	First-aid stations Fire prevention Accident procedures On-the-job use of alcohol and drugs Working conditions
Salary	Payscale Paychecks Overtime pay Holiday pay Deductions Credit union Tax shelter options	Anxiety reduction	Supervisor information Hazing games of older employees
		Physical facilities	Tour of facilities Cafeteria Entrances Parking Restricted areas Restrooms Equipment and supplies
Question and answer session			

eat lunch? How far is it to the restroom? What day do I get paid? While these concerns are normally addressed by someone in the personnel department, it never hurts to have the supervisor highlight items that might be of special concern in his or her department.

SOCIAL ORIENTATION

Perhaps one of the greatest anxieties for the newcomer is not knowing whether he or she will be accepted by the work group. Each work group has its own norms, procedures, cliques, personalities, and sometimes levels of acceptable performance. At Texas Instruments, for example, investigators found that new employees experienced much of their anxiety from the practice of hazing newcomers, the uncertainty of not knowing whether acceptable performance could be attained within the allotted time, and concern about not being able to understand their supervisor's instructions.[4]

Mild forms of hazing—such as the occasional use of a derogatory remark, being asked to perform impossible tasks, the use of nicknames, or being asked to perform certain "gofer" jobs—can be expected and may actually suggest a healthy, cohesive work group. Hazing occurs until the new employee has been accepted as a full-fledged member of the unit. The supervisor should keep a wary eye on the activities, making sure the "humor" stays within acceptable limits.

> **Hazing**

A tour of the unit, accompanied by introductions to co-workers (either one-on-one or as a group), is always a good start to social orientation. Providing that the work group isn't too large, a humorous anecdote about each member of the unit not only breaks the ice but tends to be appreciated by experienced employees. Allowing the newcomer to wander about and meet others on his or her own, or expecting experienced employees to introduce themselves, is risky. People who have tendencies toward introversion, whether they are new employees or veterans, don't make friends easily. Allowing them to wander about may only aggravate their anxieties. Sometimes a little coaxing is needed to encourage experienced employees to open up to a newcomer.

> **Use icebreakers**

Another helpful strategy for socially orienting new employees is to appoint a mentor (or sponsor) to guide the new hire. Usually an experienced co-worker is given the assignment; but sometimes a more prudent choice might be an employee who has recently completed the orientation phase and is probably more aware of the new hire's concerns and anxieties. The mentor might begin by gradually introducing the new employee to other members of the group, thus preventing information overload. The mentor would also be expected to provide specific job-related information as well as insight into the work unit's norms and procedures.

> **Appoint a mentor**

[4] Earl R. Comersall and M. Scott Myers, "Breakthrough in On-the-Job Training," *Harvard Business Review* (July-August 1966), pp. 62–71.

Conscientious mentors provide encouragement, advice, techniques, and constructive criticism.

Feed information gradually

Because the impressions formed by the new employee during the first few days are going to be around for a long time, it is critical that the immediate supervisor plan on spending more time than normal with the newcomer. During this time together, there is the tendency to want to present everything the new employee will need to know. A supervisor should avoid this temptation because new employees are often overloaded with details they can't possibly retain. Instead, space the information over a period of time. It also helps to provide both oral and written instructions regarding the task, as well as examples of performance standards that will be used.

It is important to point out the performance standards that experienced employees are expected to achieve versus what is expected of trainees. If trainees are confused about what is expected of them in terms of job performance, they may become immensely frustrated as well as tentative and unsure in their job behaviors. New employees need time to learn the task, become acclimated to the job, and become comfortable with their co-workers.

Training Decisions ————————————

DECIDING IF TRAINING IS NEEDED

Is training needed? Will it help? What kind of training would be best? Who will provide the training? If training will not solve the problem, what other supervisory action or follow-up is called for?

Assess performance

Before these questions can be answered, it is imperative that subordinates' duties and responsibilities be clearly identified, that performance standards be known, and that a frame of reference be available that makes a comparison of effective and ineffective performance possible. When these conditions have been met, the supervisor can begin looking for a "gap" between the level at which subordinates should be performing and actual performance.

What's causing the performance gap?

Identifying a gap is only the first step. The performance discrepancy may be the result of any number of factors, with training deficiencies representing just a small fraction of the possibilities. Lack of employee awareness about the job, lack of supervisory feedback to the subordinate, or some external blockage beyond the control of the employee (e.g., faulty equipment) are other avenues to be explored. However, they have one thing in common. In each case the problem is not entirely the subordinate's. The responsibility for correction rests largely on the shoulders of the immediate supervisor.

Furthermore, with the possible exception of sales training, providing subordinates with a program that is designed to motivate them to work harder is generally not cost-effective. While some supervisors consider attendance at training programs an incentive (particularly when the programs are held in exotic locations), the primary purpose of training should be to satisfy a need. Training is most effective when it is given to employees who are deficient in terms of essential job skills, knowledge, or some personal characteristic (e.g., assertiveness) deemed critical for success. It is ironic that some supervisors and managers view training as a reward to their better performers, who need it least, while depriving those who could probably most use it.

While formal training may be of some value—after all, something can be learned from even the most irrelevant instruction—there are situations in which it is not cost-effective. And training and development "at any cost" is a philosophy that few organizations can afford. It might help if each supervisor were to ask the following questions before embarking on a formal training program:

Training should satisfy a need

1. What will be the cost of the training—to the organization? to me, as the supervisor, in terms of lost time and replacements?
2. Will the cost be offset by the gain in the group's productivity?
3. What would be the cost of continuing the current situation without training?
4. Which employees should be trained first? What is the degree of urgency? How many employees need this training?
5. Are there any legal constraints? What about possible discrimination problems from those who are not selected to attend the program? Will the training satisfy the organization's legal and moral responsibilities?
6. What is expected from employees who receive the training? Has this been communicated to each participant? To the trainer?
7. How will the training be evaluated?

Questions before embarking on formal training

Too often, supervisors expect too much from a training program. Regardless of the funds invested, the quality of the instruction, and even the motivation of the participants, training cannot overcome an organization's inept recruiting and selection decisions. Participants *must* have a basic level of proficiency or aptitude before training can be a viable solution.

If training is determined to be the best answer, choosing the best kind of training is the next step.

CHOOSING THE RIGHT TECHNIQUE

Vestibule training

Off-the-Job Training. While there are numerous training techniques available to the supervisor, most of them involve some off-the-job methods. Vestibule training and classroom instruction are two such methods. In the former, a vestibule facility is designed away from the pressures of the work floor, equipment and materials similar to what are actually used on the job are brought in, and the trainee can learn the procedures and skills without causing production delays and costly mistakes. Usually the immediate supervisor is not directly involved. Instead, management frequently chooses to go with a special training staff. This type of training is not economical unless there is a continuing demand for newly trained employees. For example, for training cutting and sewing machine operators, data-entry clerks, or even computer operators, vestibule training is frequently the most reliable and efficient method available.

Formal classroom instruction

Classroom instruction and conferences represent a second popular off-the-job training technique. The training and development opportunities available to supervisory and management personnel largely involve the offerings of vocational schools and universities. The lecture approach, certainly the most common classroom technique, is a fast, efficient, and economical means for updating professional employees on state-of-the-art technical aspects of their work. However, mere exposure to data, concepts, and knowledge does not guarantee learning. Group discussions are an improvement over lectures because of their emphasis on learner involvement through active participation. Yet if the group is too large or the instructor is not adept at facilitating direction and encouraging constructive feedback, the discussion can turn into a pointless dialogue.

High transfer of learning

On-the-Job Training (OJT). This approach accounts for a large portion of all organizational training. Having the necessary equipment and facilities readily available makes on-the-job training a logical training technique, especially from the supervisor's viewpoint. Furthermore, the transfer of learning back to the job is excellent because the training experiences are closely related to the actual duties, requirements, and conditions of the job. When a new employee is provided an adequate learning period to master the necessary skills and knowledge, when the supervisor demonstrates how the task is correctly performed, and when the new employee has an opportunity to question the whys and hows of the task, OJT is hard to beat.

The organizations must reward good training

Unfortunately, one of the strengths of OJT, the availability of the supervisor as a trainer, can also prove to be its downfall. If the quality of the instruction is questionable or the training is seen by the supervisor as a secondary responsibility, the OJT program will be ineffective. Management can maximize the perception of training as being an essential part of the supervisor's job by encouraging, supporting, and rewarding the training function.

A typical OJT program is simply the creation of a learning environment in which the trainer (1) tells how the task is to be done, (2) shows it done correctly, and (3) gives the trainee a chance to clarify through questions. This process is enhanced when the learning is accompanied by visual aids, including overhead transparencies, audiovisual models, and notes.

Job Rotation. Another type of program available to supervisors in many organizations is job rotation. The technique, used to train both experienced and new employees, involves a systematic transfer of workers from one job, task, or department to another. One advantage is that it gives the trainee a total perspective, or overview, of the entire work process. From a scheduling point of view, having subordinates who are capable of performing a variety of functions is certainly an advantage. Robert Blake has identified ten rules for using job rotation; they are presented in Table 11.4.

As powerful a training tool as rotation is, there are certain constraints that limit its application. For one thing, it is costly. For another, even though the trainees may be exposed to a wide variety of jobs, there

> **Learning is by trial and error**

TABLE 11.4   Job Rotation as a Training Technique: Ten Guidelines

---

1. Make sure the employee is at ease.
2. Describe the new work area and find out what the employee already knows about it.
3. Explain to the employee the importance of the job within the department and company.
4. Place the employee in the best position for him/her to learn the new task.
5. Tell, show, and illustrate one step at a time.
6. Stress each key point.
7. Instruct clearly, patiently, and completely.
8. Present no more than the employee can master at one time.
9. Have the employee perform the job, then correct any errors.
10. Encourage questions and provide reinforcement for accomplishments.

Derived from Robert T. Blake, "The Better They Are Informed, the Better They Perform," *Supervisory Management,* February 1982, pp. 17–20.

ON-THE-JOB TRAINING?

I showed up on time my first morning at the plumbing shop, where every morning there were about fifteen men drinking coffee, picking up fittings and tools, and loading trucks. I had hoped to get on new construction, but was told to work with Reggie's crew on a rehabilitation job in a twenty-story building requiring forty new bathrooms and kitchens. Reggie was a young man in his early thirties, about six feet, clean shaven, carefully dressed in clean dungarees and a woolen shirt, and he seemed very reserved. While most of the other men were picking up tools and supplies they were expounding their views on sports, sex, and politics, but Reggie seemed pretty aloof from all the talk. He just told me what fittings to pick, then said, "Get the bag and let's go."

The bag was a huge leather tool case that looked like a mailman's bag that you slung on your back. It was full of heavy plumbing tools. It must have weighed fifty pounds, but seemed to gain a pound every ten minutes. The helper carried the bag, and it never mattered that you had such other items as the gasoline torch, a bag of fittings, and some-

times some pipe to carry—you still carried the bag. An amenity of being a journeyman plumber was to have a helper who was a combination mule, personal attendant, and general support system.

Reggie said that I was to cut floors and walls and run the roughing (the pipe that goes inside the walls). He was soft-spoken, and I liked him. He never swore nor was he abusive, which was not true of any of the other plumbers. He showed me how to cut floors and walls, using a drill, saw, hammer, and chisel. It seemed easy, until in a few hours my arm began to feel like a piece of wood. By noon I was sure it would fall off. Fortunately I was rescued by being sent out on my first plumbing supply-house pickup.

Reggie ever so patiently showed me how to cut open floors and walls to receive pipe. "Never more than you have to," he would say, "because remember, we have to close them up again." I learned how to cut and thread pipes to dimensions given by the plumber. Since the pipe vise, dies, and fittings were usually kept in the basement, there was a ceaseless muling of stuff up and down stairs,

may be a lack of sustained direction because of the number of supervisors involved. This is compounded when the trainee is rotated to another new job before he or she has had time to learn the necessary functions of the current one. Adding to these problems is that trainees may not be motivated to dig in and learn, because they know they will be moving on to something else in the near future. Yet in spite of these problems, job rotation is becoming more popular with supervisors and management.[5] Organizations are finding that job rotation is beneficial for both entry-level training and employee career development.

[5] Robert T. Blake, "The Better They Are Informed, the Better They Perform," *Supervisory Management*, February 1982, pp. 17–20.

unless I was lucky and worked in a building where I could use the elevator. As the helper I was the go-fer, running for fittings, pipe, fixtures, coffee, beer, Coke, and so forth, for eight hours every day. Reggie was good to work with. He would try to give me a bunch of assorted pipe orders so I could work out my own system of cutting and threading.

One day I was pulled off a job I was working on to help a crew with a main sewer stoppage in a 20-story building. I should have suspected that something was up as the guys greeted me with, "We'll see what this kid's made of." And, "This is a big job for a big man," and to each other, "Don't know if we got one. Well, this will tell." I was being challenged, and I knew if I shriveled and ran away, I would be shunned like a skunk. Though scared to death, I kept whistling in the dark, saying to myself, "Don't worry." This challenge has to be answered. That is that. Besides it will be good for me. I hoped.

We unloaded the tools and snakes from the truck and carried them into the cellar, which because of the stoppage was already under a foot of water with all kinds of junk floating around. One of the men said, "OK, kid, here are the boots; put them on. See that plug over there in the corner? Take it off and start working the snake into the sewer line as we feed it to you." All the men kind of hung back toward the door. That should have been a clue that there was something fishy going on. But I just forged ahead.

Off I went by myself in my hip boots across the cellar to the sewer line. The line must have been a foot in diameter. I needed a three-foot wrench just to screw out the plug. Then I took the end of the steel snake that the men were feeding to me and began to push it into the pipe. Well, it hadn't gone but six feet when the whole thing let go with a huge geyser that hit the ceiling. A deluge of toilet paper and shit rained all over that basement (and me), and it seemed like it would never stop. I ran, but there was no escaping.

Robert Schrank, *Ten Thousand Working Days* (Cambridge, Mass.: MIT Press, 1978), pp. 13–18.

Obviously, there are other techniques available to supervisors who desire to provide meaningful learning experiences to subordinates. Table 11.5 lists a few of the techniques that we've tried ourselves or heard about from supervisors. This is not meant to imply that other techniques would not work. The only limitations to identifying an effective training technique are one's creativity and persistence.

The one common thread running through the list presented in Table 11.5 is that guidance alone is insufficient. People learn as much through mistakes as through success—provided they are made aware of where they went wrong and how they might go about correcting errors. Good trainers expect to see mistakes, and they point them out tactfully to the trainee. They also make it a point to reinforce correct performance.

Mistakes are a part of learning

TABLE 11.5   Types of Training Techniques Available to the Supervisor

On-the-job training

Job rotation

Delegating

Mentoring

Special assignments

Committee assignments

Writing assignments

Work/study programs

Fact-finding assignments

SUMMARY

As far as understanding how people learn, whether they are new or experienced workers, the principles are the same. Adults are slower to pick up new skills and knowledge when these contradict established skills and habits. Therefore, the content of employee training must be made relevant and meaningful. Purpose must be clearly identified because learning is hard work. If skills are involved, the learner needs to have adequate practice opportunities to try them out. Practice builds the skill itself along with the confidence to try it out in the real world. When combined with timely and constructive feedback by the trainer, the likelihood for developing complex skills is excellent.

One of the most important times in an employee's career is his or her first few months on the job. First impressions tend to last a long time. And wrong impressions can result in an employee having an abbreviated career with the organization. The anxieties that every new employee develops with a new job, new supervisor, and new co-workers should not be ignored. The supervisor should plan to spend more time with him or her—but should not try to teach everything in one sitting. It is best to feed small bits of information, increasing the amounts gradually, instead of overwhelming the new person with details. All questions should be answered, even the most basic ones. The supervisor should also keep in mind that a big part of the orientation process involves initiating social contacts with more experienced employees. He or she should explain that a new hire can expect a certain degree of hazing from co-workers, which should not be taken seriously.

When it comes to choosing a technique for training subordinates, the most reliable methods are on-the-job training and job rotation. The reason is simple. Both involve the use of actual job conditions, not classroom instruction, thus increasing the odds that the training will readily transfer back to the job.

THE COMPANY TRAINING PROGRAM

Widget Manufacturing Company believed in providing every possible aid and encouragement to the development of its management personnel. Among the many extras that it provided was attendance for thirty or forty people each year at the Industrial Management Conference. These conferences were held in a college town and were widely attended, with as many as 1,200 people from various companies present at the annual three-day sessions. The sessions were divided into workshops and discussion groups, with a liberal sprinkling of speakers—experts in various phases of industrial management. The meetings concluded with a major speech and banquet, followed by entertainment.

When John Hamilton joined the staff of the Widget company, he was greatly impressed by the efforts of top management to provide such continuous development of its supervisory staff. He took advantage of the extension courses offered, was present at all foremen's classes, and generally considered himself lucky to be part of such an organization. When one of the supervisors approached him and asked if he would like to attend the conference, he was delighted. It seemed to him that it would be an excellent opportunity to sample some of the best thinking of men who were specialists in their fields.

Customarily the men were sent down in several cars to the conference. John Hamilton found himself in a car with three other men, one of which was Jim Warner, an old-line supervisor. He noted the holiday atmosphere from the beginning of the trip and felt that the men must indeed get a great deal out of the conferences because of the enthusiasm with which they greeted the prospect of attending. Several times on the ride to the conference John tried to draw out Jim on the subject matter of the conferences. All he got was remarks such as "You're sure to enjoy yourself, John; just relax."

Following the registration, John told Jim that he was going to his room and freshen up. He wanted to be sure and catch the first speaker. Before John could leave, Jim said, "Sure, John, just stop in room 325 before you go."

A little while later John knocked on the door of room 325 and was admitted to the smoke-filled room. Two of the desks had been pushed together and a blanket thrown over them. The supervisors he knew were sitting around in their shirt sleeves, playing poker and drinking. Before John could say anything, someone put a paper cup of lukewarm whisky and ginger ale into his hand. "There's plenty of time before the first speaker," said Jim. "Why don't you play a couple of hands."

Hamilton didn't want to miss the speech; neither did he want to antagonize the other foremen by refusing a few friendly hands of poker with them. "Okay," he said. "But I'm only going to play one deal around; then I'm taking off." Five hands later Jim asked him, "How do you like the conference?"

"Look, Johnny boy," said Jim, "this is the conference. That speech making and all the other stuff is hogwash. The whole purpose of these conferences is to give the boys a three-day vacation for a little drinking and poker playing."

"That doesn't sound right to me," said John. "From the look of the program, a lot of people have worked hard to line up a very good conference. "It doesn't make sense to me," said John, "to drive all the way down here to hear these experts speak and stay in our rooms and play poker."

"This is the way the company wants it," said Jim. "The main idea is for the foremen to get together and get to know each other better. It makes a closer spirit among the foremen."

Hamilton was in a quandary. He wanted to attend the program, but he knew that if he spurned the poker session more than half of the foremen he knew would think him a "square."

1. Is the "training program" serving a productive purpose for the company?
2. What will be the long-term effect of allowing this practice to continue?
3. Should John somehow report the events to the company's top brass? What are the risks that John faces if he should report the training truancy?

* Case prepared by Professor Kenneth A. Kovach of George Mason University. Copyright © 1980 by Kenneth A. Kovach.

DISCUSSION QUESTIONS

1. Why is training a function that supervisors, in general, are not enthusiastic about performing? What can top management do to make the function more acceptable to supervisors?
2. Identify the different ways training might be provided to employees.
3. What is it about the supervisor's role that makes the supervisor the most critical person in terms of the transfer of training back to the job?
4. Explain how adults learn differently than children.
5. What do the two learning theories mentioned in this chapter have in common? How do they differ?
6. Identify the principles of learning that a supervisor must incorporate into an on-the-job training method for a new employee.
7. Why wouldn't practice alone be sufficient when teaching an experienced employee how to perform a complex task?
8. Is empathizing the same thing as sympathizing? Explain.
9. What should a general orientation program for new employees include?
10. Explain a systematic procedure for identifying training needs.
11. Can training overcome bad selection decisions? If so, how might it be done?
12. Identify the different off-the-job training methods that might be used to train employees to become supervisors.

REFERENCES

Blake, Robert T. "The Better They Are Informed, the Better They Perform." *Supervisory Management* (February 1982): 17–20.

Craig, Robert L. *Training and Development Handbook.* New York: McGraw-Hill, 1967.

Donaldson, L., and Scannell, E. *Human Resource Development.* Reading, MA.: Addison-Wesley Publishing, 1978.

Randall, John S. "You and Effective Training; Parts 3–4: Communications, Communications Aids." *Training and Development Journal* (August 1978): 36–40.

Schneier, Craig. "Training and Development Programs: What Learning Theory and Research Have to Offer." *Personnel Journal* (April 1974): 288–293.

St. John, Walter. "The Complete Employee Orientation Program." *Personnel Journal* (May 1980): 373–378.

Zemke, Ron, and Zemke, Susan. "30 Things We Know for Sure About Adult Learning." *Training/HRD Journal* (June 1981): 45–52.

CHAPTER 12

THE LABOR OF LABOR RELATIONS

Poorly trained supervisors who have played "favorites" among employees, administered the rules as they saw fit, and failed to do their jobs as communicators and leaders have been the cause of more lost union elections than have complaints about wage and salary and benefits programs or working conditions.

—J. M. BLACK

Chapter Outline

Objectives

The term "labor relations" refers to the relationship between employer and employees. Supervisors occupy a unique position in this critical relationship because they are the link between management (the employer) and the rank and file (the employees). Supervisors must use their managerial skills to build a healthy, productive relationship between the two groups. The purpose of this chapter is to give you as a supervisor the necessary background on unions and the American collective bargaining process so that you will be able to handle the labor relations function in a positive and efficient manner. Specifically, in this chapter you will become familiar with:

1. The history of labor unions in the United States
2. The major pieces of legislation affecting labor relations
3. The nature and influence of unions in today's labor force
4. How unions get recognized and started in an organization
5. The grievance procedure and the necessary skills to operate within it
6. How to identify and overcome barriers to good labor relations

Major Concepts

Knights of Labor
American Federation of Labor
Industrial Workers of the World
Congress of Industrial Organizations
The Norris-LaGuardia Act
The Wagner Act
Unionization
Union-organizing campaign
Unfair labor practice

Authorization card
National Labor Relations Board (NLRB)
Union steward
NLRB-sponsored election
Decertification
Labor contract
Grievance procedure
Arbitration
Strike

LIVING WITH A UNION

Joanne and Les Frederick blame themselves for the unionization of their company—a Somerville, Massachusetts, custom photo lab with sales approaching $1 million a year. As Northeast Color Research, Inc., expanded from a two-person shop in 1960 to a twenty-five-person organization in the 1970s, the Fredericks failed to define pay policies or work rules. And their production supervisor, with no experience or training in supervision, never learned how to communicate with employees.

In 1980 the company's dozen production workers finally rebelled: They petitioned for a National Labor Relations Board-sponsored election and voted 9 to 3 to be represented by the United Food and Commercial Workers Union. The Fredericks negotiated their first union contract.

Joanne Frederick, who has served as Northeast's chief executive officer since the start of the union crisis, hated the idea of sharing management responsibility with a union. She felt that no union was likely to reflect the company philosophy that serving professional photographers with good craftsmanship is more important than making money. She knew that Northeast had neglected that philosophy, but she says she would rather have closed shop than give up the ideal.

The law required Joanne Frederick to deal with the union once employees had voted to make it their bargaining agent. And despite her anti-union bias, she had to admit that the professional leadership of the Food and Commercial Workers was useful to her. "The union helped us to establish and enforce discipline and teach these young employees what it means to have a job," Joanne declares.

Frederick now acknowledges that unions may not be bad for companies with varied philosophies. She says that one New York-based competitor told the Fredericks that "a union is like a mother-in-law who comes to live with you. You may not like everything she does, but she sure makes a great baby-sitter." The competitor argued that his union relationship enabled him to handle all the vexing questions of pay and benefits in a few weeks of contract negotiations.

Most entrepreneurs probably don't want to share decision-making power with a union, however. And for them the Fredericks' experience may contain an important warning. Stephen Cabot, a well-known foe of unions, argues that many employers are behaving during today's recession in ways that will lead to union-organizing campaigns when the economy improves. "They're abusing the living hell out of their employees," he declares. "Some are seeking to cut wages when they don't have to; others who must cut wages are failing to communicate why."

Cabot notes that most unions cannot organize effectively now, when employees feel there are few job opportunities available if a confrontation with management leaves them unemployed. But unless employees feel they are treated fairly during the recession, Cabot says, many will seek to organize when the economy is strong again. Many companies, he adds, could soon find themselves facing crises like the one at Northeast Color.

Adapted from R. C. Wood, "Managing People—The Decline and Fall of a Union," *INC.,* October 1982, pp. 135–136.

Unionism in America

The labor force in just about every organization is affected by unionism. Either the employees are union members or they depend on the services of other firms whose employees are unionized. Organized labor is as much a part of our society as is the family and the television. Unions have legal and social status. They are an integral part of today's organizations, and as such they should be recognized and understood. This chapter examines the role of organized labor in the modern organization. First, the chapter takes a brief look at the history of unionism in America. It next deals with the unionization process, explaining the benefits of unions and why management has a tendency to resist unions. The certification process is discussed, as is union decertification. The chapter then examines the contract administration phase of the collective bargaining agreement—the area in which the supervisor is involved on a daily basis. The discussion includes the reasons for grievances, the overall grievance procedure, arbitration, and the strike. Finally, some practical guidelines for supervisors are outlined.

A SHORT HISTORY OF THE U.S. LABOR MOVEMENT

The history of labor unions in the United States goes back to 1792, when craft unions of carpenters, printers, and shoemakers were founded to resist wage deductions. These early unions comprised workers sharing a single craft, who sought goals that are recognized today in modern craft unions: minimum wage, job security, and control of apprentice entry into the craft. By the end of the Civil War, there were almost 300 unions scattered throughout the United States.

In the period between the Civil War and the beginning of World War I, there were three major national labor organizations: the Knights of Labor, the American Federation of Labor, and the Industrial Workers of the World. These organizations, which differed in their orientation, organizational structure, strategies, and tactics, together made major contributions to the labor movement in the United States.

The Knights of Labor

Founded by Uriah S. Stephens as a secret society in 1869, the Knights of Labor (KOL) maintained secrecy until 1882 so that members would not be discharged by their employers for participating in a labor organization. One of the main concerns of the Knights of Labor was the rapid industrialization that began during the Civil War. The Knights felt that mass production reduced the employees' feelings of pride and personal accomplishment on the job. In earlier times, employees could be satisfied with their craftsmanship, a sense of accomplishment, the fashioning of goods from beginning to end. Thus the Knights were concerned with more than just the material working conditions prevalent in the factories at the time. Employers were encouraged to join the KOL, the rationale being that they would be able to influence the bankers and owners of gold, who, the KOL believed, were the ruin of industrial society, and politicians, who were motivated by self-interest. The Knights also encouraged workers to save part of their wages so that they would be in a position to purchase or establish factories that would be owned cooperatively. In this way, employees would become their own masters; and they would have a voice in decision making, which would include the fair distribution of profits. During the 1880s, the Knights of Labor saw a tremendous growth because of their orientation against the powerful industrialists and because of the fact that they became identified with the eight-hour workday—an issue that was rapidly becoming important to the nation's work force.[1]

But in the late 1880s, the KOL experienced a sudden decline. The decline came about because the Knights were more interested in social reform for American society rather than in improving the economic and working conditions of its members. They also assumed that technological advancement could be halted and possibly reversed. Although the KOL was ahead of its time in its attempt to organize unskilled employees, the leadership did not identify with the needs of the membership, and the union quickly became an insignificant organization in the U.S. labor movement.

The American Federation of Labor (AFL) started in 1881 as a group of six crafts. By 1886 there were 138,000 members of the AFL, and by 1920 over 4 million, representing about 70 to 80 percent of all union workers. Samuel Gompers was one of the major founders of the AFL and was president from its founding in 1881 until his death in 1924. Gompers, unlike the Knights of Labor, placed little emphasis on the intellectual betterment of the union members. He believed that the goals and organization of the AFL should follow directly and naturally from members' needs and not from the pronouncements of top leaders trying to structure the movement on the basis of their views of how society ought to be. The AFL's major goal was to improve the material conditions of members through the existing capitalist system. Gompers believed that workers could obtain more only if capitalism continued to flourish, since without capitalism neither the employers nor the employees would receive revenues from their labors.

The American Federation of Labor

The third major labor organization was the Industrial Workers of the World (IWW), and it was formed as an alternative to the AFL in 1905. The initial goal of the IWW was to overthrow the existing system by any means that would result in the quick destruction of capitalism. Unlike the Knights, who stressed that employees and employers have common interests and that conflicts must be resolved through peaceful means, the IWW wanted to remove any group that supported capitalism. The IWW felt that Gompers was an arrogant, power-hungry leader and that the AFL did not recognize the working class movement or hourly employees as being a class-conscious group apart from the rest

The Industrial Workers of the World

[1] Donald L. Kemmerer and Edward D. Wickersham, "Reasons for the Growth of the Knights of Labor in 1885–1886," *Industrial and Labor Relations Review,* vol. 3 (January 1950), pp. 213–220.

of society.[2] The IWW never did establish an effective organization; in fact many of its leaders never made up their minds about precisely what kind of organization should be set up. Partly for this reason and partly because of its lack of permanent membership and financial base, its inability to appeal to members' interests, and its alienation of news media and government officials, the IWW came to a rather early demise. It incurred the wrath of the federal government when it refused to support the involvement of the United States in World War I. Instead, it proclaimed that the war represented a capitalist plot.

At the beginning of World War I, the AFL was on firm ground, and it was the first nationally recognized labor organization to withstand a severe economic depression, hostile press, and hostile employers.

The Congress of Industrial Organizations

As organized labor entered the tough economic times of the 1930s, unions represented only a small, select group of workers. These workers were the best trained and best paid, not the unskilled workers found in the mass production industries. The AFL showed little interest in organizing these workers. However, the AFL in 1935 set up the Congress of Industrial Organizations (CIO), which became independent in 1938. The CIO was extremely successful in organizing industrial unions (including skilled and unskilled workers) in the steel, auto, oil, aluminum, glass, meat-packing, and rubber industries. The AFL then established rival industrial unions to compete with the CIO. Over the years, the AFL with its strong financial and organizational base and experience was able to surpass the efforts of the CIO and gain a membership lead.

The Norris-LaGuardia Act

During the period between the world wars, several important legal events occurred in relation to the U.S. labor movement. For several years after World War I, there was an increase in the cost of living, and during this time there were some major strikes in the work force. The U.S. Congress, for the most part, left policy toward the organization of workers in the hands of the judiciary during this period. In the 1930s, however, Congress passed two major pieces of legislation, which fundamentally changed public policy toward organized labor, and today form the foundation of regulation of the collective bargaining process as we know it. The first piece of legislation, known as the Norris-LaGuardia Act of 1932, freed unions from the threat of injunctions. Although the Norris-LaGuardia Act did not restrict employer efforts to prevent union organization of the workplace, unions could strike without fear of the injunction. However, there was nothing in this law that required the employer to bargain with the union or do anything that in any

---

[2] Bill Haywood, *Bill Haywood's Book: The Autobiography of William D. Haywood* (New York: International Publishers, 1929), p. 73.

way recognized the union. The act had two main features: (1) it restricted judges from issuing injunctions against strikes, and (2) it made "yellow-dog contracts" unenforceable in court. A yellow-dog contract was a signed promise by an employee not to join or support a union.

The second major law relating to collective bargaining was the Wagner Act, passed in 1935. The Wagner Act, also known as the National Labor Relations Act, helped employees and unions still further. Whereas the Norris-LaGuardia Act had removed weapons used against unions but left employers free to oppose union organizing, the Wagner Act required employers to bargain collectively with the union of the employees' choosing. More important were the provisions in the act establishing the National Labor Relations Board to administer union representation elections, defining employer unfair labor practices and enforcing the legal rights of employees to join unions.

The Wagner Act

The third major piece of labor legislation, the Taft-Hartley Act, was passed in 1947, following a turbulent year of labor disputes. The Taft-Hartley Act was to a large extent an amendment and extension of the Wagner Act. The Wagner Act was passed during a period of relative weakness for organized labor. The Taft-Hartley Act, enacted twelve years later, attempted to balance the role of the government in labor relations by establishing, among other things, unfair labor practices for labor unions. The act created new obligations for unions, such as the duty to represent employees, and new restrictions on union security, such as outlawing the closed shop and permitting states to pass more restrictive union security policies. The act also provided for a procedure to deal with national emergency strikes.

The Taft-Hartley Act

Following World War II, three major developments have occurred in relation to organized labor. There has been increased concern over collective bargaining issues, organized drives have been aimed at public and white-collar employees, and the AFL and CIO have merged. With many of the major production industries already unionized during the period after World War II, union membership growth has slowed drastically. Rivalry between the AFL and CIO has resulted more in stealing members from each other than in building additional membership. Since 1955, the postmerger period, there has been a gradual increase in the number of union members, but a gradual decrease in the proportion of employees who belong to labor unions. The only exception to this development has been in the public sector, which has been transformed from an area of sparse union activity to an area that surpassed the private sector in percentage of union membership during the 1970s. This growth in public sector unions during the period after 1960 has been aided greatly by public policies of the federal government and by many state

Developments since World War II

TABLE 12.1   America's Ten Largest Unions and Their Membership

Unions	MEMBERSHIP (IN THOUSANDS)		
	1964	*1974*	*1980*
Teamsters	1,507	1,973	1,892
Automobile workers *	1,168	1,545	1,357
Steelworkers	1,250	1,300	1,238
Electrical (IBEW)	806	943	1,041
Machinists	808	943	745
Carpenters	760	820	832
Retail clerks (RCIA)	428	651	215
Laborers (IUMA)	432	650	608
State, county (AFSCME)	235	648	1,098
Service employees (SEIU)	320	550	650

* Indicates independent unions. Others are affiliated with the AFL-CIO.

Statistical Abstract of the U.S., 1981, and U.S. Department of Labor.

legislatures, which have encouraged collective bargaining in the public sector.

UNIONS TODAY

Union membership

Reliable statistics relating to union membership in this country are not readily available. The figure of approximately 22 million workers is commonly accepted as the current U.S. union membership.[3] This total includes about 20 million U.S. members of national and international unions, and approximately 2 million members of independent local unions. It excludes approximately 1.5 million Canadians who belong to internationals headquartered in the United States. America's ten largest unions and their membership are shown in Table 12.1.

In terms of relative labor force penetration, the 22 million unionized workers represent only about 22 percent of all civilian members of the labor force in the country and account for about one-quarter of the employees in nonagricultural organizations.[4] In fact the unions have lost ground in recent years: There has been a loss of union members due to the closing of unionized plants; there has been an increase in

[3] Unofficial data furnished by the U.S. Department of Labor, Bureau of Labor Statistics.
[4] D. Seligman, "Who Needs Unions," *Fortune,* July 12, 1982, p. 64.

union losses in National Labor Relations Board elections; and there have been "give-backs" in collective bargaining and a general perception that unions are sliding toward obsolescence. In short, unions are going to have to increase their ranks in order to maintain themselves as a viable force in the labor movement. Table 12.2 shows the results of NLRB elections held in the years 1973 to 1981.

Unions have now begun to concentrate their efforts in areas of traditionally ignored union representation. For example, only 15 percent of white-collar workers in the United States belong to unions, whereas more than 39 percent of blue-collar workers do. It seems that unions are winning an increasing percentage of elections for white-collar representation. Unions that have shown the greatest gains of membership from 1978 to 1981, the period when unionism as a whole has declined, were those active in organizing white-collar workers. Organizers have also set out to represent the ever-increasing number of women working full-time. In general women lag behind men in job status and salary, and the chief issue is perceived as inequities in the wage structure. Women on the average earn only 59 percent of the wages earned by men, and this has prompted cries from women's groups and other organizations for equal pay for comparable work. Unions are finding that they can successfully ride to victory on the issues of child care, sexual harassment, job stress, and unequal opportunities for advancement as compared to those of men. As the percentage of women in the labor force continues to increase, better-educated women will be demanding equal pay and equal job opportunities, and the unions will no doubt intensify their efforts in areas where women feel they are being taken advantage of or exploited by their employers.

Another area in which the unions feel that there is a good opportunity is the changing nature of the work force. Besides the continued increase

White-collar unionism

Working women

TABLE 12.2   NLRB Elections

	1973	1974	1975	1976	1977	1978	1979	1980	1981
Total elections	8,916	8,368	8,061	8,027	8,635	8,380	7,266	8,531	7,789
Union wins	4,648	4,273	4,001	3,993	4,159	3,842	3,429	3,744	3,234
Union losses	4,268	4,095	4,060	4,034	4,476	4,538	4,837	4,787	4,555
% union wins	52.4%	50.9%	49.6%	49.7%	48.0%	46.0%	47.0%	45.7%	43.1%
Decertification	453	490	516	611	849	807	777	902	856
Loss of union employees	10,028	11,470	13,849	15,303	22,398	19,884	22,088	21,249	9,648

NLRB Annual Reports, NLRB Monthly Representation Election Reports.

in the number of working women, new entrants into the work force come with different work values than those of their parents. Many of these new workers, unused to having demands placed on them by either their schools or their parents, find the demands of a supervisor and of a job onerous. They have no inclination to be in an environment in which they have to meet someone else's job expectations. These individuals have grown up with cars, television sets, and other items that their parents considered luxuries when they were growing up. Now these luxuries have become necessities, and many individuals are susceptible to the promises of organizing labor unions.

Supervisors should be aware of the unprecedented drive by unions to add and retain members. Supervisors are a bridge between the employer and the employees. When an organization has been targeted by labor for assault, the supervisor is in a key position. He or she has to be vigilant and responsible for the concerns of the workers; otherwise, organized labor will find a very favorable environment.

The Unionization Process ■■■■■■■■

WHY WORKERS JOIN UNIONS

While many manufacturing firms have long been unionized, supervisors in the service industries and in the public sector are very likely to face union-organizing drives in the years ahead. Knowledge of the organizing process can become a very critical component of the supervisor's job. Supervisors need to be aware of how an organization becomes unionized.

Protection against arbitrary management

There are many reasons why workers join unions. First, union membership provides workers with some protection against arbitrary management actions. The union can be expected to push for curbs against what it calls managerial discrimination or favoritism on job assignments, promotional opportunities, and even continued employment with the organization. Management may be well intentioned; but the organization cannot guarantee that some of its employees or supervisors may not act arbitrarily. The union sees itself as a force that places checks on such actions.

Social needs

A second consideration for individuals joining unions is the fact that certain social needs are important for workers, and the union often satisfies this need. This is especially true when the work itself is performed in geographically scattered locations (such as truck driving, mail carrying, or railroad employment). This social need can also occur when the technology of the job minimizes on-the-job social interaction. The local union can serve as a club for the individual members, allowing the formation of close friendships that are built around a common interest. Over the years, unions have capitalized on this social need and have become increasingly ambitious in sponsoring such activities as athletic activities, adult education programs, and vacation retreats—for members only, of course.

A third reason to join a union is the social pressure applied by fellow workers. When workers are asked why they joined unions, a typical response is, "I can't think of a good reason, except that everybody else was joining." Often the pressure is more overt. An individual who is hesitant about joining the union may be hounded by unionized co-workers and finally signs up just to get them off his or her back. Figure 12.1 is an advertisement sponsored by an organization that helps workers resist the pressures to join a union.

Social pressure

A further reason why employees join unions is that the union offers an opportunity for realizing such needs as status and self-fulfillment. Individuals often join a union with the hope of gaining positions of authority within the union structure. To an individual who has leadership ambitions but lacks educational and other advantages, the union offers an opportunity to fulfill such higher-level needs.

Satisfaction of higher needs

Finally, there are the monetary gains and other benefits that unions promise workers for joining the union. Even employees with high incomes may be tempted by union offers of health insurance and pensions that help protect workers against economic adversity.

Material benefits

WHY MANAGEMENT RESISTS UNIONS

Managers in every nonunionized organization are aware of the potential for union organization of their employees, and virtually all of them wish to avoid it. The reason is simple: Management resents any encroachments on its decision-making powers. In the words of one company representative:

> Restriction on management freedom is a big issue. . . . We've got heavy responsibilities for making quick, accurate, and effective decisions. Sometimes there are considerations that we can't divulge or that wouldn't be understood if we did. We are held responsible for the success of them, but the union isn't. It takes complicated maneuvering to run a business, and all the parts have to be kept working together. You have to have a good deal of free play in the rope for that. Sometimes there is a particular restriction that gets your goat, but on the whole it's the overall sense of being closed in . . . that gets you. It's a cumulative effect of one area of freedom after another being reduced and the promise of still more that gives us concern, but you make adjustments and you go on to every particular one. It's impossi-

Loss of decision-making authority

FIGURE 12.1
An Advertisement
Sponsored by the
National Right to Work
Legal Defense
Foundation

Join The Union... Or Else.

Sammy Kirkland spends most of his time these days on a hog farm, away from his home in Ft. Myers, Fla. He doesn't answer his mail or the telephone.

He's kept a low profile ever since that terrifying day in May 1971 when a union mob nearly killed him on an excavation job, breaking three of his ribs, putting steel shavings in his eyes and threatening to cut off his arms.

Why were they out to get him? Because he refused to join a local union. Sammy Kirkland's life has been altered, forever, because he refused to abandon his right to work to union goons.

Other lives have been changed too. Four of the union agents responsible for the vicious attack were given five-year jail sentences. Kirkland also filed a damage suit against the local and international unions.

In early 1976, union officials agreed to a $165,000 out-of-court settlement, one of the largest ever obtained in a union violence case. But as Kirkland's attorney provided by the National Right to Work Legal Defense Foundation said, "No amount of money can compensate him for the damage that's been done."

Sammy Kirkland's case, shocking as it is, is not an isolated one. Herbert McGruther of Lake City, Fla., was fired from his construction job in 1975 because he refused to join another local of the same union.

McGruther was subjected to a different kind of intimidation. A union agent prominently displayed a large pistol in his belt while demanding that McGruther pay a union initiation fee and dues.

McGruther, with the support of the National Right to Work Legal Defense Foundation, has filed suit, charging the union with violating his rights and asking for punitive damages.

Sammy Kirkland and Herbert McGruther were fortunate. They found help. But how many other Kirklands and McGruthers in America need similar help?

The National Right to Work Legal Defense Foundation is a publicly supported charitable institution that provides free legal aid to employees whose rights have been violated because of compulsory unionism. The Foundation is currently assisting workers in more than 50 cases across the country.

If you want to help Herbert McGruther, and all the other McGruthers and Kirklands in our society, we'd like to hear from you.

For more information on how you can help workers like Sammy Kirkland and Herbert McGruther, write:

The National Right to Work
Legal Defense Foundation
8001 Braddock Road
Springfield,
Virginia 22160

AS SEEN IN <u>ABA JOURNAL</u>

Commentary 64 (August 1977), p. 13. Reprinted by permission of the National Right to Work Legal Defense Foundation.

ble, but you wonder how long you can go on and be able to meet your responsibilities.[5]

But the desire to retain the decision-making authority is by no means the only objection that management has to unions. Many employers tend to look on the union as an outsider, with no justifiable basis for interfering in the relationship between the company and its employees. The organization seeks to maximize profit, within certain limits; the union seeks to maximize its own membership and its general bargaining power. Management does not view these goals as being in harmony. Second, management views the union as a troublemaker, bent on creating gaps between management and workers where none would otherwise exist. When the union occupies an insecure status in the organization, its leaders often seek grievances in order to keep employees willing to pay union dues. Insecure status occurs when the union fears decertification because a large number of employees are unhappy with union-sponsored contract provisions (for example, talented employees resent promotion based on seniority). Third, a lot of managers view unions as underminers of employee loyalty to the organization. When an employer has prided himself on providing good wages and working conditions, and has shown personal concern for the individual problems of his employees (perhaps by extending unsolicited loans to meet financial emergencies or by voluntary payment of employee medical expenses), the employer is surprised when he or she learns that a majority of the work force has suddenly decided to "go union." Fourth, management is often opposed to organized labor's major values. Some of these values, such as a stress on seniority, work method controls, and decreased workloads, are threats to the decision-making ability of management. For example, job security has a far more favorable connotation to a unionist than it does to management.

Many managers of nonunionized organizations think that labor unions initiate organization attempts. However, it often happens that one employee or a small group of employees will become disenchanted with management for one of the reasons stated earlier, and what follows is a very secretive attempt to determine whether other employees share an interest in becoming a unionized organization. As one union organizer said, "We don't organize the people. The company does."[6] At this point, at an employee's request, a union will conduct a formal or informal

Conflicting goals and values

Who initiates unionization?

---

[5] E. Wight Bakke, *Mutual Survival: The Goal of Unions and Management* (New York: Harper & Row, 1946), p. 29.

[6] Joann S. Lubin, "Labor Reverses: Pugnacious Companies and Skeptical Workers Cost Unions Members," *Wall Street Journal,* October 21, 1982, p. 20.

feasibility study to determine the probability of a successful organization campaign. Included in this feasibility study will be the amount of resources needed to win the campaign and the benefits that the union will derive if the organization is unionized. For example, winning an election at this organization could provide inroads into a sparsely unionized industry, and the expenditure of union resources at this point might be considered a wise investment.

COPING WITH A UNIONIZATION ATTEMPT

Management's reactions

The most common reaction from management to the realization that employees have turned to a union is that they were caught off guard. Employers are often caught totally unaware and do not realize that their employees are unhappy. Accompanying the shock reaction are frustration and resentment, often reflected in such statements as, "We've always treated our employees well," or "We have a family atmosphere at our company." The third reaction on the part of the employer is anger, and the response when this occurs may be, "The employees have stabbed us in the back; we'll show them!" None of the above reactions is conducive to running a level-headed, well-conceived election campaign. These emotional reactions can only put management at a disadvantage. The following considerations can be used as a guide when management wants to maximize their chances of winning the election.

The union organizer

One of the biggest mistakes in the beginning of a union-organizing campaign is to underestimate a union organizer. Usually this individual is first seen distributing handbills to employees as they leave or enter the work location. The skillful organizer will not show up at the organization's front gate in a $500 suit, but rather will dress as the workers do. This frequently results in a negative first impression on management. However, management should never lose sight of the fact that the majority of these individuals are professionals, and they are in the process of doing what they do best: organizing a union. Most organizers have a relatively high degree of leadership ability, otherwise they would not hold the position that they do. These individuals are paid by the national union, and most are former local union presidents or business agents who receive their appointments as organizers on the basis of their demonstrated ability. Many organizers firmly believe that the workers would be better off if they were card-carrying union members. In short, a union organizer is a salesperson whose job it is to encourage workers to sign authorization cards and to vote yes when the election has been set up.

A responsible management cannot ignore organizing activity. Neither can it panic or do something that would commit the organization to union recognition without an employee election, regardless of the union's true position or the real wishes of the employees who are being organized. The Wagner Act, discussed earlier, is the basic law governing relations between labor unions and business organizations in the private sector. This act established the National Labor Relations Board, which administers and enforces the provisions of the act. The Wagner Act states and defines the rights of employees to organize and bargain collectively with their employers through representatives of their own choosing. The act established a procedure by which employees can exercise their choice in a secret-ballot election conducted by the NLRB.

Section 7 of the NLRA (Wagner Act) guarantees that

Section 7 of the Wagner Act (NLRA)

Employees shall have the right to self-organization, to form, to join, or to assist labor organizations, to bargain collectively through representatives of their own choosing, and to engage in other concerted activities for the purpose of collective bargaining, or other mutual aid or protection, and shall also have the right to refrain from any or all activities. . . .

These provisions basically guarantee the right of employees to form or join a union, to assist a union in organizing employees, and to go out on strike to secure better working conditions. They also guarantee the right of workers to refrain from any activity in behalf of a union.

Section 8 (a) (1) of the Wagner Act makes it illegal for an employer

Section 8 of the Wagner Act

to interfere with, restrain, or coerce employees in the exercise of the rights guaranteed in Section 7.

Thus Section 8 makes it illegal for employers to make threats of reprisal against employees for participating in union activity. It also prohibits promising benefits to employees for rejecting a union, and it prohibits the questioning of employees about their union activities. In sum, coercion and intimidation of employees by a supervisor for their union involvement are against the law.

If management or a supervisor becomes involved in one of the activities discussed in Section 8, there is a procedure for filing an unfair labor practice charge. For example, suppose a supervisor says, "If the union is elected, your wages and benefits will be cut." This statement indicates that the company will unlawfully retaliate against the employees if the union wins the election. Under these circumstances an employee or any other person may file a charge by contacting the local NLRB office. Once the charge is filed, a hearing is held before a NLRB trial examiner, who acts as the judge. If the investigation reveals that an unfair labor practice has in fact occurred, the NLRB will issue a complaint against

Unfair labor practices

the charged party, ordering him or her to cease and desist from such practice.

One thing that should be noted is that anything said or done by any management representative, including a supervisor, in connection with union-organizing activities may be considered to have been said or done by the organization itself. Supervisors must steer clear of conduct that obviously interferes with the employees' right to decide whether they wish to participate in the union's organizational drive.

HOW SHOULD THE SUPERVISOR REACT?

During the period of a union-organizing campaign, the supervisor still has the task of getting the work out. The employees are naturally interested in the union-organizing effort. Some of them will be strongly opposed to unionization, others strongly in favor of it. And some will remain open-minded or indifferent to the question.

Providing information is important

The first order of business is to remain calm and rational and to approach the campaign as objectively and unemotionally as possible. Employees will look to the supervisor for answers to many questions about unions, and since they are not usually aware of the effects of union representation at the time when the union begins its organizing attempt, the supervisor should consider it an obligation both to the employees and to management to provide all employees with the necessary information to help them make an informed choice. Supervisors should not play "antiunion"; rather, they should promote a "pro employee" position during the time of union organizing. Since employees are individuals, with different job-related needs and different questions that need to be answered, the supervisor should personalize the information given to individual employees. Above all, the supervisor should maintain credibility. Exaggerations should be avoided; the emphasis should be not on whether unions are good or bad but on whether or not the employees need or can benefit from a collective bargaining agreement.

The important thing a supervisor must remember is not to overreact. Such behavior can destroy the confidence that employees have in a supervisor. While a unionizing campaign is under way, supervisors should be guided by existing personnel policy. Sudden changes in personnel practices should not be made during union-organizing efforts, as such changes are often interpreted by the National Labor Relations Board as an attempt to bribe employees. When changes are being considered during a time of union organizing, they should be discussed with the employer's labor relations lawyer. On the other hand, supervisors cannot refuse to implement an existing practice because of the union, where the practice would normally have been implemented. This would be considered punitive and therefore unlawful.

The more informed a supervisor is about a particular union, the better he or she is able to work with or against the unionization campaign. When a union is chartered, it must file an LM-1 form with the U.S. Department of Labor. This form states the names and titles of the various union officers, the constitution and bylaws of the union, and whether the union has a right to collect additional money from its members, other than union dues. Each year unions must update this information by filing an LM-2 form, which also includes a statement of the financial status of the union. All of this information can be obtained by contacting the U.S. Department of Labor, Office of Labor Management Standards Enforcement. It is also useful to obtain information on the incidence and average duration of strikes the union has engaged in. This information is available from the Bureau of Labor Statistics. An investigation should be made to determine if the union has been found guilty of unfair labor practices, and if it has, what type of conduct has led to that charge. Such information can be obtained from the *Daily Labor Report*, which is published by the Bureau of National Affairs. Another source of information is the *National Labor Relations Board Election Report*, published monthly, which provides data on every representation election that has been held in the previous month. The company (or organization) and the union involved are indicated, as well as the number of votes cast for and against the union. In situations where the union won the election, the companies can be contacted to determine the issues and procedures that were used by the union.

> **Sources of information about unions**

Obviously unions prefer to conduct an organizing campaign in secret. But there are usually some signs that an organizing effort is under way, and supervisors are often in a position to see the symptoms of a union-organizing campaign. Recognition by the supervisor of the signs and symptoms of organizing activity is often critical to the organization's success in confronting the union challenge. The supervisor works side-by-side with employees on a daily basis and is more aware of their major concerns than any other level of management. In short, it's the supervisor who is management's front-line defense during an attempt at organization by the union.

The following are some of the signs of organizing that a supervisor can often spot:

> **Evidence of organizing**

1. The presence of strangers around the plant or at employee gathering spots at quitting time

2. An increase in employee complaints and a resurgence of problems that had been thought to be eliminated
3. Employees asking questions about unions
4. Discarded union handbills or union authorization cards found on or near the organization's property
5. Reports in your neighborhood or community that your organization is targeted for a union-organizing attempt.

Once a supervisor recognizes one or more of the symptoms of union-organizing activity, he or she should immediately contact an appropriate member of upper management. It is then upper management's decision as to what the organization's formal response will be.

Maintain fairness

Supervisors should be well informed of the issues frequently used by union organizers. Most union-organizing attempts arise from unresolved grievances or the inconsistent application of disciplinary procedures. Supervisors must also take special care to avoid treating employees known to be union sympathizers differently from those who are neutral or anti-union. When it becomes apparent that a supervisor is treating employees unfairly or in a capricious manner, the supervisor should be disciplined. Organizers will frequently approach the issues of discipline and grievances from the standpoint of the job security that a union agreement usually provides.

Make the facts available

An employee who is being solicited to join a union usually needs a great deal of information to help him or her make the choice. An employee deserves to know both the pros and the cons of unionizing, so that an informed decision can be made. The supervisor should make available all the facts—about unions in general, about the particular organizing union, and about the possible effects if the organization becomes unionized. The following are some of the questions that a supervisor should encourage and assist the employees to obtain answers to:

1. Can the union guarantee job security?
2. How often has this union called strikes, and what would be the effect of a strike on the employees and their families?
3. What rules and regulations will employees have to obey as union members, under penalty of union-imposed fines and loss of job?
4. How will the employees' dues be used if the organization agrees to go to a union contract?
5. What amounts of money will members have to pay in dues, fines, fees, and additional charges and assessments?

Most prospective union members are unaware that a union has the power to demand additional money over and above their regular dues and initiation fees. One use for these additional funds is to supplement the union's strike funds. These are the types of facts that should be made known to the employees.

As is well known, 30 percent of employees in a proposed bargaining unit must sign union authorization cards before the NLRB will conduct an election. More likely, the organizer will seek about 60 to 70 percent support before filing a petition for an election. Management should be aware, though, that this is not necessarily indicative of a high degree of support. Employees who sign authorization cards prior to a hearing of both sides may change their minds after such a hearing.

Employees should be made aware of the fact that an authorization card carries with it far-reaching implications. It is important that a supervisor discuss these implications at the first hint that the cards are being distributed among the employees. As indicated, once 30 percent of the employees have signed authorization cards, the union may petition the NLRB and hold an election. If 51 percent of the employees sign authorization cards, then any of the four following events can occur:

The authorization card

1. The employer can recognize the union as the employees' representative, even without holding an election.
2. The union and the employer can agree to have a third party verify the signatures and, if they are found to be genuine, can agree that the union will now be the employees' representative, without an election.
3. The union can take the cards to the government and accuse the employer of commiting unfair labor practices and preventing a fair election, and have the government declare the union to be the employees' representative, even without an election.
4. The union can call the employees out on strike until the employer recognizes the union as the employees' representative, without an election.

In short, if supervisors do not react quickly and decisively once they sense that an organizing attempt is being made at their organization, the union's organizing campaign can be successfully completed even before top management is aware of it.

Supervisors often have to set the record straight for employees. Unions basically use promises to organize. They also play on employee fears, and they will criticize current pay practices, rules, working conditions, discipline, or supervisory actions that the employees perceive as being unfair or showing favoritism. One popular misconception among employees is that once a union becomes their representative, the employer will be forced to give them additional wages and benefits. It's up to

Set the record straight

the supervisor to point out that all wages and benefits are open to negotiation and that neither the union nor the company can predict the outcome. In some cases wage rates may go up; in other cases they may go down. It is possible for employees to end up with the same or even less in terms of the total package of wages and benefits that they receive.

The bargaining process

Related to this is the fact that bargaining on a union contract does not start from where the employees are now. All present benefits and working conditions can be a part of the negotiation, just as much as the union demands for new wages and benefits. Employees may soon discover that in order to get new benefits, the union will trade off some of the present conditions and benefits. Unions may sometimes try to generate fear among employees concerning whether a benefit or practice will continue if the employees don't unionize. Supervisors have the responsibility to meet this challenge by reviewing the company's history of maintaining and increasing benefits and making these facts known to the employees.

The risks of striking

Supervisors should also notify employees of the risks they take when they strike. Striking employees may not be fired because they are engaging in a strike that is considered lawful. Therefore it would be incorrect for a supervisor to tell an employee, "If you go out on strike, you will be fired." However, the supervisor should remind employees that strikers can be permanently replaced, and that if replaced, the employee who ceases striking and wishes to return to work will be hired only if a vacancy in his or her job occurs. The correct way for a supervisor to discuss this with an employee is to point out that as a union member the employee has a right to strike, but that the company has a right to replace permanently any employee who strikes. Some other misconceptions concerning the strike relate to employee fringe benefits. Some employees think that all of their fringe benefits will continue to be paid by the employer during a strike. Some even think that the employer is prohibited from continuing to operate, and that when it comes to a strike, the union possesses all the collective bargaining power.

Unions have their own interests

The supervisor should also point out, in an unbiased way, that the union has its own interests, that the first loyalty of many union organizers is to the union and not to the employees of the organization. Union policy covers more than one organization, and it could be implemented to the detriment of the employees' own organization. The supervisor should give his or her subordinates all views on unionization so that the employees can make a wise decision. This will avoid the situation where the employee feels management and the supervisor are fighting the union. Supervisors should understand employee desires and requests for information and should try to provide candid and honest opinions without interfering with employee rights. This will generate an atmosphere that will help the employees make the best choice.

THE ELECTION

The NLRB election marks the termination of the union's organizing activities. The election follows weeks of preparation and activity on the part of both the union and the management. Speeches have been made, letters mailed, posters hung, and individual sessions held to give answers to the numerous employee questions. There are many besides the supervisors who are waiting for the election results; they include union officials, the few employees who may become union officials, and the many employees who perceive a personal gain or loss because of unionization. The NLRB, the employer, and the union agree on where the election will be held. Balloting is usually held at the workplace, in order to ensure a large turnout. The polling place is located near a cafeteria or rest area; the NLRB tries to avoid areas near management offices. Basically, they look for a reasonably private area that is free from any intimidating influence. The NLRB sets up portable election booths, and employees vote by marking one of two squares on a paper ballot—either yes or no. The election results are determined by the majority of votes cast. The union does not need to get a majority of all eligible employees; all they need to do is get a majority of the votes cast. The ballots are counted by the NLRB agent immediately after the polls close.

Polling

Sometimes a voter's eligibility is challenged—because someone thinks that the voter is a supervisor, is not employed by the company, or was hired after the voter eligibility cutoff date. When a vote is challenged, the ballot is placed in an envelope that is then sealed and deposited in the ballot box. No one sees the marked ballot, and the NLRB agent at the election site tries to resolve the challenge before the counting of the ballots. If it is resolved, then the challenged ballot is mixed in with the other ballots and counted. If the challenge is not resolved and the challenged ballot makes a difference in the outcome of the election, a decision is made later by the NLRB regional office as to whether the challenged voter had a right to vote.

Who gets to vote

Even after the ballots have been counted, the result of the election can still be in doubt. The NLRB has procedures that allow either the employer or the union to object to the manner in which the election was run or to the conduct of some party during the preelection campaign. Objections must be filed within five working days after the election. Unions typically challenge results by charging that the employer committed such unfair labor practices as questioning the employees on how

The election challenge

they intended to vote or promising the employees a raise if the union is defeated. Employers challenge the results by showing that the union misrepresented important facts so close to the time of the election that the employer had no time to respond to the allegations. The election challenge procedure entails the NLRB's regional director investigating the allegations. If there are found to be some unusual issues, then a hearing will be held, with the regional director issuing a decision. There are also other appeals that both the union and the employer can use if the election is still in dispute. During the appeal process, employees may become confused, and it is up to the supervisor to keep them informed about why all this came about, what is being done, and how long the legal process could take. The supervisor should make a point of continuing to communicate with the employees, particularly new employees, so that he or she will have their confidence and trust, whether the election is reheld or upheld. It's important that the supervisor avoid actions during this interim period that can later become a source of collective bargaining problems.

When the union loses, the organization can return to business as usual. The supervisor has the responsibility to ensure that no one is discriminated against because of her views during the union campaign.

Following a successful election, the supervisor should meet with management (or workers) to see if any policies or work-related rules should be examined for clarification and modification. Since the first-line supervisor is the one who will have to implement new policies, he or she should participate in the review process that management initiates following an NLRB election. But in the event of a union victory, a supervisor is not prevented from continuing to direct his or her employees or even to discharge them should the need arise. Win or lose, the role of the supervisor remains critical, and whatever the resulting policy becomes, it's up to the supervisor to make sure that it is properly implemented.

DECERTIFICATION OF A UNION

Establishing reasonable doubt

The first thing many employers want to know after they have lost an NLRB election is when and how the union can be decertified. For decertification to occur, employees must believe, by the turn of events, that the union is not what it was cracked up to be. In short, they must reach a conclusion that they would be better off without a union. Decertification may be initiated by either the employees or the employer. The process involves submitting an NLRB petition with evidence showing that at least 30 percent of the organization employees want a decertification election. The following types of facts have been accepted as sound considerations for supporting an employer's "reasonable doubt" that the union represents the majority of the employees:

1. There is a marked decline in the number of employees subscribing to the union dues checkoff.
2. The majority of employees have not supported the union during a strike.
3. There has been a substantial employee turnover subsequent to the union certification.
4. The union has admitted a lack of majority support.
5. The union has become less and less active in representing employees.
6. The employees have verbally repudiated the union.[7]

More than one of the above is needed to establish a reasonable doubt as to the union's status, and the claim has to be documented.

The important thing to remember with a decertification attempt is that even when a labor contract has not been executed, the law obligates the employer to continue to bargain with and recognize the union for at least twelve months after the certification election. During this time, the employer cannot contest or dispute the union status. Only after the twelve-month period has expired may the employer file an NLRB representation petition for a decertification election. Another point relating to the labor contract is that the employer is obligated to recognize the union and follow the union contract provisions for the duration of the agreed contract.

When the majority of employees have made it clear that they do not wish to have union representation, chances of decertification are good, provided the employer is able to avoid problems on the way to the decertification election. But management should be cautioned that the preelection gripers and grumblers do not always vote the way they talk.

> The 12-month proviso

The Labor Contract

IMPLEMENTING THE CONTRACT

Once management and the union have agreed on a labor contract, this agreement becomes the major document under which both parties will operate for the period of time specified in the contract. Supervisors

> Know the labor agreement

[7] William A. Krupman, "Withdrawal of Recognition Based on Objective Evidence—Reckoning by Starlight," *Delaware Journal of Corporate Law*, vol. 1, no. 2 (1976), pp. 288–298.

have the obligation to manage their departments or units within the framework of the labor agreement. This requires that supervisors develop a thorough knowledge of the provisions of the agreement and how these provisions should be interpreted. It is the supervisor's responsibility to become familiar with the wages and working conditions—including hourly rates, incentive pay, hours of work, overtime, vacation, seniority, and leaves of absence—stipulated in the agreement. The contract will include some provisions for grievance and complaint procedures, which the supervisor should also become familiar with. It is not in the best interests of the union-manager relationship for the supervisor to try and "beat the contract," even when supervisors feel that they are doing the organization a favor. In short, once the agreement has been reached, supervisors should implement it; they should not attempt to ignore or reject it.

GRIEVANCES

Arbitration

In almost all labor agreements there is a section devoted to the process of solving labor disputes through the grievance procedure. (The procedure itself is discussed in the next section of the chapter.) The collective bargaining agreement defines a system of governance at the workplace. The agreement is a contract that binds both parties should disagreements occur concerning the precise terms and conditions that are specified in the contract. Unlike a legal contract, however, a collective bargaining agreement is not enforced or interpreted by the courts. Instead, a neutral person, following guidelines designated by mutual agreement (the collective bargaining contract) of both the union and management representatives is chosen to mediate the dispute. The neutral person, usually called an arbitrator, gets his authority from the parties. In almost all contracts, the arbitrator's decision is binding on both parties. When the union and management representatives cannot agree on the meaning of a particular phrase in the collective bargaining agreement, and all other grievance steps have been exhausted, the issue goes to arbitration. Along with this, in almost all collective bargaining agreements the employer receives a no-strike agreement from the union in return for agreeing to binding arbitration; binding arbitration is the cost of a binding no-strike pledge from the union. Arbitration is a means to resolve a dispute without resort to economic force. The arbitrator's decisions are not necessarily permanent, since if either party is dissatisfied they can attempt to negotiate a change when contract renegotiation comes up.

When labor and management officials negotiate a labor contract, they are principally concerned with agreement over major issues. These negotiators are not particularly concerned with determining the precise meaning of every word in the contract, and they generally cannot predict all of the unique situations that can potentially distort or may fall outside the negotiated terms of the labor contract.

Some grievances do not actually protest the violation of the labor agreement; instead, they stress that management has obligations beyond the scope of the labor agreement. Most grievances over safety hazards fall into this category. An employee may realize that there is no contractual violation but still file a grievance to communicate concern to management over a safety issue. Unions on the other hand may file a grievance to draw attention to a problem in hopes of setting the stage for future labor agreement negotiations. In fact, a union may file several grievances over a particular issue to show or document its demands during the negotiation of subsequent labor contracts.

Types of grievances

Another reason why grievances are filed is that they permit, and in some cases encourage, an employee to protest alleged wrongs committed by a management official. Filing a grievance in effect enhances the perceived status of the employee by calling his or her organizational superiors on the carpet for an explanation of their actions. This type of grievance may be filed when there is a supervisor who flaunts authority unnecessarily, thereby causing tension and stress among the employees. Grievances also provide a forum where the union steward can demonstrate his or her verbal and intellectual capabilities to management and to other union officials. There are other reasons why employees file grievances. Their motives can be as varied and complex as their personalities and life experiences.[8] Sometimes uncovering the motive behind the grievance may be helpful to management so that the climate may be improved in the entire organization. It should be noted that management must process a grievance even when it feels the employee's motives are improper or illegitimate.

THE GRIEVANCE PROCEDURE

The grievance procedure has evolved as a very effective tool for processing grievances. The procedure can be viewed as simply a means of correcting single issues for individuals, or it can be viewed as a process to reduce or make more manageable the tensions that arise between different levels in the organization. The labor agreement usually defines a grievance as a misunderstanding arising from the application or interpretation of the

Objectives of a good grievance system

[8] W. W. Ronan et al., "The Studies of Grievances," Personnel Journal 55 (January 1976), pp. 33–38.

current contract. Theoretically, then, a grievance can occur only when a provision of the contract appears to have been violated. However, this is not always the case, as was mentioned, and there are a wide range of issues that are processed through the grievance procedure even though there is no explicit contract language on the particular matter. There is therefore a need to have a grievance procedure that can perform a larger role than interpreting exactly what the contract calls for, one that can respond as needed to such issues as a wildcat strike or a slowdown.

Although grievance procedures vary from organization to organization, an effective system has been shown to have the following characteristics:

1. An immediate response to the issue
2. Settlement of the issue at the lowest step possible in the grievance procedure
3. Resolution of the grievance in the most objective and consistent manner possible
4. The use of neutral arbitration as the final step in the settlement of the issue

A typical procedure, and one that appears in many contracts, is shown in Figure 12.2.

Step 1

Step 1 actually consists of two phases. First the employee and the union steward discuss the concern with the employee's supervisor. If agreement is not reached among these three individuals, then a written grievance is filed by the employee, or by the union steward acting on the employee's behalf, and the supervisor responds with a written reply.

Step 2

Step 2 of the procedure involves bringing together the union's grievance committee representative and management's industrial relations representative to discuss the supervisor's first-step grievance answer. Both representatives are aware of administrative procedures throughout the entire plant, and their main role is to determine whether the grievance should be resolved at this stage on the basis of acceptable working conditions and established rules in the shop.

Step 3

Step 3 involves the same individuals as Step 2, plus the industrial relations manager and another management official (such as a general supervisor, an assistant plant manager, or a superintendent). From labor's side there are also additional members of the union's grievance committee. These individuals are added at this stage because the grievance answer at this level could affect the entire operation, and both management and union representatives wish to obtain as much input as possible before a decision is arrived at, and, since the additional union and manage-

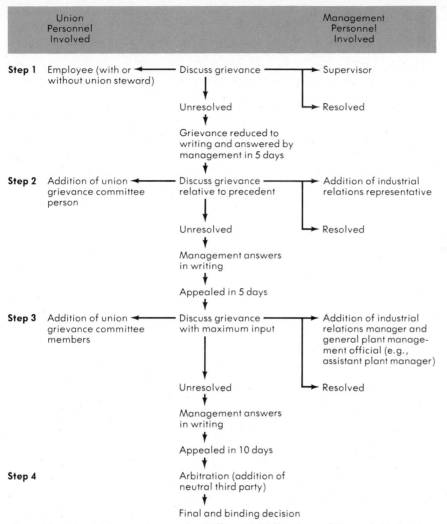

From *The Labor Relations Process* by William H. Holley, Jr., and Kenneth M. Jennings. Copyright © 1980 by the Dryden Press, a division of Holt, Rinehart and Winston, Inc. Reprinted by permission of CBS College Publishing.

ment officials are not personally involved in the grievance outcome, they are better able to assess the merits of the case with relative objectivity. From the union's point of view, the addition of individuals at Step 3 can also be used as a training or educational device for relatively new union officers. Since many labor agreements require paid time off for grievance meetings, a new union official can learn the complex issues and strategies involved in a grievance procedure at the company's or organization's expense. The union grievance committee can also serve a tactical purpose, in that the sheer number of individuals on the committee can impress on the employee who is filing the grievance that the union is forcefully representing his or her interests. This third-step addition has yet another function—it can serve as a buck-passing device for both sides. If the grievance is lost, the union steward or the committee representative can inform the employee that he or she did everything possible to win the grievance but was overruled by other members of the committee. If the grievance is won, supervisors can claim to their managerial counterparts that they were merely sold out by higher-level management officials in subsequent steps of the grievance procedure. The final part of Step 3 usually involves a policy statement written by the industrial relations manager, because the decision will probably have organization-wide implications and applications.

Step 4—arbitration

Step 4, arbitration, is the final step in the grievance procedure. It generally involves the same individuals as Step 3, but with the addition of a neutral third party. At this stage of the grievance, the union and management both work diligently on preparation of a case to be submitted to arbitration, so as not to appear to be "losers." The arbitration procedure is a nonlegal yet legalistic proceeding, in which the impartial third party, selected jointly by the union and management, renders a final and binding decision.

The decision

The arbitrator

The first step of Step 4 is the selection of an arbitrator to function as the neutral party in resolving the dispute. The selection is usually made from a list supplied by a government agency or by the American Arbitration Association. Next, the issue to be resolved is presented to the arbitrator in a document that summarizes the questions on which the neutral party is to focus. It is normally considered inappropriate for the arbitrator to go beyond the issue or issues presented by the parties. In fact, many contracts have provisions that prohibit the arbitrator from making an award that would change the terms of the existing labor contract. The arbitrator's role is to decide if the contract language has been breached. It is definitely not to write new language into the contract. Generally, informal arbitration hearings are conducted so as to permit both management and the union the opportunity to present their case. Where necessary, this may involve on-site inspection, witness testimony, cross-examinations, and oral arguments. Thirty to sixty days after the hearing has been closed, the arbitrator makes an award and submits a written opinion giving the reasons for his or her decision. This decision is final and binding, and the case that started the grievance is now closed. The result is that the contract language may have a new interpretation, the employee has had a fair hearing, and the frustration around the issue is finally dissipated. One final note regarding the finality of the arbitrator's decision: Courts have accepted arbitrator decisions, primarily because the employer and the union have voluntarily agreed to this procedure and the courts have long respected the desires of those who will consent to a mutual agreement. Therefore, under most circumstances the arbitrator's interpretation of the contract cannot be appealed to the courts.

THE STRIKE

Even after the union has become the certified bargaining representative of the employees, the labor law does not require that the employer agree to the demands made by the union or make any concessions at the bargaining table. In fact, there is no legal requirement that a labor contract or agreement has to be reached. After the union is certified, both the employer and the union must analyze their position and decide what they will do in order to force the other side to make concessions. The union's chief weapon is the strike—a test of strength between the employer and the union in which the union basically tries to shut down the business. The strike is usually used in conjunction with picketing, which tries to prevent the delivery of supplies to and the shipments of goods from the plant to prevent nonunion and replacement workers from continuing operation. The union also has other weapons that can be used, such as protest marches, media protests, a mass sick call, a slowdown, a sitdown on the job, refusal to work overtime, and a total compliance with the stated regulations. The strike is generally used when these other methods become ineffective.

Other union weapons

Employers faced with a strike are far from powerless. One of the main tools of management is that striking employees can be permanently replaced. The supervisor must be careful when explaining to employees the difference between being permanently replaced and being fired. Ignorance of this distinction can cause many problems for supervisors. The NLRB has said that employees have the right to strike, but also that employers have the right to replace strikers. The supervisor must avoid saying, "If you strike, you will be fired" because the NLRB views such a statement as a threat to an employee's lawful union activity. The correct approach is to say, "If you strike, you may be replaced"; the supervisor would then be acting within the law.

Management's weapons

The supervisor has a difficult job during a strike. He or she may have to cross picket lines to and from work, and sometimes this requires courage beyond what is ever called for on the job. The strikers' hostility may be vented on the picket line and directed toward their own supervisors. Besides having to cross the picket line, the supervisor has additional

The supervisor's role during a strike

responsibilities during a strike. Once inside the plant, the supervisor may have to perform the duties of the subordinates and work longer hours. If replacements are sought and hired, then the supervisor may have a major training task to complete before the replacements are fully productive. If the strike is still going on while replacements are being hired and trained, the training effort may be complicated by the fact of new employees being harassed crossing the picket line, and they may quit rather than endure such harassment. During this time the supervisor should try to create a productive atmosphere. He or she should be willing to pitch in and perform employee tasks when necessary to help the new employees become productive as soon as possible.

And after a strike

Not all strikes lead to the replacement of employees, and once a strike is settled, a supervisor has some additional problems to contend with. Often the supervisor has to deal with any remaining hostility among the strikers or misperceptions of their employer. Sometimes strikers blame the employer for the strike and for the lost wages that they incurred because of the strike. The important thing to remember is that nothing is gained by allowing the bitterness and resentment to remain. Supervisors should help to create a more positive attitude by welcoming the strikers back to the job. They should point out to the employees that no resentment or ill will exists, that the strike is behind everyone, and that the employees should pick up where they left off before the strike occurred. The supervisor has the job of getting the employees back to working as a team so that the overall plant or organization will again be a productive entity.

Practical Guidelines for Supervisors

Working with unions

In many cases, a labor union already exists in an organization. However, when union-organizing attempts occur, the supervisor is often a critical factor in determining whether or not an individual employee group does select a union to represent them. This is usually a period of tension; it is also a period in which constructive solutions to problems are difficult to attain. Once a union becomes a bargaining representative, the union and management usually learn to live with each other after a time. A supervisor who has never worked in a union environment before must keep in mind that a union is just another institution that has potential for either advancing or disrupting the common efforts of the organization. From the supervisor on up, it is in the interests of management to develop a labor-management climate that directs this potential toward constructive ends. The supervisor plays a key role in achieving this goal. There is no magic formula. From the supervisor's point of view it takes wisdom, sensitivity, and hard work to show that the union is going to be accepted and is as responsible as the organization itself. It's the supervisor's day-to-day action with the employees that makes the labor agreement a living document, which can turn out to be for better or worse. Management also has a responsibility in this, in that there must be periodic training of supervisors concerned with the operating fundamentals of the collective bargaining agreement.

Most of the supervisor's union contacts will be with the union steward. The union steward, sometimes referred to as a shop committeeman or committeewoman, is an elected official of the union—elected by fellow workers to be their official spokesman to management and to the union local. But in most organizations the union steward is also an employee who is expected to perform a full day's work for the employer. Thus the steward must serve two masters. As an employee, the steward is expected to perform satisfactory work for the employer by following the orders and directives of the organization; yet as a union official, the steward has a responsibility to other employees and to the union. The union steward wants to be a "partner" with the supervisor in running the department, or at least to be perceived as such by the employees. For the union steward, there is employee pressure to lessen management work demands. This causes the steward to put pressure on the supervisor, who often finds the steward's demands to be in direct conflict with his or her own managerial task. The resulting tension and conflict can often neutralize an effective supervisor.

The union steward

For the supervisor, adjusting to a union environment can be a difficult task. Supervisors may find that their authority and orders are constantly being challenged by the steward. The union steward may be looking over supervisors' shoulders and trying to second-guess what they plan to do, and there may often be some questioning of the intent of their actions. These repeated challenges, especially from an overaggressive shop steward, may cause some supervisors to stop making decisions and stop taking action. Sometimes the challenges become a grievance, and this will consume many hours of a supervisor's time in the form of meetings, grievance investigations, and arbitration hearings.

It is often difficult for a supervisor who has been used to having the last on every issue to adjust to a new union. Employees may decide that the spirit of cooperation between them and their supervisor is a thing of the past. Now employees may hesitate in carrying out an order, by consulting with the union steward to see if his or her advice concurs with that of the supervisor. In addition, relationships with employees

Adjusting to a new union

may become more formal. And the situation may be aggravated if the union steward tends to foster a "we versus them" atmosphere which implies that employees should keep their distance from the supervisor.

Motivating employees who are affected by the union-inspired clauses of the contract may be difficult. The supervisor may be prohibited from rewarding productive employees with pay raises, more interesting assignments, and promotions. Unions attempt to treat all employees equally and to base personnel decisions on seniority rather than on a worker's performance. And when a supervisor lacks the tools to motivate employees, maintaining productivity becomes a problem.

In spite of the attempts by unions to slow down productivity, supervisors must keep in mind that they have a responsibility to management and to their employees; the job must be done. Supervisors must try not to allow unionization to hamper their efforts to create a highly productive environment, to maintain good working relationships with the employees, and in general to do the job the organization is paying them to do.

Good supervisors can minimize the number of grievances. Supervisors have enough decision-making power to be able to settle most employee complaints. When problems involving organization rules and policies occur, they can often be settled quickly if the supervisor uses diplomacy and tact.

SUMMARY ━━━━━━━━━━━━━━━━━━━━━━━━━━━━━━

The chapter provides the supervisor with the necessary background on unionization in the United States, labor laws, and the collective bargaining process. Labor relations involve the relationships between the employer (management) and the employee (labor). Supervisors occupy a unique role in labor relations because they are caught in the middle between management on the one hand and the rank-and-file employees on the other. Union growth in recent years has occurred in the nonmanufacturing or service areas, such as educational institutions and government agencies. Since many supervisors will be dealing with unions in one way or another, they should fully understand how unions operate.

Workers join unions for a number of reasons. First of all, workers feel that a union will protect them against managerial discrimination and favoritism on job assignments, and provide them with continued employment at high wages and with exceptional benefits. Second, workers join unions to satisfy certain social needs. Third, individuals join unions because of social pressure applied by fellow workers. Finally, workers join the union because it offers them an opportunity to realize needs for status and self-fulfillment.

Management typically resist unions because they have a desire to retain the decision-making authority of the organization, and they feel the union is a trouble maker that creates gaps between management and the workers.

Upper management negotiates the labor-management agreement; however, it is the supervisor who must work with the agreement on a day-to-day basis. It is up to the supervisor to use wit, persuasiveness, and charm to get management and the rank and file together for a healthy, productive relationship. One of the greatest tests of a supervisor's ability to maintain a productive relationship occurs when employees band together to form a union.

After the employees are unionized, the supervisor can no longer deal directly with employees over wages, working conditions, and hours but instead must deal with the union on these matters. A supervisor may want to fire a worker for being late three days in a row. However, if the labor-management agreement states that employees must be given a written warning before termination, the supervisor must adhere to this. The supervisor may want to promote a good worker who lacks seniority; but if the labor-management agreement states that promotions must be made on the basis of seniority, the supervisor must adhere to this as well.

A strong managerial tool in a unionized environment is the collective bargaining agreement. This agreement defines a governing system at the workplace. The labor agreement typically contains the provisions for a grievance procedure to handle problems that have not been specifically negotiated in the labor contract. The procedure generally involves a four-step procedure that may lead to resolution of the dispute by an arbitrator or mediator.

HOWARD EVANS

On a Tuesday afternoon during the spring busy season, Roger Lester, general production foreman of Petri's main plant, received his production quotas for the subsequent two weeks. Since the production of silver nitrate in building 11 was being increased substantially, Lester had requested five additional people who held the job-classification title of "chemical operator." Lester sought assistance from the personnel department to select people for these jobs who had previous experience in producing silver nitrate. Among the people assigned to Lester for the silver-nitrate production was Howard Evans, twenty-six years old, a chemical operator with six years' experience at Petri.

On Thursday Evans received a copy of the posted working schedule for the next week. The schedule indicated that he was to report to building 11 the following Monday morning to work on the silver-nitrate process. About 3:30 that afternoon, Evans walked into Roger Lester's office.

EVANS: Why didn't you pick on someone else to work on silver nitrate? I want to remain on my present job. I was transferred to building 24 only a few weeks ago. I've just gotten to the point where I understand my new job. Now you are taking me away and putting me back on this job.
LESTER: In other words, Howard, you feel that I am imposing on you by requesting your transfer?
EVANS: I am beginning to believe that you bosses are damn inconsiderate around here. Do you realize that I have been moved six times in the past five months? I haven't been able to learn any of these jobs well. Just as I get to the point where I'm beginning to be able to do the work, one of you guys hauls me off to a different department.

Does everyone get moved around as much as I, or is there something wrong with me? Am I doing such a poor job that all my bosses are trying to get rid of me?
LESTER: Remember, Howard, I did request that you be assigned to my department. And you do have the job title of "chemical operator," which means that we can use you as the demands of our business dictate, so long as you work in jobs that are basically similar in nature. We've always done it this way. You've had prior experience in the silver-nitrate production process, and I felt we needed people like you to get over the spot we're in now.
EVANS: Can't you fellows plan your work? This is a poor way to run a department. No one shows any consideration for chemical operators. We get moved around like men on a checkerboard. And don't tell me that it's done fairly. No one ever asks us what we want to do.
LESTER: I am sorry to learn that you feel this way about my department. I always thought that we clicked it off in a good manner.
EVANS: Tell me, how long will I be here? Can I count on staying in this department from now on? Or am I going back to building 24 next week?
LESTER: I can't promise that you will stay here. All I know is that we need production in silver nitrate for at least the next two weeks. I don't know what will happen after that.
EVANS: I think I am getting a raw deal here.

I'm going to see my union steward to file a grievance.

Howard Evans had worked in building 24 for five weeks before being transferred back to building 11, his former department. He had an excellent work record; in fact, most of his supervisors had given him a top rating on his semiannual employee evaluations. In recent months, however, several foremen had commented that his previous enthusiasm and spirit on the job had diminished somewhat.

Two days following his conversation with Evans, Roger Lester received a written grievance from the union steward that protested the "indiscriminate transferring of chemical operators from job to job in violation of the contract." In studying Evan's grievance, Lester reviewed the union contract sections governing job transfers in the plant. The most pertinent clauses read as follows.

Section 1: Management Rights

(a) Cooperation between parties and the observance of the contract is the basis of all enduring agreements. The parties to this agreement recognize that stability in wages, working conditions, production, and competency and efficiency of workers are essential to the best interests of both employees and management and agree to strive to eliminate all factors that tend toward unstabilizing such conditions. It is understood that the administration and operation of the plant including but not limited to the assignment, transfer, and discipline of workers and the establishment of production-control procedures is the responsibility of Management. . . .

Section 21: Transfers

The transferring of employees is the sole responsibility of Management subject to the following. . . .

(b) It is the policy of Management to cooperate in every practical way with employees who desire transfers to new positions or vacancies in their department. Accordingly, such employees who make application to their foreman or the personnel department stating their desires, qualifications, and experience will be given preference for openings in their department provided they are capable of doing the job. . . .

Lester pondered what his reply to the grievance should be and what course of action he should take.

1. Explain the grievance procedure Roger Lester will follow.
2. What might have been done to avoid the filing of the grievance in the first place? Does the union contract restrict management's flexibility?
3. What should foreman Roger Lester do?

E. L. Hilgert, P. Schoen, and W. Towle, *Cases and Policies in Personnel: Human Resources Management,* 4th ed. (Boston: Houghton Mifflin, 1982), pp. 343–345. Used with permission.

DISCUSSION QUESTIONS

1. Compare the Knights of Labor with the American Federation of Labor. What are some reasons the AFL succeeded where the KOL did not?
2. Why should a supervisor in a nonunion organization be concerned with unions?
3. What legal obligations does an employer have when faced with union intervention?
4. Once a majority of workers have joined a union, what are the primary obligations the union has toward employees and employers?
5. What are some current issues facing the unions today, and how do these affect a supervisor?
6. Some organizations, such as Motorola, have made successful efforts to prevent their employees from joining unions; how do you suppose this is done?
7. How do unions get organized within a company, and what are some practical ways management should handle the situation?
8. In the event of an impending strike, what are some bargaining advantages a supervisor may have? What are some things the union may have in its favor?
9. Where does arbitration fit in the grievance procedure, and what are the qualifications and duties of an arbitrator?

REFERENCES

Angel, Marina. "White-Collar and Professional Unionization." *Labor Law Journal* 33, no. 2 (February 1982): 82–101.

Carney, Christopher F. "What Supervisors Can Do About Union Organizing." *Supervisory Management* 26, no. 1 (January 1981): 10–15.

Davey, H. W.; Bognanno, M. F.; and Estenson, D. L. *Contemporary Collective Bargaining.* 4th ed. Englewood Cliffs, NJ: Prentice-Hall, Inc., 1982.

Hagburg, E. C., and Levine, M. J. *Labor Relations: An Integrated Perspective.* St. Paul: West Publishing Company, 1978.

Holley, William H., and Jennings, K. M. *The Labor Relations Process.* Hinsdale, Ill: Dryden Press, 1980.

Hoover, John J. "Union Organization Attempts: Management's Response." *Personnel Journal* 61, no. 3 (March 1982): 214–219.

Lubin, Joann S. "Labor Reverses: Pugnacious Companies and Skeptical Workers Cost Unions Members." *Wall Street Journal* 107, no. 79 (October 21, 1982): 1+.

Seligman, D. "Who Needs Unions." *Fortune* 106, no. 1 (July 1982): 54–66.

Sloane, A. A., and Witney, Fred. *Labor Relations.* 4th ed. Englewood Cliffs, NJ: Prentice-Hall, Inc.: 1981.

Swann, Jr., James P. "The Decertification of a Union: The Rules of the Game." *Personnel Administrator* 28, no. 1 (January 1983): 47–51.

CHAPTER 13

PERSONAL COMPUTER BASICS FOR SUPERVISORS

"I only ask for information"

—"Miss Rosa Dartle"
Charles Dickens

Chapter Outline

Objectives

Computers play an increasing role in modern life. Kids request them—their mothers and fathers often end up using them. Furthermore, computers are all around us—in schools, banks, stores, and at work. Many people first play with them at home; then they become "hooked" and buy or request one for the organization where they work. Or they become so pleased with them at work, they take them home for fun. In short, many people are quickly losing their fear of computers. However, interested first-time users soon realize that some education is needed so that they can get the most for their time and money. At the supervisory level, supervisors must become familiar with computers and computer systems so that they will be willing to use them in every suitable application. This chapter provides a basis for understanding the role that personal computers can play in organizations. Specifically in this chapter you will become familiar with:

1. Why personal computers have become so popular in recent years
2. The functions of a personal computer
3. Some common business applications for personal computers
4. The components of a personal computer
5. Some elementary computer programming concepts
6. A common-sense approach for acquiring and installing a personal computer

Major Concepts

Computer hardware
Computer software
Management by exception
Information processes
Feasibility study
"K"
Byte
Read-only memory (ROM)
Read-and-write memory (RWM)
Random-access memory (RAM)
Microprocessor

Binary digits
Floppy/fixed disks
Systems/application software
Packaged/custom software
Batch/real-time processing
High-level languages/machine
    language
BASIC
Integer/floating point mathematics
Interface
Interpreter

DEALING WITH COMPUTER HARD-SELL

I did not purchase any computer ware—hard or soft—during the holiday season.

It was, of course, terribly irresponsible of me, especially with our media seemingly almost totally dependent on the computer industry for advertising support.

But don't think I'm not suffering. When a guy refuses to join the communications revolution, word gets around. This is 1984, after all.

The first knock on my door came at 6 A.M. on December 26. It was Kelly, the Commodore man. Thinking it was someone less offensive— an auditor from the IRS, perhaps, or a representative of the Larry Flynt for President campaign—I opened the door.

"Who ratted?" I asked.

"We have our sources," he said, pulling a readout from his pocket. He motioned to the tricycle in the driveway. "How old is the kid?"

"Four," I said.

Kelly shook his head with a mixture of sadness and disgust. "Four," he repeated. "And no computer. I suppose he can't even read or write."

I nodded in shame.

"Illiteracy is a terrible thing," he said. "You're lucky I got to you in time. Buy our computer and he'll be translating the Bible into five languages by Easter."

I finally got rid of Kelly by telling him that I was an Amway distributor and excusing myself to get my display case. But I knew it was going to be a long day. I shut the curtains and turned out the lights, but that didn't stop Watson, the next salesman.

He arrived with a backpack carrying his computers. There was grain stuck to his pants.

"You must be from Texas Instruments," I said.

"Yes, but it's not my fault," he said. "Home computer salesmen run in the family."

"I really don't want a computer," I said.

"No one does," said Watson. "Help us out. Take just one."

"How much?"

"Nineteen dollars," he said.

"Too much," I answered.

"Thirteen fifty," said Watson. He pulled out a picture of his family. I reached for my checkbook.

"Just one thing," said Watson. "No rebate."

I closed the door in his face and hung up a "Quarantined" sign on the door, but that didn't stop Alan Alda. He put on a surgical gown and mask and knocked on the door.

I wasn't about to let him in, but my wife had other ideas. Before I could get a word in, he was sipping coffee and booting up an Atari.

"Too much money," I said, trying to lure Alda's dog from my best chair.

"Maybe," Alda replied. "Maybe you can put a price tag on the gift of knowledge."

"He's so sincere," my wife whispered. "Just like he was in MASH."

I found myself considering it. Alda pressed on. "All of our educational programs are nonsexist," he said. "I see to that personally."

I said something about having to go to a Sons of the American Revolution meeting, and Alda and his dog left.

As I was boarding up the windows and leashing my new guard dogs, I heard a tramping outside. It was Chaplin, the IBM man.

"You," he said, "are in luck."

I kept pounding the nails, but he didn't stop.

"We are strongly inclined to let you buy a PC Junior," he said. "We have assembled a complete psychological profile of you and your family and we believe that you will uphold the IBM tradition. All you have to do is pass a brief test."

Naturally, I was flattered. "How much does the PC Junior cost?" I asked.

Chaplin retreated toward his limousine.

"Sorry," he said. "You just failed the test."

Adapted from Howard Gelfand, "Dealing with Computer Hard-Sell," *Wall Street Journal,* January 24, 1984, p. 28.

*I*n general, computer-related technology has been slow to make its mark on the average organization. This delay has been mainly due to the cost and complexity of implementing the computer and its related equipment. Word processors, for example, were one of the first innovations and have taken over fifteen years to arrive in significant numbers on the organizational scene. However, personal computers and electronic calculators have been exceptions to this rule. It took calculators just over five years to replace the old adding machines in many organizations. The personal computer is showing signs of gaining a strong foothold in business in an even shorter period of time. Computers are fast becoming an important information processing tool for many non–data processing supervisors, managers, and professionals.

There are a number of reasons for this quick success. First, the cost of hardware (equipment) and software (programs) is now relatively low. Today's simple game-playing personal computers come with a price tag that would have been impossible just a decade ago. The second reason is the perceived simplicity of the equipment. A personal computer, having come from the game-playing environment, is perceived by many potential users as simple to use and operate. Companies selling personal computers do not have to go into gyrations to sell the product or provide user handholding as they have done in the past. Finally, personal computers now come with a wide variety of software. These third-party packages allow the first-time user to apply a personal computer to a great many business and organizational tasks without having to learn programming. A large number of these packages are currently being marketed by reputable software sales organizations.

Often personal computers have gained entry into organizations without the blessing of upper management. In fact, many managers are unable to say just how many are currently installed within their organizations or in what ways they have been used to improve productivity in the organization.

There was a time when supervisors didn't have to think about computers. Mainframe computers were too big, too complex, and too expensive, and they were mainly used by the data processing department or strictly limited to large operations. Times have changed, and personal computers are now within the budget of many organizations. They can fit right into the existing organizational space, and they are simple enough to be used by clerks or typists who are already employed by the organization. Supervisors are often able to survey their departments and find areas where people could be more productive if they had more complete,

> **Today's computers—low-cost and simple**

> **Computers make better use of employees**

accurate information at their fingertips. The computer is ideal for helping people complete repetitive tasks. When a clerk prepares an invoice, he or she can type in the account number and a computer can automatically fill in bill-to and ship-to addresses and any other standard information, saving the clerk several minutes on each invoice. The computer also helps provide better information and lets organizations make better use of their employees. Other examples might include a dispatcher who can work out a system to combine backhauls with deliveries, a supervisor who can use a computer to schedule work in a way that minimizes machine breakdowns, and a warehouse worker who can get packing slips printed in the order of bin locations.

The computer can make supervisors more efficient in handling many of the day-to-day matters that often bog them down. Supervisors can establish guidelines—such as credit limits, inventory reorder points, and discount structures—and the computer can alert them only when the guidelines are exceeded. This allows the supervisor to practice management by exception. The computer also enables supervisors to make better management decisions by giving quicker access to more accurate information. Once basic data are stored in a computer's files, it is relatively easy to summarize, reformat, and perform analysis utilizing calculations on the stored data. The result is that the supervisor can extract information that is more useful for solving the task at hand.

Allow for management by exception

Using Computers at Work

THE BASIC FUNCTIONS OF A COMPUTER

Before describing how computers can be utilized in the work environment, it seems appropriate to describe the basic functions of a computer.

The computer's basic functions

1. Capture data. As in manual systems, the computer can store data that are deposited directly into its files. For example, when a purchase order is written, data are created that affect several different computer files, such as an inventory status file, a billing file, and a delivery file. A well-designed computer system can capture all of the necessary information, right from the originating document, and post it off into the appropriate computerized files automatically.
2. Process data. Computers can perform many complex calculations in a fraction of a second with complete accuracy. Besides completing mathematical calculations on stored data, a computer can also sort and move data from one place to another. Furthermore, the data

can be summarized, analyzed, and verified with little expenditure of human time and effort.

3. Print output. Any piece of paperwork that an organization needs to have generated can be produced with the aid of a computer, provided the necessary information is in the computer's files. This includes end-of-month statements, operating and management reports of all kinds, payroll checks, and inventory status reports.

4. Interact with people. A more recent popular addition to the computer field has been the concept of interactive processing. Computer terminals in remote locations—such as a supervisor's office, a billing department, or the shipping dock—are linked to the computer through a telephone line or by a direct computer line. These terminals can access a computer's data files so that updates and calculations can be carried out whenever they are needed.

5. Store information. As indicated earlier, a computer has the ability to store information that will be needed at a later time. An important part of this ability is the fact that the computer can retrieve stored data at very fast speeds and can index this information in a wide variety of ways, making it much easier to retrieve than manually stored data.

6. Perform editing chores. Many computer programs have been designed to automate the operation of the computer and other activities. For example, certain programs can handle various tasks going on within the computer itself, so that several individuals can interact with the computer simultaneously. These programs are generally called operating systems. They vary considerably from computer model to computer model. Internal editing routines can check data that people want to put into computer files by verifying codes, checking calculations, and examining the information for errors before it gets into the file itself. Furthermore, there are identity-code-checking routines that can be used to restrict access to certain files whose data are confidential or proprietary.

Since computers can perform the same operations that are done manually, the management of a growing organization is faced with the choice of either hiring more personnel or buying computer capability to do the additional processing for the organization.

Information processes

Organizational tasks such as order entry, payroll, and inventory control are information processes. Each of these tasks involves collecting, processing, and reporting information about the organization. Computers are ideally suited to perform these functions, and they can do so with great accuracy and speed. When complex processing on large amounts of information is required, a computer can be a very cost-effective way to carry out these functions.

BUSINESS APPLICATIONS FOR COMPUTERS

Business applications for microcomputers are varied, ranging from simple reporting functions to complex scheduling and forecasting tasks. The following are some typical applications listed by major business functions.

ACCOUNTING
Accounts payable
Accounts receivable
Payroll
Financial statements

Some typical applications

FINANCE
Project analysis
Projected cash flow statements
Investment return reports

MANUFACTURING
Production scheduling
Production cost of goods manufactured
Quality control reports
Raw material availability
Bills of material
Inventory economical order quantity analysis
Purchasing analysis and forecasting

SALES AND MARKETING
Shipping control and analysis
Commission reporting
Sales analysis and projected sales

The above list is by no means exhaustive. While reading, you may already have thought of several of your own organizational procedures that would benefit from computer implementation. The important thing is to consider each of your current procedures and how the organization might benefit from an increase in their speed and accuracy. Specifically, let's look at an application in the area of order entry. A clerk may take an average of ten minutes to process an order. This processing includes:

Speed and accuracy

Looking up a customer's identification number, credit status, and ship-to and bill-to address

Verifying the model number and price of items ordered

Verifying the total amount of the order

Preparing an order acknowledgment

Preparing an internal document from which the order is filled and shipping instructions are to be carried out

When a computer system is implemented, this procedure might take about twenty-five seconds, since all the clerk needs to do is enter into the computer a customer's identification number plus the quantity and model of each item ordered. This procedure involves about twenty seconds of the clerk's time, after which the computer will automatically do each of the above steps. In addition, it can store this order information so that periodic reports can be generated. Such reports might include:

Daily sales

Year-to-date sales by customer

Monthly sales by model number and product

The computer will take about five seconds to complete the above five steps and store the order data. This is an example of how a computer can increase speed and how valuable management reports can be generated from the data stored within the computer.

Cost-effectiveness

Procedures such as those outlined above can be very cost-effective. Thus supervisors need to make a list of their organization's procedures and from that list determine which tasks, if computerized, would benefit the organization and reduce costs. If it seems at this point that the organization might really benefit from having a personal computer, then it is time for action. One approach is to hire a management consultant to analyze the organization's procedures, problems, and goals. The consultant will produce a feasibility study containing a recommendation as

Three alternative courses

to whether or not you need a personal computer. This might be a valuable course of action, but it will also be expensive. A study of this type usually takes one or two weeks and costs between $50 and $100 per hour. A second course of action is to call the local sales offices of several computer manufacturers. Discuss with them your interest in purchasing a personal computer to help with a particular task that you have. Typically a salesperson will visit your premises, help you analyze your computer needs, and of course answer any questions that you may have. But the important thing to keep in mind is that these are salespeople, in business to sell their company's products. Typically, they stress the importance of the computer equipment they are peddling, which may or may not meet the needs of your particular application. However, they are an excellent and valuable source of information.

A third alternative is to consult the organization's accountants or auditors. Since they have a basic familiarity with your system, they can offer views regarding their professional requirements. In addition, if the organization has a data processing department, it may have a systems analyst who may be willing to discuss the details of your particular problem and offer some advice as to whether a personal computer would be helpful or whether the problem would be more readily solved using the organization's centralized computing facilities.

The Components of a Personal Computer

The personal computer is the smallest version of a computer, both in size and in capabilities. It is composed of a microprocessor, input/output units, one or more storage units, and the interconnecting circuitry.

COMPUTER MEMORY

A computer's capacity is measured in terms of "K." In the metric system, the letter "k" (kilo) represents a thousand. When used with computers, "K" always represents 1,024. Therefore, a computer with a memory capacity of 32K can store 32,768 bytes of data. A byte is either a number or a letter represented by the computer in 1s and 0s. When data are entered through a keyboard, the system decodes the alphabetic or numeric characters into an electrical representation. The same process occurs in reverse when the computer is ordered to print out the results of processing; it translates the electronic representation back into English.

"K"

There are two basic types of memory inside a personal computer. One is called read-only memory (ROM), and the second is called read-and-write memory (RWM). Computer instructions for a particular application are usually stored in read-only memory and read into the processor for execution. The computer industry uses the term RAM for the read-and-write memory. RAM stands for random-access memory, which means that each area of the memory used for data storage is directly accessible— as opposed to sequential (or program) memory, where units of instruction must be processed in sequence. One way to distinguish between ROM and RAM is to remember that the contents of RAM are continuously

RAM and ROM

FIGURE 13.1
The Organization of the
ROM, RAM, and
Microprocessor
Components of a
Personal Computer

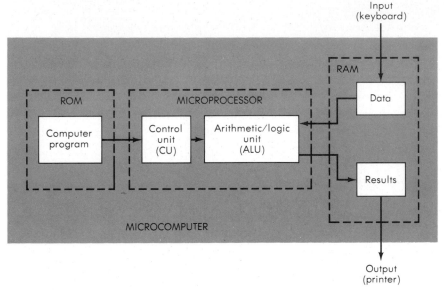

Adapted from J. Daniel Couger and Fred R. McFadden, *First Course in Data Processing with BASIC,* 2nd ed. (New York: Wiley, 1984), p. 178.

being changed as the computer operates, whereas the contents of ROM remain fixed. Usually, ROM is used to store computer programs that will be used repeatedly; since these programs are not modified, they can be effectively used in the read-only device. Figure 13.1 shows the relationship between RAM and ROM. A computer program is stored in ROM. When an operator enters on a keyboard the data to be processed, the logic for completing the operator's request is accomplished in a set of instructions, called a computer program, that has been stored in ROM. The instructions in ROM are executed by the microprocessor in sequence until a solution is obtained. The result is then output on a printer device.

COMPUTER HARDWARE

**Hardware: Four
essential parts**

Like any other computer, a personal computer is made up of hardware and software. The hardware, that is, the physical components of the system, is composed of electronic or electromechanical devices. In any microcomputer system there are four essential parts:

    Microprocessor
    Input devices

Storage devices
Output devices

Data are entered into an input device and then moved to the microprocessing and/or storage unit. Processing results in a new form of information, which can either be stored or be transformed through an output device. Data that have been previously stored may be retrieved from storage for processing or transferred to an output device—such as a line printer, a terminal display, or a typewriter.

The Microprocessor. The microprocessor is the heart and brain of a computer system. It contains the arithmetic/logic and control units that interpret and execute the program instructions. The microprocessor is equivalent to the central processing unit (CPU) of a large-scale computer. It is typically manufactured from a single silicone chip containing both the arithmetic/logic unit and the control unit of the personal computer. The microprocessor's function is to receive data in the form of binary digits (0s and 1s) called "bits," store the data for later processing, perform arithmetic and logic operations in accordance with previously stored instructions, and then deliver the results to the user through an output mechanism such as a cathode ray tube (CRT) unit. Microprocessors are inexpensive to produce, and because they can be mass produced, are readily available. In addition, they require little power and take up little space.

| The heart and brain |

Input Devices. An input device is the link or connection by which the user communicates with the personal computer system. There are many devices designed for this purpose, including keyboards, optical character readers (OCR), and card readers. Some of these devices do both input and output.

Storage Devices. A storage device is a device into which data may be fed and from which data may be retrieved at a later time. Some examples are magnetic tape, cassettes, and magnetic disks. Personal computers utilize two different types of magnetic disks. First, and most common, is the floppy disk, which can be readily removed and replaced with another disk as needed to execute a program. Floppy disks (sometimes called diskettes or mini disks) are flexible and are about the same size as a 45-rpm phonograph record. They are thin disks made of polyester film coated with a metal oxide compound. They are mounted and rotate freely within a jacket that prevents their being damaged. A second type, called a fixed disk, consists of units that can read or write data at a

| Floppy disks |

| Fixed disks |

much faster transfer rate than the floppy disk and have a much greater storage capacity.

Output Devices. An output device is the link by which the computer system communicates with the user. Some examples of output devices are typewriter terminals, visual display terminals, line printers, and rapid display terminals. All of these devices present information or data to the user in some sort of readable form.

Expert advice is needed

Selecting Hardware Components. The selection of hardware devices for building a personal computer system requires some technical knowledge. The recommendation of specific hardware components is best left to a systems analyst or salesperson who is aware of the capabilities of the equipment and its suitability for the user's applications. Some major factors to consider are cost, processing speed, information storage capacity, reliability, and expandability. Obviously the user wants a system that can process and store all the necessary information at a satisfactory transfer rate and at a reasonable cost. The last factor, expandability, requires that the capacity of the system be easy to increase by adding more components.

COMPUTER SOFTWARE

Systems software

Software is defined as the instructions or programs that direct the personal computer's operation. These are written by programmers. There are two types of software: (1) systems software and (2) applications software. Systems software is a set of instructions for performing many basic computer functions. These functions include the control and execution of the application programs, the scheduling of computer resources, and the operation of the various input and output devices. Systems software, which resides on a systems disk, has been thoroughly tested by the manufacturer so that the system will perform all the basic functions necessary for your application needs.

Applications software

Applications software is the set of optional programs that performs your particular processing need. This software determines whether or not your task can be effectively completed. Applications software can be either "packaged" or "custom." Packaged programs, designed to handle standard applications, are intended to be sold virtually unchanged to many users. Custom software is written directly to your specifications and is intended to satisfy your precise needs. Obviously, packaged software is a less expensive alternative, since the cost of development is spread over the many users who purchase the program. A second advan-

Packaged versus custom software

tage of purchasing packaged software is that it is more likely to be error-free. Manufacturers guarantee that the package will perform standard business functions, for example, order entry, in a standard way or provide a choice between several standard methods. However, when the organization's procedures do not follow a standard method, then a standard software package cannot be utilized. In this case, it may be possible to get the package modified; if that is not feasible, then custom software must be written for your particular application.

The advantage of custom software is that it can be designed exactly to meet the existing methods of operation of your organization. However, because it is customized, it tends to be expensive. The cost is not spread over many users. Furthermore, an extensive testing period is necessary to find and fix all errors that may exist in the program. Custom software is provided by a software house—a company that specializes in programming.

Packaged software is available from several sources, including computer vendors—sometimes for purchase or lease. A third possibility is to use in-house programmers to do the job. This alternative is not recommended unless you have access to an experienced staff.

The manager may have to decide between two types of applications software, "batch" and "real-time." In batch processing, transactions are collected as a group for input. For example, inventory transactions may be collected daily and then posted, as a group, into the inventory file at the end of the workday. One disadvantage of batch processing is that errors and incorrect data are not corrected until the entire set of data has been keyboarded and submitted to the computer for running. This problem is avoided in real-time or structure processing, because the computer indicates the presence of errors as the data are entered. In real-time processing, data may be entered into the system at any time, and all necessary processing is done immediately. The result is that current, updated information can be retrieved at any time. For example, inventory transactions can be entered as they occur, and the inventory file will immediately reflect the most current inputs and outputs to the system.

Batch versus real-time

An Introduction to Computer Programming

Almost all personal computer manufacturers provide at least one high-level programming language with their system. High-level languages are "people-oriented"; they permit programmers to write instructions in the

High-level languages and machine language

language of the problem to be solved (e.g., in mathematical notation and in sentence-like notation). High-level language must be translated into machine language, which is composed of digital codes that match bit patterns etched in the computer's microprocessor. High-level languages increase programmer productivity, are easier to read, and can significantly reduce programming errors. The use of these languages requires another piece of software, also included with the language package, which is called either a compiler or an interpreter. A compiler is a computer program that translates the entire program written by a user or a programmer into a machine language version that the computer will execute at a later time. An interpreter, on the other hand, translates and executes a program line by line. Compilation is more efficient when programs are run repeatedly, because the program can be set up so that the translation occurs only once. Interpreters are more efficient for developing programs, since the errors are pointed out to the programmer as they occur.

Although computers have become, in effect, push-button machines much like home stereo systems or video cassette recorders, computers have one important difference: They are programmable. Programs enable the user to accomplish a wide variety of tasks that have been specifically set up by the user.

Thousands of programs have been written and continue to be written for practically every kind of personal computer. But even these thousands don't now—and may never—cover everything that you want a personal computer to do or in the way that you want it done. Rather than giving up and ignoring a personal computer, you can learn to program your personal computer yourself. If you don't want to learn to program, you can purchase commercial software and software packages. You may have to spend time searching through back issues of computer magazines to find packaged programs that fit your needs. If you find one, then all you need to do is purchase the disk or tape, insert it into the machine, and have the program put into the computer. If it doesn't match exactly, you will have to know some programming to make minor changes in the computer program. These changes can be time consuming, and as a result some people have found it simpler to write their programs themselves. A knowledge of programming will enable you to get more use out of your personal computer and save you money.

When people reach the point of purchasing a personal computer, they often begin to despair. They've heard stories from friends who have excited them with the prospects of a marvelous electronic helper, and then the friends indicate that the new user has to learn to program computers—a year's tuition and boring night classes at some fancy com-

Compilers and interpreters

The search for software

puter training school. Nothing could be further from the truth. Many books and articles have been published in the last five years that will help you learn the principles of BASIC (a popular microcomputer beginner's programming language) at home with about eight or ten hours of self-teaching.

BASIC was developed at Dartmouth College in the middle 1960s, and it has become the most popular language for personal computers because it is easy to use, easy to learn, and easy to implement. Although BASIC will be emphasized in this short account, the fundamental approaches to programming do not depend on which high-level language you use. Once the fundamentals are learned, they can be applied to any computer language.

BASIC: A high-level language

The important thing to remember is that computers need a high-level language to be able to read and execute programs. (The list of instructions that tells the computer how to operate is called a program.) However, the machine operates by its own internal machine language. As a high-level language, BASIC, which closely resembles English words, cannot address the computer directly. If you talk to your computer in BASIC and it understands only machine language, then there is a communication problem, and the computer will not cooperate and utilize the instructions that you have given it. Each personal computer, therefore, must have an interpreter that translates BASIC into machine language and vice versa.

Interpreters

BASIC interpreters vary widely. The simplified ones such as tiny BASIC can accept only less complicated instructions and do not have some of the features that BASIC-plus and extended BASIC have. These latter two versions have borrowed certain features from more advanced high-level languages such as APL (a programming language) and Pascal. Pascal has become very popular in recent years because it is able to use abbreviated commands that the computer understands as if they were the full commands.

Types of BASIC interpreters

The power and capability of the language interpreter are determined by the amount of memory it utilizes. Practically every language interpreter has a notation such as "16K BASIC" or "Microsoft 64K BASIC." These notations inform the user how much memory the interpreter itself needs when it is loaded into the personal computer. If the computer has a 16K RAM and the interpreter is an 8K BASIC interpreter, then the user has a maximum of 8K RAM with which to write a program. Many word processing packages require at least 32K of RAM. Some accounting packages need at least 64K and may require two disk units.

Typically, each personal computer requires a specific BASIC variation. A program written on one personal computer requires an interface so

Interfaces

that it can be translated with different interpreters and be understood by other computers. Interfaces, which are computer programs (software), are readily available. Another recent development by personal computer manufacturers is to have the interpreter etched into the microprocessor circuitry along with the computer's operating system. In this case, the interpreter is resident in the personal computer's memory and need no longer be stored on a cassette recorder or disk drive for loading into the computer.

COMPUTER PROGRAMMING USING BASIC

BASIC's advantage

Integer versus floating point

Before BASIC was introduced, the only computer languages were for advanced scientific, business, and mathematical uses. The most popular scientific and mathematical language was FORTRAN (Formula Translating System). Business applications for the most part were written in COBOL (Common Business Oriented Language). The obvious advantage of BASIC is that it is easily learned by beginners. BASIC is a flexible language, and as a result many variations are used in personal computers now on the market. Without getting into the specifics of each interpreter, some variations are oriented toward more scientific and mathematical functions, such as algebraic, geometric, and trigonometric functions. For example, each BASIC interpreter will indicate whether it handles integer or floating point mathematics. Integer can handle only whole numbers; floating point can handle numbers with decimal points. Users need to know whether their personal computer handles floating point or integer mathematics. The user's manual or the dealer from which the personal computer is purchased can provide this type of information.

BASIC programming operations

Regardless of the variation supplied with a personal computer, each BASIC language covers five kinds of operations: (1) Input/output commands tell the computer to accept, transmit, or print information. (2) Arithmetic operations involve the use of special symbols that indicate mathematical operations such as multiplication, addition, subtraction, division, and exponentiation. (3) Control commands tell the computer to execute various procedures associated with the operation of a computer program. RUN, LOAD, and LIST are some of the more commonly used control commands. (4) Library commands perform special advanced mathematical functions that reside in the BASIC interpreter. They are sets of commands that are used frequently to perform a specific task such as finding the square root of a number or variable. (5) Extensions are included with BASIC interpreters to make them faster and more versatile. Most extensions are used in advanced BASIC programs. One of the more popular extensions, called PEEK AND POKE, allows a user to look at a specific memory location inside the RAM and change its contents as desired.

Each of the above operations can work in two modes. The first, called direct mode, operates when the user gets an immediate response from the computer after he or she has typed a line and entered it. For example a user can type:

Direct and indirect modes

PRINT "TODAY IS WEDNESDAY"

and then press the carriage return or return key. The computer will then show

TODAY IS WEDNESDAY

The second is indirect mode, which allows the user to write a complete program and execute, or RUN, the program at a later time or when the user has completed it.

HOW TO WRITE A BASIC PROGRAM

Every program contains a series of programming lines. Each line consists of a line number and a statement. Line numbers identify each line on a program and indicate the sequence in which instructions are to be carried out. What is entered or written after each line is called a statement. For example, the following is a BASIC line:

Line numbers and statements

20 PRINT "THE TEMPERATURE IS +10 OUTSIDE"

When quotation marks are used, they denote a string. A string can have letters, numbers, and/or special characters, including commas, periods, and mathematical operators. The quotation marks enclose the string but are not part of the string itself. Before examining a complete BASIC program, a few features should be noted:

1. Each line or statement of a BASIC program must have a number. These line numbers can have any value; however, programmers usually space them by at least 10 (e.g., 10, 20, 30) so that additional lines can be inserted at a later time if necessary without having to renumber existing lines.
2. The computer executes the individual instructions or statements in numerical sequence by line number (e.g., 30 after 20).

Features of a BASIC program

3. Lines can be entered in any order. The computer arranges the statements in numerical order automatically, thus allowing the user to insert lines at any point, provided that gaps have been left in the line numbers.

4. If the user makes a typing error or some other mistake, he or she can rectify it by entering the correct line along with the original line number. BASIC erases the old incorrect line automatically.

5. Besides statements, BASIC also has commands that do not require line numbers. The most common of these commands are:

COMMAND	DESCRIPTION
NEW	Clears the computer and indicates a new program for memory
LIST	Lists the program (prints all statements by ascending line numbers)
RUN	Executes the program starting with the lowest line number
SAVE	Preserves and stores the program in its secondary storage system (i.e., on disk)
SCRATCH	Directs the computer to delete a program from primary storage; used when the user wants to delete an old program and enter new statements in its place
BYE or LOG OFF	Terminates the session with the computer; it may also take the computer out of the program
RENUMBER	Causes the computer to renumber automatically all statements in the program usually by 10s beginning with 10

6. Each statement or command must be concluded with a (carriage) RETURN. This is a special key on the computer keyboard marked ENTER or RETURN for this purpose.

7. Lines are deleted by just typing the line number followed by RETURN.

8. Variable names consist of a letter or a letter followed by a digit.

9. BASIC uses a slash (/) for division and an asterisk (*) for multiplication. These signs cannot be omitted; for example, the computer treats *xy* as an error, not as *x* times *y*.

The following is an example of a complete BASIC computer program:

```
ENTER (type in or press on keyboard)
NEW                                               RETURN
10   REMARK *** A SIMPLE MULTIPLICATION TABLE RETURN
20   PRINT "MULTIPLICATION TABLE FOR 5"           RETURN
30   FOR J = 0 TO 9                               RETURN
40   PRINT J; "TIMES 5 ="; J * 5                  RETURN
50   NEXT J                                       RETURN
60   END                                          RETURN
RUN
```

The RUN command tells the computer to execute the program, and as a result the computer will display the following:

```
MULTIPLICATION TABLE FOR 5
0 TIMES 5 = 0
1 TIMES 5 = 5
2 TIMES 5 = 10
3 TIMES 5 = 15
4 TIMES 5 = 20
5 TIMES 5 = 25
6 TIMES 5 = 30
7 TIMES 5 = 35
8 TIMES 5 = 40
9 TIMES 5 = 45
READY
```

The READY at the end of the output display signals that the program is completed and the computer is ready to accept a new program. If the user wants to see a listing of his or her program after RUN has been pressed, the user need only type in LIST and press RETURN, and the computer will display the program listing as it is stored in the computer.

The common BASIC statements are listed below:

STATEMENT	DEFINITION
PRINT	Types or displays normal strings or numbers
REM or REMARK	Denotes explanatory information in a program listing; does not tell computer to do anything
FOR . . . . NEXT	Establishes and executes a loop
END	Marks the end of the BASIC program; every program must have an END statement
LET	Assigns a definition to a variable

DATA	Contains lists of values; the computer uses the values in the order in which they were typed on a line
READ	Tells the computer to get values for variables from DATA statements
GO TO	Tells the computer to execute the specified line number rather than continuing its normal sequence
INPUT	Allows the user to enter data from the keyboard while the program is running; an INPUT statement tells the computer to print a question mark and wait for the user to respond

A SAMPLE INTERACTIVE BASIC PROGRAM

Interactive programming

An interactive type of program allows the user to interact with the program while it is running, allowing a student, for example, to answer questions on arithmetic sums. A simple interactive BASIC program is illustrated below. This example involves using the computer as a calculator. Data are provided in the program; the program reads two numbers from a DATA statement, displays the two numbers, and asks the user to enter an answer. When the answer is entered, the program checks to see if it is correct and responds by displaying YOUR ANSWER IS CORRECT or YOUR ANSWER IS WRONG. The process is repeated, with the program using the next two numbers in the DATA statement.

On some versions of BASIC interpreter, the program will stop after the last two numbers have been read and processed. On other versions, after the last two numbers have been read, the computer will go back and reread the first two numbers. So that the user can terminate the session, the program also contains a series of statements that allows the user to stop the program. If the user enters a zero (0) when asked for the sum of two numbers, the computer proceeds to line 999 and stops.

See the sample program below:

```
10    REM THE ARITHMETIC QUIZ PROGRAM
20    DATA 10, 6, 4, 3, 7, 15, 12, 9, 8, 4
30    DATA 5, 15, 4, 21, 8, 3, 14, 6, 9, 3, 1, 7
```

```
40   REM READ TWO NUMBERS AND FIND THE CORRECT
     SUM
50   READ A, B
60   LET C = A + B
70   PRINT "DO YOU WANT TO CONTINUE (ENTER 0 FOR NO,
     PRESS RETURN FOR YES)"
80   INPUT D
90   IF D = 0 THEN 999
100  REM ASK USER TO ENTER THE ANSWER
110  PRINT A, "+", B, "="
120  INPUT E
130  REM CHECK ANSWER AND RESPOND TO USER
140  IF C = E THEN 170
150  PRINT "YOUR ANSWER IS WRONG"
160  GO TO 50
170  PRINT "YOUR ANSWER IS CORRECT"
180  GO TO 50
999  END
```

The PRINT is called an input/output statement. Three other such statements are READ, DATA, and INPUT. The READ statement, which works together with DATA, instructs the computer to accept information and store it in memory locations specified by READ statement variables. When a READ statement is executed (line 50), numbers are taken from the DATA statement in the same order in which they were entered by the READ statement. For example:

```
20   DATA 10, 6, . . . . . . . .
50   READ A, B
```

after the initial READ at line 50, A is equal to 10 and B is equal to 6. The next time line 50 is executed, the next two DATA variables will be read so A will equal 4 and B will equal 3, and so on.

The INPUT statement can be used as an alternative to the READ/DATA statements. For example:

```
120  INPUT E
130  REM . . . . . . . .
140  IF C = E THEN 170
```

The computer understands that the INPUT statement implies that the user will add information. With a prompt symbol (usually a question mark is displayed on the screen), a user could then type in

(prompt) 16

and the computer would understand that the user meant D is equal to 16.

The sample program also shows the two most important control operations in BASIC. They are the GO TO and the IF THEN. Lines 150 and 160

```
150   PRINT "YOUR ANSWER IS WRONG"
160   GO TO 50
```

mean that the computer will print out YOUR ANSWER IS WRONG and then go to line 50.

The IF/THEN operation establishes a *conditional* statement and moves control from one line to another. It can be used to establish a loop, end a loop, or end the program, depending on whether or not the condition in the IF/THEN statement is satisfied.

Learning BASIC

The use of these statements, commands, and operations just begins to explore the BASIC language. However, the reader can see that BASIC is not impossible to learn and in fact may be quite easy to learn if the user is willing to spend a little time and effort. Anyone who understands the sample program can be writing BASIC programs within a few days. An easy way for a beginner to learn BASIC is simply to buy a textbook and start studying. Every personal computer with a BASIC interpreter provides a programming manual. With a personal computer, the vendor-supplied manual, and a textbook, the user can begin learning BASIC. In addition, BASIC courses are regularly offered through local schools, universities, and at some retail computer stores.

One warning should be noted by beginning programmers. Computers do not automatically check to see if the data or the results make sense. The computer has no common sense at all; that has to be put in by the programmer. Therefore, the programmer needs to check the data and the results and provide for program warnings if the values are unreasonable.

Acquiring and Installing a Personal Computer ■━━━━━━━━

The supervisor's role

So far, the chapter has dealt with the basic functions of how to operate and program a personal computer. Now it seems appropriate to consider some guidelines and some techniques that can be used to help in the selection of a personal computer. The role of the supervisor in this process is most essential. The supervisor must clearly define the desired results that the organization is seeking from the system. The supervisor examines what changes he or she wants to implement and which of these a computer is most able to perform. Thinking through this process will allow the supervisor to give a clear direction to the development of the personal computer system, and in the end to get a better system to help achieve the departmental and organizational objectives.

Any computer acquisition should be preceded by a feasibility study— a careful examination of the organization's current procedures to find out what it now costs to process information. This involves a detailed survey of each application area that is being considered for computerization. Data must be gathered on the number of transactions handled every day and on all the steps involved in each transaction. Furthermore, the analysis must take into account the people and equipment presently required, plus the forms currently used and any other relevant factors. Often the computer offers unique benefits that can't be realized by simply adding additional staff. For example, the computer might generate reports that are not now available, and it might use more sophisticated mathematical or business techniques. Furthermore, the processing time for transactions may be shortened, freeing up clerical and management talent for other areas. A good analysis will set a value on these potential benefits and weigh them in the analysis. A feasibility study is carried out so the user can competently conclude either that buying a computer is now worthwhile or that the purchase should be delayed.

Feasibility study

Once the determination to go ahead with a computer purchase has been made, the next step is to perform a thorough systems study. A systems study involves two steps. First, a study must be made of the current operations to see if there are any changes that need to be made which are not related to the installation of a computer. Some organizations may want to take advantage of this period of change from a manual operation to a computerized operation to make additional changes in their personnel or procedures. The second step is to identify specific problems for the computer to solve. These problems should be assigned priorities so that a sequence can be determined for attacking them.

Systems study

Another factor to consider in the purchase of a computer system is what dollar savings the organization can expect from the expenditure. The following are some questions that should be asked:

Figuring the savings

1. Will a computer system avoid problems that have lost sales or customers in the past? Can a dollar amount be assigned to the organization by eliminating previous lost sales or customers?
2. Will a computer system help to increase sales via more customers, or at least allow sales volume to increase without incurring significant

additional expenses such as hiring additional personnel? Can this increase be quantified in terms of dollars, units, or customers, and over what period of time will this increase occur?

3. Will a computer system enable the organization to perform tasks in-house that have previously been sent out or subcontracted? If the answer is yes, then what cost differential will occur between the subcontracted and the new in-house cost?

4. Will a computer system save time? Whose time? And how much? What will the time reduction be worth per hour?

5. Will a computer system save materials? How much? What is the value of these materials? And what do past records show relating to the usage of these materials? What can the organization expect to save in the future regarding these materials?

Once you've reached the point where you are able to list several areas where computerization may be a source of improvement, then the next step should be to number these areas according to priority. This step is very important because it allows you to attack computerization in a logical and structured manner.

Don't stretch justifications

A word of caution should be noted regarding these evaluations: Don't try to stretch each justification. If you find that you are digging fruitlessly for a few more dollars to justify the purchase, then you should perhaps look in other areas for savings. In addition, if the anticipated savings are large in relation to the investment, then you should seek the advice of a tax consultant or an accountant to decide on exactly how much the savings would be worth after taxes are taken into account. To summarize, the average person in business can make the right decision the first time, with marvelous results if he or she makes up and follows a plan. Even if the plan leads to a negative decision and the individual decides not to buy, this may be the right decision. If the budget does not permit a large enough expenditure for the right system, then no system at all might be better than being forced into a "live with it" situation by buying a less than adequate system.

Selecting the equipment

Selecting a supplier

Buying a computer involves more than just determining what tasks and jobs should be computerized, since the equipment to perform the tasks selected must also be evaluated. Help is available from independent computer suppliers, who have become a growing force in the retailing of computers in recent years. Suppliers can be found by looking under "Computers" in the yellow pages of the local telephone directory. They can bring understanding—as well as actual experience—to an examination of your current operations and requirements. These suppliers can provide "turnkey" systems. As the name implies, a turnkey system in-

---

TABLE 13.1   The Personal Computer Buyer's Check List

---

1. Look at a working version of the personal computer you intend to acquire.

2. Is the computer easy to use? Make sure that
   a. the keyboard is not too small
   b. the instructions are satisfactorily explained in the user's manual
   c. the size of the monitor screen is not too small

3. Check out the vendor's hardware. Is the product highly regarded?

4. Call or visit the computer supplier's customers with similar hardware to determine if their experiences have been good. Ask about
   a. equipment reliability
   b. their maintenance/repair experiences
   c. the availability of service

5. Is there a large number of programs available for the computer so that the user will not have to write all the programs that will be needed?

6. If commercial software is being purchased also, ask the supplier about ongoing software maintenance, in case the user asks for changes to the proposed applications.

7. Is the computer capable of handling the complexity of problems that must be run on it? Ask how long it takes programs to be processed.

8. Can the system grow with your needs? Make sure that the system is expandable by adding on memory and disks rather than by expensive conversions to larger systems.

9. Can the computer communicate with other computers so that a user can use other data bases and programs?

10. Take delivery of your hardware with at least some working applications.

---

volves little start-up effort by the user. The supplier studies the user's requirements, offers standard application packages, and installs the system complete and ready to run. The process of selecting a supplier is essentially the same as selecting a law or accounting firm. Suppliers should have a sound business reputation and a track record of success with systems similar to the one your organization is considering. Table 13.1 has been prepared to help in the evaluation of an independent supplier. For best results, evaluate more than one supplier.

A FINAL WORD OF CAUTION

The personal computer has now become the status symbol of our times. Unfortunately, many people have purchased their personal computer without any clear-cut objectives. Often this purchase requires a sizable investment, complicated by the fact that obsolescence is sometimes mea-

> Investigate potential uses carefully

sured in weeks, rather than months or years. When making an investment of this nature, supervisors should take the time to investigate what a personal computer can do to help make their own and their subordinates' jobs easier or more productive. Personal computers are great for repetitive or mathematical tasks and for the storage of some types of information. If the supervisor or her subordinates repeat the same tasks hour after hour each day, or if they need to get at considerable amounts of specific stored information, then a personal computer is worth considering.

Use specialists where appropriate

It is very important to take a close look at your business before taking a close look at a computer. The following are some critical considerations. First, can the task that you want to do on your personal computer be done better or cheaper on someone else's specialized computer? This is the old make versus buy decision, in which one needs to evaluate whether others can perform the same task at a greater speed or at reduced cost. The key consideration in this analysis is whether there is sufficient volume to justify computerization, or whether the task should be done outside the organization. For example, in the case of bookkeeping, should the task be done by a small business bookkeeping service? Payroll would be a similar example, since there are companies that specialize in this single function. Potential users must keep in mind that computers don't solve business problems. In fact, they may create a whole new set of problems, as a support group must be created to enter data into the computer system; because of the nature of their work, the organization may have only very limited control over this group.

Computers don't communicate with everyone

Second, the employees and supervisor must realize that the computer isn't literate yet and doesn't communicate well with most people. No doubt some of these problems will be reduced as computer manufacturers overcome the difficulties of making their products communicate effectively with people.

Computers don't do everything better

A third consideration involves some of the major problems in the application of computers to general business. The computer typically has made its entrance into organizations through the accounting functions. Most of the mature applications are in the accounting area. But the computer doesn't do everything better. For example, the electronic spreadsheet was developed to do business school cases, but many accountants can do a spreadsheet manually with greater speed and utility. The computer can easily draw bar graphs and pie charts, even in color; but one must consider that the drawing of bar graphs and pie charts manually has been a standard technique for over 100 years. The computer often adds little except increased cost to this technique, and electronically produced charts shouldn't be expected to revolutionize one's organization or business.

Before getting involved with the purchase of a computer, start with a task and work toward the alternatives—not the other way around. Instead of figuring out uses for a computer, first see if you could figure out what you're doing without a computer, then determine if a computer could help you do it better. Since computers are going to be with us for a long time to come, begin the introduction of computers into your organization in an organized, cost-justified way, rather than yielding to the urge to rush out blindly to purchase your first personal computer.

SUMMARY

As more people become intrigued with the power and capabilities of microcomputers, one of the first questions they often ask is: "How can I put one to practical, cost-effective use on a regular basis?" At the present time there are many uses for a microcomputer. These uses include: solving problems, making plans, building schedules, maintaining files, and accessing information sources. The multipurpose benefits of microcomputers are made possible by a wide variety of versatile, productive programs that are currently available from computer manufacturers and software vendors.

A computer system consists of hardware and software. Hardware is the machines, devices, mechanisms, or physical equipment used to process information. Software is the programs, computer languages, documentation, and procedures necessary to operate the hardware to process information.

A common computer language available on many microcomputers is BASIC. BASIC was designed as an easy-to-learn, interactive language for student use. An interactive language allows the programmer to interact directly with a program during its execution. Besides becoming one of the most widely used languages in schools, colleges, and universities, it is rapidly becoming a widely used language for business and scientific programming.

In addition to general guidelines, the chapter included step-by-step procedures for most of the tasks involved in determining whether an organization can justify purchasing a microcomputer.

RESISTANCE TO CHANGE

Mildred is a first-class legal secretary for one of Denver's oldest law firms. She is responsible not only to the firm's attorneys but also to paralegals who handle the firm's routine assignments as well as background research. She is sixty years old and has worked for the firm for over thirty years. She has a reputation in the office for being able to do anything and get it done yesterday. When it comes to whether to do something her boss's way or Mildred's way, she usually wins, and she is usually right.

When the firm decided to automate to the extent of bringing in a microcomputer for word processing, accounts payable, and payroll, Mildred didn't refuse to cooperate; it would not have been consistent with her characteristic desire to be a dedicated loyal employee. But her efforts to master the new equipment were unsuccessful. The firm even sent her to a special intensive three-day microcomputer training program sponsored by the computer manufacturer. The instructors reported back that Mildred seemed to get a handle on the equipment although she didn't ask nearly as many questions as the other participants.

After two weeks of complaints, work schedule problems, and equipment breakdowns with the new computer and software programs, Mildred asked whether she could continue to use her old typewriter and time-proven methods to get the work out. Her boss, recognizing that he was probably making a mistake, could not think of a way to deny her request. After all, the work load was backing up and something needed to be done.

Now, six months later, Mildred continues to be an asset to the firm, but no longer an unmixed one. Just a year ago she was considered fast. Now she can no longer cope with the entire work requirements of the department to which she is assigned. The paralegal in that department, whom Mildred should be typing for, is willing and able to use the word processor and does most of her own text production rather than asking Mildred, who should be doing it. Unfortunately, this sets a bad precedent for other secretaries in the firm who do not believe they should be providing secretarial service to paralegals at all.

Mildred's boss has been reluctant to confront her with the problem because he is afraid that she might leave. He prefers to wait until she retires, which could be years in the future. In the meantime, he is working around the problem.

1. Why is Mildred so reluctant to learn and use the new equipment?
2. What mistake did Mildred's boss make in allowing her to revert back to her typewriter?
3. What type of incentives and motivational strategies could be used to encourage Mildred to use the new system?
4. Can the current situation continue and what effect might it have on co-workers?

DISCUSSION QUESTIONS

1. What are the basic functions of a computer?
2. Define the term "microcomputer."
3. What is a computer program?
4. Name four types of organizations that process data and might be able to use microcomputers.
5. What is computer hardware? software?
6. What are the components of a personal computer?
7. Differentiate between batch and real-time information processing.
8. What is a high-level computer language? Name a few of them.

REFERENCES

Andrew, John. "Terminal Tedium—As Computers Change the Nature of Work, Some Jobs Lose Savor." *The Wall Street Journal* 108, no. 89 (May 6, 1983): 1+.

Brajer, P., and Panrone, Gary R. "Selecting a Small Business Computer." Marlburo, Mass.: Data Systems Publications, 1977.

Couger, J. Daniel, ed. "Development to Facilitate Managerial Use of the Computer." *Computing Newsletter,* 16, no. 8 (April 1983): 1–2.

Couger, J. Daniel, and McFadden, Fred R. *First Course in Data Processing with BASIC.* 3rd ed. New York: John Wiley & Sons, Inc., 1984.

Falvey, Jack. "Don't Count Too Heavily on That Personal Computer." *The Wall Street Journal* 109, no. 178 (August 15, 1983): 12.

Larson, James A. *Tutorial: End User Facilities in the 1980s.* New York: The Institute of Electrical and Electronic Engineers, Inc., 1982.

Leventhal, Lance A., and Stafford, Irvin. *Why Do You Need a Personal Computer.* New York: John Wiley & Sons, Inc., 1981.

Perry, Robert L. *Owning Your Home Computer: The Complete Illustrated Guide.* New York: Everest House, 1980.

Sippl, Charles J., and Dahl, Fred. *Computer Power for the Small Business.* Englewood Cliffs, NJ: Prentice-Hall, Inc., 1979.

Wohl, Amy D., and Carey, Kathleen. "We're Not Really Sure How Many We Have. . . . How Are Corporations Responding to the Onslaught of the Personal Computer? A Survey." *Datamation* 28, no. 12 (November 1983): 106–109.

CHAPTER 14

SURVIVAL TACTICS

All the world's a stage, and all the men and women merely players.

—SHAKESPEARE

Chapter Outline

The Informal Organization
  Building Networks
  Rules, Norms, and Sanctions
The Socialization Process
Impression Management
  Recipe for Impressing Others
  Crisis Management
Building Commitment
  Defining Commitment
  Rites, Rituals, Heroes, and Corporate Culture
  Commitment Strategies for the Supervisor
Recognizing and Dealing with the Dark Side
Reading the Organization's Climate

Objectives

This chapter focuses on the social pressures that are at work in every organization. The subject throughout is the survival tactics that organizational participants use in dealing with each other to get what they want. Specifically, in this chapter you will become familiar with:

1. The informal organization, including networks, rites, rituals, heroes, and culture
2. The need for norms and sanctions
3. The impact impression management has on people
4. The opportunities available in decisively handling a supervisory crisis
5. Strategies for building employee commitment
6. The dark side of management practices that lead to dysfunctional performance and low morale
7. Organizational climate—its influence on job performance and how it can be analyzed

Major Concepts

Network building

Socialization

Organizational rituals

Heroes

Rules

Norms

Sanctions

Commitment

Loyalty

Competence

Motives

Impression management

Perception

Crisis management

Organizational climate

Win-lose philosophy

Win-win philosophy

Dark-side tactics

Game-playing

FURNITURE FACTORY

My third or fourth week at the factory found me earnestly launched in my quest for holding the job but doing less work—or working less hard. This was immediately recognized and hailed by the men with "Now you're gettin' smart, kid. Stop bustin' your ass and only do what you have to do. You don't get any more money for bustin' your hump and you might put some other poor bastard outa a job." Remember this was the depression. Most workers, while aware of the preciousness of their jobs, felt that doing more work than necessary could be putting someone else, even yourself, out of a job. "Only do what you have to" became a rule not only to save your own neck but to make sure you were not depriving some other soul like yourself from getting a job.

In the next few years, I was to be taught a second important lesson about working. One day while picking up sawdust, I began to "find" pieces in the sawdust or behind a woodpile or under a machine. The first few times, with great delight, I would announce to the operator, "Hey, look what I found!" I should have figured something was wrong by the lack of any similar enthusiasm from the operator. Sam was a generally quiet Midwesterner who never seemed to raise his voice much, but now when I showed him my finished-work discovery behind his milling machine he shouted, "Who the f--k asked you to be a detective? Keep your silly ass out from behind my machine; I'll tell you what to pick up. So don't go being a big brown-nosing hero around here."

Wow, I sure never expected that. Confused, troubled, almost in tears, not knowing what to do or where to go, I went to the toilet to hide my hurt and just sat down on an open bowl and thought what the hell am I doing in this goddamned place anyway? I lit a cigarette and began pacing up and down in front of the three stalls, puffing away at my Camel. I thought, What the hell should I do? This job is terrible, the men are pissed off at me. I hate the place, why don't I just quit? Well, it's a job and you get paid, I said to myself, so take it easy.

While I'm pacing and puffing, Sam comes in, saying, "Lissen, kid, don't get sore. I was just trying to set you straight. Let me tell you what it's all about. The guys around, that is the machine operators, agree on how much we are gonna turn out, and that's what the boss gets, no more, no less. Now sometimes any one of us might just fall behind a little, so we always keep some finished stuff hidden away just in case." The more he talked, the more I really began to feel like the enemy. I tried to apologize, but he just went on. "Look, kid, the boss always wants more and he doesn't give a shit if we die giving it to him, so we [it was that "we" that seemed to retrieve my soul back into the community; my tears just went away] agree on how much we're going to give him—no more, no less. You see, kid, if you keep running around, moving the stuff too fast, the boss will get wise about what's going on." Sam put his arm on my shoulder. (My God! I was one of them! I love Sam and the place. I am in!) "So look," he says, "your job is to figure out how to move and work no faster than we turn the stuff out. Get it? OK? You'll get it." I said, "Yes, of course, I understand everything." I was being initiated into the secrets of a work tribe, and I loved it.

How are employees initiated into groups? Who develops the work norms and standards to which groups religiously adhere? How is a fair day's work determined? These are just a few of the questions to which supervisors need to figure out answers if they are going to survive politically within their respective organizations.

This chapter is about the real organization. It is not a discussion on structure, chain of command, or line-staff relationships. Rather, it is about the subtle, and not so subtle, social pressures at work in organizations and how these pressures can influence productivity, morale, and employee commitment.

Our purpose is to provide the new (or aspiring) supervisor with a realistic perspective on the informal relationships within organizations and what it might take to function effectively with them and in them. Because the events that occur in organizations aren't always what they seem to be, we will describe and analyze what actually goes on, good and bad, ethical and unethical.

A successful supervisor has to be more than technically competent and proficient. At least a part of being successful depends on how well the supervisor has learned to read organization events in terms of the content, symbols, politics, and impressions that are important, the informal relationships that make up a network, and the prevalence of dark-side management practices.

The Informal Organization

Chart is often misleading

While almost every organization, public and private, has an organizational chart, the novice quickly learns that the relationships depicted on the chart don't correspond to how things really get done. The organizational chart is simply a formal attempt to present graphically the many positions (i.e., territory and title) and ranks (i.e., level) using a top-down format. While it is the most common method for presenting relationships, it is by no means a reliable or accurate portrayal of how organizations operate. One reason is that charts recognize only the *formal* relationships among positions. Actual work relationships may well differ from what is suggested on the chart.

While work relationships are not always clear on the chart, neither are authority relationships. Subordinate X may appear to report to supervisor Y, but in actuality most of what subordinate X does may depend on personnel from another unit. A bank clerk dealing with special accounts, for example, supposedly reports to a floor-clerk supervisor; yet most of her banking transactions necessitate a close working relationship with the loan officer. The organizational chart, however, would depict no relationship between the clerk and the loan officer. And often people seek out others who are willing and in a position to help them do their jobs more effectively. It doesn't matter whether the person being sought out has direct line responsibility over the one needing assistance or not. The only requirement is that the person have the knowledge, skill, motivation, or connections that are deemed useful.

BUILDING NETWORKS

Part of learning to survive in the organization involves identifying those people who could be most useful when a problem is encountered or a favor is needed. In fact, the informal organization is composed of a network of cooperative relationships among co-workers, outsiders, and a variety of people above, below, and diagonally related (see Figure 14.1).

How these relationships are formed and maintained is still not clear. Sometimes management consultants will even go so far as to say that network building is nothing more than a waste of time. Examples of network time wasters are cited, such as keeping office doors open, personally taking all incoming calls, and discussing topics with co-workers that seem to be unimportant. According to John Kotter, network building

Network activities appear inefficient but aren't

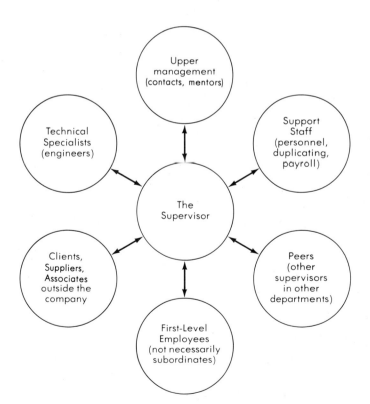

FIGURE 14.1
Hypothetical Network
for a Supervisor

may appear to be inefficient, but this appearance is misleading.[1] One never knows when or where a contact is going to be needed when a crisis occurs. Consequently, the more contacts that are developed, the better the likelihood of having an effective network. From the perspective of the network builder, taking an extra few minutes to chat with Joe, who works in duplication, might save a whole lot of time later if, for some reason, a crisis occurs that involves the need for some urgent duplication. Effective networks are an excellent device for getting things done expeditiously, by-passing formal channels and cutting through red tape.

Guidelines for network building

A supervisor who does not already have a network should consider building one for the future. You could begin by joining a trade or professional association and taking an active part in meetings and programs. Or you could volunteer to serve on company committees. The other committee members often make excellent contacts down the road because of the commonality of purpose that was once shared while serving together. Becoming actively involved in various community projects, such as the United Way campaign, will expand one's network. It is amazing how often a contact that initially occurred outside the company (e.g., church, Boy Scouts, American Cancer Society) may ultimately lead to new contacts within the company. However, before a network can be truly useful, the members of your network must be willing to help you out in a pinch. That means you, as the network builder, must create a sense of obligation in them toward you. One way to do this is by performing favors for them when they are in a pinch. Another way is to point out to them personal characteristics, attitudes, values, and/or perspectives that you happen to share with them. Yet another way is to create (using the principles of impression management) a professional reputation, or expertise, deemed important in the eyes of others, thus making yourself a valuable component of others' networks.

Whatever strategy one chooses, however, it is important to note that network building is a voluntary process. While it involves a wide variety of indirect influence techniques, it will rarely involve a supervisor ordering others around.

RULES, NORMS, AND SANCTIONS

Another big part of learning to identify the informal organization, especially for new supervisors, is picking up on the workplace customs, rules,

[1] John P. Kotter, "What Effective Managers Really Do," *Harvard Business Review*, November–December 1982, p. 160.

and norms. Not taking the time or trouble to learn workplace customs can bring disaster to the supervisor. Subordinates tend to feel insulted when their norms are ignored. Strikes have occurred for less reason. The hard part is that while some of these customs appear obvious to the veteran (just "good common horse sense"), to the new supervisor, they might appear rather peculiar.

Every company has its own set of written rules specifying what is and is not acceptable behavior for employees: what time one needs to be at work, length of breaks, where and when one may smoke, what time one may leave for the day. Usually these rules are included in company policy manuals or posted where they are highly visible.

But in every organization, there are also norms—unwritten rules— that go beyond the written rules. Norms exist because the formal policies and procedures are incomplete; something more detailed and definitive is needed. These norms might be nothing more than a shared understanding of what is acceptable work behavior for certain groups of employees. Electricians, for example, may expect apprentices to perform only the simplest of tasks. Personnel staff may expect various tasks to be rotated among themselves. Engineers may adhere to a code of conduct among themselves that is much more rigorous than the company's.

> **Norms represent agreement on acceptable work behavior**

Contrary to the idea that group norms restrict one's independence and freedom to act, norms may actually make people, especially new recruits, less tense and more comfortable with their work environment. Take, for example, the employee who's new on a job that involves outside sales calls. "How many should I make? How many do my co-workers make? Do I go along with my boss?" People want a predictable work environment. Likewise, they are uncomfortable with the uncertainty as to what is a fair day's labor. One of the most common types of workplace group norms, and one that is usually established early in group formation, is identifying the appropriate level of effort. Group norms may quickly, and unequivocally, identify ten calls per day as the standard. The new employee, not wishing to incur the wrath of his or her co-workers, will soon bring his or her performance into agreement with the group's. Norms provide structure and clarity in the work environment (something new employees desperately want) by creating shared expectations of what is fair and/or acceptable job behavior.

> **People want a predictable work environment**

While norms usually reflect what is acceptable behavior in work groups, they may also reflect organizational values. For example, organizational norms may make it perfectly normal and expected for employees to stay late or come in on weekends simply because "that's the way we do things around here." Dress codes, work ethics, even attitudes, once they are accepted by organizational members as expected, become norms.

> **Norms reflect organizational values**

Violators will be sanctioned

Violators of norms, especially if they are aspiring supervisors, may be taking large risks with their careers. An employee who continually violates a work group norm is likely to incur the sanctions of his or her co-workers. A sanction is the group's way of administering internal punishment to norm violators. It may take the form of social ostracism (i.e., silent treatment), subtle and not so subtle warnings and messages, verbal abuse, or in some cases, physical violence. Every once in a while a deviant will persist to the point where sanctions are dropped (in a few rare cases, admiration is even grudgingly bestowed on the deviant), and the deviant is accepted anyway. More usually though, the deviant will tire of the sanctions and either conform or exit the group.

The Socialization Process

Consider for a moment what might occur if the military did not have basic training. Certainly, the physical conditioning of recruits would suffer. Most likely, the time it takes to learn military terminology, tactics, equipment, and all the other aspects of warfare would be lengthened. But undoubtedly the gravest loss, at least to the generals and admirals who control the services, would be the lack of discipline in the troops.

Instead of soldiers responding to orders in a crisp and decisive manner, the recruit would probably ask why. Instead of military units who think like soldiers, the units would be made up of individualists who think like students. What would an army or navy be worth if enlisted personnel started engaging in group decision making and acting like a democracy? The point is, people are normally not conditioned to think and act like soldiers. Something must be done to them, and quickly, to get them to behave in predictable ways.

The organization needs predictable employees

Basic training is the method used by the military to teach the recruit how to think and act like a soldier (see the accompanying box). Management, like the military, has many of the same concerns. Organizations need employees to act and behave in predictable ways. It is especially important that their employees willingly embrace the organization's basic principles and values. New employees, like military recruits, cannot be left on their own to adopt at their own speed the ways of the organization. Some people with only a little prodding by management may accommodate the organization by immediately embracing its basic values and principles. Others will need to be convinced (or enticed) before they are willing to make such a commitment.

BASIC TRAINING

Any of our readers who have ever served in the armed forces can recall the dramatic change in their lives that enveloped them the moment they stepped off the bus and were introduced to their first sergeant. Chances are he was abusive, arrogant, unfriendly, and dictatorial in his demeanor toward you. It didn't take long for your attitude toward the sergeant to be just as unpleasant as his was toward you. For most people, this period in their lives marked a whole new life style (if you can call it that)—new rules, attitudes, and norms—none of which bore any resemblance to old experiences. The things one was ordered to do—taking equipment and gear apart only to put it back together again, digging holes only to fill them back up again—seemed completely pointless. Moreover, individualism and personal privacy were discouraged. Instead, teamwork and unquestioning obedience were emphasized. Life during these long weeks of intense indoctrination and physical abuse was tough.

Near the end of this period, however, your perceptions began to change. While the sergeant was still an authority figure, there were some things that both you and he had in common. You may even have had a brief but entertaining conversation or two with him. By golly, you thought, the sergeant doesn't appear to be nearly the beast he once was. You couldn't believe the magnitude of the change in him. Moreover, the once ridiculous orders to dig holes and dismantle gear now took on a whole new meaning. It didn't matter why anymore. All that was important was to satisfy the sergeant.

Only after one has had a chance to reflect on these experiences does it gradually occur that maybe the sergeant didn't really change, that the tasks once thought pointless were, at the end, still the same meaningless tasks. The change, surprising as it might seem, had occurred in you, the recruit. What that change amounted to was socialization.

In the military, physical and mental duress are used to help mold the soldier. In organizations, the technique is more subtle. Nevertheless, the process and objectives in both cases are the same—to take a stranger, a person who is totally unfamiliar with the organization, and make him or her a committed and loyal participant. The process will point out what needs to be learned and what is important. The process will give once trivial symbols a new degree of importance. It will substitute new values for old. This process is called socialization.

Socialization:
Molding the new
recruit

In a nonmilitary organization, the socialization process may be lengthy—several years may be needed before the new member is fully accepted by those who control it. For a few unsuspecting new employees, the process may bring dramatic change and culture shock (although usually not to the same extent as to the military recruit).

427

Rites and rituals play a part

Part of the process may involve activities much like those of a student pledging a fraternity. Usually a ceremony and possibly some minor degree of hazing will accompany the initiation (e.g., having to run for coffee and conduct errands for more senior co-workers). By participating in these rituals, the individual is asking to be admitted as an accepted member of the group.

Socialization takes time

Participation in the socialization process is a means of building commitment. If it is too short in duration and demands too little in the way of sacrifice from the new member, it may open the door to unwanted change. Usually the longer the process takes, the more the participants feel they have something personal invested in the system—as it is. "After all," members may say, "since I had to go through it, why shouldn't they have to as well?"

Only deviants bring change

Some new employees find the required changes in behavior, values, and thinking unacceptable. A few of these will exit the system. Others will stay yet never completely accept the system—although behaving in ways that keep the heat off. A very few of these deviants may persist long enough to begin instituting changes in the socialization process. When this does occur, they will themselves have begun to create a new set of rites, rituals, and values. Their success, however, will depend on there being others with similar ideas, beliefs, and values to etch the new process firmly into place.

Impression Management

Anyone who has spent any time at all working in an organization can recall the anxiety and uncertainty that was experienced during the first days of employment. These concerns centered around not knowing what the boss would think of you personally, how co-workers would react to you, and whether or not you would come across as competent and confident. Chances are that you were also trying to figure out these people as well. "What kind of boss is he? Does he know what he's doing? Is he sincere? Can I believe him?" As far as your co-workers were concerned, you probably most wanted to know if they were friendly, open, and easy to talk to.

Past experiences help to get one through unfamiliar situations

People are often uncomfortable in unfamiliar situations, especially when they are with strangers. Their behavior is fragmented because they do not know what is expected and customary. Past experiences will be depended on to help them through. But for some, past experiences hold little in the way of useful memories. For most people, however, there are always bits and pieces of experiences that can be related to their current situation, thus providing some idea of appropriate behavior. With time, people will gradually add new information or ignore experiences that don't appear relevant. Older employees who have been "around the track" a few times have seen it all, so there is usually little in the way of new or novel information garnered by them for deciding how to behave.

Impressions are the perceptual process of screening the environment for cues that suggest how some new bit of information might be evaluated. It is a way that uninformed people make judgments about how to behave in situations. If one's new boss talks to one in a warm and friendly manner, uses a tone of voice that is soothing, clear, and confident, and body language that suggests interest in one, the impression is likely to be of a supervisor who is supportive, trustworthy, and decisive.

The perceptions that are formed may be the result of associations between personality traits, such as dependability, and resultant behaviors, such as promptness. Specific associations between behaviors and traits are common in our society. For example, if you see a supervisor who rushes around the office, always in a hurry, and thrives on crises, you will likely perceive the supervisor as decisive. Whether or not they are perceived as competent, however, will depend on whether the crises were manufactured by these same supervisors in the first place and on how successfully they handle these crises. Until new information replaces the old, this impression will probably remain with you.

Impressions—about superiors, co-workers, and subordinates—are formed all the time. It's almost frightening the number of judgments that are made about people's motives, attitudes, and worth to the organization based on the flimsiest evidence. One supervisor noted: "Gee, Sally sure jumped when I asked her to work overtime this weekend. That kind of attitude gets a new person noticed in our company." However, once an impression is formed, it could lead to a mistaken or biased rating later, perhaps during the employee's performance appraisal.

People who attempt to control others' impressions are engaging in impression management. Image creation, much like the marketing of a company's product, can be well planned and deliberate. It can also be misleading. But people who try to create a favorable impression that is false will, over time, revert to their true selves. A supervisor who wants to be perceived as competent, for example, had better be able to handle problem situations, not just act it out. The results of one's actions often make a difference in terms of correcting or reinforcing impressions.

RECIPE FOR IMPRESSING OTHERS

Credibility is the key

In spite of the chance one takes in trying to be something one is not, there are a few impression management guidelines supervisors might consider for presenting themselves positively to subordinates. The key to coming across in a believable fashion begins with credibility. It is the bottom line of impression management.

If a supervisor has always been dominant and autocratic, for example, then chances are that changing roles from boss to discussion leader is not going to be believable. The supervisor will probably experience discomfort and, in his awkwardness, do or say things that negate the spirit and purpose of the meeting. He may respond defensively to ideas proposed by employees, feeling he should have thought of the ideas himself. At other moments in the meeting, he may slip into an evaluative mode by pointing out the weaknesses in employees' suggestions, with the effect of shutting off the discussion.

Start with competence

Building credibility is, essentially, the basis of good impression management. It should begin with competence. Supervisors, like all employees, must know their own jobs well and perform them well. While supervisors don't need to be specialists themselves, they do need to be able to discuss characteristics of their subordinates' jobs intelligently—using the terminology of the workplace. Knowledge about matters that are of companywide concern, as well as an ability to communicate this information, is also a key part of appearing competent.

Add a cup of character

Character is another characteristic that others are quick to notice in a supervisor. Character would include: openness, honesty, fairness, and consistency. Openness is seen in the supervisor's willingness to clarify expectations and to provide specific, honest, and accurate feedback. Honesty is keeping promises made to employees, even in such small things as being sure to get an answer back to an employee regarding some matter. Furthermore, a supervisor who honestly calls it as he or she sees it is always appreciated. Fairness is simply not playing favorites. Treating everyone the same is a behavior that is quickly noticed by the work unit. Finally, since people are most comfortable in predictable work environments, consistency in the supervisor helps to remove some of the insecurities experienced by employees (e.g., knowing how the boss is going to react to a question might make it easier to ask). Consistency is also noticed in how supervisors handle problem employees. Does the punishment fit the crime? Do all violators receive the same penalty? Each of the traits mentioned, when taken together, tends to form that elusive human quality referred to as "character."

Make sure intent is not self-serving

A boss who will stand up and go to bat for an employee, especially at great risk to herself, will quickly build loyalty from her group. However, putting your neck on the line is not always appreciated. If employees perceive the supervisor's action as nothing more than a tactic to make herself look good in the eyes of management, the action will backfire. Supervisors whose motives, or intent, can be summed up as self-serving and manipulative will almost always be viewed with suspicion. Certainly supervisors want to do well, and many *would* like to advance their careers, but to tell employees continually, "I'm doing this for your good" is just hypocritical. The way out of this dilemma is to tell employees candidly that when the group looks good, the supervisor is going to look good, too.

Richard Ritti describes yet other qualities of supervision that are worth passing on.

> Superiors must project the image of the generalist, knowing the stuff of many specialties, but *only* enough to make the necessary decisions. The superior must display an appropriate *sense of urgency.* His manner must be *crisp* and *hard hitting.* Why, you ask? Because few know, and fewer still are able to judge, the work that has actually been done.[2]

Ritti makes a good point. People who maintain high visibility, poise in handling adversity, and enthusiasm even when dealing with the routine, and who take a dynamic, forceful approach when tackling a problem are people who become noticed. This is not to suggest that *form* is always more important than *substance.* But sometimes the impression one leaves others with is more important than the activity which created that impression.

Put in a dash of enthusiasm

The last quality, and one that should be present in all of us, is integrity—a soundness of moral character. Perhaps integrity is best described as that certain human quality someone else has that we would like to have. Perhaps, too, the path to integrity can be traveled only by acquiring the preceding human characteristics. If that should be true, then integrity may be the most elusive of the group.

Add a touch of integrity—your secret ingredient

Before concluding on impression management, one warning should be given. When attempting to shape impressions to fit a desired image, be careful that the image desired is characteristic of the role of the presenter. Characteristics such as age, sex, and position may be critical to image projection. Chances are a twenty-two-year-old college graduate is not going to be well accepted if he presents himself as an expert on employee relations when standing in front of a room of veteran supervisors. It is important to study the role, know what is traditionally expected

Desired impression should fit the role

---

[2] R. Richard Ritti and G. Ray Funkhouser, *The Ropes to Skip and the Ropes to Know,* rev. ed. (Columbus, Ohio: Grid Publishing, 1982), p. 37 (emphasis added).

from the role-player, practice when opportunities present themselves, and be alert to the reactions of the observers.

CRISIS MANAGEMENT

For readers who have been on the firing line of supervision for a few years, putting out fires on a daily basis may seem like no big deal. Some might even admit that they thrive on the excitement and intensity of a crisis—it seems to make the day or the week go by so much more quickly.

Crisis management involves some of the same principles as impression management. Those who are generally successful in handling crises would tend to view crises as *opportunities* to impress others with their competence. But for newcomers to supervision, the very idea of a crisis may seem frightening.

A crisis may be an opportunity

Of course, the kinds of crises we are talking about are not life or death situations. They involve dealing with sudden or unexpected deadlines, undertaking special projects, or coping with routine assignments with less than the normal complement of resources (as during a strike). It might be hard for the newcomer to view a crisis as an opportunity to show one's stuff. But in fact coping well with a sudden serious and extraordinary occurrence allows a leader to be recognized as competent and capable. (It is also a good opportunity for impression management.) Crises may also provide the leader opportunities to learn and grow.

Steps in handling a crisis

Predictable responses to crisis follow a pattern: shock, denial, gradual acknowledgment, then an attempt at adaptation. While quick response is essential, it is important not to act with too much haste. Many "crises" go away if left alone. Allan R. Cohen suggests the following crisis management guidelines for determining what to do and when to do it, as well as for leaving the desired impression.[3]

Define the crisis

First, the supervisor must analyze the situation and answer the question, Is there really a crisis? This requires gathering information wherever possible to determine if the impression of a crisis is localized or widespread. It is important to define the crisis. If many people think there is a crisis, that in itself may pose a crisis situation. But be on the lookout for the person who is constantly crying wolf, and monitor your own tendencies to over- or underdramatize the situation.

Is action needed?

Once it's determined that there is a crisis, the next step is deciding whether or not to act. This includes evaluating whether or not the crisis will blow over on its own. Sometimes the best approach at this

[3] Allan R. Cohen, "Crisis Management," *Management Review*, November–December 1982, pp. 186–197.

point is to stall for time. If in doubt, listen to all involved parties. However, be prepared to act quickly and decisively if that is what it's going to take.

Having decided to act, the third decision is *when* to act. Take advantage of fortunate accidents; look for ways to solve several problems simultaneously; and act quickly, especially when it will allow you to slip in under an opponent's defenses. Taking a crisp and hard-hitting approach tends to reduce uncertainty, tension, and the ambiguity of an unsettled crisis.[4]

On the question of who should be involved, there are different guidelines for different situations. When speed is necessary, involve as few people as possible. But where company commitment is needed, involve as many people as is feasible. Where the resolution of the crisis needs to be of high quality, choose experts. But where developing subordinates is an important goal, involve them. In general, choose supporters from among the most powerful individuals, while dividing opponents of the solution.

Crises can be turning points for both the organization and the individual handling them. They represent opportunities to demonstrate competence, to shape the organization, and to face up to important issues. The ability to keep cool under fire when everything is collapsing is most impressive. Yet a crisis is a situation that is not without its risks.

| Know when and how to act |

| Know when to involve others |

Building Commitment

DEFINING COMMITMENT

How many times does one hear the phrase, "We've got to build commitment around here," or, "We are counting on the commitment of our employees"? The word "commitment" plays a central role in the workplace vocabulary of both management and the supervisor.

Commitment means the intention to follow up or perform in a way that will ensure the success of a project. The word is often incorrectly used to state a belief. "I'll come in on Saturdays until this project is completed" is a statement expressing commitment. On the other hand, the statement "I believe working Saturdays is needed" is only an expression of belief. The distinction is important.

Take the case of a supervisor being trained to use management by objectives (MBO). She continually expressed her support for the program

| Commitment is more than a belief |

---

[4] Ritti and Funkhouser, *The Ropes to Skip,* p. 37.

for the duration of the training (four separate sessions). During each session she would praise the program as "the best thing management's done yet." Yet when it came time for implementation, this supervisor never really gave it a chance. She had probably been expressing only a belief, not a commitment. She believed the program to be important but failed to see a part in it for herself.

Pretended commitment

Organizational game-playing is a tactic that is sometimes used to suggest commitment. Supervisors who do not believe they can commit themselves to a project may show interest anyway. When others (especially their bosses) seem genuinely interested in pursuing a new project, these individuals don't want to create the impression of not being "team players." Such an impression is usually perceived negatively and will do no good in terms of maximizing one's rewards. Over time, however, a lack of involvement by these individuals may be all that is needed to subvert the program. The result is that they look good for giving their "full support" to a project even when they didn't lift a finger to help it.

Game-playing may also occur in the guise of time utilized on a project. It is frequently assumed that the amount of time spent on a task or project is a measure of commitment. For example, "Why, I spent half of the day getting out the Jenkins report" might leave the impression to unsuspecting co-workers that the speaker was committed. But be cautious—commitment is not so much a function of how much time was spent as of *how* it was spent.

RITES, RITUALS, HEROES, AND CORPORATE CULTURE

Corporate culture

A recent wave of popular books has supposedly unlocked the secrets to corporate success.[5] A point on which they all agree is that one of the keys to increased profitability is employee commitment. But commitment, in turn, depends on a strong corporate culture.

Deal and Kennedy maintain that every workplace possesses a culture— a "way we do things around here"—that is based on the principles important to the people in the organization.[6] Examples of how culture affects employees' routines might be the way meetings are conducted, the way offices are arranged, the stories people tell, and how people (e.g., customers and new recruits) are greeted at the door.

---

[5] For example, Thomas J. Peters and Robert H. Waterman, Jr., *In Search of Excellence* (New York: Harper & Row, 1983); William Ouchi, *Theory Z: How American Business Can Meet the Japanese Challenge* (Reading, Mass.: Addison-Wesley, 1981); Terrance E. Deal and Allen A. Kennedy, *Corporate Cultures: The Rites and Rituals of Corporate Life* (Reading, Mass.: Addison-Wesley, 1982).

[6] Deal and Kennedy.

But having a culture does not in itself guarantee strong employee commitment. The culture must support the organization's basic principles. A supervisor who is in charge of conducting a meeting, for example, may not *really* be committed to accomplishing what ought to be accomplished. It is not a question of not knowing how but simply the absence of purpose. Culture provides the purpose—even if it is nothing more than the statement, "That's just the way we do it around here." Chaotic meetings may simply be the way it is done in some organization cultures.

Weak cultures provide little purpose

A strong culture, on the other hand, might discourage members (especially the leader) from misdirecting their efforts. The basic principles a company stands for, and practices, provide a pattern of behavior for the supervisor to follow. The conduct of meetings, for example, probably follows a strict set of procedures—perhaps beginning with the supervisor expressing firm beliefs about what ought to be accomplished. A strong culture would also provide a set of rules regarding conduct at meetings that is largely shared by the people in attendance.

Strong cultures follow a purpose

Catchy slogans, such as "Work smarter, not harder," are insufficient. Several companies have adopted this slogan only to regret it later. It implied to employees that quality and hard work were outdated and unimportant. In some cases, employees took the slogan to heart and began engaging in deceitful tactics because that is what they thought "working smarter" meant. A good slogan must capture the principles and values of the organization's culture.

Catchy slogans don't make a strong culture

Heroes, too, are a part of every culture. They play the role of model— someone to be imitated and admired. Organizations with strong cultures will almost always have stories being circulated among new recruits about some corporate hero. Doesn't every company have at least one story about the CEO who worked his way up through the ranks or the salesman who was so good that he could have sold refrigerators to Eskimos?

Heroes provide a model

Supervisors play a key role in perpetuating and embellishing the company's heroes, by encouraging employees to appreciate the hero's dedication to the company. When the employee is urged to be more productive or do better, or is faced with an unfamiliar situation, the corporate hero gives the employee something to imitate.

COMMITMENT STRATEGIES FOR THE SUPERVISOR

It seems obvious that organizations need a committed work force. It should be no less obvious that supervisors need a personal commitment from their subordinates. Whereas organizations build commitment through a strong culture, supervisors build personal commitment by using their interpersonal skills. While the process of building commitment

Interpersonal skills are the key

can begin at any time, perhaps the best time to start is during the new recruit's orientation.[7] Essentially, the supervisor's strategies are three-fold.

Identify compatible goals

First, help subordinates identify work goals that are compatible with their own personal goals and aspirations. When this is accomplished, each subordinate will develop a vested interest in seeing that these goals are achieved.

Provide for participation

Second, commitment is also a by-product of employee participation in task-related decisions. The more subordinates know about what it is they're doing, about how it fits into the bigger picture, and that input from them is not only acceptable but expected, the more likely it is that they will participate.

Cultivate loyalty

Loyalty, the third and perhaps the most basic ingredient for building commitment, is the strength of attachment and support of the subordinate toward the supervisor, the work group, and the organization. New employees, while in many ways the easiest group to motivate, will not have a strong sense of loyalty because loyalty, like good wine, takes time. It tends to grow with service and cannot be easily rushed. Loyalty can be spawned, nurtured, and strengthened in new subordinates only through the supervisor's sincerity in matters that relate to the employee's personal well-being and professional growth. Keeping the employee's best interests at heart is probably one of the soundest strategies for building loyalty.

Recognizing and Dealing with the Dark Side

By now it should be clear that supervision can involve a great deal of organizational game-playing. Participants working under the guise of "This is for the good of the company" may be behaving in ways that will improve their own positions. Certainly, many of these organizational games *do* benefit the organization. But in too many cases, the benefits returned in the form of higher profits and/or goal achievement also bring with them a high cost in the long run.

Gamesmanship pervades our society

Gamesmanship—the art of psyching out an opponent—is practiced as much in organizations as it is in golf, basketball, or racquetball. Why do so many organizational participants indulge in this practice? Most

---

[7] New employee orientation is discussed in detail in Chapter 11.

assuredly the thrill of competition explains part of it. In our society, competition plays as big a part as does the work ethic. It is woven into our social fabric from early childhood and lasts through retirement. Another reason for gamesmanship is that some organizations encourage it—either by direct or by indirect means.

Some organizations attempt to capitalize on the natural tendencies of their employees by promoting competition among them. There is certainly nothing wrong with competition—until it goes too far. Some authors have referred to carrying competition too far as the "dark side of management" [8] (a take-off on the recent movie hits that introduced the notion of "the Force" and its never-ending struggle with evil—the dark side). Playing on the scarcity of valued rewards (e.g., pay, promotion, prestige), top management deliberately structures situations in such a way that only a few can win. This is what scholars refer to as a win-lose philosophy, implying that when one person wins, another must lose.

The dark side

The win-lose philosophy

Supervisors are likely candidates for getting caught up in "the game"— after all, this is their first step on the management ladder. If they have ambitions to move higher (and most do), they may be playing into the hands of dark-side tactics.

Essentially, dark-side tactics begin with a "carrot" approach. As individuals climb the organizational ladder, fewer and fewer opportunities are available (e.g., promotions are more infrequent because there are fewer openings). Because many participants are vying for just a few "carrots," management is tempted to play off one participant against another, holding out the possibility of a promotion, higher salary, more status, and greater influence. As a result, an intensely competitive climate is created that may result in participants getting carried away with winning.

Scarcity heightens competition

Instead of concentrating their energies and resources on improving their own performance, these overzealous participants may adopt tactics that unfairly interfere in a competitor's performance. Wording memos to a superior that imply a co-worker is not loyal to the company, not providing all the information a co-worker needs to do his or her job, not giving proper credit to a co-worker—these are just a few of the unethical tactics and dirty tricks that dark-side management tends to spawn. Supervisors so caught up may even begin pressuring their own subordinates to become accomplices in these "games."

Dark-side tactics

A major flaw in the logic behind dark-side practices is the assumption that there must be losers. Organizations are rarely limited in valued resources. In fact (as pointed out in Chapter 4), there is no limit to the rewards an organization can make available to its employees. Material

The win-win philosophy

[8] Frank Machovec and Howard R. Smith, "Fear Makes the World Go Round: The Dark Side of Management," *Management Review*, January 1982, pp. 8–17.

rewards (such as money) may be scarce; but others (such as recognition and praise) are not. Thus management (and including the supervisor) does not have to behave in ways that encourage carrying competition to extremes. For one thing, it can refuse to reward members who employ devious and unethical tactics. For another, it can begin developing win-win strategies by encouraging and rewarding cooperative efforts among employees, departments, plants, and agencies. A win-win philosophy proposes that there don't have to be any losers. Whereas competition is a natural part of sports, organizations artificially create losing situations using dark-side tactics. Instead of penalizing participants who fall short of the finish line, why not reward them for what *was* accomplished? Focusing on accomplishment rather than deficiencies is the win-win strategy.

Guard against creating win-lose situations

Even with the adoption of win-win strategies, managers can still occasionally expect individual competition that goes too far. After all, why should individuals whose lifetime values have been programmed for competition suddenly lose this drive when they enter the working world? Furthermore, supervisors may unknowingly create win-lose situations for their own people, complete with "carrot" rewards and dark-side practices. Without realizing the implications, a supervisor might be giving the "juiciest" assignments as a reward to deserving subordinates in a work group composed of highly competitive individuals. If the supervisor isn't careful, the spirit of cooperation and cohesiveness may get trampled and lost in the stampede for the best assignments.

Use win-win strategies

One way out of this dilemma is to develop group goals and group rewards when managing a group of highly competitive individuals. Taking the group out to dinner when a project is completed and putting the group's picture in a company newsletter are only two of the ways a supervisor might go about building cohesiveness and team spirit. Individual competitiveness does not have to be snuffed out; the energy simply needs to be rechanneled using win-win strategies.

Reading the Organization's Climate

Organizational climate

Each organization has its own unique climate. Organizational climate might be thought of as the atmosphere or personality of an organization. It is very much a product of the overall leadership of the company. It is also a product of the people who work within the organization. Supervisors help to create the organization's climate by the way they lead, bring about change, encourage cooperation, deal with conflict and crises, and communicate with their subordinates.

Understanding the organization's climate is important to the supervisor because the type of climate can affect the success of various motivational approaches, which in turn can influence the productivity and morale of the work force. For example, assume that a supervisor is charged with the responsibility of instituting an MBO (management by objectives) program for his or her work group. Assume further that management has tied various incentive plans to the MBO scheme. Also, for the sake of simplicity, assume that this represents a first attempt by the organization to identify and reward individual performance.

Climate affects productivity and morale

Will the strategy work? Will employees be motivated to perform at higher levels? Logic would suggest that it should. After all, any strategy that links high performance to desired rewards seems sound, at least on the surface. However, if management has had a history of labor/management turmoil and mistrust, if the organization's climate can be described as secretive or unsupportive, and if management's motives are viewed as manipulative and self-serving, then chances are that the strategy will be doomed before it is off the drawing board. The first reaction of the work force toward the MBO strategy will be one of suspicion: "What's management up to?" "What's my supervisor trying to pull?" and "What are 'they' getting out of this?" are some of the thoughts that will be in the minds of affected employees. The "we versus they" mentality is symptomatic of an adversarial relationship. Like combatants in a chess game, each side is trying to understand the motives behind the moves.

The climate, or atmosphere, has to be supportive of change, because it is the climate that determines how things will be done. Consequently, motivational strategies, incentive systems, and new productivity programs must be designed with the climate in mind if they are to have any chance of success. Otherwise, office politics and organizational games tend to make short work of management's best intentions.

Is the atmosphere right for change?

A criticism often directed at the organizational climate concept (and its advocates) is that it is too nebulous to be practical. When asked to identify the climate of their work units, supervisors will usually depend on their gut-level reactions, with little if any supporting evidence. Climate surveys may help; but they are not always the most reliable because of the ease with which they may be faked. Moreover, surveys must be constructed, administered, and scored—calling for skills more suited to staff personnel than supervisors. However, most supervisors are in a position to gather some hard data that will suggest how employees feel about their work and the organizational climate.

Assessing climate

SUPERVISOR'S GUIDE FOR SIZING UP THE ORGANIZATION'S CLIMATE

Most supervisors, because of their leadership position, are in a unique position to influence some of the elements that make up the organization's climate. Yet most new supervisors (and many veterans) either do not realize this important fact or are unaware of how to create a more positive work climate. While there is no limit to the number of characteristics that together make up the work environment, perhaps the following questions and suggestions will help in sizing up your organization's climate.

How strong is the *sense of belonging* in the organization? What is the degree of loyalty? Are there "in" groups (i.e., groups that have relatively higher status among peers)? Perhaps the easiest place to identify trouble with employee loyalty is to look for high rates of sick leave, turnover, union discord, grievances, and work slowdowns. Such symptoms usually indicate that management's actions are being perceived as manipulative and self-serving. A more subtle symptom of trouble is the prevalence of cliques (i.e., small informal groups) in which the loyalty toward the subgroup is stronger than that toward the unit, department, or organization.

What *degree of openness* is normal in the organization? How safe are employees in expressing their true thoughts, feelings, and concerns? An organization that punishes employees for open communication will face several problems. Employees will resort to gossip, character assassination, and secretiveness. Managers will place stronger emphasis on formal rules, restrictions, and procedures, and will work to hide their own and the organization's weaknesses.

What *level of cooperation* exists in the organization? What is the big picture, and how do individual jobs fit together? When cooperation is missing, difficulties arise. For one

Look for hard data

A few factors that might be considered are attendance, turnover, safety, grievances/complaints, suggestions submitted by employees, scrap rate, response time, accidents, and overtime. Note that each of these items can be observed, enabling records to be compiled and reviewed over a period of weeks, months, even years. The choice of items to be included depends on the kind of organization and the work being done. And some items may be more important than others. Greater weight might need to be given to the more critical items, as well as greater care in collecting and analyzing the trends of those items.

Hard data are the preferred form of evidence to support what could otherwise be interpreted as subjective opinions. Once a trend has been identified (for example, when there is an increase in the number of grievances filed per month), the supervisor might recall the events that led up to the grievances and try to analyze them for causes.

The accompanying box highlights some critical climate variables and offers a few useful guidelines for informally sizing up the personality of the work unit.

thing, management tends to assume planning responsibility. Also, look for individuals and subgroups competing with one another instead of cooperating for the mutual good.

To what extent is *mutual support* expressed in the organization? How much authority is delegated? How closely are people directed? If mutual support is not encouraged, there will appear to be too much red tape and too many "sign-offs" will be required. Supervisors will feel like message carriers for upper management. Procedures will seem oppressive, and company watchdogs will be regarded as enemies.

How is the *competence of management* viewed by the employees? Has the organization grown beyond the capabilities of present management to handle the business? When management recognizes this problem, it may resort to excessive controls, reduce personal risk taking and self-disclosure, and fail to del-

egate responsibility. Employees will joke about the organization's competence and products and make comparisons with more successful competitors. They may express doubt about the ability of the organization to reach its goals. Members of the organization who were formerly open and trusting will begin using political strategies and making deals.

How well does the organization adjust to change? Is the firm a leader in its industry or barely keeping up with modern technology? When the method for coping with change is unresolved, the company faces many problems. Employees may find themselves sitting at empty desks or working on meaningless tasks. They will begin job hunting because they sense the uncertainty about their job future. Management that is *resistant to change* avoids making decisions, depends on past experience, and withholds relevant information.

SUMMARY

In order to function effectively, supervisors must learn to play organizational games. In part, this means they need to project facts about themselves that they think are important to their image. Often these projections come across as credible. But when they misrepresent the truth, the true image usually surfaces over the long run.

"Commitment" is defined as the intention to perform in a way that will ensure the success of a specific project. Supervisors can help build employee commitment by identifying compatible goals, providing for participation, and cultivating loyalty.

A strong organizational culture helps to en-

sure commitment. The organizational culture is maintained by a socialization process which ensures that employees behave in ways that are predictable and that change doesn't occur too rapidly.

The dark side of management refers to top management playing one employee against another when rewards are scarce and employees' competitive tendencies are strong. While competition is perfectly acceptable, when it encourages an overzealous attitude of winning at any cost it is usually counterproductive. Competition needs to be tempered with good judgment.

A MAN HAS GOT TO KNOW HIS PLACE

Scott Korman was not your ordinary doctoral student. At age thirty-five, he was ten years older than most other students in the Ph.D. program. Unlike his contemporaries, he held no teaching assistantship. In fact, he made no secret that he did not need financial assistance as did his peers. Scott's Pierre Cardin shirts, Gucci loafers, and $40,000 Mercedes didn't do much toward helping him blend into the role of the struggling student.

Scott's background is well-known around the university. He had his B.A. and M.A. degrees in English literature from Stanford University by the time he was twenty-three. Scott then took a job at a junior college in Virginia and taught English literature and creative writing. In his spare time, he wrote. His first novel was published when Scott was twenty-seven. It was favorably received by critics and the book-buying public. The book sold nearly 60,000 copies in hardback and over 2 million in paperback. At twenty-nine, Scott published his second novel. Selected by several major book clubs, this novel sold over 300,000 in hardback, and 3 million in paperback. It was also sold to Hollywood for $500,000, though it never was made into a film. His third novel, published last year, was on the best-seller list for twenty-two weeks. The paperback rights alone were purchased for $1.6 million.

Success to Scott was more than selling lots of books and making millions of dollars. Scott wanted the academic life. He dreamed of being a professor of creative writing at a quality eastern university and sharing his ideas with young people. But such a goal requires a doctoral degree—the Ph.D. So Scott has decided to go back to school to earn his doctorate.

The first semester back was difficult for Scott. It was not easy for him to sublimate a lot of his opinions on writing. Unfortunately, many of his ideas did not agree with those held by his professors. But he was learning to play the student role. The more pressing problem was something Scott couldn't control. That was the way the faculty reacted to him. Not surprisingly, they were not used to having a best-selling author around, especially as a lowly graduate student. One young assistant professor, who himself could not have been much over twenty-six years old, told Scott directly, "You don't belong here. You don't have any talent. Your books may sell a lot and you may be the darling of Madison Avenue, but I'm going to do everything I can to see that you never get your degree."

At one level, Scott felt like laughing. Why would these people—established academics with all the appropriate credentials—care that he had written three successful novels? He wasn't a novelist here; he was a student! At another level, Scott realized that whether he got a Ph.D. or not rested with the professors in his department and they apparently didn't enjoy playing second fiddle, in reputation, to a graduate student.

1. Analyze Scott's dilemma in terms of the various types of rites, rituals, norms, and sanctions that appear to be operating in the doctoral program.
2. Scott's refusal to accept the role of "ordinary doctoral student" is creating conflict between him and his professors. Should Scott give in to the traditional expectations and roles that students play? Explain.
3. What could Scott do to increase the likelihood of obtaining his Ph.D.?

Source: Stephen P. Robbins, *Organizational Behavior: Concepts, Controversies, and Applications,* 2nd ed. (Englewood Cliffs, N.J.: Prentice-Hall, Inc., 1983), pp. 357–358.

DISCUSSION QUESTIONS

1. How is the informal organization different from the organization depicted on the organizational chart?
2. What is network building? What are its advantages and disadvantages?
3. Why is socialization important to an organization? What is the supervisor's role in the socialization process?
4. Explain why impression management is not the same thing as misrepresentation.
5. Crisis management, as a strategy, is sometimes used by supervisors as a substitute for long-range planning. Discuss.
6. Explain how a supervisor might go about building commitment in his or her subordinates.
7. What role does the supervisor play in strengthening a company's corporate culture?
8. How might competition—a truly American trait—lead to dark-side management tactics? What can a supervisor do to prevent or minimize dark-side tendencies?
9. What should a supervisor look for when attempting to assess the type of organizational climate operating in his or her work unit?

REFERENCES

Allen, Robert; Madison, Dan; Porter, Lyman; Renwick, Patricia; and Mayes, Bronston. "Organizational Politics: Tactics and Characteristics of Its Actors." In *Organizational Behavior and the Practice of Management.* 4th ed. by D. Hampton, C. E. Summer, and R. Webber. Glenview, Ill: Scott, Foresman & Co., 1982: 659–666.

Byrd, Richard E. "Developmental Stages in Organizations: As the Twig Is Bent, So Grows the Tree." *Personnel* (1982): 12–25.

Goffman, Erving. *The Presentation of Self in Everyday Life.* New York: Doubleday, 1959.

Kindler, Herbert S. "The Art of Managing Differences." *Training and Development Journal* (January 1983): 26–32.

Klein, Stuart, and Ritti, R. Richard. *Understanding Organizational Behavior.* Boston: Kent Publishing Co., 1980.

Kotter, John P. "What Effective General Managers Really Do." *Harvard Business Review* (November–December 1982): 156–167.

Lippitt, Gordon L. "Managing Conflict in Today's Organizations." *Training and Development Journal* (July 1982): 67–74.

Machovec, Frank, and Smith, Howard R. "Fear Makes the World Go Round: The Dark Side of Management." *Management Review* (January 1982): 9–17.

Ritti, R. Richard, and Funkhouser, G. Ray. *The Ropes to Skip and the Ropes to Know.* 2nd ed. Columbus, Ohio: Grid Publishing, 1982.

Schein, Edgar H. "The Individual, the Organization and the Career: A Conceptual Scheme." *Journal of Applied Behavioral Science* 7 (1971): 401–426.

Sheppard, Thomas. "Rite of Passage . . . Women for the Inner Circle." *Management Review* (July 1981): 8–14.

SUPERVISOR'S ACTION GUIDE

Individual Skills

Planning the Work
Setting Goals and Standards
Making Decisions
Running a Meeting
Giving a Speech
Managing Stress

People Skills

Being an Effective Communicator
Issuing Orders
Managing Conflict
Counseling the Problem Employee
Handling Gripes, Grievances, and Complaints
Interviewing Candidates for Employment
Disciplining Employees
Terminating an Employee

Organization Skills

Supporting Desired Performance
Being an Effective Trainer
Breaking in New Employees
Dealing with Sexual Harassment
Protecting Privacy

Often, the daily routine of the supervisor's job doesn't give him the opportunity to get away and think through a problem that may be facing his department. The supervisor needs a quick source of information to help him get things back on track. Out of this need grew the idea of a supervisor's action guide. The purpose of the guide is to provide you, the supervisor, with a convenient reference to help solve some common supervisory problems. To obtain additional insight into a particular problem, you can select a chapter or two in the main body of the text or use some of the references. When time is of the essence, the guide will get you headed in the right direction.

The topics dealt with in the guide appear under three main headings. "Individual Skills" deals with problems that the supervisor as an individual will face on and off the job. "People Skills" addresses situations that involve the supervisor interacting with her fellow workers (i.e., both her own supervisors and the employees she supervises). "Organization Skills" contains material designed to help the supervisor compete effectively within the organization. Each topic ends with a list of easy-to-remember do's and don'ts and some additional references.

INDIVIDUAL SKILLS

PLANNING THE WORK

Planning is a basic supervisory activity. It consists of projecting a course of action for the future that is consistent and coordinates with the goals and objectives of the organization.

Planning in general involves long-range, standing, single-use, and short-range plans. All plans are designed to provide guidance over some period of time. However, the definitions of long-range and short-range planning will depend on the employee's level in the organizational hierarchy, the kind of organization, and the type of enterprise. Most people define short-term planning as that which covers a time period up to one year. Long-range planning typically involves a time period of five, ten, or more years.

Standing plans are used for activities that are carried on without much change from year to year. They cover such things as health and safety, purchasing procedures, employment practices, and other matters related to the overall operation of the organization. Single-use plans are—as the name implies—used only once and then discarded or revised. Common examples are department budgets and operating schedules, which are good for a month or year and then are replaced with new ones.

While long-range, standing, and single-use plans are helpful to a supervisor in a general sense, short-range techniques are most useful and applicable to supervisors. These involve planning and scheduling routine, day-to-day activities under the control of the supervisor.

Lack of planning often shows up in missed delivery dates or work not done because the supervisor forgot to schedule it. Other sure signs are idle employees, idle equipment, slow production pace because employees have too little to do, and crash programs with lots of expediting. When supervisors fail to plan their own jobs, they are continually having to put out fires. These supervisors complain that they must be in five places at the same time and need thirty hours per day to complete their jobs. Such situations arise either because of poor planning or because the supervisor doesn't understand his or her job.

The following techniques are most useful for short-range planning:

1. **Check lists** are the simplest and most direct device for short-term planning. Each morning the supervisor should take ten minutes to list the things that need to be accomplished that day. Once listed, each item should be ranked and given a priority. Once the priority has been given, the supervisor should work through the list in the determined order. As items are completed, they should be crossed off; as new problems arise, they should be added, but new problems should not be worked on unless they have a top priority.
2. **Calendars** are an indispensable tool for daily planning. Tasks and meetings that must be conducted at particular times should be recorded in the appropriate time slots. The calendar can also be used for short notes to help the supervisor remember critical items that must be included in weekly reports and performance appraisals. A calendar can also serve someone else as a guide to tasks and duties, in the event that a supervisor is absent or called away for a special project or meeting.
3. **Gantt charts,** which relate tasks or jobs to time sequences, are also useful for daily planning. They are particularly helpful when the work of one employee depends on the work of another employee.

DO'S
- Review plans regularly.
- Explain the plan to all concerned in language they understand.
- Consider the goals of the entire organization, not just your own department.
- Set aside time for planning: ten minutes daily / thirty minutes weekly / one hour monthly

DON'TS
- Forget to keep in mind your limitations in manpower and resources.
- Attempt anything new or try any changes without prior planning.
- Trust your memory; jot down reminders of things you need to do.

Gantt Chart

A. Schedule at First of Week

	Monday	Tuesday	Wednesday	Thursday

Carpentry

Paint crew

Cleanup crew

B. Progress after One Day

	Monday	Tuesday	Wednesday	Thursday

Carpentry

Paint crew

Cleanup crew

C. Progress after Two Days

	Monday	Tuesday	Wedesday	Thursday

Carpentry

Paint crew

Cleanup crew

For additional information see pages 33–42 and the following references:

Baker, H. K., and Holmberg, S. H. "Stepping Up to Supervision: Planning for Success." *Supervisory Management* 26 (November 1981): 12–18.

Humes, G. K. "Better Planning, Fewer Crises." *Supervision* 43 (July 1981): 5–7.

Jones, W. D. "Characteristics of Planning in Small Firms." *Journal of Small Business Management* 20 (July 1982): 15–19.

Kahalas, H. "Planning Types and Approaches: A Necessary Function." *Managerial Planning* 28 (May/June 1980): 22–27.

SETTING GOALS AND STANDARDS

Setting goals and standards is part of the planning process in an organization. Often it is the responsibility of the supervisor to examine plans that were developed largely by upper management and then to translate the plans into specific actions. At the supervisory level, goals are usually targets that a particular department must aim for to assist the organization in reaching a profit goal or in living up to its service commitments. Typically, departmental goals are short-range. These goals pin down quality, quantity, and cost performance targets for the coming week, month, or quarter.

Goal setting begins by estimating the strengths and weaknesses of a department. The supervisor should consider how these strengths and weaknesses help or hinder meeting organizational goals. Goals should be reasonable, and they should be arranged in a list of descending importance—that is, the most important ones at the top. Use numbers and dates wherever possible. Goal achievement works best when employees know what is required of them. Pin down assignments of the various individuals needed to meet a particular goal. Explain the goal to all concerned, since employees who know why are more likely to cooperate. Finally, goals should be reviewed periodically because circumstances, restrictions, and resources change. Goals may need to be changed or modified depending on the results of the periodic review.

Good results depend on high motivation and attainable, clear-cut goals. The supervisor's task is to make sure that the department's goals are clear and to motivate his or her employees to achieve them.

DO'S
- Tell employees what their objectives are.
- Spell out what you expect of them, in clear measurable terms, so that arguments are unlikely.
- Ask questions to ensure that employees understand what they have to do and what standards you expect of them.

DON'TS
- Assume that employees know their objectives.
- Set lower standards for unsatisfactory performers than you do for other employees.
- Set unrealistic goals.

For additional information see pages 107–112 and the following references:

Mendelow, A. L. "Setting Corporate Goals and Measuring Organizational Effectiveness: A Practical Approach." *Long Range Planning* 16 (Fall 1983): 70–76.

Olivas, L. "Adding a Different Dimension to Goal-Setting Processes." *Personnel Administrator* 26 (October 1981): 75–78.

"Setting Goals Can Ease Office Stress." *ABA Banking Journal* 74 (December 1982): 20.

MAKING DECISIONS

If supervisors were asked to give a short definition of their job, many would reply that they are paid to make decisions or solve problems. A problem exists when there is a gap between what the supervisor expects to happen and what is actually happening or going to happen. Supervisors are confronted with problems as part of their daily activities and often, through experience, they develop routine solutions for minor problems.

Trouble may occur when a supervisor is confronted with a major problem and finds it difficult to decide on a course of action. Trouble may also occur when a supervisor is required to find solutions to problems that are caused by unusual circumstances or changing conditions.

There is no universal agreement as to what constitutes the exact steps in the decision-making process. In fact, if you ask supervisors how they make decisions, the answer might be: "I don't know, I just do what I feel has to be done, given the situation." Despite what is said, good supervisors typically follow a number of steps in the decision-making process. Those steps involve:

1. Defining the problem and its causes. State or write the problem as clearly and specifically as possible. It might be necessary to delve deeper in order to locate the real problem and define it. Defining a problem is typically a time-consuming task, but it is time well spent, since the supervisor cannot proceed in the decision-making process until the problem or circumstances relevant to the situation have been defined. The supervisor may have to gather data on materials used, design specifications, employee performance, and equipment functions. At this point the supervisor should list every feasible cause for the problem. Then, using the process of elimination, she should select the most likely causes for further analysis. During this process she should also consider any intangible factors—such as reputation, discipline, or personal biases—that may play an underlying but significant role in the situation.

2. Develop alternative solutions by suggesting ways for removing the problem causes. The task here is to experiment with different resources and try to determine the outcome of the various alternatives. An evaluation is then required based on the facts that have been presented.

3. Select an alternative from among the feasible possibilities. The supervisor should keep in mind both the degree of risk involved in each course of action and the available resources—such as tools, records, facilities, and manpower. The overall objective is to give the best result for the least amount of effort or resources expended. If all

the alternatives are unsatisfactory or have too many undesirable effects, the supervisor must think of new alternative solutions.

4. Implement your choice when the strengths of your solution exceed its weaknesses. It's the supervisor's job to spell out a plan of action to carry out the solution. The supervisor should be careful to involve the group in this implementation phase. He should also avoid the assumption that once the decision has been made, it is final. Throughout implementation, the supervisor must analyze the effectiveness of the course of action that has been selected. When follow-up indicates that something is wrong or the results are not as anticipated, the decision-making process must begin over again.

DO'S

- Take time to define the problem carefully.
- Realize that the burden of decision making can be eased by seeking the advice of others.
- When decisions are made, put them into practice.
- Prepare a fallback position so that you will have a way to alter plans and at least attain part of the objective.
- Guard against wishful or biased thinking when making choices.

DON'TS

- Overcommit your resources on one problem when you may need them later for an unanticipated problem.
- Reach too high by setting your objectives at the very top; allow room for mistakes.
- Make decisions without the responsibility to solve a particular problem.

For additional information see pages 13–18 and the following references:

Delaney, W. A. "Why Are People Indecisive?" *Supervisory Management* 27 (December 1982): 26–30.
Himes, G. "Solving Problems—Making Decisions." *Supervision* 45 (January 1983): 15–17.
Murnighan, J. K. "Group Decision Making: What Strategies Should You Use?" *Management Review* 70 (February 1981): 55–62.
Redford, L. G. "The Positive Side of Unpopular Decisions." *Supervisory Management* 27 (November 1982): 10–12.

RUNNING A MEETING

A common complaint in almost any organization is that there are too many meetings and committees that take up too much time. The fact is that without meetings, it would be impossible for most organizations to operate efficiently. Meetings supply employees with information they need to carry out their jobs. They are also a way for management to receive ideas and opinions from its employees. Since meetings are an important tool of management, the supervisor must be familiar with the workings of a departmental meeting or committee.

The success of any meeting or committee depends largely on the chairperson's ability to guide the group to reach an optimal solution in the least amount of time with the greatest amount of agreement possible. Depending on the type of meeting, the chairperson's role will vary. An informational meeting requires a good speaker, one who can get ideas across and who can get the group to agree with what the chairperson is selling. The opinion-seeking meeting requires someone who can get people to express their ideas. This involves asking questions that will stimulate the group and convince them that their ideas are wanted. The problem-solving meeting requires a skillful chairperson who has the ability to get ideas accepted. He must get discussion going so that members will give their ideas and at the same time keep the meeting moving on track. He must tactfully silence those who want to talk all the time and get the quiet ones into the discussion. The objective of the problem-solving meeting is to get members to agree on a solution— a unanimous solution if possible. Unanimity avoids the difficulty of some members having to carry out an action they do not support. However, unanimous solutions should not be sought if this will excessively prolong the meeting or fragment the group.

Before a well-led meeting gets under way, the chairperson does a number of things to ensure success. Planning a meeting involves determining which time of day, place, and people will be the most productive. The meeting should meet the needs of the group. Before the meeting, the chairperson should thoroughly acquaint herself with the subjects to be considered. She should try to anticipate situations and questions that may arise. Items on which the group will agree should be first on the agenda.

A good chairperson individualizes the meeting by checking into the background, interests, and problems of the group members. She won't let aggressive talkers dominate the meeting. She will draw out quiet people who might have something to say. Above all, she will maintain eye contact with the participants.

DO'S
- Hold meetings only when they are necessary.
- Always let others know the purpose of the meeting by distributing an agenda prior to the meeting.

- Check out audiovisual equipment ahead of time.
- Start on time.
- Tell people what to bring.
- Play the appropriate leader role depending on the type of meeting.

DON'TS
- Place the most complex and controversial items at the end of the agenda.
- Start over again if someone arrives late for the meeting.
- Invite people to the meeting who have no reason to be there.
- Lose sight of the purpose of the meeting and let discussions wander.
- Schedule your most important meetings on Fridays at 4:00 P.M.
- Go past the adjournment hour.

For additional information see pages 41–42 and the following references:

Brown, L. K. "How to Conduct a Productive Meeting." *Supervision* 44 (July 1981): 5–6.

O'Neill, H. "How to Run Meetings—And How Not To." *Management Today* (March 1982): 41–43.

Roy, J. O. "Avoiding Conflicts in Meetings." *Personnel Journal* 60 (September 1981): 677.

GIVING A SPEECH

The best advice when you are faced with the task of giving a speech is to do your homework and take care of the details before getting up in front of your audience. The first thing a speaker should find out is what is expected of him. This means knowing his audience. He must find out who they are, where are they from, and how many of them will be there. After this has been established, the speaker should find out from the person who asked him to speak whether he is supposed to give a humorous, informational, or motivational speech. Then he should seek to know about twice as much about the topic as will be required. If a speech is scheduled for fifteen minutes, be prepared to talk for thirty minutes. The speech will proceed much faster when it is presented to an audience.

Preparing thoroughly involves three steps. First, the speaker should write notes and be prepared to elaborate on them. Second, he should find a quiet place and read the material from beginning to end. And third, he should actually stand and deliver the speech aloud in an empty room. The use of a cassette recorder can be helpful. More often than not, the speaker is his own severest critic. If the third step is repeated for seven consecutive days, the speaker will have committed the bulk of his talk to memory, and although he hasn't memorized it (which should be avoided), he will be very comfortable presenting the material.

DO'S
- Make appropriate use of body language, gestures, and voice inflections.
- Keep track of time and pace yourself.
- Stay away from professional jargon; it tends only to cloud the issue.
- Get right into what you have prepared.

DON'TS
- Assume that just because you know your subject, you can deliver a speech.
- Give a canned speech.
- Worry if you have a little stage fright before getting up before the audience; that's normal.
- Try to quote from memory.

For additional information see pages 342–343 and the following references:

Hammer, M. M. "Giving an Effective Speech." *Supervisory Management* 28 (January 1983): 34–38.
"How to Give a Speech." *Practical Accountant* 14 (June 1981): 47–49.
"Speaking of Speaking." *Management Review* 70 (September 1981): 2–3.

MANAGING STRESS

Recently, much has been written about stress and its effect on individuals, both on and off the job. Many things about stress are unknown at this time; however, the medical and psychology professions have made many observations about stressful behavior and stress management that can be useful to the supervisor.

Individuals, families, and groups inevitably go through periods of stress: a death in the family, for example, or a move to a new job 600 miles away. Every organization is likely to have some of its personnel passing through an emergency from time to time. The supervisor must learn to recognize stress symptoms and to act in a way that will minimize the employee's anxiety and decline in job performance.

When an individual is going through a stressful period, he will exhibit a special type of behavior of which he is often unaware. First, the person behaves erratically and is unable to concentrate on any single task. Second, his relationships with friends, family, and employees are loosened, and the individual is likely to develop new attachments, friends, and social activities.

Long-term stress generates such diseases as stroke, ulcers, alcoholism, and drug addiction, which in turn may lead to social breakdown. These medical problems can lead to low productivity, absenteeism, hospitalization, and even premature death.

People should realize that it's possible for an individual to psych himself into believing he is under significant stress. To avoid this, the individual should dismiss the assumption that a situation is inherently stressful and recognize that one's perceptions of the situation will determine to a considerable extent the stress that one feels. The following do's and don'ts are designed to help anyone—supervisor or employee—lead a less stressful life.

DO'S
- Learn to plan and to set reasonable limits for projects that must be completed.
- Periodically have fun and escape from the pressures of life.
- Get exercise on a regular basis—exercise that's enjoyable as opposed to a program that involves drudgery.
- Learn to tolerate and forgive.
- Regularly (once a month) take time to reflect on the stressfulness of your situation.
- Get a regular physical checkup.

DON'TS
- Be a negative person.
- Keep your troubles inside.
- Ignore physical symptoms of stress (i.e., ulcers, high blood pressure, irritability, nervousness, etc.).
- Assume that you can handle stress just as well or better than your co-workers.
- View stress as always negative or undesirable.

For additional information see pages 256–263 and the following references:

"Dealing with Stress." *Management World* 11 (April 1982): 24.

Hayes, J. L. "Executive Stress and You." *Security Management* 26 (January 1982): 16–17.

Pesci, M. "Stress Management: Separating Myth from Reality." *Personnel Journal* 27 (January 1982): 57–59.

BEING AN EFFECTIVE COMMUNICATOR

An essential component of a successful supervisory style is the ability to create an atmosphere that supports open and honest communication. This means making sure that there are opportunities for input, feedback, and correction. Communication is not only speaking and listening but reading and writing as well. However, for supervisors, nothing can beat face-to-face communication.

Despite the recognized need for good communication, even in organizations with the best management and the best workers, communication is often bad. And poor communication results in dissatisfied customers, increased costs, hard feelings, waste, and other inefficiencies. While not all problems associated with communication can be eliminated, there are some guidelines available to achieve a greater level of success in this area.

Communication begins with the decision to tell somebody something. Some supervisors are indiscrete and they overcommunicate. Don't violate confidentiality, and don't waste your time communicating information that employees don't need or want. Talk about things employees want to know and about things that affect them and their work. Supervisors must communicate organization rules, pay procedures, opportunities for advancement, employee benefits, and appraisals of how well employees are doing on the job. Supervisors should also discuss departmental and organizational matters while they are current news.

Supervisors—and employees too—should practice two-way communication: speaking and listening. People won't listen to you if you won't listen to them. There are no specific rules for listening; however, some suggestions are appropriate. Listen without evaluating or passing judgment. This involves being noncritical and understanding. Try to look for the reason that the other person wants your attention. If the employee begins to wander in her discussion, return her to the main point with directed questioning. When an employee comes to you with a problem and the solution is obvious, reply with a straightforward answer. When there is time, permit the employee to develop a solution on her own that can be discussed later.

DO'S
- Speak or write on the basis of facts, not rumors or assumptions.
- Present your message quickly. Avoid a lengthy historical recap before getting to your main point.
- Use language that is familiar to your employees.

DON'TS
- Use face-to-face communication when emotions are high or the financial stakes are great.
- Convey several messages at one time.
- Let rumors grow and develop because of the lack of official news.

For additional information see pages 148–170 and the following references:

Hunter, W. L. "Eight Steps to Better Communication." *Management World* 10 (December 1981): 36–37.
Pancrazio, S. B., and Pancrazio, J. J. "Better Communication for Managers." *Supervisory Management* 26 (June 1981): 31–37.
Tracy, L. "Do Actions Speak Louder Than Words?" *Personnel Journal* 61 (December 1982): 882–883.

ISSUING ORDERS

The job of being a supervisor directly implies exercising authority. The supervisor directs and controls the activities of subordinate employees by issuing orders, directives, and instructions. Probably the most important dimension of issuing orders is to support the directive with the right climate. The right climate consists of an atmosphere of help and voluntary cooperation. Direct orders and commands are the tools of an immature supervisor.

Good orders are reasonable; that is, they can physically be accomplished without unreasonable danger, difficulty, or delay. Reasonableness is a matter of degree, so it is up to the supervisor to make sure that an order can be successfully carried out by the employee to whom it is given. Good orders are understood by the employee who must carry them out. Keep in mind that communication problems develop, and that everyone doesn't get the same meaning from words. To reduce the possibility of a failure in communication, the supervisor should give the employee an opportunity to ask questions. It may be a good idea to ask the employee to repeat to you in his or her own words what you want done.

Good orders are also compatible with the purposes and objectives of the organization. When an order does not appear to facilitate organizational objectives, the employee may be reluctant to carry it out correctly, or he or she may not execute it at all. When a possible conflict exists, the supervisor must explain why such action is necessary.

DO'S

- Repeat orders or instructions to be certain the employee understands them completely.
- Handle each employee individually and tailor your leadership to fit the particular employee.
- Watch out for conflicting instructions.
- Get feedback as soon as possible so that misunderstandings and resistance will surface before situations get out of control.

DON'TS

- Let anyone else give orders to your employees unless you have expressly asked someone else to pass along orders to your people.
- Give orders, if you can avoid it, when you're angry.
- Assume the worker understands and needs no opportunity to ask questions and voice objections.
- Assume you're the big shot and flaunt your authority. Cracking the whip is not the way to get respect and cooperation; rather, it tends to diminish your authority.

For additional information see pages 130–137 and the following references:

Baker, H. K. "Stepping Up to Supervision: Mastering Delegation." *Supervisory Management* 26 (October 1981): 15–21.
Heller, G. C. "Laying Down the Law—Progressively." *Supervisory Management* 26 (August 1981): 14–16.

MANAGING CONFLICT

Most of us probably prefer to think that conflict doesn't or shouldn't exist and that everything in our organizations is running smoothly. However, this head-in-the-sand attitude doesn't change the fact that conflict does occur. Managers spend an average of 20 percent of their time dealing with conflict. Those who seek ways to deal with conflict and those who take a positive attitude toward it will manage conflict and not be managed by it.

Conflicts arise for several reasons. Competition for status often leads to conflict. An example of this type of conflict occurs when a young, highly educated person is called on to supervise the work of older employees who have gained their status through years of experience. The older workers may resent their supervisor, thinking of him as a "young upstart."

People with different backgrounds and different value systems perceive things from different viewpoints, and this is a possible cause of conflict. Also, when people have mutually exclusive goals—that is, goals that cannot be reached simultaneously—conflict is generated. A case in point would be where employees of equivalent ranking compete to replace the boss who is moving to another job. Conflict can also occur when individuals or groups are committed to reaching their goals but are limited by the resources available.

On the positive side, conflict promotes competition, encourages creativity, and identifies problem areas that need attention. Each incident that involves conflict seems to give rise to a unique set of circumstances; therefore, specific suggestions for managing conflict cannot be offered. However, the following do's and don'ts should be helpful for managing conflict on the job.

DO'S

- Provide each employee with clearly defined communication as to what is expected of him or her.
- Attempt to avoid uncertainty and fuzziness in employees' minds concerning their activities, functions, or objectives.
- Reward good performance and productivity with genuine appreciation and recognition.
- Provide a sense of pride in excellence of performance.
- Provide relaxed and consistent discipline within your area. This will eliminate looseness, idleness, and unnecessary argument.
- Promote a healthy attitude toward conflict.
- Provide channels for conflict to be addressed and resolved.

DON'TS

- Provide an atmosphere of reluctance to change.
- Promote an environment that inhibits constructive controversy.
- Use a win-lose approach in decision making that results in hostility and a personally humiliating outcome.
- Seek secondhand information from people in your office.

For additional information see pages 56–68 and the following references:

"Making the Most of Conflict." *Management Review* 71 (January 1982): 5–6.
"Reducing Conflicts." *Management World* 11 (December 1982): 23.

COUNSELING THE PROBLEM EMPLOYEE

Problem employees are those individuals who for no apparent reason are not performing as they can or who display sudden changes in behavior: preoccupation, unusual irritability, or increased accidents or absences. The cause may be drugs, drinking, mental problems, or a traumatic personal experience, such as the loss of a loved one.

Handling the employee who has become a problem is not an easy job; in fact, it can be downright unpleasant. Thus it's only natural to evade the responsibility. However, this is a key supervisory responsibility that must be dealt with. But pampering the problem employee may serve only to increase her demands and at the same time aggravate the severity of her difficulties.

The supervisor should focus attention on job performance while remaining ready to listen and to help if the employee opens up. Tell the employee how much her current difficulty is affecting her job and where the limits of organizational tolerance are drawn. If the employee brings the problem to the supervisor, he or she can help most by listening in a nonevaluative manner. This means no interruptions, solutions, prescriptions, or preaching. Listen, and then in a supportive way aid the troubled employee in finding help for the underlying cause. However, it may be desirable to schedule a counseling session.

At the supervisory level, a counseling session is aimed at helping the employee unburden herself. The objective is for the employee to gain confidence in the supervisor so that the employee doesn't vent her frustrations on the supervisor. Allow at least fifteen minutes for a session; however, it is much better to allow up to an hour.

The supervisor should find a quiet place where his or her discussion with the employee won't be interrupted or overheard. The supervisor should try to make the employee feel at ease. This may involve talking casually about things that have no connection with work and then permitting the employee to describe her reactions to the job itself, the people she works with, and the working conditions. This approach avoids the employee's feeling that she alone is responsible for her dissatisfaction. Try to get the employee to lead the conversation to the subject that is on her mind. Specific legitimate complaints should be investigated. End the session with a commitment from the employee to a solution to the problem and a timetable for carrying out the solution.

DO'S

- Recognize that handling the problem employee is your job and you can't run away from it.
- Listen to the employee in an understanding manner.
- Ask leading questions; restate the employee's remarks in your own words, both to be sure you understand them and to encourage the employee to enlarge on previous statements.
- Give the employee every opportunity to help herself.
- Encourage the employee to come up with a solution.
- Reach an agreement on what specific things the employee is going to do to eliminate the problem.
- Set a date for a future meeting to review the progress that has been made.
- Suggest professional help or refer the employee to the organization's personnel office if the problem is not job-related.

DON'TS

- Give the employee the impression you are looking for an excuse to get rid of her.
- Offer hasty advice on the employee's problem.
- Look for immediate results.
- Mix a counseling interview with some other action you need to take, such as a disciplinary conference.
- Apologize for confronting the employee about the situation.
- Lecture.
- Be afraid of silence and refuse to give the employee a chance to answer.
- Issue orders or threats.
- Give advice on off-the-job problems.

For additional information see pages 258–268 and the following references:

Axmith, M. "Coaching and Counseling: A Vital Role for Managers." *Business Quarterly* 47 (October 1982): 44–53.

Smith, T. L. "Coaching the Troubled Employee." *Supervisory Management* 26 (December 1981): 36.

Uniz, P. M., and Chasnoff, R. "Counseling the Marginal Performer." *Supervisory Management* 27 (May 1982): 2–14.

HANDLING GRIPES, GRIEVANCES, AND COMPLAINTS

A very natural part of a supervisor's job is handling employee complaints about working conditions or on-the-job relationships. A supervisor is paid to make decisions, not all of which are acceptable to every employee. Supervisors should treat gripes seriously because the employees believe their complaints have merit; otherwise they wouldn't call attention to them. Where a union environment exists, a formal procedure for the processing of grievances will be spelled out in the bargaining agreement. However, the supervisor often gets involved before the situation reaches the grievance level. The following guidelines are useful for handling complaints or gripes at early stages.

1. Listen with undivided attention. Look beyond what the employee is saying to find out what is really bothering him. Be calm and don't let the meeting degenerate into an emotional confrontation. If a confrontation occurs, the individual will stop talking about the complaint to his supervisor and will go to his friends. Then the individual's problem has the potential for becoming a group problem.
2. Give the employee an opportunity to present a solution that seems fair to all concerned and that will make him happy.
3. Get all the facts from the employee, check the organization's policy on the disputed issue, and if necessary check to make sure your interpretation of policy is correct on this matter.
4. Set a date by which a decision will be made.
5. Give your decision at the time promised and explain the reasons for it. Also explain to the employee how he may appeal to the next step in the grievance procedure.
6. Regardless of the outcome, check with the employee after a reasonable time to assess his attitude regarding the problem and to reaffirm that you want your employees to keep coming to you with their complaints.

DO'S
- Conduct grievance discussions in a businesslike manner.
- Talk to the employee in a place where you're free from interruptions and distractions.
- Keep control of your temper, even if the employee or union steward loses control.
- State your decision in such a way that there is no mistake about what you mean.

DON'TS
- Treat the complaint as a public matter.
- Discuss personalities.

- Delay your decision when responding to an employee request. A prompt no will be less troublesome than a long-delayed yes.
- Discuss your evaluation of other employees with the complaining employee.
- Forget to explain to the employee who is dissatisfied with your decision that he may appeal to the next step in the grievance procedure.

For additional information see pages 366–371 and the following references:

Briggs, S. "Beyond the Grievance Procedure: Fact Finding in Employee Complaint Resolution." *Labor Law Journal* 33 (August 1982): 454–459.
Swann, J. P., Jr. "Formal Grievance Procedures in Nonunion Plants." *Personnel Administrator* 26 (August 1981): 66–70.

INTERVIEWING CANDIDATES FOR EMPLOYMENT

Since they are frequently involved in selecting and interviewing potential employees, supervisors must be familiar with the interview and its role in the selection process. The objective of the job selection process is to find an employee whose skills, motivation, abilities, and knowledge closely match the requirements for the job. The job interview is an important step in assessing a candidate's qualifications. To get the most out of the interview, however, the supervisor must do some planning. Besides finding a quiet room where there will be no interruptions, the supervisor should prepare some possible questions for the interview, do some research on wages and benefits if necessary, and review the applicant's resume and job qualifications.

During the interview, the supervisor should be aware of many things in sizing up an applicant. She should look for the fairly obvious attributes: self-confidence, articulateness, openness, and acceptable personal appearance. However, the supervisor should also try to assess the candidate's maturity, interests, motivation, attitudes, and judgment. The way the applicant answers questions gives an idea of how well the individual will fit into the job. In short, a well-directed interview will enable the supervisor to learn a lot about the applicant's background, previous work experience, hobbies, interests, and education.

Being a good interviewer requires having a complete understanding of your organization and the relationships that exist among divisions, departments, and groups. The supervisor must be able to show how jobs relate to one another, and she must be able to explain what is required for the job that currently needs to be filled and the route to and opportunities for promotion.

A good way to begin the interview is to offer a short description of the job, briefly outlining the major duties, qualifications, and responsibilities. This approach also allows the candidate to make a good selection decision. Being a good listener is also part of the interviewing process, and the supervisor should let the candidate know that she is interested in learning as much as possible about him or her. Supervisors who are able to limit their own talking will find that even a quiet individual will talk if given the opportunity. The interview should end with the supervisor telling the candidate when the selection decision will be made and just where the candidate stands in relation to other applicants.

DO'S

- Prepare a schedule or plan for the interview.
- Come prepared with questions and knowledge about the individual before the interview.
- Put the applicant at ease by creating an atmosphere of informality.
- Ask the candidate to give a brief explanation of his or her particular strengths with respect to the job.
- Be fully familiar with aspects of equal opportunity and fair employment practices.

DON'TS

- Ask questions of the candidate in relation to his or her religion, national origin, marital status, race, color, or sex.
- Conduct a one-way (supervisor to applicant) questioning process.
- "Oversell" the job by telling the applicant about rewards that are available for exceptional employees only.
- Require qualifications that far exceed the requirements of the job.

For additional information see pages 299–317 and the following references:

Acuff, H. A. "Employee Selection Simplified." *Management World* 11 (November 1982): 26–29.

Bloom, R., and Prien, E. P. "A Guide to Job-Related Employment Interviewing." *Personnel Administrator* 28 (October 1983): 81–82.

Gallagher, P. "The Interview: Luring Good Candidates." *Chain Store Age: General Merchandise Edition* 59 (September 1983): 103–104.

Turecamo, D. A. "Would You Hire Yourself?" *Supervision* 45 (February 1983): 3–5.

DISCIPLINING EMPLOYEES

Disciplining employees is probably the most difficult and unpleasant part of a supervisor's job. However, discipline must be maintained so that employees do their jobs properly. For many workers, the only discipline they receive during their entire working careers comes from the training and coaching they receive from their supervisor. Today, management theories stress positive strategies; but discipline problems still arise, and generally it's the supervisor who has the responsibility of taking the necessary action to correct the problem so that the employee returns to being a good worker.

The traditional approach to discipline has stressed the use of progressive punishment (warnings, threats, written reprimands, suspensions, demotions, and if necessary termination) when attempting to change an employee's behavior on the job. The supervisor normally has been responsible for handing out these punishments to an unsatisfactory employee. Newer approaches to discipline stress a more positive and supportive approach when dealing with disciplinary problems. Punishments are still used, but only after the supervisor has made sure that the employee knows his job, that he has been advised of the problem, that there are no unreasonable obstacles preventing the employee from doing his job, and that the employee has received some periodic feedback as to how well he is doing.

Employees need to know that the supervisor means what he or she says and that punishment is certain and impartially applied. There is a tendency to concentrate on those individuals causing problems and to overlook those who are cooperating and doing a good job. Yet the majority are hurt by the abuses of a few. Too many absences or excessively long coffee breaks can make the organization uncompetitive, and then all employees suffer.

Supervisory discipline involves teaching an employee to accept the rules of the organization and modeling the correct behavior. The key to disciplining is how it is done (i.e., the methods used). Ask yourself if your disciplinary methods contribute to or threaten good group control. Keep the disciplinary conference as informal as possible, and give the employee an opportunity to tell his or her side of the story. When all the facts have been obtained, the disciplinary action should be fair and expressed in a calm manner.

DO'S
- Make discipline your last resort when an employee breaks a rule. Instead, search hard for the reason the employee acts the way he or she does.
- Establish discipline through good leadership, and avoid negative discipline by scoldings and suspensions.
- Issue written warnings because they become valuable evidence should a union grievance be filed.

- Remember that disciplinary problems, left unchecked, grow worse over time—and the defiance and disrespect that cause them tend to spread to other employees.
- Take into account mitigating circumstances and the past record of the person involved.
- Be sure the employee knows exactly what the offense was and why you are taking the action.
- Keep the disciplinary interview on an objective basis.
- Keep adequate records of warnings and reprimands.
- Remember that the purpose of disciplinary action is to correct unacceptable behavior, not to punish.

DON'TS

- Take your job as a disciplinarian lightly; it's a responsibility that requires good judgment and impartiality.
- Take any disciplinary action when you are boiling over. Do not argue with the employee.
- Discipline an employee in public.
- Give punishment that is too severe, especially for first offenses.
- Act emotionally and fail to get all the facts.
- Delay addressing suspected discipline problems; these problems usually get worse.

For additional information see pages 263–275 and the following references:

Asherman, I. G. "Corrective Discipline Process." *Personnel Journal* 61 (July 1982): 528–531.

Discenza, R., and Smith, H. L. "What's New in Discipline: A Supportive Approach." *Supervisory Management* 23 (September 1978): 14–19.

Harrison, E. K. "Legal Restrictions on the Employer's Authority to Discipline." *Personnel Journal* 61 (Fall 1982): 136–141.

Lippert, F. G. "Preventive Discipline." *Supervision* 44 (March 1982): 17–18.

TERMINATING AN EMPLOYEE

The supervisor's authority is often limited by the organization's policies and by its agreements with a labor union if the employees are unionized. Some employee offenses are worse than others. Such actions as drinking or sleeping on the job, destroying property, gross insubordination, fighting, falsifying time cards, and smoking in restricted areas often result in discharge. These incidents have one thing in common; they are single events that require immediate action by the supervisor.

One way to handle these serious offenses and still leave a door open is to give a suspension. To suspend an employee, the supervisor can say, for example, "You appear unfit to do your job, and you could be subject to termination for being in this shape. You're suspended for the remainder of the day. I'll talk to you tomorrow about this problem." Avoid making statements that convey judgment or diagnosis. A suspension shows the employee that you are willing to enforce your authority. You protect yourself and the organization from looking weak and indecisive. Tomorrow, after consultation with your boss and with the personnel administrator, a decision can be made whether to terminate the employee or take him or her back.

There may come a time when you decide to fire an employee for unsatisfactory performance. This point is reached when a positive approach has failed—when the employee's behavior problems continue uncorrected after suspension has been carried out. The supervisor should investigate the situation thoroughly and review it with his or her boss and the personnel manager before taking action.

After reviewing the situation, a meeting should be held to inform the employee of her termination. The best time to hold the termination meeting with the employee is at the end of the workday. The discussion should focus on the employee's performance, not on the individual. The meeting should be held in a private area, with a union representative present if requested by the employee. Tell the employee she is being terminated and the reasons why. Give the employee any information she needs on continuation of benefits and insurance. Be sure to ask for any questions the employee may have, then collect from her all the organization's property (keys, tools, uniforms, manuals, etc.). Either give the employee her final paycheck or explain how she can obtain it. Finally, and most important, end the meeting on a positive note by mentioning the positive contributions the employee has made and expressing your confidence that she will do better in another organization or in another line of work. Let the employee know that the job and the employee did not match, but there is other employment where she can probably perform more effectively and happily.

DO'S
- Examine the situation calmly and objectively before deciding to fire an employee.
- Consult with another supervisor whose opinion you respect and with your own superior before making a decision.
- Be sure the employee understands the reason for termination.
- Keep a written record of your actions.

- Get the assistance of the personnel department, and follow organizational policies and procedures for termination.

DON'TS
- Let anger or emotion cause you to act before you have all the facts.
- Discharge an employee except as a last resort.
- Say anything you're not ready to back up in court should it come to that.

For additional information see the following references:

Coulson, R. "Fine Art of Informing an Employee: You're Fired." *Management Review* 11 (Fall 1982): 37.
Lissy, W. E. "Changes in the Employer's Right to Fire." *Supervision* 44 (March 1982): 19–20.

ORGANIZATION SKILLS

SUPPORTING DESIRED PERFORMANCE

In order to be successful, the supervisor must effectively influence employees so that they become positively motivated and contribute fully to the objectives of their department and the organization as a whole. This involves interpersonal relationships, which can be handled a number of ways, depending on the situation and the individual involved. Human relationships are complex. There are many variables that influence an individual's desire to perform well—such as environment, education, and work experience.

A happy worker and above-normal productivity do not necessarily go hand in hand. By setting high work standards and trying to motivate employees to achieve them, the supervisor may generate tension and disagreement over work expectations among his or her employees. But when resolved through a successful exchange of views, these conflicts can strengthen supervisor-employee confidence and keep morale high.

Good interpersonal relations must be nurtured by the supervisor. Supervisors should realize that employees need and expect good working conditions, fair pay, and a sense of achievement. Competitive forces and government regulations usually force employers to provide acceptable working conditions and good wages. These are sometimes referred to as lower-level needs. However, employees also have higher-level needs, such as self-fulfillment. It is one of the supervisor's major responsibilities to satisfy these needs.

The higher-level (human growth) needs can be satisfied on the job through promotion opportunities, interesting work, greater responsibility in work assignments, and professional growth. No single supervisory strategy is appropriate for all employees. Supervisors often claim that they know what employees want. In reality, they may not have a clear idea of what motivates a particular employee. An employee's needs for achievement, recognition, and responsibility may be met through such supervisory strategies as delegating, job enrichment, and positive reinforcement. The supervisor should use any of these approaches selectively. Everyone likes to be treated as an individual, rather than as an interchangeable component in the production process.

DO'S

- Encourage people who are trying to do a good job.
- Praise employees for the *parts* of their jobs that they are doing well.
- Remember that employees who are new to the work force need more frequent encouragement than seasoned workers if they are to develop self-confidence.
- Provide support to improve the self-image of employees.

DON'TS

- Dwell on poor performance.
- Assume that employees will know that they're doing well if you don't tell them.
- Take the attitude that "they're just doing their jobs."

For additional information see pages 86–97 and the following references:

Foegen, J. H. "Basing Benefits on Employee Performance." *Administrative Management* 42 (November 1981): 60–63.
Grant, P. C. "How to Manage Employee Job Performance." *Personnel Administrator* 26 (August 1981): 59–65.

BEING AN EFFECTIVE TRAINER

Most job situations require either general or specific training. The training may involve nothing more than exposing a new employee to specific departmental procedures. Or it may involve helping employees to improve their attitudes, skills, and knowledge to perform their jobs.

Training employees has many benefits. Besides shortening the learning period, training makes new employees feel that the supervisor is concerned for them and their welfare. This typically results in improved attitudes and feelings toward the organization, which in turn usually reduces absenteeism, tardiness, and turnover. Training employees also helps them to upgrade their earning ability—either within the organization or with competitors, thus making employees feel more secure in their jobs.

Training can be either one of the most pleasurable jobs or one of the most difficult aspects of being a supervisor. Good trainers follow four fundamental steps.

1. Learning requires that the trainees be properly prepared to learn. Therefore, the supervisor should get the employee in a frame of mind to learn. Stress why the training is important and how it fits into the overall scheme of things. Try to create an eager frame of mind for the task ahead.
2. Demonstrate how the job should be done by saying, "Watch how I do it," and then showing the correct procedure. The best approach is to lay out the task in a step-by-step manner, stopping at the end of each step to see if the trainee has grasped it.
3. Let the employee try to perform the job, staying with her until she has gotten the knack of it. The mistakes made while you are watching are invaluable because they show you where the trainee hasn't learned and provide the best opportunity to offer pointers on how the trainee can avoid repeating the errors.
4. After the trainee has demonstrated that she can do the job reasonably well while you are standing by, let her do it on her own. But return at frequent intervals to see if she needs help. As her mastery improves, check her less frequently.

DO'S
- Relate the purpose of the training to organizational objectives.
- Get to know the trainees as individuals.
- Start training exercises first thing in the morning.
- Start trainees off on an activity in which you know they will succeed.
- Follow up on the trainees' performance at a later time to see if they've got it.
- Be patient.
- Recognize even the slightest improvement or evidence of learning.

DON'TS
- Hand out materials that are poorly prepared.
- Smoke, chew gum, or jingle change in your pockets while teaching.
- Criticize the person when mistakes occur.

For additional information see pages 328–346 and the following references:

Drake, R. T. "Better They Are Informed, Better They Perform." *Supervisory Management* 27 (Fall 1982): 19–20.

Levine, H. Z. "Employee Training Programs." *Personnel* 58 (July/August 1981): 4–11.

McAfee, R. B. "Using Performance Appraisals to Enhance Training Programs." *Personnel Administrator* 27 (November 1982): 31–34.

BREAKING IN NEW EMPLOYEES

Perhaps the most impressionable time for an employee in any organization is his first few months on the job. The employee enters the new work environment with few preconceptions about the organization; thus any information about the job, co-workers, rules, benefits, and general work environment is rapidly absorbed and retained until more valid information becomes available. During this period generalizations are formed about the organization, the management, the immediate work setting, and most of all about the supervisor. The new employee will depend on these "beliefs" to help him predict how others will behave and as a guide to responding to them appropriately.

The supervisor plays a critical role in breaking in new employees because he or she influences their attitudes toward the job and the organization. As a naturally powerful authority figure, the supervisor must exercise caution in not overwhelming the employee. A genuinely warm greeting helps to create a good first impression. If the employee happens to have an unusual name, an effort should be made to pronounce it correctly. It seems to help, too, when the supervisor informs co-workers about the new employee's arrival and work assignments, and gives them a little background information about the new person.

Supervisors who are good at breaking in new employees tend to have three things in common: (1) good interpersonal skills, (2) accessibility, and (3) candor. Taking the time to break in the new employee the right way is a smart investment when one considers that nearly half of all employee turnover occurs during the first few weeks on the job.

DO'S

- Provide a simple explanation of the organization's philosophy, purpose, and history.
- Describe the general functions and operations of the department or division. Let the employee know where he or she fits.
- Point out special regulations, rules, procedures, and policies that will affect the employee.
- Define the employee's job duties and responsibilities.
- Learn to be a "positive Pygmalion" by establishing challenging yet realistic expectations about the new employee's capabilities.
- When possible, assign a mentor to help the employee learn the job and the ropes of the organization.
- Give the employee time to attend orientation meetings.

DON'TS

- Forget to take the time to introduce the new employee to co-workers.
- Expect too much in the way of capability or performance.

For additional information see pages 340–344 and the following references:

Denton, K. "Giving Instructions: It's Not as Easy as It Seems." *Supervisory Management* 28 (September 1983): 32–35.

Guild, P. B. "How to Involve Learners in Your Lectures." *Training* 20 (April 1983): 43–45.

Kraft, C. L. "Low Budget Training: Beating Recession, Meeting Competition." *Supervision* 45 (October 1983): 3–5.

Morrisey, G. L., and Wellstead, W. R. "Supervisory Training Can Be Measured." *Training and Development Journal* 34 (June 1980): 118–122.

DEALING WITH SEXUAL HARASSMENT

Sexual harassment is a relatively new concern for supervisors. This behavior has probably occurred for as long as people have supervised others in the work environment. Many employers dismiss it as a nonissue. However, recent court decisions indicate that there is a growing concern about sexual harassment and the legal and psychological problems it generates.

One of the difficulties with sexual harassment is that people cannot agree on how to define the problem. The distinction between "hanky-panky" and sexual harassment is often unclear. Employees and supervisors may have widely different views of what sexual harassment is. Often there is little evidence to substantiate the accusations. When a third party (i.e., the supervisor) enters the dispute, wider disagreement may occur between the two individuals originally involved, and they in turn may persuade friends and associates to take sides. In some cases, those offended may be unwilling to report sexual harassment if they believe public exposure and mandatory punishment of the offender will occur. In such cases, employees will talk to the supervisor only under the condition that no public action be taken.

Nearly always the offended person simply wants the harassment to stop. The supervisor can assist in this process by explaining several factors to the harassed individual. From a legal point of view, sexual harassment cannot be pursued under Title VII of the Civil Rights Act of 1964 unless there is a definite relationship between the male employee's advances and the female's employment status. To receive a favorable judgment when pursuing sexual harassment charges in an Equal Employment Opportunity Commission hearing or in federal court, the plaintiff (the harassed person) must generally prove three conditions. First, the plaintiff must show that the sexual harassment is specific to one sex (usually female) while the opposite sex is unaffected. Second, the harassment must be a condition of employment. (For example, a supervisor threatens to fire his secretary if she refuses his advances.) Third, the conduct must have occurred with either the explicit or tacit approval of the employer.

The supervisor should encourage the employees to resolve the problem themselves if possible. One method that should be tried, especially after verbal requests have failed, is to have the offended person write a letter to the accused. This should be a low-key and polite letter containing three parts. Part one should be a detailed statement of the facts as the writer sees them. Precise dates and times should be included. The second part of the letter should describe what damage has been done and what action has been taken to eliminate the harassment, such as requesting a job transfer. The writer should also mention any time taken off or misery associated with the harassment. The third and final part of the letter should contain a short statement of what the accuser would like to have happen next. This statement is typically a request that the relationship between the involved individuals be a purely professional one.

The offended person should, if possible, deliver the letter in person to verify when and how it arrived. When necessary, a security person or some other witness should accompany the offended person. The letter more often than not results in an end to the harassment. A good letter can also be used as legal evidence if the offended person feels the need to appeal to upper management or to the courts.

DO'S

- Make sure that your employees understand the written policies and special grievance procedures dealing with harassment.
- Give the accused a chance to defend himself.
- Provide the offended employee a chance to resolve the harassment problem without starting a public action.
- Suggest to the offended person that she keep a careful log of incidents and her reactions.
- Recommend that the victimized person get together with others who understand the problem. Women's organizations can give support and direction.

DON'TS

- Fail to give aggressors who do not understand what they are doing a fair warning.
- React by creating an intimidating or hostile work environment.
- Forget to document the relevant facts while maintaining the confidentiality of employee supervision records.

For additional information see pages 242–248 and the following references:

Dreyfack, M. "Sexual Harassment: Can You Afford Not to Clamp Down?" *Supervision* 44 (April 1982): 8–10.

Linenburger, P., and Keaveny, T. J. "Sexual Harassment: The Employer's Legal Obligations." *Personnel* 58 (November/December 1981): 60–68.

"Sexual Harassment and the Manager." *Management World* 11 (April 1982): 24.

PROTECTING PRIVACY

Supervisors are often asked questions about their subordinates by outsiders. Credit agencies, insurance companies, law firms—even law enforcement agencies—will from time to time ask questions about a specific employee. Answers to these questions may, at times, border on violating employee confidentiality. Although federal employees are protected by the Privacy Act of 1974, organizations in the private sector will usually voluntarily adhere to the guidelines of the Federal Privacy Protection Commission. Essentially, the guidelines discourage organizations from disclosing anything more than directory information, such as dates of employment, title and position, wages, and location of job site. However, a properly identified law enforcement official can ask for and receive information regarding an individual's home address and dates of attendance at work.

How much do employees have to know? While there is no federal requirement that employees be provided access to their personnel files, seven states have passed such laws (i.e., California, Connecticut, Ohio, Oregon, Maine, Michigan, and Pennsylvania). It stands to reason that individuals must be allowed access to any personnel records about them. Supervisors need to be discreet and reasonably sensitive when employees request to see their own records. Sometimes special "incidents files," often kept by supervisors for documentation purposes, need to be opened up to the employee in question. The guidelines recommend that supervisors' files be purged each year for non–job performance information.

DO'S
- Make sure information collected is relevant to the job.
- Ensure the confidentiality and proper use of employees' medical and disciplinary records.
- Allow employees to see and amend the information kept on them.
- Set up safeguards to keep confidential information secure.
- Review and purge employees' files at least once each year.

DON'TS
- Attempt to hide employee records.
- Release information—other than routine directory information—to third parties without the employee's consent.
- Allow employee records to be passed internally from one department to another.

For additional information see pages 270–275 and the following references:

Duffy, J. "Employee Privacy: A New Challenge for Personnel." *EEO Today* 9 (Autumn 1982): 53–65.
———. "Privacy in the Work Place: Defamation." *Employment Relations Today* 10 (Autumn 1983): 67–80.
Moldt, K. R. "Psst! Worker Privacy Deserves Scrutiny." *Iron Age* 224 (March 11, 1981): 39–41.
Walsh, F. "What Companies Should Know About Employees and the Right of Privacy." *Public Relations Journal* 39 (May 1983): 5.

INDEX

About the Authors

Norb Elbert is currently the Brown and Williamson Chairholder and professor of management at Bellarmine College. He has taught human resource management at the University of Denver and at Northern Arizona University. He received his B.S. and M.B.A. from the University of Louisville, and his D.B.A. from the University of Kentucky. He has contributed over thirty articles to scholarly journals, including *Decision Sciences, Health Care Management Review, Academy of Management Journal,* and *Journal of Marketing Research.* An accredited personnel specialist in personnel research, Professor Elbert is also an active consultant to the state of Colorado and to the Arizona Department of Economic Security.

Richard Discenza, a sociology professor at the University of Colorado in Colorado Springs, received his Ph.D. from the University of Oklahoma, his M.B.A. from Syracuse University, and his B.S.F. from Northern Arizona University. He previously taught at Northern Arizona University, at the University of Maine, and at the University of Oklahoma. Before obtaining his Ph.D. Professor Discenza worked several years in industry and in universities as a research assistant and associate. A specialist in operations and systems management, he has published numerous articles, and is certified by the American Production and Inventory Control Society and the Data Processing Management Association.